T0260051

The Industrial Internet
of Things (IIoT)

Scrivener Publishing
100 Cummings Center, Suite 541J
Beverly, MA 01915-6106

Advances in Learning Analytics for Intelligent Cloud-IoT Systems

Series Editors: Dr. Souvik Pal and Dr. Dac-Nhuong Le

Scope: The role of adaptation, learning analytics, computational Intelligence, and data analytics in the field of Cloud-IoT Systems is becoming increasingly essential and intertwined. The capability of an intelligent system depends on various self-decision making algorithms in IoT Devices. IoT based smart systems generate a large amount of data (big data) that cannot be processed by traditional data processing algorithms and applications. Hence, this book series involves different computational methods incorporated within the system with the help of Analytics Reasoning and Sense-making in Big Data, which is centered in the Cloud and IoT-enabled environments.

The series seeks volumes that are empirical studies, theoretical and numerical analysis, and novel research findings. The series encourages cross-fertilization of highlighting research and knowledge of Data Analytics, Machine Learning, Data Science, and IoT sustainable developments.

Please send proposals to:

Dr. Souvik Pal
Department of Computer Science & Engineering
Sister Nivedita University
(Techno India Group)
Kolkata, India
souvikpal22@gmail.com

Dr. Dac-Nhuong Le
Faculty of Information Technology, Haiphong University, Haiphong, Vietnam
nhuongld@hus.edu.vn

Publishers at Scrivener
Martin Scrivener (martin@scrivenerpublishing.com)
Phillip Carmical (pcarmical@scrivenerpublishing.com)

The Industrial Internet of Things (IIoT)

Intelligent Analytics for Predictive Maintenance

Edited by

R. Anandan
Suseendran Gopalakrishnan
Souvik Pal and Noor Zaman

Scrivener
Publishing

WILEY

This edition first published 2022 by John Wiley & Sons, Inc., 111 River Street, Hoboken, NJ 07030, USA and Scrivener Publishing LLC, 100 Cummings Center, Suite 541J, Beverly, MA 01915, USA
© 2022 Scrivener Publishing LLC
For more information about Scrivener publications please visit www.scrivenerpublishing.com.

Wiley Global Headquarters
111 River Street, Hoboken, NJ 07030, USA

For details of our global editorial offices, customer services, and more information about Wiley products visit us at www.wiley.com.

Limit of Liability/Disclaimer of Warranty
While the publisher and authors have used their best efforts in preparing this work, they make no representations or warranties with respect to the accuracy or completeness of the contents of this work and specifically disclaim all warranties, including without limitation any implied warranties of merchantability or fitness for a particular purpose. No warranty may be created or extended by sales representatives, written sales materials, or promotional statements for this work. The fact that an organization, website, or product is referred to in this work as a citation and/or potential source of further information does not mean that the publisher and authors endorse the information or services the organization, website, or product may provide or recommendations it may make. This work is sold with the understanding that the publisher is not engaged in rendering professional services. The advice and strategies contained herein may not be suitable for your situation. You should consult with a specialist where appropriate. Neither the publisher nor authors shall be liable for any loss of profit or any other commercial damages, including but not limited to special, incidental, consequential, or other damages. Further, readers should be aware that websites listed in this work may have changed or disappeared between when this work was written and when it is read.

Library of Congress Cataloging-in-Publication Data

ISBN 978-1-119-76877-7

Cover image: Pixabay.Com
Cover design by Russell Richardson

Set in size of 11pt and Minion Pro by Manila Typesetting Company, Makati, Philippines

10 9 8 7 6 5 4 3 2 1

Contents

Preface

It is with immense pleasure that we introduce this book on intelligent analytics for predictive maintenance through the industrial internet of things (IIoT), with the objective of fostering advancements and disseminating results concerning recent applications in the field.

Since the internet of things (IoT) dominates all sectors of technology, from home to industries, automation through IoT devices is remarkably changing the processes of our daily lives. For example, more and more businesses are adopting and accepting industrial automation on a large scale, with the market for industrial robots expected to reach 73.5 billion US dollars by 2023. The primary reason for adopting IoT industrial automation in businesses is the benefits it provides, including enhanced efficiency, high accuracy, cost-effectiveness, quick process completion, low power consumption, fewer errors, and ease of control. Therefore, every smart entrepreneur undoubtedly has the vision of automating office processes to match the latest technological innovations. However, it is not so easy to use these same innovations to automate industrial processes. Which is why the IIoT, a key element of a smart factory, was created to bring together modern cloud computing, the IoT, and AI to design intelligent, self-optimizing industrial equipment and facilities.

Since engineers, both current and future, need systematic training in industrial automation in order to keep up with and advance the rapidly evolving field of applied control technologies, expert systems with IoT capabilities make for more versatile and innovative handling of problems. However, since security of both physical devices and administration applications is basic to the activity of the IoT and is imperative for its success, this book was designed to provide students with an opportunity to explore knowledge concerning the security frameworks of the IoT that are dependent on new specialized norms. Therefore, new security plans are discussed which highlight these new norms.

This book showcases industrial automation through the IoT by including case studies in the areas of the IIoT, robotic and intelligent systems, and web-based applications which will be of interest to working professionals and those in education and research involved in a broad cross section of technical disciplines. The diverse topics covered in the 15 chapters herein are briefly described below.

- Chapter 1 provides an updated overview of the IoT and IIoT, addressing its evolution along with AI technology and its potential in the industry, approaching its relationship with a concise bibliographic background, and synthesizing the potential of the technologies.
- Chapter 2 discusses the major challenges in securing IoT devices and the data being exchanged over the network. It also covers the manufacturers of IoT devices and the standards they follow. Security challenges such as privacy, confidentiality, integrity and reliability are also discussed in a broader manner.
- Chapter 3 extensively covers the challenges concerning smart automation, and smart and grid management.
- Chapter 4 focuses on how advanced forms of automated data processing connect with new types of computer vision (CV) applications that directly influence safety, thereby protecting human lives and physical assets in hazardous places.
- Chapter 5 explains the use of precise system modeling along with appropriate objective function that can offer optimal solutions, along with the financial implications of using soft computing techniques.
- Chapter 6 provides insightful knowledge on antenna designs, which can further help in future wearable antenna design research to fulfil the requirements of best wearable electronics.
- Chapter 7 briefly reports on the numerous IoT devices used in daily life. Since the data generated by these devices are huge, there is a discussion on how it should be monitored, controlled, and acted upon using IoT data transmission protocols in data centers using various computing methods such as Fog, Cloud, Edge, and distributed computing along with machine learning techniques. Challenges faced in data centers and the IoT are also presented.
- Chapter 8 provides insight into the challenges of drone delivery system and the use of IoT to overcome them.

- Chapter 9 studies IoT-based water management system, including investigations of rate impediments in biophysical and geochemical measures to help biological system administrations concerning water quality.
- Chapters 10 and 11 further emphasize the numerous advantages of the industrial IoT.
- Chapter 12 introduces a novel neural predictive classifier for improving the prediction rate of adverse drug reactions (ADRs), which is proposed to identify ADRs using the IoT.
- Chapter 13 explains the impact that COVID-19 has had on the IIoT and gives an overview of IoT's role in COVID-19, the benefits and challenges of the IIoT, and the effects of COVID-19 on industrial manufacturing and its impact on IoT-connected applications and digital transformation, and also the influence of COVID-19 on IoT application in general.
- Chapter 14 paves the way for a comprehensive composite smart ambulance booking and tracking system using the IoT for digital services.
- Chapter 15 discusses the increasing demand to solve health issues affecting the elderly, where the use of new IoT technology is completely changing their everyday lives, and promises to revolutionize modern healthcare by enabling a more personalized, preventive and collaborative form of care. Embedding devices with a cloud server and the sensor-cloud paradigm will give the elderly a more versatile facility. So, by analyzing security problems, such as authentication and data protection to protect the privacy of the elderly, an intelligent and safe health control system is proposed in this chapter with an IoT sensor focused on cloud storage and encryption.

In conclusion, we would like to extend our appreciation to our many colleagues and give our sincere thanks to all the experts for providing preparatory comments that will surely motivate the reader to read the topic. We also wish to thank the reviewers who took time to review this book. Also, we are very much grateful to our family members for their patience, encouragement, and understanding. Special thanks are given to the many individuals at Scrivener Publishing who contributed their talents and efforts in bringing this book to fruition. Finally, any suggestions to improve the text will be highly appreciated.

R. Anandan
Suseendran Gopalakrishnan
Souvik Pal
Noor Zaman
January 2022

1

A Look at IIoT: The Perspective of IoT Technology Applied in the Industrial Field

Ana Carolina Borges Monteiro[1], Reinaldo Padilha França[1]*, Rangel Arthur[2], Yuzo Iano[1], Andrea Coimbra Segatti[2], Giulliano Paes Carnielli[2], Julio Cesar Pereira[2], Henri Alves de Godoy[2] and Elder Carlos Fernandes[2]

School of Electrical and Computer Engineering (FEEC), University of Campinas – UNICAMP, Av. Albert Einstein, Barão Geraldo, Campinas – SP, Brazil
Faculty of Technology (FT), University of Campinas – UNICAMP, Paschoal Marmo Street, Jardim Nova Italia, Limeira, Brazil

Abstract

The advent of solutions with AI (Artificial Intelligence) technology means tools and software that integrate resources that automate the process of making algorithmic decisions. Simply put, AI consists of systems or machines that mimic human intelligence to perform tasks improving iteratively over time based on the information collected. Thus, IoT currently matches a series of hardware that works connected to the internet, from a refrigerator to a wearable watch that measures heart rate and sends this data to an application. In this sense, it is possible to interpret what part of these devices uses, even on a small scale, AI technology. This technological innovation connects everyday intelligent devices or even intelligent sensors, to the internet, linking the physical world increasingly closer to the digital world. In this scenario, the world is experiencing a digital transformation, and related to it, the Industrial Internet of Things (IIoT) aims to connect different devices to collect and transmit data present in an industrial environment. Performing this communication through essential industrial variables related to smart devices, effecting communication, data, and data analysis. In this sense, this chapter is motivated to provide an updated overview of IoT and IIoT, addressing its evolution along with AI technology and potential in the industry, approaching its relationship, with a concise bibliographic background, synthesizing the potential of technologies.

Keywords: IoT, IIoT, industrial, IoT applications, sensors

Corresponding author: padilha@decom.fee.unicamp.br

R. Anandan, Suseendran Gopalakrishnan, Souvik Pal and Noor Zaman (eds.) The Industrial Internet of Things (IIoT): Intelligent Analytics for Predictive Maintenance, (1–30) © 2022 Scrivener Publishing LLC

1.1   Introduction

The concept behind the Internet of Things (IoT) is to connect several devices, through the internet which can exchange information with each other. Considering that this technology can be applied to industry, it makes this connection between these different devices generates Industry 4.0, which is reputable as the Fourth Industrial Revolution, being the new trend that is being adopted by large corporations to get ahead in the market, characterized by the introduction of information technology in the industry [1].

IoT in Industry 4.0 is basically responsible for the integration of all devices inside and outside the plant, considering that the concept represents the connection as it is a network of physical devices (objects), systems, platforms, and applications with embedded technology to communicate, feel or interact with indoor and outdoor environments [1, 2].

Industry 4.0 is the complete transformation of the entire scope of industrial production through the fusion of internet and digital technology with traditional industry, being motivated by three major changes in the productive industrial world related to the immense amount of digitized information, exponential advancement of computer capacity, and innovation strategies (people, research, and technology) [2, 3].

When it is said that the internet is in the industry, these changes allow everything inside and around an operational plant (suppliers, distributors, plants, and even the final product) to be digitally related and connected, affording a highly incorporated value chain, from the factory floor, is important to relate this to an environment where all equipment and machines are connected in networks and uniquely providing information [3, 4].

For Industry 4.0 to become feasible, it requires the adoption of a technological infrastructure made up of physical and virtual systems, aiming to create a favorable environment for new technologies to be disseminated and incorporated by the industry, with the support of Big Data Analytics technology (Figure 1.1), automated robots, simulations, advanced manufacturing, augmented reality, and the IoT, employing the monitoring of technological trends, assisting managers throughout the entire industrial chain [3, 5].

The Industrial Internet of Things has an IoT and IIoT layer in the industry, provoking a prognostic model, since automation, which in general already exists, answers questions regarding what is happening, what happened, and why it happened, considering its network of physical devices (objects and things, among others), systems, platforms, systems, and

Figure 1.1 Big data analytics illustration.

applications with embedded technology in industry sectors, aiming to promote automation of manufacturing and, thus, increase the productivity of production lines, generating greater competitiveness with the international industry through intelligent factories (smart manufacturing) [6].

Generating an increasing number of connected devices (in some situations, it even include unfinished products), since the digitization of data from machines, methods, processes, procedures, and intelligent devices, integrates and complements the operational layer of an industrial plant, enabling communication and systems integration and controls and allowing responses and decision-making in real time. Thus, IIoT becomes a prerequisite for Industry 4.0 [1, 7].

The difference between IoT and IIoT is in the sense that the first relates systems that connect things, complement information, normally only produce data, and can be used in any sector of the industry, transforming the second, to manage assets and analyze maintenance trends [8–10].

IIoT forms a critical layer of the production process and can directly connect a product supplier in real time on the production line, which analyzes the quality and use of your product, as well as connecting the input and output logistics chain of materials and control production, in real time, at the optimum point of operation, becoming an application of production and consumption of data, with a critical profile [8–10].

The use of IoT and IIoT proposes the digital factory bringing benefits to productive plants as an improvement in the use of the asset, reduction of operations or asset cycle cost, improved production, reduction of operations or stoppages, improving asset use (performance), increased speed in decision-making, allow the sale or purchase of products as a service, generate opportunity for new business, among several others. Thus, the premise of digitizing all information can lead to a question about the reason and reason for digitizing so much data, since this information is all digitized and there are all the means (networks) for them to travel and exchange information with each other, it is expected that decisions can be made not only between operators and machines, but also between machine and machine, this is called M2M, Machine to Machine, which before were not available in real time and are now needed [8–11].

Thus, the architectures of industrial automation systems, which have adherence to Industry 4.0, manage to integrate different devices in favor of industrial evolution, with more and more sensors, cameras, and systems that will be monitoring the entire industrial production process, evaluating and supervising the performance of equipment, and providing, in addition to the already known layers of operational control and the entire control framework, the IoT and IIoT layer, where it will converge all this data into a Big Data, delivering operational control possibilities (Figure 1.2), with decision-making in prognoses and with the possibility of autonomous actions [10–12].

Optimizing the production process of the industry is the main reason for the application of IoT in the production line of the factories, since the IoT technology and its IIoT aspect allows the equipment that makes up the industrial yard of a company today that can be connected in a network. With the data collected and stored in the cloud, it allows the decision-makers of the companies to have quick and easy access to all the information of the company and its collaborators; in other words, this makes all the

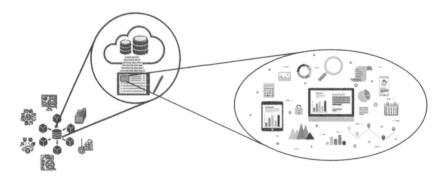

Figure 1.2 Big data illustration.

industrial machinery work automatically through of highly programmable intelligent sensors [13, 14].

Wherefore, this chapter is motivated and has the purpose to originate an updated overview of IoT and IIoT, addressing its evolution and branch of application potential in the industry, approaching its relationship with current technologies and synthesizing the potential of technology with a concise bibliographic background.

1.2   Relationship Between Artificial Intelligence and IoT

The emergence of solutions and tools with AI (Artificial Intelligence) technology means solutions, tools, and software that have integrated resources that automate the process of making algorithmic decisions. The technology to be used can be anything from independent databases employing Machine Learning to pre-built models that can be employed to a diversity of data sets to solve paradigms related to image recognition and text analysis. Applied in the industry, it can help a business achieve a faster time to evaluate, reduce costs, increase productivity, and improve the relationship with stakeholders and customers [15, 16].

Machine Learning is only part of AI, that is, it is an AI application in which it accesses a large volume of data and learns from it automatically, without human intervention. This is what happens in the case of recommendations on video streaming platforms and facial recognition in photos on social media pages. AI is a broader concept that, in addition to Machine Learning, includes technologies such as natural language processing, neural networks, inference algorithms, and deep learning, in order to achieve reasoning and performance similar to that of human beings [15, 16].

An AI system is not only sufficient and capable of storing, analyze, and manipulating data, but also of acquiring, representing, and manipulating information and knowledge. Including the characteristic to infer or even deduce new knowledge, new relationships between data-generating information about facts and concepts, from existing information and knowledge and to use methods and procedures of representation, statistical analysis, and manipulation to solve complex questions that are often incognito and non-quantitative in nature [17].

The increase in mass data collection over the years, related to IoT devices, has boosted AI, given that the volume of information produced by people has been growing exponentially. But allied with Big Data technology to understand this massive set of data, which serves as a basis for learning the most diverse software, such as Machine Learning. This data revolution favored the AI scenario, i.e., with more information available, more intelligent, and automated ways to process, analyze, and use the data [18, 19].

Big data is the term employed to refer to the enormous amount of data that is produced and stored daily, evaluating that from this abundance of information, there are intelligent systems created to organize, analyze, and interpret (that is, process) the data, which are generated by multiple sources [19, 20], still pondering on predictive analysis as the ability to identify the probability of future results based on data, statistical algorithms, and machine learning techniques. From Big Data, it is possible to do this type of analysis, identifying trends, predicting behaviors, and helping to better understand current and future needs and, finally, to qualify decision-making in machines, equipment, and software, taking technology to a new level. AI is impacting society with machine learning systems, neural networks, voice recognition, predictive analysis, and natural language processing (NLP) and continuously remodeling new aspects of human life [19, 20].

Forecasting and adaptation are possible through algorithms that discover programmed data patterns, the solutions learn and apply their knowledge for future predictions. If a sequence of bits exists, then the AI recognizes the sequence and predicts its continuity. This is also able to correct spelling errors or predict what a user will type or even estimate time and traffic on certain routes in transit (autonomous vehicles based on AI) [17].

Decision-making through data analysis, learning, and obtaining new insights is able to predict or conjecture a more detailed and faster decision than a human being. But it helps to increase human intelligence and people's productivity. Through continuous learning, AI can be considered a machine capable of learning from standards [21].

Also related to its characteristics in the ability to build analytical models from algorithms, learning to perform tasks through countless rounds of trial and error. In the same sense, NLP provides machines and computing devices the capability to "read" and even "understand" human language [22].

1.2.1   AI Concept

Another characteristic of the basic types of AI is purely reactive, since it acts after the perception of the problem, exemplifying an AI software that identifies the chess pieces on the board and their movement, but has no memory of past movements, ignoring everything before the current movement, that is, it only reacts to the position of the pieces on the board. In the legal field, lawyers focus on more complex aspects of law practice, given the use of text analysis, Jurimetrics, text review, data mining, contract analysis, computational argumentation, and other possible AI-derived features [17, 23], still pondering the characteristics of AI-related to its capacity for intelligent perception, such as visual perception, speech perception, auditory perception, and processing and learning of perceptual information. Reflecting on autonomous cars and virtual assistants, there is not only a programmed answer to specific questions but answers that are more personalized [23–25].

Through AI solutions, it is possible to eliminate boring tasks that may be necessary, but with machine learning, it performs basic tasks, considered human-computer interaction technologies, or even related to the more robust use found in conversational interfaces that use machine learning to understand and meet customer needs [23–25].

Even through AI solutions, it is possible to concentrate diffuse problems where data inform all levels of the operation of a modern company, i.e., it has a lot of material to interpret, so it is necessary to consume this amount of information at scale. Since the extent of the data available today has gone beyond what humans are capable of synthesizing, making it a perfect job for machine learning. Through the data, the information is extracted from various sources of public and private data, still comparing them and making changes when necessary [25].

Through AI solutions, it is possible to distribute data, given that modern cybersecurity leads to the need to compare terabytes of internal data with a quantity of external data. With machine learning, it can automate the process of detecting attacks as cybersecurity problems change and increase, vital for dealing with distributed data problems, assessing that humans are unable to involve their actions around a distribution so wide of information. AI solves dynamic data, which is a valued characteristic, given the major obstacle related to addressing individual employee characteristics, or dynamic problems of human behavior. Through AI, it is possible to use determining complex patterns to help organizations move more quickly and respond better to the changing needs of each employee [26].

Or even, through AI, industrial systems integrate robotics powered by AI, 3D printing technologies, and human supervision, building interactive robot systems leading by AI technologies. This process not only decreases costs and increases efficiency but also generates much safer industrial environments for human workers. The dangerous elements of industrial activities are surpassed by machines [27, 28].

In simpler terms, AI technologies consist of intelligent systems or intelligent machines that mimic human intelligence to operate tasks and can improve iteratively supported on the information it collects. AI technologies manifest itself in various ways in modern contemporary society as chatbots to understand customer issues more quickly and provide more efficient responses or smart assistants to analyze critical data and information from large sets of free-text data to improve programming, or even at home, through recommendation mechanisms providing intuitive recommendations for TV programs supported on users' viewing habits. However, AI technologies are not deliberate to replace human beings but aims to substantially improve human skills and actions, tasks, and even contributions [17, 23, 24].

AI is related to application areas that involve expert systems or systems based on knowledge, natural language comprehension/translation, intelligent systems/learning, speech comprehension/generation, automatic programming, or even image and scene analysis in real time, among many others. Therefore, it can be evaluated that the technological AI field aims to emulate human beings' capabilities including problem-solving, understanding natural language, computer vision, and robotics, considering systems for knowledge acquisition, and even knowledge representation methodologies [15].

To obtain the full value of AI, Data Science is necessary (Figure 1.3), consisting of a multidisciplinary field that employs scientific methods to collect and extract value from data, combining skills such as statistics, probabilities, frequency of occurrence of events, observational studies, and computer science, with business knowledge to analyze data gathered from distinct sources [29, 30].

The central principle of AI technologies is to replicate, and then exceed, the processes and conduct humans perceive, notice, see, and react to the world, fueled by several forms of Machine Learning techniques that recognize patterns in data to allow prognosis and predictions. Propitiate a better comprehensive understanding of the wealth of available data, information, and predictions to automate overly complex or ordinary tasks, improving productivity and performance, automating tasks or processes that previously demand human energy, and also making sense of the data on a superhuman scale [31].

Data science makes it a priority to add technological value to business intelligence and advanced analysis as the main technology differential for companies, through the use of demographic and transactional data to foresee and predict how much certain customers and users will spend over their business relationship with a company (or even the customer's lifetime value), price optimization supported on preferences and customer behavior, or even utilizing image recognition techniques to analyze X-ray digital images searching for signs of cancer [30].

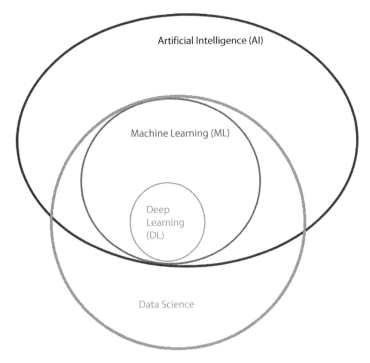

Figure 1.3 AI and data science illustration.

Three elements are leading the development of AI technologies across all sectors, which are the computational high-performance, affordable, and even processing capacity available, assessing the abundance of computing power in the cloud technologies allowing easy access to affordable and high-performance computing power. Large volumes of data available for conduct training, given that AI, require to be trained on a lot of data available to generate the correct predictions, also relating the emergence of distinct tools for labeling data, in addition to the ease and accessibility of storing and processing structured and unstructured data, to train AI algorithms [31].

The benefits of operationalizing AI are related to the cognitive interactions of machine learning techniques with conventional business applications, methods, and processes that can greatly increase productivity and user experience, or even considering AI as a strategic method and competitive advantage related to greater efficiency in processes, doing more in less time, and increasing customer loyalty, creating customized and attractive customer (user) experiences, and predicting commercial results to generate greater profitability [23, 24, 32].

AI applications in people's daily lives are based on an app that recognizes the content of images and allows a search by typing the name of an object or action, or streaming platforms transcribing audio and generating subtitles for videos, or in an email offering automatic responses smart; or even with regard to online translators who translate texts from signs, labels, and menus with the cell phone camera; or even pondering about streaming platforms that use AI to understand users' preferences and recommend music and movies, respectively, still relating autonomous cars that drive alone, or even in medicine, advancing cancer studies [26].

The application of AI is present in various segments of the economy; in industry, automation is a keynote for machines that keep getting smarter. With AI, the equipment manufactures and checks the products without having to be operated by a human, that is, it performs repetitive work and has no limitations for their use. Through the GPS (Global Positioning System), the routes suggested by online applications, generally, point out the best path, considering that the AI interprets data provided automatically by other users about the traffic on the roads. Online retailers, using online store algorithms, recognize user purchasing patterns to present offers according to their preferences. Financial institutions use AI algorithms to analyze market data, manage finances, and relate to their customers [33].

Thus, the first industrial revolutions created equipment that replaced manual labor, carrying out the work of many men with greater efficiency and less cost. Currently, in several cases, through the AI employee in tasks, they have been previously seen as "intellectuals". In any case, the important thing is that AI theater is a reality. In this regard, the understanding of its mechanisms and the understanding of the possibilities that this provides must be expanded. The concept of AI refers to the creation of machines, not necessarily with physical bodies (software that can abstract, create, deduce, and learn ideas), with the ability to think and act like human beings and aim to facilitate everyday tasks [7, 34].

1.2.2   IoT Concept

IoT in the early days corresponded to the connection via the internet in physical objects, such as a toaster, especially sensors. Over the years, the concept of connecting the physical material world with the virtual world has evolved into a technological revolution in order to connect all the objects that people use on a daily basis to the internet (Figure 1.4), describing a scenario in which several things are connected and communicate, through technologies like Wi-Fi. The result is a smarter and more responsive planet [35, 36].

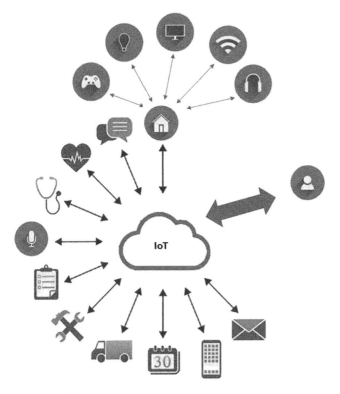

Figure 1.4 Internet of Things.

Thus, IoT currently matches a series of hardware that works connected to the internet, from a smart TV to a running watch that measures heart rate and sends this data to an application. However, it is possible to interpret what part of these devices uses, even on a small scale, AI. This technological innovation connects everyday items (smart devices), or smart sensors, to the internet, making the physical world increasingly closer to the digital. Thus, the technology describes the physical objects (things) connected and communicating (transmitting) with each other and with the user, transmitting data (information) to a network, as if it were a broad digital nervous system, i.e., a structure that allows the exchange of information (data) between two or more points [17, 18, 37].

Still pondering that every day, more appliances, watches, means of transport, and accessories are connected to the Internet and other devices, such as smartphones, tablets, and mobile devices that transmit signals and appear to each other. Still pondering that through a connected network, these devices can be connected via the internet with cars, refrigerators, microwaves, trains, airplanes, among other thousands of artifacts (Figure 1.5) [18].

The field of IoT practices has been diversified over time, and currently, the field of applicability and use of IoT is very broad, reflecting on numerous technological resources that have been used to provide connection of devices. Like Bluetooth technology, communication by proximity field (short-range wireless technology, which allows the exchange of information between devices with enabled and compatible NFC) is also a feature used in IoT. Making the devices "talk digitally" to each other, generating more productivity, comfort, information, knowledge, and practicality in general, and their uses and application can include health monitoring or leading real-time information about city traffic, or yet the number of parking lots available in parking, even indicating activities, reminders, or even content on their connected intelligent devices [38].

Nowadays, everyday "things" become intelligent and have their functions and role expanded by crossing data (information), seeing a virtual assistant crossing data from connected intelligent devices to inform, even if not requested, the time (travel duration) it will take to get to work when leaving the house, also relating the interconnectivity of smart IoT devices around the environment and making a digital assistant learn a user's routine, their times, their location via GPS connection, the connection (link)

Figure 1.5 IoT illustration.

to the car's Bluetooth at a singular time (Figure 1.6), and the circumstance that this context has been repeated many times [18].

The IoT exchanges information is essentially derived from three elements that require to be associated with an application to work which are the intelligent devices, the network (structure), and a digital control system. The intelligent devices are all those imaginable equipped with sensors and antennas, among others, providing communication with the other elements such as lamps, bedside lamps, refrigerators, microwaves, cars, coffee makers, and watches, television, among others (Figure 1.7). The network is the means of communication such as Wi-Fi, Bluetooth, mobile data, and fiber optics, among others. The control system causes all data (information) captured from the devices (things) to be processed and then sent (transmitted) to a digital system that controls each aspect analyzed and evaluated [36, 39].

Big Data is the driving technology of IoT, related to data are currently the great creators and destroyers of business value. Since the IoT devices connected to the network are constantly sending, receiving, exchanging, and crossing data, i.e., constantly producing data. As a result, the accumulation, analysis, and use of Big Data are more significant, especially for

Figure 1.6 Connection to the car's illustration.

Figure 1.7 IoT devices.

companies, which have the most expressive production of data with IoT, as it has a large number of objects that can be connected or already connected. In addition, with data and information in hand, companies make fewer mistakes, produce more, and win more customers. To make sense (means of storing, tracking, analyzing, and making use of this large amount) of all this data (information), Big Data analysis has a fundamental role, which is critical for companies of all sizes [19, 40].

Still pondering the seven main attributes that define and differentiate a normal object or device from an item that is part of the great mass of IoT connectivity, these devices and systems include sensors that track and measure activity worldwide. Internet connectivity will be in the item itself (thing/device), probably collecting information over time through sensors, exchanging messages, and files with a Cloud platform. Like any computer, the devices will have some built-in processing power, even if only to analyze and transmit data. Although many of the IoT devices are not yet equipped with special features to become really powerful in processing [41–43].

Efficient energy consumption is related to these devices being able to operate for a certain time or more on their own, using stored energy or staying connected only while used. Cost x benefit ratio is linked to the premise that several objects with sensors (must be relatively inexpensive to purchase and implant) distributed on a large scale to be really efficient,

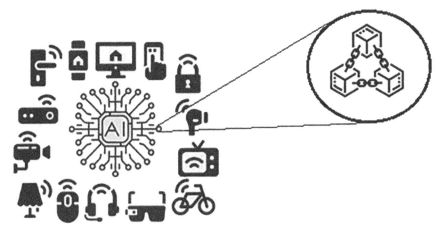

Figure 1.8 IoT and blockchain illustration.

as in the case of food products in supermarkets that must have an indication of validity. Quality and reliability are related that many of the devices must operate exposed to harsh climates for long periods of time [41–43].

Security is given that IoT machines and devices transmit private and detailed information, such as that related to the user's health, still reflecting that the change from previously inert objects to a reality based on connectivity transforms businesses, products, and workflows to suit consumer trends and needs. In this respect, blockchain technology can promote more digital security (Figure 1.8), so that objects connected to networks are not hacked [41–43].

However, the main potential of IoT is to carry out communication between objects, and people are given the practical nature, via the internet, "things" exchange signals with each other, i.e., mobile and fixed objects gain autonomy to interact with each other and with users. One of the greatest examples of this digital transformation in recent years is the increased use of IoT in homes and work relationships. Another technology that enhances the growth of IoT is AI, guaranteeing more autonomy and learning for objects connected to the internet [44].

1.3 IoT Ecosystem

IoT is basically things, i.e., it is all types of equipment/device/sensor that can be connected in different ways, from a truck to monitor the displacement of product transport fleets, use of sensors in tractors that measure the soil situation and send data to systems responsible for processing this information, and make suggestions for the best areas or times for planting, a boiler temperature sensor in a factory, or the adoption of devices at home, such as thermometers, energy consumption regulators, or home appliance managers, who allow the householder to control this equipment remotely, or even microsensors that monitor the status of patients remotely in hospitals or outside them [45].

In IoT, it is consistent with an environment whose rules deal with both connection and intelligent data collection and processing, since applications allow the coordinated and intelligent use of devices to control various activities, from monitoring with cameras and sensors to managing spaces and of productive processes. The IoT ecosystem is a system composed of a digital space of interaction including digital tools related to data analysis and modeling, as well as digital elements that integrate and interact within it. It is through these interactions and the exchange of information that AI allows these elements to work in an integrated manner, composing an intelligence potential far superior to what each of its elements has separately. The IoT ecosystem involves different agents and processes, such as smart objects [sensors, appliances, cars (Figure 1.9), and factory automation equipment], smart modules (processors and memories), connectivity services (access to the internet or private networks that connect these devices), integrators (systems that combine applications, processes, and devices), enablers (control systems, collection, and processing of data and commands involving objects), and even providers of IoT services [45, 46].

Figure 1.9 Maintenance IoT vehicle illustration.

Within an IoT ecosystem, applications that integrate IoT technologies with Big Data technologies are operated, enabling the collection and analysis in real time of large data sets, allowing the development of predictive models for a variety of situations, from consumer behavior to the prevention of factory failures, and optimizing activities on the most varied fronts of activity. IoT technology brings changes both in the development of more pervasive connectivity and in the increase of data processing, derived from the refinement of sensors that allow data collection in different environments. All of this is associated with some practical solution allowing for increased efficiency, reduced human intervention, or even new business models [45], still evaluating that the AI generates a layer to enhance the value generated by the analysis of the different information captured and combined; allowing the automation of the decision-making process and actions in specific situations; bringing significant benefits to the increase in the speed of processes, reduction of the error rate due to human interference, and reduction of costs per transaction, in addition to the possibility of greater absorption of insights at each interaction that feedback and "teach" the AI algorithms (Machine Learning as an example); and making this incrementally more efficient [31].

In the digital transformation of the industry (relating the advent of the Fourth Industrial revolution), AI associates IoT with the combination of the ecosystem for data transmission between devices and the technology for analyzing this information independently, still conceptualizing the emergence of Artificial Intelligence of Things (AIoT). Considering that the IoT concept is related to the various IoT devices that collect data and create a network for transmitting critical information to administrators, on the other hand, AIoT data is processed by resources that analyze the standards providing only the information necessary for making a decision and can even make the necessary decisions without human involvement [17].

Pondering on AI, this uses algorithms to analyze data and resources through aspects such as Machine Learning by automating processes without manual intervention, incorporating with IoT gaining connectivity and capacity for data exchange. The great advantage of the IoT concept is in the various solutions involving machine-to-machine communication, integrated into a single network, where it publish and consume information. Thus, it is through the integration of IoT, with the analysis of broad data sets (Big Data Analytics), and with the performance in ecosystems using AIoT that it is possible to exceed the limits that each of these technologies has individually, developing an advanced solution to support operational management, offering predictive maintenance, and consequently increasing control, quality, and efficiency in business operations [35].

1.3.1   Industry 4.0 Concept

Industry 4.0 is considered as Fourth Industrial, also characterized by the introduction of information technology in the industry, representing the total transformation of the entire ambit of industrial production through the unity of digital technology and the internet (connection) with conventional industry, deriving from IoT as a connected network, which alone has immense amounts of connections between industrial cells [1].

IoT in Industry 4.0 is basically responsible for the integration of all devices inside and outside the industrial plant, relating the digital transformation and the function of the IIoT, together with developments in mechanics, engineering, and manufacturing [2].

Consider that the IoT is a network of physical objects, platforms, systems, and applications with incorporated technology to communicate, feel, or interact digitally with internal and external environments. The IoT on the shop floor is related to an environment where all equipment and machines are connected in networks and providing information in a unique way; therefore, different industrial cells have different purposes, having different functions and applicabilities, but they are united under the same network. Thus, IIoT is a subcategory of IoT, which also comprises user-oriented applications, such as usable devices, machine devices, and infrastructure with integrated sensors that transmit data (collected information) via the internet and which are managed by software, technology for smart homes, and even cars autonomous [3].

However, this industrial revolution is not yet a reality, even so, it is being motivated by three major changes in the productive industrial world related to the exponential advance of the capacity of computers, the immense amount of digitized information, and also new innovation strategies in relation to research and technology [4].

The connections generated by IoT in the industry generate opportunities create a large circle of added value to products and services as integrated monitoring, generating data that communicate in real time through what can be considered a large unified database or even scheduled maintenance stop on the production line before this is intensified. From this generated database, automatic decisions are made through online communication between interconnected devices correlated to event monitoring. Based on the decisions taken through the global view, the production process becomes more efficient, reducing negative impacts and maximizing the value chain of a given industrial sector [5].

The benefits of IoT in Industry 4.0 for industrial plants can be understood in the following aspects related to operational efficiency and maximizing profits by introducing more flexible automation, connectivity, and production techniques. In addition, scalability, time, and cost savings help to maximize profits for industrial organizations. Pondering about the aspects that increase the operational efficiency of a plant is reducing production stops, reducing the cost of the asset cycle, improving the use of the asset, and even improving the production [46].

Even listing the benefits of new services and business models given that IoT in Industry 4.0 allows the creation of new sources of revenue by creating new connected services. Hybrid business models allow both digital products and services to be used. In an applicable context, a vehicle manufacturer can take advantage of the raw data obtained to provide car condition service in real time as a source for preventive maintenance. This use of digital services also improves the relationship with the customer, since it allows different points of contact that generate valuable information for the customer, creating a relationship of trust and loyalty [47].

Even the benefits related to greater knowledge for decision-making arising from the analysis of industrial data, allowing and facilitating the making of better decisions due to a more accurate view of the industry's performance. To top it off, IIoT's network of smart devices allows industrial organizations to connect all of their employees, data, and processes from the shop floor to executives and managers, further assisting the productivity of department leaders and decision-making [48].

It is important to emphasize that more than facilitating decision making, Industry 4.0 aims to promote that these decisions are made automatically by intelligent techniques, toward an autonomous reaction of the machines. From the point of view of systems and equipment, these steps correspond, respectively, to a vision of what is happening (data), to know why it is happening (analysis, knowledge), and to predict what will happen (based on standards and AI). After that, analyze the implementation of a strategic plan, requiring a clear roadmap in relation to the processes, security, and necessary technologies [7].

1.3.2 Industrial Internet of Things

The world is experiencing a digital transformation and the IIoT aims to connect different devices to collect and transmit data in an industrial environment. Performing this communication through essential variables related to the devices, the communication between the devices, the data, and the data analysis. The concept is the same as the IoT used for home appliances; however, for IIoT, the connection is between industrial machines, legacy systems, and other devices related to the world of production. This can be applied in sectors such as facility management, supply chain monitoring, healthcare, and retail, among others [8].

The application of IIoT is through a network of devices and intelligent objects that collect, through sensors, and share large amounts of data. This forms a technological layer that can directly connect a product supplier in real time on the production line, which analyzes the quality and use of your product. This through intelligent data consumption creating a critical profile can connect the logistic chain of input and output of materials and control production, in real time, at the optimum point of operation [9].

The main challenges of IIoT are interoperability, security, and a high volume of data exchange. Interoperability is the ability of different systems and organizations to work together, considering the difficulty on the appearance of devices from different brands is a challenge and it is necessary to develop technological initiatives to unify these systems. Security is a challenge because companies need to know that their data is safe, and it is necessary to guarantee the necessary infrastructure for an exponential explosion of data [10].

Thus, IIoT comprises of machines connected to the internet and advanced analytics platforms (digital structure) that process the data produced, and IIoT devices range from complex industrial robots to tiny environmental sensors; however, the technology also includes agriculture, financial services, healthcare, retail, and advertising, among others. To get the most out of the benefits of IIoT, three technological capabilities related to sensor-oriented computing, industrial analytics, and the application of intelligent machines are needed [49].

IIoT technology can be applied in various sectors such as production where most of the technology is being implemented and employed, derived from machines that can autonomously monitor, analyze, and predict potential problems, meaning less downtime and more efficiency in general, or even simpler and safer facility management with sensor-driven climate controls. In addition, intelligent devices that monitor facility entry points and react quickly to potential threats improve facility security, or even supply chain with sensor-managed inventory taking care of supplies orders before stocks run out. This reduces waste, while keeping the necessary goods in stock and freeing workers to focus on other more specific tasks [49–51].

This large industrial data generation machine will be an opportunity to explore capacities related to sensor-driven computing, thus enabling the measurement of temperature, pressure, speed, and several other parameters. Given that all this information is valuable to innovate in services, it is usually data that customers do not have access to [51].

With regard to Industrial Analytics, the data generated through the sensors allows the industrial analysis to transform this data into valuable insights, managing to extract all the information from the thousands of data generated daily and then serving for decision-making and action plans, as alarms that constantly signal for abnormalities of processes. Still evaluating that the raw data are transformed into valuable insights into the conditions of the industrial plant, this will allow it to control the plant with greater precision, increasing productivity and decreasing losses [50, 51]; or even applying intelligent machines, i.e., machines that do not have only mechanical functions, considering that this will be the driving force for the generation of new revenue streams, reinforcing the concept of a hybrid business model; or even, the advancement of technology is making it possible to compose physical intelligent devices and their monitoring software with third-party services [52, 53].

With IIoT technology, the production process is differentiated, that is, there is greater communication between what is produced and the machine, aiming that any inconsistency can be detected during the production process, thus greater quality control. Inventory control is also more efficient with the use of IoT sensors, which can verify the need for parts replacement. Thus, in addition to accurate inventories, there is a streamlining of processes and savings, both for employee time in controlling inventory and to avoid wasting unnecessary purchases [52–54].

1.4   Discussion

The application of AI in the industry has been increasingly optimizing its results, in an attempt to reach its maximum degree of efficiency. AI advent is the arrangement of several technologies, which allow machines digitally to perceive, understand, act, and learn on their own actions or complement human activities, which has become a broad technology used for machine learning, predictive analytics, augmented reality, robotics, performance diagnostic software, and many others.

With entire procedures performed by machines capable of making decisions based on data, agility and increased productivity are natural consequences. Through AI, industrial production has become faster and more effective compared to human labor. Still considering the possibility of the machines performing tasks that a person would not be able to do, as is the case with dangerous raw materials or microscopic components.

AI works through the integration of factors such as the use of IoT sensors, Cloud Computing, and other technologies present in Industry 4.0, working in sync, devices equipped with AI create complex systems, which correlate the information collected and, with this, seek the best ways to carry out the activities for which they were scheduled. These new technologies are developed to work using the least amount of resources possible, whether in terms of raw material or energy consumption, still relating the point of cost reduction, the mitigation of errors, and waste of the operation.

When addressing AI applications, it is worth mentioning IIoT as a critical technological layer added to the production chain, which allows even the connection with suppliers and the analysis of the performance of its raw materials, still pondering the potential of AI in relation to security alerts, which point to the need for maintenance and performance reports in real time, indicating the best measures to be taken.

Still pondering the aspect in which machines can withstand extreme conditions that would be harmful even if perceived only in the long term for the health of the employees of industry, such as cooling cameras, chemical processes, and management of explosive materials, among others, that can be carried out almost entirely through automation.

The aspects in Industry 4.0 in relation to the digitization processes that guarantee the collection of data that were previously lost, the mitigation of risks in decision making, the optimization of operations, and the gain of agility, among others, are also mentioned. The implementation of complex AI algorithms has been enabling industries to assess and enable problem-solving and decision-making in a more complex and secure way.

Assessing that each sector of the industry receives contributions from AI in a different way, as a logistics and inventory structure can benefit from technology for identification and control of demand, for example; or industries with production chains that have different machinery, as is the case with the automotive industry, since with the use of predictive analysis, they can identify the need for maintenance on their machines.

The benefits are not the only ones since the industry receives an extremely positive impact on the use of AI in its processes. Given that it is possible to point out an increase in the quality of products and services, since AI reduces execution errors and subsequently uses operation data to analyze performance and make improvements; or even more effective new products and services, since the development can also be supported by AI to evaluate the proposed designs, identifying the material variables, the weaknesses to be improved, and the possibility of using augmented reality to make tests before actually putting it into production; or even through data analysis, it is possible to get an agile response to new market demands, considering that the needs and interests of consumers are changing with great velocity.

AI brings great advantages to the industry related to the reduction of errors, because after being trained, intelligent algorithms are able to perform very well tasks that are susceptible to errors in processes executed by humans. The reduction of costs since e-commerce stores or banks use robots (chatbot) for customer service, this allows employees to be allocated in more strategic areas, which can increase profit. So, with fewer errors and employees focused on more important processes, the company will have more time to think about the business and leave other tasks to AI.

Thus, AI through an automated process uses large volumes of data to make decisions, dispensing with human intervention and increasing productivity in different activities.

1.5   Trends

Adaptive Intelligence is about helping to generate better business decisions by integrating the computational power of internal and external data in real time with the computing infrastructure and highly scalable decision science. In this type of systems, relating the adaptive learning, the characteristics are monitored so that there is an adjustment in order to improve the process. The efficiency of these systems depends on methodologies adopted to collect and diagnose information related to needs and characteristics, in relation to how this information is processed to develop an adaptive context. These applications essentially make businesses smarter, allowing them to provide customers with better products, recommendations, and digital services, all of which generating better business results [55].

Digital twins are related to the practice of creating a computer model of an object, such as a machine or even a human organ, or yet a process like a climate. By studying the behavior of the digital twin, it is possible to analyze, understand, and predict the behavior of its counterpart in the real world and to solve issues before they occur. However, to take full advantage of the digital twin's potential, real systems need not only be networked with each other but also need to develop the ability to "think" and act autonomously [56].

This development tends toward AI, from simple mutual perception and interaction to independent communication and optimization, also requiring integrated information systems that allow a continuous exchange of information, still demanding powerful software systems that can implement them along the entire value chain, and planning and designing products, machines, and plants, in addition to operating products and production systems. The technology of digital twins allows users to act in a much more flexible and efficient way, as well as personalize their manufacturing [57].

Intelligent Edge refers to the place where data is digitally generated, interpreted, analyzed, and treated, i.e., the use of this technology means that analyses can be managed more quickly and that the probability of data being unduly intercepted or leaked is considerably less. This technology refers to the analysis of data and the development of solutions in the place where the data is generated, reducing latency, costs, and security risks, making associated businesses more efficient, still pondering that the three largest categories of Intelligent Edge are the edges of operational technologies, IoT edges, and IT edges [58].

The use of Intelligent Edge technology helps to maximize business efficiency, since instead of sending data to a data center or even to a third party to perform processing, the analysis is performed at the location where the data is generated. This means not only that the analysis can be performed more quickly, but it also means that companies are much more self-sufficient and do not depend on potentially flawed network connections to do their job [58].

Predictive maintenance is one of the most promising branches for industrial applications based on the use of data received from the factory to avoid production failures. This type of system eliminates unnecessary maintenance and increases the probability of avoiding failures, which involves a machine or even a component with sensors capable to collect and transmit data and then analyze it, and perform storage in a database. Then, this database offers comparison points for events, as they occur [59, 60].

The predictive maintenance model aims to periodically monitor the operation of machinery, equipment, and parts in a factory, in order to detect failures before they occur and prevent interruptions in the production line, relating IoT and AI in order to assist in the survey and management of data from all sectors of production, integrating the company's departments, performing analyzes to take advantage of the useful life of industrial equipment, indicating the real conditions of its operation, detecting possible deterioration of parts and components, and ensuring the reliability and availability of services. This information obtained is used to support decisions and present suggestions for actions and interventions, generating better results than with the use of raw data [59, 60].

1.6   Conclusions

IoT refers to the network of intelligent devices that are concerned with issues of connectivity, competition, and protocols, among other aspects.

Relating the respective AI to the branch of cognitive computing caring for principles of data analysis, statistics, and other aspects. Considering that when applied together, it brings results related to the data generated by the IoT and can be processed by an AI software, which will optimize decision-making and contribute to the increase in the agility of the processes.

From the historical point of view, objects (things), people, and even nature, emitted a huge amount of data; however, humanity just could not to perceive, i.e., see, hear, or make sense of them. However, through the IoT and the data collected, humanity began to see, understand, and use it to its advantage with technological advances in practically all sectors of society. It is in this aspect that the IoT came to change the reality of the contemporary and modern world, considering that everything around the environment has intelligence and is interconnected, so that through this technology, it is possible to have access to data, or better, information. Having access to this sea of data, which through the technological potential brought by AI is able to put digital intelligence and transform them into information, i.e., knowledge, and finally, into wisdom.

Starting from the premise that it is possible to perceive the patterns of all these data, society will become more efficient, effective, increasing productivity, enhancing the quality of life of people, and the planet itself. Reflecting on the possibility of generating new insights, new activities promoting even more technological innovation. In this respect, the bridge between data collection (information) and the suitable sharing of that data, with safety and protection digital for all parties, abides the key in technological evolution.

Reflecting on the industrial sector, it is possible to identify a behavioral trend and anticipate the application of a new idea, and this premise shows that the world is heading toward the Fourth Industrial Revolution. This represents the introduction of information technology in industries, correlating a hidden potential that is the use of data, since the good use of this data increases operational efficiency, better decision-making, and even creates new business models.

Finally, IIoT brings together different technologies correlating the Information Technology (IT) initiative for resource management, planning, and decision support systems, Operations Technology (TO) that monitors, analyzes, and controls field equipment, manufacturing, and production procedure, through AI. One of the applications of this is predictive analysis, which makes it possible to forecast a given situation in the future based on information from the past and probability. From this, it is possible to get an AI to perform a certain action corresponding to a specific sensor in the IoT network indicating a specific state of the shop floor, optimizing this activity with increased precision.

Still reflecting on the digitization of processes and the entire production chain of the industry, it is the basis of Industry 4.0, with the layers of IoT and IIoT enabling the planning, control, and even tracking of production, both by digital simulation and virtualization, winning decision-making time and cost reduction. Thus, AI and IoT are tools that drive business and guarantee a competitive advantage with the possibility of generating automated and more agile services, consequently impacting the final consumer.

References

1. Gilchrist, A., *Industry 4.0: the industrial internet of things*, Springer Nature Switzerland AG., 2016, https://link.springer.com/book/10.1007%2F978-1-4842-2047-4
2. Vaidya, S., Ambad, P., Bhosle, S., Industry 4.0–a glimpse. *Procedia Manuf.*, 20, 233–238, 2018.
3. Rojko, A., Industry 4.0 concept: background and overview. *Int. J. Interact. Mob. Technol. (iJIM)*, 11, 5, 77–90, 2017.
4. Xu, L.D., Xu, E.L., Li, L., Industry 4.0: state of the art and future trends. *Int. J. Prod. Res.*, 56, 8, 2941–2962, 2018.
5. Ardito, L. *et al.*, Towards Industry 4.0. *Bus. Process Manag. J.*, 2019.
6. Sanders, A., Elangeswaran, C., Wulfsberg, J.P., Industry 4.0 implies lean manufacturing: Research activities in industry 4.0 function as enablers for lean manufacturing. *J. Ind. Eng. Manag. (JIEM)*, 9, 3, 811–833, 2016.
7. Gunal, M.M. (Ed.), *Simulation for Industry 4.0: Past, Present, and Future*, Springer Nature Switzerland AG., 2019, https://link.springer.com/chapter/10.1007/978-3-030-04137-3_16
8. Jaidka, H., Sharma, N., Singh, R., Evolution of IoT to IIoT: Applications and challenges. *Proceedings of the International Conference on Innovative Computing & Communications (ICICC)*. 2020, https://papers.ssrn.com/sol3/papers.cfm?abstract_id=3603739
9. Yu, X. and Guo, H., A Survey on IIoT Security. *2019 IEEE VTS Asia Pacific Wireless Communications Symposium (APWCS)*, IEEE, 2019.
10. Mathur, P., Overview of IoT and IIoT, in: *IoT Machine Learning Applications in Telecom, Energy, and Agriculture*, pp. 19–43, Apress, Berkeley, CA, 2020.
11. Leminen, S. *et al.*, Industrial internet of things business models in the machine-to-machine context. *Ind. Mark. Manag.*, 84, 298–311, 2020.
12. França, R.P. *et al.*, Improvement of the Transmission of Information for ICT Techniques Through CBEDE Methodology, in: *Utilizing Educational Data Mining Techniques for Improved Learning: Emerging Research and Opportunities*, pp. 13–34, IGI Global, Pennsylvania, USA, 2020.

13. Franca, R.P. *et al.*, Better Transmission of Information Focused on Green Computing Through Data Transmission Channels in Cloud Environments with Rayleigh Fading, in: *Green Computing in Smart Cities: Simulation and Techniques*, pp. 71–93, Springer, Cham, 2021.

14. Al-Gumaei, K. *et al.*, A survey of internet of things and big data integrated solutions for industries 4.0. *2018 IEEE 23rd International Conference on Emerging Technologies and Factory Automation (ETFA)*, vol. 1, IEEE, 2018.

15. Monteiro, A.C.B. *et al.*, Development of a laboratory medical algorithm for simultaneous detection and counting of erythrocytes and leukocytes in digital images of a blood smear, in: *Deep Learning Techniques for Biomedical and Health Informatics*, pp. 165–186, Academic Press, Cambridge, Massachusetts, EUA, 2020.

16. França, R.P. *et al.*, Potential proposal to improve data transmission in healthcare systems, in: *Deep Learning Techniques for Biomedical and Health Informatics*, pp. 267–283, Academic Press, Cambridge, Massachusetts, EUA, 2020.

17. Al-Turjman, F. (Ed.), *Artificial Intelligence in IoT*, Springer Nature Switzerland AG., 2019, https://link.springer.com/book/10.1007%2F978-3-030-04110-6

18. Hosseinian-Far, A., Ramachandran, M., Slack, C.L., Emerging trends in cloud computing, big data, fog computing, IoT and smart living, in: *Technology for Smart Futures*, pp. 29–40, Springer, Cham, 2018.

19. França, R.P. *et al.*, A Proposal Based on Discrete Events for Improvement of the Transmission Channels in Cloud Environments and Big Data, in: *Big Data, IoT, and Machine Learning: Tools and Applications*, p. 185, 2020.

20. Cielen, D., Meysman, A., Ali, M., *Introducing data science: big data, machine learning, and more, using Python tools*, 320 pp., Manning Publications Co., New York, USA, May 2016. ISBN 9781633430037, https://www.manning.com/books/introducing-data-science

21. Sangaiah, A.K., Thangavelu, A., Meenakshi Sundaram, V., Cognitive computing for Big Data systems over IoT. *Gewerbestrasse*, 11, 6330, Springer, 2018.

22. Deng, L. and Liu, Y. (Eds.), *Deep learning in natural language processing*, Springer Nature Switzerland AG., 2018.

23. Jackson, P.C., *Introduction to artificial intelligence*, Courier Dover Publications, Mineola, New York, USA, 2019.

24. Flasiński, M., *Introduction to artificial intelligence*, Springer Nature Switzerland AG., 2016.

25. Arrieta, A.B. *et al.*, Explainable Artificial Intelligence (XAI): Concepts, taxonomies, opportunities and challenges toward responsible AI. *Inf. Fusion*, 58, 82–115, 2020.

26. Semmler, S. and Rose, Z., Artificial intelligence: Application today and implications tomorrow. *Duke L. Tech. Rev.*, 16, 85, 2017.

27. Ardito, L., *et al.*, Towards Industry 4.0: Mapping digital technologies for supply chain management-marketing integration. *Bus. Process*

Manag. J., 2019, https://www.emerald.com/insight/content/doi/10.1108/
BPMJ-04-2017-0088/full/html?journalCode=bpmj

28. Raj, M. and Seamans, R., Primer on artificial intelligence and robotics. *J. Organ. Des.*, 8, 1, 1–14, 2019.

29. Zhu, L. and Jim Zheng, W., Informatics, data science, and artificial intelligence. *Jama*, 320, 11, 1103–1104, 2018.

30. Carlos, R.C., Kahn, C.E., Halabi, S., Data science: big data, machine learning, and artificial intelligence. *J. Am. Coll. Radiol.*, 15, 3, 497–498, 2018.

31. Acemoglu, D. and Restrepo, P., *Artificial intelligence, automation and work*, National Bureau of Economic Research, Cambridge, MA, 2018.

32. Nadimpalli, M., Artificial intelligence risks and benefits. *Int. J. Innov. Res. Sci. Eng. Technol.*, 6, 6, 2017.

33. Sola, D., Borioli, G.S., Quaglia, R., Predicting GPs' engagement with artificial intelligence. *Br. J. Health Care Manag.*, 24, 3, 134–140, 2018.

34. Delamater, N., *A brief history of artificial intelligence and how it's revolutionizing customer service today*, SmartMax Software, Inc, Tulsa, OK, 2018. https://images.g2crowd.com/uploads/attachment/file/73099/expirable-direct-uploads_2F469f2619-a917-446d-b2b8-14cf8f8d2c4e_2FChatBotWhitePaper2017.pdf

35. Olson, N., The Internet of things. *New Media Soc.*, 18, 4, 680–682, 2016, https://journals.sagepub.com/doi/abs/10.1177/1461444815621893a?journalCode=nmsa

36. França, R.P. *et al.*, Improvement of the Transmission of Information for ICT Techniques Through CBEDE Methodology, in: *Utilizing Educational Data Mining Techniques for Improved Learning: Emerging Research and Opportunities*, pp. 13–34, IGI Global, Pennsylvania, USA, 2020.

37. Osuwa, A.A., Ekhoragbon, E.B., Fat, L.T., Application of artificial intelligence in Internet of Things. *2017 9th International Conference on Computational Intelligence and Communication Networks (CICN)*, IEEE, 2017.

38. Zeng, Xuezhi *et al.*, IOTSim: A simulator for analysing IoT applications. *J. Syst. Archit.*, 72, 93–107, 2017.

39. França, R.P. *et al.*, Intelligent Applications of WSN in the World: A Technological and Literary Background, in: *Handbook of Wireless Sensor Networks: Issues and Challenges in Current Scenario's*, pp. 13–34, Springer, Cham, 2020.

40. Erl, T., Khattak, W., Buhler, P., *Big data fundamentals: concepts, drivers & techniques*, Prentice-Hall Press, Hoboken, Nova Jersey, EUA, 2016.

41. Balali, F. *et al.*, Internet of Things (IoT): Principles and Framework, in: *Data-Intensive Industrial Asset Management*, pp. 1–19, Springer, Cham, 2020.

42. Lakhwani, K. *et al.*, *Internet of Things (IoT): Principles, Paradigms and Applications of IoT*, BPB Publications, New Delhi, India, 2020.

43. Tran, C. and Misra, S., The Technical Foundations of IoT. *IEEE Wirel. Commun.*, 26, 3, 8–8, 2019.

44. Shovic, J.C., Introduction to IoT, in: *Raspberry Pi IoT Projects*, pp. 1–8, Apress, Berkeley, CA, 2016.
45. Peng, S.-L., Pal, S., Huang, L., *Principles of Internet of Things (IoT) Ecosystem: Insight Paradigm*, Springer Nature Switzerland AG., 2020.
46. Bröring, A. *et al.*, NOVA: A Knowledge Base for the Node-RED IoT Ecosystem. *European Semantic Web Conference*, Springer, Cham, 2019.
47. Okano, M.T., IOT and industry 4.0: the industrial new revolution. *International Conference on Management and Information Systems*, vol. 25, 2017.
48. Kanagachidambaresan, G.R. *et al.*, *Internet of Things for Industry 4.0*, Springer International Publishing, 2020.
49. Boyes, H. *et al.*, The industrial internet of things (IIoT): An analysis framework. *Comput. Ind.*, 101, 1–12, 2018.
50. Reddy, B.R. and Sujith, A.V.L.N., A comprehensive literature review on data analytics in IIoT (Industrial Internet of Things). *HELIX*, 8, 1, 2757–2764, 2018.
51. Jacob, J.J. and Thamba W., Meshach, Industrial Internet of Things (IIoT)–An IoT Integrated Services for Industry 4.0: A Review. *Int. J. Appl. Sci. Eng.*, 8, 1, 37–42, 2020.
52. Mathur, P., Overview of IoT and IIoT, in: *IoT Machine Learning Applications in Telecom, Energy, and Agriculture*, pp. 19–43, Apress, Berkeley, CA, 2020.
53. Kim, D.-S. and Tran-Dang, H., An Overview on Industrial Internet of Things, in: *Industrial Sensors and Controls in Communication Networks*, pp. 207–216, Springer, Cham, 2019.
54. Nicolae, A., Korodi, A., Silea, I., An Overview of Industry 4.0 Development Directions in the Industrial Internet of Things Context. *Rom. J. Inf. Sci. Tech.*, 22, 183–201, 2019.
55. Sternberg, R.J., A theory of adaptive intelligence and its relation to general intelligence. *J. Intell.*, 7, 4, 23, 2019.
56. El Saddik, A., Digital twins: The convergence of multimedia technologies. *IEEE Multimed.*, 25, 2, 87–92, 2018.
57. Müller, V.C. and Bostrom, N., Future progress in artificial intelligence: A survey of expert opinion, in: *Fundamental issues of artificial intelligence*, pp. 555–572, Springer, Cham, 2016.
58. Patel, P., Ali, M.I., Sheth, A., On using the intelligent edge for IoT analytics. *IEEE Intelligent Syst.*, 32, 5, 64–69, 2017.
59. Mobley, R.K., *An introduction to predictive maintenance*, Elsevier, Amsterdam, Netherlands, 2002.
60. Selcuk, S., Predictive maintenance, its implementation and latest trends. *Proc. Inst. Mech. Eng. Part B: J. Eng. Manuf.*, 231, 9, 1670–1679, 2017.

Analysis on Security in IoT Devices—
An Overview

T. Nalini[1]* and T. Murali Krishna[2]†

[1]Dept. of CSE, Dr. M.G.R. Educational and Research Institute,
Chennai, India
[2]Dept. of CSE, Srinivasa Ramanujan Institute of Technology, Ananthapuramu, India

Abstract

Internet of Things (IoT) is becoming an evolving technology being a part of day-to-day activities of human life. The number of IoT devices is expected to rise up to 30–35 billion by 2022. As the connectivity to World Wide Web is highly available at affordable price, which leads to more number of internet users. Therefore, an enormous number of electronic gadgets that are connected to Internet are producing huge amount of data. This creates a biggest challenge in IoT sector such as securing the IoT devices and data that is been exchanged over the network.

The user's private information is transferred among the gadgets, and several security challenges such as privacy, confidentiality, integrity, and reliability issues need to be addressed. Several industries are manufacturing different IoT devices at various standards. Incorrectly configured IoT device (faulty apps on mobile device) can cause excessive data traffic over Internet Protocol and device batteries are getting drained faster. This research is mainly focused on different issues such as analysis of present research in IoT security, and this analyzes the communications behavior of IoT devices and mobile apps, security threats on IoT technology, various IoT tools, IoT manufacturers, and the simulators that are currently used.

Keywords: IoT technology, authenticity, confidentiality, privacy, simulation

*Corresponding author: drnalinichidambaram@gmail.com
†Corresponding author: murali2007tel@gmail.com

R. Anandan, Suseendran Gopalakrishnan, Souvik Pal and Noor Zaman (eds.) The Industrial Internet of Things (IIoT): Intelligent Analytics for Predictive Maintenance, (31–58) © 2022 Scrivener Publishing LLC

2.1 Introduction

The promising IoT connects various kinds of devices through the Internet so as to reap data formulated by sensor(s), end devices connected at longer distance, buildings, vehicles, etc. [1]. In the last year, IoT devices have radically increased in number with variations and nearly 50 billion of them being connected to web by end of 2020 [2]. IoT devices are distributed across all environments and several kinds like "smart cities, grids, health, retail, watches, supply chain, farming, TVs, and so forth". While designing IoT, important aspects to consider are security and privacy services. Unfortunately, there is a chance for the IoT devices to be inadequate or deficiently structured security systems. Moreover, security assaults can infiltrate into IoT devices and destroy the communications; hence, such security dangers must be aware of in IoT network.

In order to evade cyber assaults, during IoT devices design, security must be looked upon as a vital segment [3]. But, the various types of IoT constituents interrupt unfolding of well recognized techniques for reassuring Security in IoT systems [4, 5]. The foremost challenging aspects of IoT devices are quantification, energy, storage, and communication capabilities. Just about, it is very delicate to build cyber-security among the IoT end users and manufacturers. Incidentally, most of the IoT equipment companies hold lowered cost for actuator and sensors in the market. Such devices were primarily intended to operate in disconnected networks, where the security threats are substantially less prevalent.

As a consequence, some of the designer are not capable enough on cyber security and might be ignorant of the security dangers relevant to their real world devices. Hence, with the need to lower expenses and the time on advertisements related to IoT networks commercialization, security is overlooked [6].

The objective of this paper is therefore to focus on current IoT cyber security issues and get familiarized with the dangers posed by IoT devices. The paper discusses about the characteristics of such dangers and the possible infringements. The issues recognized with IoT related cyber security have been presented in various works in the literature as in, e.g., [7–9]. As compared to such papers, here, we address the theme from an increasingly down to earth viewpoint. Commonly, "Zigbee, 6Lo-WPAN, LoRa-WAN, and Bluetooth Low Energy" are eventually utilized as communication protocols in IoT devices.

We quickly review the security methods supported by every protocol and, consequently, investigate the attack surface, additionally revealing a progression of genuine assaults against eminent business IoT devices as instances of the dangers related with inadequately planned security components. Moreover, we depict the "formulating units, communication protocol, and cryptographic equipment, and programming" utilized around business arrangements, to bestow preparatory processes as of now embraced in the market. This examination would then be able to be valuable to readers and specialists intrigued to get a handle on the more functional ramifications of IoT security.

2.2   Security Properties

Security is an inevitable issue that must be addressed in anything we do, anyplace we do, and whenever we do. There is a digital information about individuals and about what individuals do, what individuals talk, and where they go, and details about their arrangements and so on and so forth. What is more, with a plan to go ahead with IoT, the aggregates of this information will be augmented comprising sensitive data about user's conducts and behaviors. So, it might lead to undesirable outcomes on account of unprotected information.

For data protection, the major concept is that of security policy—it combines several services like confidentiality, integrity, as well as accessibility. These notions collect the elementary security objectives for both data and computational services. Furthermore, authenticity, non-reputation, and then privacy are security services, too [10].

1. Confidentiality: This denotes protecting exchanged content acquired by IoT devices.
2. Integrity: When anticipated recipients must be able to verify if the exchanged things have been modified or not within themselves.
3. Availability: The data must be available to authorized parties at all point of time. Partial resources, functionalities, or other services produced or attained by the network may be endangered and it is not accessible within the peers of the network.
4. Authenticity: This indicates that the system is not accessed by unauthorized users. Authentication mechanism helps establishing proof of identities without which fabrication is possible.
5. Non-repudiation: It does not permit the sender of a specific message to refute the claim of not directing that message.

2.3   Security Challenges of IoT

There are three classes of IoT related risks encompassing the risks that are as follows:

1. Characteristic to any web oriented system
2. Pertaining to devices dedicated to IoT systems
3. Critical to implement safety such that no danger is posed by misusing devices, for example, industrial actuators.

Customary ways such as securing of open port(s) on units fit in the first group. The second type comprises of issues particularly relevant to IoT computer hardware. Also, any scheme that can link to Internet holds an operating system—embedded positioned in respective firmware and most of these are not intended with security as their main concern.

Although the IoT presents features that are already present in other computer networking paradigms, we strongly believe that the IoT presents a completely different scenario and thus novel research challenges, especially as far as the security field is concerned. We believe the following points summarize the main reasons that should spur novel and transformative IoT security research in the near future.

1. Size of Device and Network: Management of absolute size of the IoT is a main issue based on security view, as it is prevailing security conventions and tools were not built to scale up higher. Besides, the rigorous budget constrictions of IoT companies enact restricted memory as well as power of computing. Most significantly, as replacing battery can be very difficult or incredible, such processes turn out to be greatly exclusive and time overwhelming. Therefore, augmenting energy depletion gets basic. To reword, the utter volume of devices together with the confines in energy, computation, and memory competences intensely stimulate the necessity for design and implementation of fresh security tools skilled with offering their features without stately extreme computing or loading problem on the devices but again intended to be exceedingly scalable.
2. Manual components: Unified machine-human communication is one of the most troublesome aspects of IoT. Very small sensor devices are able to flawlessly supply medications and acquire biometric details remotely, additionally

providing medical specialists with a thorough view of health related conditions. Also, the data exchange would be shared and interweaved. On the contrary, sharing data about everyone, either home or occupational grounds, may transform as a responsibility accessible by mean users—third parties. Hence, control of access and privacy convert as basic feature in IoT. Another problem exists where human beings are major actors of the detecting systems in IoT. But, there is no warranty that they will create not information unreliably, for instance, since they do not wish to or not be able to. To handle this major issue, different faith and reputation means are needed, with a scale up to huge population.

3. Diversity: IoT is a complicated ecosystem interrelating smart gadgets people and routine entities into a larger-scaled interrelated network. Due to this broad variety of components, a superfluity of various IoT conventions, methods, and standards may essentially co-occur, specifically in the networking field. While some industrialists adopt IoT standards that are open these days, most of IoT is on basis of legacy-oriented systems that depend on exclusive technology, eventually leading to anti-model concept called as Intranet of Things. Additionally, most of prevailing researches assume that existence of fixed association among IoT and resources along with the environmental entities. In contrast, the IoT setup is extremely varied and vigorous and IoT devices might undergo erratic mobility, resulting in rapid dissimilarities in communication aptitudes and positions with time. Such a setup resolves for accessible IoT devices which is a challenging job.

In this section, the paper projects the varied security challenges with respect to IoT domains. The usual attack method includes negotiating original IoT devices and perform counterfeit activities toward some another network [11]. A broad overview of classification of security levels and IoT layered architecture are discussed in detail as below.

2.3.1   Classification of Security Levels

This fragment presents a classification of requirements related to IoT system security based on operational levels, namely, at the levels of Information, Access, as well as Functional [12].

2.3.1.1   At Information Level

The following security requirements should warrant in this level:

- Integrity: During data transmission, the received data should not have been altered.
- Anonymity: Hide the data source's identity from the non-member parties.
- Confidentiality: To exchange protected information, a straight forward association has been imposed among the gadgetry to avert third parties from fetching confidential data.
- Privacy: During data transmission, sensitive information about the users should not be revealed.

2.3.1.2   At Access Level

This specifies security methodologies to control the access to the network. Some of the functional abilities of Access level listed below:

- Access control: Access control grants permission only for authorized users to access the IoT devices and the various network tasks.
- Authentication: Authentication mechanism helps launch right identities in the IoT network. This is an important aspect in IoT network in order to cooperate with other devices [13]. The devices need to be provided with validation systems to avoid security dangers. For instance, for all the IoT gadgets from similar manufacturers that are configured with analogous confirmation accreditations, the hacking of one gadget may lead to violating security at the data level.
- Authorization: Only authorized IoT devices can hold the right to use the network services or resources.

2.3.1.3   At Functional Level

It describes security requirements in terms of the following features:

- Resilience: Resilience provides IoT security during assaults and failures due to the provided network capabilities.
- Self-association: It indicates the system's ability to adapt unaided to be viable while there is a failure of certain parts of the systems due to intermittent break down or malicious assaults.

2.3.2   Classification of IoT Layered Architecture

Other than the above mentioned security stages, it is indispensable to focus on the vulnerabilities and assaults for varied modes of communication. As discussed in [14], the IoT communication architecture can be categorized as (i) Edge-Layer, (ii) Access-Layer, and (iii) Application-Layers.

2.3.2.1   Edge Layer

It pertains to side channel assaults [15]. The objective of assaults is to reveal details of the scrutiny of adverse events like consumption of power, discharges pertinent to electricity, and transmittance time, with nodal points effectuating encryption policies. The consumptive power of the units is one of the major susceptibilities among easy guesses to decrypt secret keys. Here, assaults force IoT devices deplete battery or jam the communications.

2.3.2.2   Access Layer

Eavesdropping, dishonest packets injections, and conversations that are not authorized are some of the major weaknesses. Based on the routing assaults, an assailant can try spoofing, redirecting, misdirecting, or drop packets.

2.3.2.3   Application Layer

Assaults in this layer affect the integrity of machine learning algorithms by altering the training process of learning algorithms software running on the IoT devices.

Some of the major frailties are showcased in [12] and [16] and examine all the facets and provide optimization at miscellaneous layers, from the unit to the cloud frontier. Assaults against IoT devices are shown in [17]. The authors define four possible methodologies, as given below.

i.   Functionality-Ignoring: Assaults ability is to associate with the web to exploit vulnerability. For instance, IoT devices can be utilized to make to enter into the sufferer's network and then pollute users PCs.

ii. Functionality-Reducing: the assailant attempts to reduce objectives of the device, so as to disturb the person or to make breakdowns the entire coordination. For instance, the mode of attack is coordinated to workings like smart

TVs and refrigerators, with the intention to stall their working devices so as to extort currency after the sufferer for reestablishing their regular conduct.

iii. Functionality-Abuse: IoT elements are meant to be convenient to administrator. For instance, an assailant might alter "Heating, Ventilation, and AC control" and spoil the domain by unnecessarily diminishing the temperature. In the same way, the attacker takes overall control of the smart devices and overwriting the victims' orders.

iv. Functionality-Extending: The IoT device is taken for service to accomplish all kinds of functionalities. For instance, in living environment, an alarm signal may be utilized for watching the site of the sufferer even when the alarm is off.

2.4   IoT Security Threats

By way of consistent refinement of speculative familiarity and growth of every day applicable conditions, security concerning issues uncovered using IoT innovation seem to be increasingly unambiguous. The threat of IoT security has continuously drawn in exploration and examination by researchers widely. In the midst three-layer IoT design, few researchers suggested every layer associating with conventional three-layer assembly relating with most threats. The physical layer includes IoT terminal, WSN, and RFID security [18]. The above supposed classes take not only physical but also network relevant concerns of security. Issues with network layer are rooted in "security and authentication", while privacy and reliability pose problems in application layer [19].

Unsurprisingly, the various leveled investigation method for IoT security threats as disclosed by the conventional design has lost its real-world importance. This strategy cannot wholly sum up the IoT security threats experienced in the disaster stage. Hence, quests at this stage just view this order as a characterization strategy. In [20] ordering of security intimidations by "active and passive" assaults, methods for labels that are inhibited, distorted, shaped, replayed, and captured. Anyhow, this grouping plan just comprises of data security in the IoT domain.

As of now, a few have proposed security threats for edge processing [21], and a few characterized them as designated by definite attributes of IoT structure. For example, as shown by the decent variety of IoT, it is separated into two types of threats in IoT security [22]. Classification is done as per multiplicity and interoperability [23]. These have brought in a perfect classification of particular dangers in systems; these are explicit and not all factors are inclusive to a specific component classification. It will describe three aspects of IoT security threats, namely, "physical device, network communication, and finally data threats".

2.4.1   Physical Device Threats

Conservative digital security risks incorporate mask, prohibited association, unapproved access, denial of service, withdrawal, see page of information, analysis traffic, and data destruction. The major IoT and conventional network security has huge issues with IoT devices.

2.4.1.1   Device-Threats

An end-point device plays a major role at the time of data gathering. In IoT network, identity is substantial between devices to secure devices from several kinds of attacks [21]. In IoT network, security is enhance do wing to various trending technologies like cryptography mechanism. Despite, IoT devices and sensors are impacted by the numerous threats. Normally, RFID has vulnerability to physical assaults, along with the damage of the node by itself. RF tags are attacked by Assailants order for altering the tag contents and communication channels blocked [24]. In appalling cases, the whole network will be in a damaged condition. Besides, in the network holding wireless sensors, the individual nodes have limitations with respect to battery as well as storage.

2.4.1.2   Resource Led Constraints

Devices being attacked portray [21] that IoT devices hold resources limitations. This resource limitation will compel the quantification of nodes, not being able to perform complicated quantifications, and thereby, finally, it leads to threatening the entire technology. This form of restriction mainly dominates the analyses of edges, restricting the system refinement.

2.4.2   Network-Oriented Communication Assaults

In IoT security formation, physical threats form part and parcel of the IoT security. Fundamentally, the IoT has qualities of "interoperability and operability"; nevertheless, it exposes all weaknesses of "controllability and heterogeneity". While designing IoT systems, communication among network elements transmit save as well as prepare the data communicated through the hidden layer.

2.4.2.1   Structure

Primarily, the greatest differences spanning IoT network and the conventional one lie in the details where previous one has traits of sensibility and powerless controllability. This has carried extraordinary complications to the advancement of the IoT and it should be connected with the Internet. The specialized strategy in the three layers of the IoT [18] is not just wired communication but it is remotely connected association and via Bluetooth, Wi-Fi, Ethernet, ZigBee, etc. IoT has a bonding with a massive number of varied intense components. But looking at the other side, this diversity marks network management mechanism for incredibly complicated equipment [25].

Other side, conservatively the three layer system, namely, the hidden WSN exhibits weak controllability. "Controllability and manageability" aims to accomplish the "dissemination and content of information". Considering the standard type of propagation and proliferation content observation, the most ordinary model is the hosting of password strategy. Here, the encryption algorithm is stringent in accordance with the necessities about controllability. The software outlined networking application in IoT's security [26] is the arrangement that emulates handling of the IoTs.

Howsoever, this mechanism has not been wholly advanced for current situations. The important test is facing of threats. In IoT, centralized control frequently turns into its confinement, and again in the most cynical scenario, it might turn into the tailback of the whole network. Its control node is immobilized against any harm. When the control hub is negotiated, a corrupted node can exploit this vulnerability to attack the network. Examples of such assaults are "DoS assaults, alteration of data, black hole assaults, and side channel assaults" [27].

2.4.2.2   Protocol

Every time IoT data is available over the network, it should be "transmitted, prepared, as well as have them stored". Innumerable procedures are applied for the interactions. They are characterized as "transmission and communication protocols". "REST/HTTP, MQTT, CoAP, DDS, AMQP, XMPP, and JMS" are the some of the foremost protocols in addition "MQTT, AMQP, and XMPP" are cloud servers under communication, many types of IoT communication protocols acknowledged in MQTT protocol, etc [28]. MQTT is a M2M light weighted convention and it will work on minimum-bandwidth approach. CoAP enables an assailant to transmit a small UDP packet to a CoAP user and gets a bigger packet as response. In this manner, it is powerless against DDoS assaults. The cause is that the protocol itself does eliminate session management and encryption processing requirements. Both the "AMQP protocol and the XMPP protocol" hold read object spoofing weaknesses.

2.4.3   Data-Based Threats

Data securing methods consists of five qualities in terms of "confidentiality, integrity, availability, controllability, and non-repudiation".

2.4.3.1   Confidentiality

It refers to the attributes that data is not exposed to or employed by unauthorized users. Explicit IoT security threats are deceiving, with unlawful connections, unauthorized access, data disclosure, DoS, refusal, traffic examination, invalid data stream, and data altering. Individual authentication intimidations in IoT security mention to mock assaults taking validation credentials to access unapproved service. In IoT, hoaxing of IP address will prompt DoS assaults to make a botnet. DoS assaults are operative by utilizing in numerable traded off PCs. Some of the IoT devices are tainted with malware, at that point converting every device into a bot.

At last, bot group can remotely organized by assailant, which is known as bots. The cavity assault linked using a bogus route exploits malevolent nodes in order to use the unbelievable way as the ideal path to coordinate data traffic. Instantaneously, any specific transfer attack is likewise a data led assault manner [30]. Any assailant unambiguously sends pernicious packets while rejecting genuine noteworthy data packets [22].

The IoT mechanism has benefitted us but has lots troubles to maintain data confidentiality. It is big trial for to sustain user as well as developer's privacy issues. These days, network scheme is not fitting and even a least knowledgeable person can fetch data through unlawful means, with important data transferred to web regularly with a chance to leak valuable data such as passwords, finger prints, address, and credentials, with data frequently saved in the cloud.

2.4.3.2   Availability

In the IoT network, because of assuring the availability, heaps of data can be transmitted successfully and dependably. As the system data is running, it can be effectively read. When the system is negotiated, instantaneously resolve such conditions, to improve performance. The routing data swapped can be counterfeit or altered when there is a fake attack of route. Replay attack [24] infers that the assailant directs a packet that the destination has acknowledged to complete spoofing the system; its target is to terminate the user authentication. This type of replay assault is tough to compete with regardless of how it is encoded.

2.4.3.3   Integrity

Integrity refers to the fact that transmitted data cannot be modified by anyone in the network, with the aim that data can be precisely created, terminated, and transmitted. This showcases definite problems to data security. Customary schemes integrate symmetric key methods and public key infrastructure (PKI). Blockchain will give guarantee data integrity maintenance due to its distributed nature.

To shield customers, businesses, and various devices, decision-making experts should be attentive about the exclusive risks of IoT systems. These include the following:

1. Customer information exposures: Most IoT devices quantify and transfer sensitive information. There are many gadgets that can communicate information that can be employed malevolently.
2. Corporate information exposures: When linked straightaway to a concern's information focus, IoT devices exposed security sections basically outside of knowledge of most in built Information Technology members. These may lead to appalling susceptibility and information loss.
3. Physical devices impairments: A lot of IoT components have an actuator that, when incorrectly triggered, may physically damage clients systems.
4. Higher risk-oriented downtimes: Several IoT services may pose serious issues in case of failure of services. Interconnected medical equipment should still operate properly when not online.
5. Comprehensive liabilities: Hacking of IoT can produce liability for all physical damages above information loss or identity holdup. Hacking of these elements can have interrupt shelf life and properties liabilities.

6. Reputations and trademark damages: Trademark aimed businesses can agonize due to immense losses due to security assaults. With increased online and offline outlets, clients have higher impact and opinion. Corporates must protect against larger scaled information events ruining reputations.

2.5   Assaults in IoT Devices

In view of the chapter, the assaults on IoT features are classified as well as cited accordingly. In order to have devices as smart secure devices, it is a stimulating task to designers for various constraints analysis largely at the time of design, even though the system gets more complex which contributes to many assaults and threats. The assailants are easily manipulating the devices. Accordingly, the major determination of the assailant is to effortlessly get compromised with the security services of the system. So that, the core motto of the IoT device is to guarantee with the security services like confidentiality, integrity, and availability.

In the IoT network, every smart device is connected with the web, they indirectly getting the weaknesses of such structure like DDoS, replay assaults, eavesdropping, and web-application threats [31]. Consequently, assaults are classified into three sorts on the basis of the IoT infrastructure and registered here.

2.5.1   Devices of IoT

Devices of IoT are used to obtain data from its domain with the aid of internet connection. Some of the assaults scheduled and discussed below.

i. Brute force attack: The main objective of the attacker is to get authentication credentials of the smart device by employing guessing mechanism. When some of the devices have login credentials that are default and the assailant is aware about it, then he can easily get those devices' sensitive information using default password set obtainable on the web. In IoT devices, botnet attack reasons for such susceptibility [32].

ii. Buffer overflow attack: It happens owing to uninformed faults during coding leading to this attack [33].

iii. BlueBorne attack: This attack occurs when communication medium is Bluetooth-it is employed by smart TV, printer and washing machine etc. There is likelihood to hold this attack even as Bluetooth is incapable to pair up with any further devices. Once misused, the assailants can achieve whatever the task assigned [34].

iv. Sybil (related to sensor networks) attacks: Fake devices can be used to create chaos in the system and the device performance gets weakened. Any harmful node can perform this assault by communicating over diverse personalities creating chaos [35].

2.5.2 Gateways and Networking Devices

For transmitting data to the destination through gateways and networking devices, wireless protocols are utilized by the gateway to communicate, and then the assailant can link to the gateway via wireless assaults. Some of the attacks listed below.

i. Injection attack: In the communication procedure, assailants use weakness and pervade the data into network. While protocol is verifying data integrity, assailant can alter data injected and obtain overall control from the system [36].

ii. Man-in-the-middle attack: It scouts the traffic streaming between the device and the gateways. If the assailant is unable to perceive the outgoing traffic, then this attack can be stopped. Accordingly, the employment of encryption in the convention is essential [29, 37].

iii. DNS poisoning: Whenever the assailant can damage the records belonging to DNS from the corresponding server, any information across devices get transferred across goal planned. Then, malign servers fetch the info from the units [38].

iv. Replay assaults: In this assault, the assailant surveys and saves replica of the traffic for later use. Afterward, devices can be accessed by operating on recently discoursed traffic. The approved traffic data is consumed over and over in an alternate background [39].

v. Wormhole attack: Wormhole attack will generate issues and cause overcrowding in the network in order to direct data from one place to another and form heavy traffic [40].

2.5.3   Cloud Servers and Control Devices

This section compacts how data are stored and well-ordered remotely in IoT infrastructures. There is a probability to exploit servers when the cloud servers are improperly connected as well as end-point devices.

i.   SQL injection: It occurs if the web application does not approve any contribution of the client appropriately. However, without approval, the user response is given to the server program and it might execute whatever the response given the outbreak on SQL server. Consequently, data required is gathered by attacker. This situation leads to huge loss for that particular company who has this issue [41].

ii.   DDoS: It renders the service unreachable by the client by engulfing the system with heavier traffic. This incapacitates system assets and devices execution. This attack takes place by negotiating massive equipment available across modeling bots [42].

iii.   Weak authentication: Due to weak verification system, the system can be signed in using brute force technique and via default passwords. Huge mainstream of the devices are weak authentically in the absence user and designer [43].

iv.   Malicious applications: If any user comprises pernicious application in the cell phone, at that point, there are chances of regulating the application activities. Thus, the assailant can control all the devices coordinated with the telephone [44].

v.   Back doors and exploits: As the representatives download non-trusted applications down the web, the PC can be destabilized and undermining system. From this time, it might demand money related transactions organization's name [45].

The countermeasures for the assaults are to assure integrity, secrecy, as well as accessibility in the system. The vast main stream of the IoT devices are obligatory to act in the ideal working environments, the countermeasures need not impact the exhibition or the comfort of use of the framework to the clients. The application of interruption discovery and counteraction systems can confirm a large portion of the remarkable system assaults [46].

Information can be seen travelling over system decoding calculations using best practices. Again, a great portion of the frameworks are destabilized by the improper installation by the framework managers. Lightweight conventions must be employed for upgrading the system exhibition with no cooperating security [47]. Suitable assessment must be completed to exterminate the basic and critical susceptibilities in the framework. Therefore, the assailant reason is that it is simple to misappropriate by brute force. System's integrity is conceded if device is installed imperfectly.

The IoT system is unprotected to various varieties of assaults. Currently, a substantial number of the assailant target IoT devices. For example, Mirai bot involves the IoT devices associated with the internet. Privacy, integrity, and accessibility should be protected in the IoT. Similar to this, the usage of cryptography stays elementary for safeguarding from assailants. Requirements for cyber-security are decisive in protecting the system from catastrophes. Futuristic explorations depend on execution upgrades and complex computation usage for security.

2.6   Security Analysis of IoT Platforms

Nowadays, IoT market considerably rises its growth as well as concurrently security subjects are also increases. Particularly, in IoT mechanism platforms, foremost stimulating task is about security. Some of the IoT mechanism platforms listed and labeled below [48, 49].

2.6.1   ARTIK

ARTIK is formed by Samsung and is a merged IoT stage. This stage integrates based on OCF confirmation novelty and IoT components, for example, "equipment, programming, cloud, security, and environment". Still, it is an average based on cloud IoT stage that performs security methodology including data trade and confirmation. The "MQTT, CoAP, and Websocket" are augmented as the application convention. The AES and RSA cryptography calculations are endorsed for information privacy. Moreover, the ARTIK module contributes a cryptographic motor to encryption and decoding.

In protected correspondence, classification as well as verification is noteworthy. Along these lines, ARTIK utilizes PKI to craft and have outstanding authentications and key sets to every component in the accumulating procedure. Besides, in receipt of the ECDH calculation as a scheme for identifying key in oder to secure IoT devices. Additionally, it fortifies

JTAG administrations for phase troubleshooting and secure OTA administrations for secure apprise or formation of the stage.

2.6.2   GiGA IoT Makers

It refers to open IoT stage reliant on oneM2M shaped via media communications organization. This stage is explicitly objectified by the elements of layers. It extends its security work in need of the security administration given. Along the lines, they have copious basic security mechanisms, no matter how the system seems extraordinary. Furthermore, GiGA IoT Makers is reinforced by the AES and RSA cryptography designs for information privacy. GiGA IoT Makers fortify REST API and diverse mechanical conventions, for instance, "HTTP, MQTT, CoAP, and TCP". All correspondence consumes TLS-transport conventions, and AES is contained as encryption techniques to warranting information confidentiality. Every cryptographic oriented calculation follows Cipher block chaining and counter style confirming with the data characteristics.

2.6.3   AWS IoT

It is all about cloud linked IoT stage delivering bidirectional correspondences through Amazon enabling gadgets interact with AWS IoT to efficiently engage with software and different gadgets. In AWS IoT, each allied gadget need to have security certifications to get to the administration and security accreditations must be reserved securely to transport safely. The REST interfaces are sustained as the entrance policy for exploiting assets of approved customers. AWS IoT accepts TLS-transport conventions to ensure with time make about information correspondence. As well, the PKI framework could be functional to guarantee validation same as trustworthiness confirmation and non-disavowal evading.

2.6.4   Azure IoT

It is platform formed through Microsoft envisioned to support forming IoT applications. The stage deals an assortment of highpoints to work as "SaaS (software as a service) answers for PaaS (platform as a service) and intelligence Edge". "HTTP, MQTT, and AMQP" are established as application conventions. TLS is received as a vehicle convention to guarantee information safety. AES and RSA guarantee information with twofold encrypting technique.

Azure IoT security is the significant part of this perception is the Hub and permits secured communication among the stage as well as gadgets operating gadget explicit security approvals. |PKI framework deals essentially with guarantee information trustworthiness, verification, and nondenial. Notwithstanding confirmation strategy x.509 declarations and "HMAC-SHA256", there is technique—OAuth to substantiate and support customers employing accesses tokens. Platform as a service includes dynamic index to superintend get to control, Azure universe DB, an all-around distributed database administration, and stream exploratory to differentiate information changes uninterruptedly to secure accessibility.

2.6.5   Google Cloud IoT (GC IoT)

GC IoT is a stage for perceptive IoT administrations that supervises information circulation, information handling, and IoT devices assumed over the globe. It warranties safe associations with components. Customer employs the REST application interfaces to reach stage's assets and backing "MQTT and HTTP" agreement. To anticipate associations with maleficent devices, it operates on "JWT (JSON web token)" in form of a system verifying components. This methodology can restrict consequences on a solitary gadget instead of manipulating complete gadget.

Also, this technology bolsters "RSA and ECC cryptography" computations that have solid mark key size. Details are encoded with "AES-128 or AES-256", but lesser information necessitating confirmation is applied in "CBC with AES and HMAC". Likewise, duplicated artifacts are run in CTR with HMAC and AES. Another characteristics such as "PKI and OAuth", where PKI innovation is functional to warrant information respectability along with validation and OAuth innovation developing access related tokens are useful to validate customers.

In general, the complications and the level of IoT require enacting novel, all-inclusive tactic to IoT security, where safety is approached in practical way and threats are handled in a mountable and consistent manner. The IoT expertise of current day is too complicated and unsettling for security as against insecurely-assimilated solutions. But, security needs be profoundly rooted in each stage of production round, ranging from products designing to development and then deployment. Very often, safety inclines to be an addendum in growth, and though there may be exceptions, in most cases absence of risks awareness lead to businesses pushing IoT devices without regard for safety to market.

Hence, the perception of safety-by-design must be a major driving factor in futuristic IoT security led researches. It is an attitude that has been conventionally practical to software as well as hardware creation. It looks for making systems free of susceptibilities and resistant to attacks as probable before the system is truly on the rampage to market. It is normally attained by measures like broad testing and adopting best of practices in software design. The security through designing models is in contrast with less vigorous techniques inclusive of security via obscureness, minority, and obsolescence. Precisely, it brings about are solution-oriented security models focusing on knowledge on what the IoT applications must perform rather than that the attackers perform.

Equally from other technical arenas, attaining security via design in IoT is suggestively thought-provoking, assuming that the network measure and diversity of IoT units. So, we require an applied yet inclusive and operative framework that may aid motivating implementation of security with design ideologies in the quick-paced, changing IoT background. Hence, there is need for novel framework wherein security is considered as a control issue of an IoT self-motivated system.

Every IoT system needs maintenance to be ahead of emerging safety risks. The below features as well as actions are aid in preventing future exposures.

1. Ethical hacking: Industries can be ahead of up-to-date hacking systems by recurrently testing systems with security academics and setting possible vulnerabilities when they evolve.
2. Reviews of firmware applications: Security authorities can cleanse application faults during firmware advancement, averting lethal application errors at a client level.
3. Mechanisms for security updates: Security procedures alter and improvise through time, permitting quicker firmware deployments for every device at the same time increases security.

The actual challenges for clients are the cost of identifying devices they create with exclusive IDs, addresses of MAC, keys, and then certificates, on production front or at the time of ground deployment. Nearly technical resolutions on personalization most often offer an extra toolset having provision to the greatest level of security at no added cost.

The enterprise-oriented architectures and safety measures have amended for wired computers to entirely wireless gadgets but same is not with connected components. These days, concerns look forward to linking to several devices via secure public as well as private network segments.

2.7 Future Research Approaches

Cross-cutting security competences casing the complete lifecycle of IoT systems and its modules are looked-for forthcoming IoT application systems. Advance of fresh threat scrutiny and risk running and, in addition, self-regeneration proficiencies to perceive and over throw probable attacks are vital. Accumulating, assimilating, and handling heterogeneous facts from diverse sensors, equipment, as well as systems would require new amalgamated individuality and access managing solutions. Imminent IoT systems must be able to swiftly and properly respond to dangers and attacks, include and study from different threat data, and progress and endorse thread vindication plans. The aptitude to obligingly analyze difficulties and implement safety plans for different subsystems that might be owned by dissimilar entities is also necessary.

Future systems of IoT should as well be able to safeguard manageable information ownership through enterprise borders. To reserve the confidentiality of customers or even enterprises during large volumes of data being processed, innovative data analytical procedures and varied cryptographic approaches are required. Distribution of threat astute information by means of diverse systems allows accommodating security actions that can realize more consistent awareness of the existing and impending attacks.

Methods to assess as well as manage risks for the total lifecycle of intricate IoT systems need new skills to gather and process any data that is related to aspects of security and to accomplish online and dynamic risk-based analyses for that information. New methods grounded on machine-learning systems are wanted to achieve real-time analytics pertaining to threats. The obligatory fresh techniques must yield warnings with greater precision and minimum number of false alarms. They must also be robust against confrontational attacks that may purposely compromise and destabilize learning information in order to regulate the performance of the machine learning methods. New supportive systems for handling risks and security contracts are needed to enable initial caution sin future systems.

Evolvement of test and monitoring-oriented uninterrupted security assessments supporting dynamic valuation of real-time safety levels of systems will be needed. These unremitting audit systems must to be able to evaluate various diverse IoT workings using a wide choice of solutions, from lightweight and minimal-intrusive methodologies for thin components to wide-ranging security appraisals of platforms and edge constituents.

Internet of Things has added a lot of acceptance in reduced time. Likewise, the progresses in Machine Learning as well as Artificial Intelligence have eased the automating process of IoT devices. Essentially, AI in addition to ML agendas is mutual with IoT devices to provide them appropriate automation. Because of this, IoT has also extended its area of usage in several sectors. New research techniques alongside research are discussed in terms of the IoT security in the sections presented below.

2.7.1   Blockchain Technology

Blockchain is a technology employing an individual or organization to maketransactions on a system without the requirement of any third man. The transactions made on blockchain are fullysecured. The solid PC codes utilized in blockchain confirm that no record of the transaction can be changed. Blockchain novelty has been made use of by plentifulfinancial and governmental institutions, business people, customers, and industrialists. This is one of the most typical IoT outlines to manufacture specialized devices.

BC is a distributed database for multitude of records. BCT normally applied for financial transactions, for the Bitcoin Cryptocurrency. The distributed BCT records transactions without exclusion with the aid of online ledger system. BCT is a decentralized, stable, transparent, consistent, and quickly reacting to public as well as private. Because of the accomplishment of Bitcoin, individuals presently commence to apply blockchain technology in abundant fields, for example, casting a ballot, clinical treatment flexibly chain, budgetary market, and security for IoT [50]. BCT creates secure mesh networks, and IoT devices interrelate to evade threats like impersonation, device spoofing, etc.

The system will gauge up to support a cumulative volume of devices without need for added resources [51]. There is a vast enthusiasm for "Ethereum, as a blockchain" technology for what is to arrive.

Exploring potentials of blockchain wherein the blockchain is utilized to offer a privacy-retaining IoT contracting platform. Explicitly, the information extracted by IoT devices is available from peripheral service providers and while at same instant assuring obscurity of IoT devices and producing profits for device owners. As it assures defense against data meddling, it can be efficaciously used to authenticate reliability and legitimacy of software. For example, the technology is employed to authenticate the diverse firmware sorts implanted on IoT system devices. It is also used in smart homes and industrial set-ups to guard indigenous IoT networks then normalize traffic across distributed verification tools.

Also, it is shown that blockchain unavoidably produces calculation overheads because of mining algorithms that finally rises both consumption of energies as well as processing delays. Just in case, any malevolent nodal point retains minimum of 51% of general computing power, it may be able to exploit the consensus contrivance and disrupt the reliability and dependability of the entire network.

2.7.2   5G Technology

IoT protocols are induced by 5G networks design, precisely at perception as well as network layers [52]. Munoz *et al.* [53] established that generating 5G, necessitates without its own on progressing acceptance of usual traffic formation in addition to integrate heterogeneous systems from "End to End (E2E)" with suitable cloud assets to deliver E2E IoT and mobile services. The "MIMO (multiple-input and multiple-output)" expertise arranged in 5G and basic supportive of "QoS" and "Quality of user Experience (QoE)" aware services [54, 55].

2.7.3   Fog Computing (FC) and Edge Computing (EC)

Cloud computing is impractical for certain IoT applications, thereby succeeded by the fog computing. FC is a decentralized computing substructure with regard to data sources and cloud. It improvises cloud computing along with implicit facilities, to network's edge and makes the cloud an emerging tool for efficient data processing. The main goal of the fog computing is to improvise efficiency and lower the data amount transferred.

Information preparation happens in smart device, which is then transmitted to sources for preparing and retransmission, along these lines lowering the data transmission payload for the cloud. The bidirectional communication affects performance and security of the resources. Every time data is sent to the cloud and awaiting response takes a lot of time. By ensuring the fog nodes with the analogous controls, policies, and techniques over various sections of networks, security is managed well [56].

The supreme accomplishment with edge computing is refining activities. Chiefly, there are two classes of security in edge computing: One is the security in edge computing that is improved than any other technologies because data does not move across the network. Next is security that required in edge computing is comparatively higher because the edge devices are themselves are more vulnerable to security faults [57].

IoT expertise is immature yet to a higher extent and it is very much helpful in being little suspicious on the security aspects. Beforehand, the security problems must be researched and be informed prior to developing any IoT led systems. There are higher chances for trade-offs such as UI with poor quality but good security, and there is need to balance on these scenarios.

Also do not be in the rush to bring your product in the market without proper planning for long term support. IoT devices are cheap so chances are very high that manufacturers do not pay enough attention to provide security updates and patches. This is not a sustainable development model for internet of things.

As an IoT application developer always beware of threats. Security breaches are almost bound to happen and you should be ready for them. You should always be ready with an exit plan to secure maximum data in case of an attack.

Despite IoT having undisputable benefits, the realism is that safety is not in accordance with the speed of novelty. With the IoT prevalently expanding, it is anticipated that its heterogeneousness and measure will enlarge prevailing Internet-based security intimidations. As soon as human beings, sensor devices, vehicles, robots etc., are capable to flawlessly interrelate with one another from any part of the globe by IoT, many dangers that we cannot envision these days will be revealed. If compulsory defences are not taken, then malevolent individuals will influence the ubiquity of IoT to disturb communications and achieve substantial financial benefits or physically injure people. For instance, researchers have identified that acute susceptibilities in a wide spread series of IoT monitors to watch babies and which can be controlled by hackers to do number of despicable activities, comprising approving further users for remotely viewing and controlling the monitor. Certain most troublesome circumstances of IoT hackings, nevertheless, include medical devices which can have lethal concerns on the health of the patients.

Fortifying IoT systems is one of the noteworthy obstacles to IoT attainment of its complete potential. In order to really defend devices inflowing, security must be measured at the actual start of devices designing. Shielding IoT units and resources necessitates vigilant analysis of assets since when security is not well-thought-out straight, industries, and operators of IoT might later discover organizations conceded, jeopardizing revenue, and even undergo serious problems. The future state of IoT systems may expose many opportunities along with different security pertinent risks as well as considerations that might be addressed appropriately.

References

1. Zanella, A., Bui, N., Castellani, A., Vangelista, L., Zorzi, M., Internet of Things for smart cities. *IEEE Internet Things J.*, 1, 1, 22–32, Feb. 2014.

2. Evans, D., The Internet of Things. How the next evolution of the Internet is changing everything, in: *Cisco Internet Business Solutions Group, Tech. Rep*, Apr. 2011, accessed on Jun. 2019. [Online]. Available: https://www.cisco.com/c/dam/en_us/about/ac79/docs/innov/ IoT_IBSG_0411FINAL.pdf.

3. Warner, M.R., Internet of Things cyber security improvement act of 2017. *S. 1691, 115th US Congress*, Sep. 2017.

4. Granjal, J., Monteiro, E., Silva, J.S., Security for the Internet of Things: A survey of existing protocols and open research issues. *IEEE Commun. Surv. Tutor.*, 17, 3, 1294–1312, Jan. 2015.

5. Hossain, M.M., Fotouhi, M., Hasan, R., Towards an analysis of security issues, challenges, and open problems in the Internet of Things, in: *Proceedings of IEEE World Congress on Services*, pp. 21–28, Jun. 2015.

6. Kolias, C., Kambourakis, G., Stavrou, A., Voas, J., DDoS in the IoT: Mirai and other botnets. *Computer*, 50, 7, 80–84, Jul. 2017.

7. Xu, T., Wendt, J.B., Potkonjak, M., Security of IoT systems: Design challenges and opportunities, in: *Proceedings of the IEEE/ACM International Conference on Computer-Aided Design*, Nov. 2014, pp. 417–423.

8. Ammar, M., Russello, G., Crispo, B., Internet of Things: A survey on the security of IoT frameworks. *J. Inf. Secur. Appl.*, 38, 8–27, Feb. 2018. [14] Frustaci, M., Pace, P., Aloi, G., Fortino, G., Evaluating critical security issues of the IoT world: Present and future challenges. *IEEE Internet Things J.*, 5, 4, 2483–2495, Aug. 2018.

9. Zhou, W., Jia, Y., Peng, A., Zhang, Y., Liu, P., The effect of IoT new features on security and privacy: New threats, existing solutions, and challenges yet to be solved. *IEEE Internet Things J.*, 6, 2, 1606–1616, Apr. 2019.

10. Atac, C. and Akleylek, S., A Survey on Security Threats and Solutions in the Age of IoT. *Eur. J. Sci. Theol.*, 15, 36–42, March 2019.

11. Marketwired, *Proofpoint uncovers Internet of Things cyberattack*, 2014, Jan, Accessed on Jun. 2019. [Online]. Available: https://www. proofpoint.com/us/proofpoint-uncovers-internet-things-iot-cyberattack.

12. Fremantle, P. and Scott, P., A survey of secure middleware for the Internet of Things. *PeerJ Comput. Sci.*, 3, e114, May 2017.

13. Sicari, S., Rizzardi, A., Grieco, L., Coen-Porisini, A., Security, privacy and trust in Internet of Things: The road ahead. *Comput. Netw.*, 76, Supplement C, 146–164, Jan. 2015.

14. Pielli, C., Zucchetto, D., Zanella, A., Vangelista, L., Zorzi, M., Platforms and protocols for the Internet of Things. *EAI Endorsed Trans. Internet Things*, 15, 1, Oct. 2015.

15. Singh, A., Chawla, N., Ko, J.H., Kar, M., Mukhopadhyay, S., Energy efficient and side-channel secure cryptographic hardware for IoT-edge nodes. *IEEE Internet Things J.*, 6, 1, 421–434, Feb. 2019.
16. Mosenia, A. and Jha, N.K., A comprehensive study of security of Internet of Things. *IEEE Trans. Emerg. Topics Comput.*, 5, 4, 586–602, Oct. 2017.
17. Ronen, E. and Shamir, A., Extended functionality assaults on IoT devices: The case of smart lights, in: *Proceedings of the IEEE European Symposium on Security and Privacy*, pp. 3–12, Mar. 2016.
18. Li, L., Study on security architecture in the internet of things, in: *Proceedings of 2012 International Conference on Measurement, Information and Control*, vol. 1, IEEE, pp. 374–377, 2012.
19. Han, J.-H., Jeon, Y., Kim, J., Security considerations for secure and trustworthy smart home system in the IoT environment, in: *2015 International Conference on Information and Communication Technology Convergence (ICTC)*, IEEE, pp. 1116–1118, 2015.
20. Vorakulpipat, C., Rattanalerdnusorn, E., Thaenkaew, P., Hai, H.D., Recent challenges, trends, and concerns related to IoT security: An evolutionary study, in: *2018 20th International Conference on Advanced Communication Technology (ICACT)*, IEEE, pp. 405–410, 2018.
21. Alrowaily, M. and Lu, Z., Secure edge computing in IoT systems: Review and case studies, in: *2018 IEEE/ACM Symposium on Edge Computing (SEC)*, IEEE, pp. 440–444, 2018.
22. Chaabouni, N., Mosbah, M., Zemmari, A., Sauvignac, C., Faruki, P., Network intrusion detection for IoT security based on learning techniques, in: *IEEE Communications Surveys and Tutorials*, 2019.
23. Al-Fuqaha, A., Guizani, M., Mohammadi, M., Aledhari, M., Ayyash, M., Internet of things: A survey on enabling technologies, protocols, and applications. *IEEE Commun. Surv. Tutor.*, 17, 4, 2347–2376, 2015.
24. Kim, J. and Kim, H., Security vulnerability and considerations in mobile rfid environment, in: *2006 8th International Conference Advanced Communication Technology*, vol. 1, IEEE, pp. 801–804, 2006.
25. Bedhief, I., Kassar, M., Aguili, T., Sdn-based architecture challenging the IoT heterogeneity, in: *2016 3rd Smart Cloud Networks and Systems (SCNS)*, IEEE, pp. 1–3, 2016.
26. Kalkan, K. and Zeadally, S., Securing Internet of Things (IoT) with software defined networking (sdn). *IEEE Commun. Mag.*, 99, 1–7, 2017.
27. Sidki, L., Ben-Shimol, Y., Sadovski, A., Fault tolerant mechanisms for sdn controllers, in: *2016 IEEE Conference on Network Function Virtualization and Software Defined Networks (NFV-SDN)*, IEEE, pp. 173–178, 2016.
28. Shi, Z., Liao, K., Yin, S., Ou, Q., Design and implementation of the mobile internet of things based on td-scdma network, in: *2010 IEEE International Conference on Information Theory and Information Security*, IEEE, pp. 954–957, 2010.

29. Conti, M., Dragoni, N., Lesyk, V., A survey of man in the middle assaults. *IEEE Commun. Surv. Tutor.*, 18, 3, 2027–2051, 2016.
30. Tumrongwittayapak, C. and Varakulsiripunth, R., Detecting sinkhole attack and selective forwarding attack in wireless sensor networks, in: *2009 7th International Conference on Information, Communications and Signal Processing (ICICS)*, IEEE, pp. 1–5, 2009.
31. Strba, S., *Internet of Things Security: Ongoing Threats and Proposed Solutions*, 2018.
32. Jesudoss, A. and Subramaniam, N., A survey on authentication assaults and countermeasures in a distributed environment. *Indian J. Comput. Sci. Eng. (IJCSE)*, 5, 2, 71–77, 2014.
33. Gadaleta, F. *et al.*, Instruction-level countermeasures against stack-based buffer overflow assaults. *ACM International Conference Proceeding Series*, Francesco Gadaleta, 2009.
34. Lonzetta, A. *et al.*, Security vulnerabilities in Bluetooth technology as used in IoT. *J. Sens. Actuator Netw.*, 7, 3, 28, 2018.
35. Newsome, J. *et al.*, The sybil attack in sensor networks: analysis and defenses. *Third international symposium on information processing in sensor networks, 2004. IPSN 2004*, IEEE, 2004.
36. Huang, Y. *et al.*, Bad data injection in smart grid: attack and defense mechanisms. *IEEE Commun. Mag.*, 51, 1, 27–33, 2013.
37. Data, Mahendra, The Defense Against ARP Spoofing Attack Using Semi-Static ARP Cache Table. *2018 International Conference on Sustainable Information Engineering and Technology (SIET)*, IEEE, 2018.
38. Alharbi, F. *et al.*, Collaborative Client-Side DNS Cache Poisoning Attack. *IEEE INFOCOM 2019-IEEE Conference on Computer Communications*, IEEE, 2019.
39. Ding, D. *et al.*, A survey on security control and attack detection for industrial cyber-physical systems. *Neurocomputing*, 275, 1674–1683, 2018.
40. Ma, R. *et al.*, Defenses against wormhole assaults in wireless sensor networks. *International Conference on Network and System Security*, Springer, Cham, 2017.
41. Qian, L. *et al.*, Research of SQL injection attack and prevention technology. *2015 International Conference on Estimation, Detection and Information Fusion (ICEDIF)*, IEEE, 2015.
42. Wang, B. *et al.*, DDoS attack protection in the era of cloud computing and software-defined networking. *Comput. Netw.*, 81, 308–319, 2015.
43. Alomar, N., Alsaleh, M., Alarifi, A., Social authentication applications, assaults, defense strategies and future research directions: a systematic review. *IEEE Commun. Surv. Tutor.*, 19, 2, 1080–1111, 2017.
44. He, D., Chan, S., Guizani, M., Mobile application security: malware threats and defenses. *IEEE Wirel. Commun.*, 22, 1, 138–144, 2015.
45. Vukalović, J. and Delija, D., Advanced persistent threats-detection and defense. *2015 38th International Convention on Information and Communication Technology, Electronics and Microelectronics (MIPRO)*, IEEE, 2015.

46. Anwar, S. *et al.*, From intrusion detection to an intrusion response system: fundamentals, requirements, and future directions. *Algorithms*, 10, 2, 39, 2017.

47. Lee, J.-Y., Lin, W.-C., Huang, Y.-H., A lightweight authentication protocol for internet of things. *2014 International Symposium on Next-Generation Electronics (ISNE)*, IEEE, 2014.

48. Lina, Y., Lee, G., Kim, H., A Study on the Lora Systems. *KICS Proceedings of Symposium of the Korean Institute of communications and Information Sciences*, vol. 6, pp. 217–218, 2017.

49. Garam, K., Ahn, H-b, Kim, G.-B., Lee, J.E., Lee, S.-M., Lee, J.-H., *IoT service development starting with Thingplug*, pageblue, Korea, Nov 2015.

50. Underwood, S., Blockchain beyond bitcoin. *Commun. ACM*, 59, 15–17, Oct. 2016.

51. *How blockchain can change the future of IoT*, 20 Novemver 2016, [Online]. Available: https://venturebeat.com/2016/11/20/how-blockchain-can-change-the-future-of-iot/. [Accessed 2018].

52. Chiang, M. and Zhang, T., Fog and IoT: An overview of research opportunities. *IEEE Internet Things J.*, 3, 854–864, Dec 2016.

53. Munoz, R., Mangues-Bafalluy, J., Vilalta, R., Verikoukis, C., Alonso-Zarate, J., Bartzoudis, N., Georgiadis, A., Payaro, M., Perez-Neira, A., Casellas, R., Martinez, R., Nunez-Martinez, J., Esteso, M.R., Pubill, D., Font-Bach, O., Henarejos, P., Serra, J., Vazquez-Gallego, F., The cttc 5g end-to-end experimental platform: Integrating heterogeneous wireless/optical networks, distributed cloud, and IoT devices. *IEEE Veh. Technol. Mag.*, 11, 50–63, Mar 2016.

54. Yang, N., Wang, L., Geraci, G., Elkashlan, M., Yuan, J., Renzo, M.D., Safeguarding 5g wireless communication networks using physical layer security. *IEEE Commun. Mag.*, 53, 20–27, April 2015.

55. Xu, L., Xie, J., Xu, X., Wang, S., Enterprise lte and wifi interworking system and a proposed network selection solution, in: *2016 ACM/IEEE Symposium on Architectures for Networking and Communications Systems (ANCS)*, pp. 137–138, March 2016.

56. Fog Computing and the Internet of Things: Extend, in: *Cisco*, [Online]. Available: http://www.cisco.com/c/dam/en_us/solutions/trends/iot/docs/computing-overview.pdf, pp. 5. [Accessed 2018].

57. Rouse, M., *Edge computing*, August 2016, [Online]. Available: http://search-datacenter.techtarget.com/definition/edge-computing. [Accessed 2018].

3

Smart Automation, Smart Energy, and Grid Management Challenges

J. Gayathri Monicka[1] and C. Amuthadevi[2*]

[1]*Department of Electrical and Electronics Engineering, SRMIST, Ramapuram, India*
[2]*Department of Computer Science and Engineering, SRMIST, Kattankulatur, India*

Abstract

Energy production is transformed dynamically, and the basic infrastructure containing information and technology is gradually being built. The Internet of Things (IoT) can be an assembly of individual objects at anytime, anywhere, to anyone, to everything, by means of any network and service. Consequently, IoT can denote an enormous, active international configuration of a network of Internet-connected objects through network tools. The further most significant and important claims of IoT are smart grid (SG). SG can be a data net united into the power grid to assemble and analyze data that cannot be inherited as of transmission lines, distribution, and customer substations. With the development and modernization of smart electronic devices in traditional energy grids and their revolution in SGs, there is a prerequisite for retrieving and processing information from these devices in real time or near real time. In addition, data mining requires that field devices can also communicate with each other through a central reference point. Owing to the interoperability of the IoT within smart networks, communication between devices not normally designed for the fullest possible exchange of information, information that will be available from anywhere with Internet access. It works better and quicker than the first transmission and distribution systems. Building computerization is the adopted flow chart of the automated and intelligent events essential in any building/shopping center, i.e., temperature regulator, door regulator, and pressure controller. IoT is a platform for testing networks of various sensors/actuators on the Internet. Safe and fast communication and management is probable from anywhere in the world;

Corresponding author: camuthadevi@gmail.com

R. Anandan, Suseendran Gopalakrishnan, Souvik Pal and Noor Zaman (eds.) The Industrial Internet of Things (IIoT): Intelligent Analytics for Predictive Maintenance, (59–88) © 2022 Scrivener Publishing LLC

this is the foremost application of IoT. The IoT facilitates the storage and analysis of information as well as third-party intervention.

Keywords: IoT, smart grids, building automation, machine to engine, network management, cybersecurity

3.1   Introduction

An innovative scientific solution is desirable to achieve increasingly rare infrastructure resources, particularly given the challenges of population growth, usually with limited capital. Internet of Things (IoT) technologies and principles enable the safe and better management of resources for many resources related to city life, including product evolution, clean, and public transport. When large-scale cities are distributed, advanced information and communication technology (ICT) with IoT technologies are called "smart cities". IoT aids can be reinforced, i.e., augmenting energy consumption and maximizing effectiveness, thereby improving and maximizing the quality of life in the city in terms of living opportunities and resource efficiency. At the skill level, there is interest in authentication, but evolutionary technology itself will use the general cyber security architecture, standards, and requirements. The technology is used to measure sensors and network analysis.

Architecture is about tapping things together with hierarchy. Standards relating to the possibility of installing technology in an extremely systematized way, ensuring easy and reliable end-to-end compatibility, in addition to the machine-to-machine (M2M) standards and methods. However, smart city applications are endless for smart automation systems including qualitative response, transport automation, smart grid (SGs) and buildings, product manufacturing, and logistics applications. Cities are integrating with new knowledge over the years, but recently, technology adoption has increased, especially in supervision, traffic management, electricity, and street lighting [1, 2].

In most cases, the IoT can act to provide some form of communication between devices as well as control their Internet activity. This makes it easy to use for automation and control of electrical and electronic devices. IoT applications are not limited to specific fields, but have expanded the range of applications such as electric vehicles, home automation, industry, smart cities, medicine, and agriculture. To increase security, IoT devices are used to monitor and control all intelligent electrical and electronic systems at residential and construction sites.

- Smart cities
- Mobile applications through the wireless network
- WIFI street lamp
- Intelligent management and automation
- Security and surveillance systems
- Home management

Lately, the complete application has been unified with the IoT in a SG. SCADA is one of the major areas of IoT application, providing central monitoring and control of data transmission and distribution and the connection with linked objects of IoT is represented in Figure 3.1.

SG maximizes available power by generating and distributing electricity according to load. In this chapter, the specific challenges and claims of IoT for smart cities are discussed, particularly challenges, technical solutions, and technical challenges related to extensive IoT training in the areas of intelligent automation, intelligent energy, and municipal network. Smart cities are not based on any precise or distinctive IoT technology and nevertheless cover solely types of IoT technologies, complete with relevant analytics networks and sensors, altogether of which might depend on a specific vertical conventionally, even in smart city applications, IoT is considered to providing a large number of devices with relatively low bandwidth, especially in M2M environments such as electricity meters and industrial control. However, new trends in smartphone and video applications that have incoming streams are increasing the resolution of ultra-high-definition images. These new IoT applications are called IoT built transfer applications (IoTMM) [3, 4].

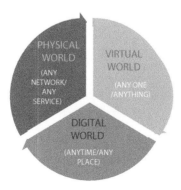

Figure 3.1 Connections and linked objects of IoT.

3.2   Internet of Things and Smart Grids

Most of the physical resources have been digitized and joint to meet the needs and requirements of multiple organizations. The extend use of the IoT is apparent in industrial areas known as Industrial IoT "IIoT" for intelligent applications such as smart agricultural, smart well-being, industrial computerization, smart retailing, and power system [5].

Figure 3.2 shows an example. Autonomous robots are used in countless industries, including manufacturing. When the robot is connected to the server and logic, the robot's actions are automatically linked to each other more than ever before. Since all resources or components are digitally connected, all activities are performed intelligently with little human intervention and physical robot movement and they are also portable.

In IoT, the configuration of all sensors and actuators periodically collects real-time data (homogeneous/heterogeneous) in the environment and sends it to servers distributed in the remote network model. Security must be ensured when transferring data between IoT devices and servers. More recently, more risks have been highlighted in the use of sensitive data, such as video recordings, real-time personal location, corporate access control, manufacturing processes, and obtaining medical information

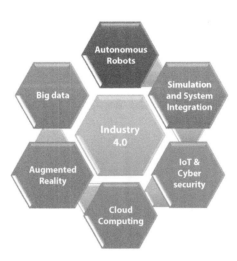

Figure 3.2 Autonomous robots with Industry 4.0.

[6]. In addition, some commercial IoT devices have been attacked and are attracting public attention.

In addition to the technical side of IoT and IIoT, all stakeholders (especially manufacturers and end users) need to be aware of the risks and implement cybersecurity challenges. Because many IoT devices are manufactured by a variety of low-cost vendors (such as smart TV devices), each set of sensors is designed to work in autonomous systems with few or no vulnerabilities. Therefore, many manufacturers may not be aware of the dangers of using them on the Internet. This leads to the fact that when developing a new product, and more tests are needed before commercialization [7]. Sometimes, end users may not even train, so they risk losing or stealing data.

3.2.1   Smart Grid in IoT

The IoT will support SG technology. Comprehensive IoT detection and processing capabilities will enhance SG capabilities such as processing, alerting, self-improvement, disaster recovery, and consistency. The convergence of IoT and SG is largely influencing the emergence of smart stations, meters and sensors, hardware, and communication strategies.

1. The IoT is used to reliably transfer information over a wired and wireless infrastructure between multiple SG components (power group, transmission lines, distribution, and feeding/deployment) as in the field of energy production, IoT will get used to monitoring energy production from various types of power plants, e.g., solar wind biomass and coal, gas emissions, and energy consumption for storage and forecasting the power needed to supply consumers.

2. The IoT is used to collect data on electricity consumption, distribution, monitoring and protection of power lines, substations and towers, and to switch and monitor. IoT is used in the customer's approach in sensible meters to work with various smart parameters.

3. The IoT will be used via the customer approach in sensitive meters to measure various parameters, intellectual energy feeding, power on completely diverse nets, charging and discharging of rechargeable vehicles, management of energy, and energy 2 IoT application.

3.2.2   IoT Application

Main features of IoT applications are listed below:

1. High reliability AMI: AMI can be a key part of SG. The IoT will be used in AMI to collect information, test for anomalies in SG, exchange information among sensitive meters, view power quality and distributed energy, and analyze consumer consumption patterns.

2. Functional house: Smart house is castoff to move with consumers and SG, improve SG amenities, meet advertising claim, recover quality of service, manage sensitive equipment, display collected energy consumption information from sensitive meters, and monitor renewable energies.

3. Monitoring of power lines: With wireless broadband technologies persecuted, transmission lines will be monitored for faults and repaired.

4. Assistant electric vehicle (EV) control system: Auxiliary power unit control systems include a charging station, an electric vehicle, and a monitoring center. Using GPS, operators can find close charging stations and parking information. GPS can mechanically guide car driver in the direction of the utmost apt charging station. The monitoring center accomplishes car batteries, chargers, and charging positions and makes optimal use of resources.

To use IoT on SG, always follow certain technologies and meet some of the needs listed below:

(i) **Communication technology:** Communication technologies will be familiar with receiving and transmitting non-existent information on the condition of SG equipment. Standards for short and long-range communication technologies like ZigBee wireless technology, Bluetooth, and ultra-broadband technologies remain as short-range intelligence technologies. Extensive distance communications use cables, optical fibers, 3G and 4G wireless cellular networks, and satellite communications.

(ii) **Information fusion methods:** The properties of the IoT terminal such as bandwidth batteries and memory are inadequate; it is impossible to refer all information to the destination. Therefore, information consolidation techniques are used to collect and combine data to improve data collection capacities.

(iii) **The process of collecting energy in houses:** Since most IoT devices use a battery with their primary power, there is home power. This technique is extremely important in IoT applications, such as finding completely diverse sensors and cameras toward examine different components of the SG.

(iv) **Work in difficult conditions:** IoT devices connected to high voltage power lines and substations must create a harsh environment. Therefore, to spread the life of their sensors under these circumstances, it is always necessary to have high resistance, anti-electromagnetic, or waterproof vasoconstrictor.

(v) **Dependability:** IoT applications in many surroundings can meet diverse needs for reliability, self-assembly, or self-repair. Therefore, with the support of a specific location, the corresponding IoT device requirement is elite to solve environmental problems, e.g., as soon as some devices are unable to send information due to a power failure, it is essential to find a new route for the information in order to maintain the reliability of the network at a certain level.

(vi) **Security:** Security policies should be used in conjunction with IoT layers to transfer, store and achieve information, and prevent data leaks.

(vii) **Sensors:** Real-time sensor sizes are compatible with temperature, voltage current, light, frequency, power, and variable signals and provide raw information for processing, transmission, and analysis. Lately, the science of engineering has been used to produce an excellent material which encompasses very different device applications and contributes to the development of the sensor.

3.2.3 Trials and Imminent Investigation Guidelines

To attain the procedural goals of using IoT in SG, there are numerous problems that need to be addressed separately in imminent analytical directions. Since completely different environments will have to be added to IoT devices, which will have severe environments, e.g., high or low temperatures, high voltage, revelation toward magnetic waves, and swimming in water, so they essential respond to needs under such conditions that they like reliability of Compliance. In various applications, IoT devices and sensors support batteries, i.e., diverse sorts of sensors castoff to monitor transmission lines, consequently appropriate home harvesting methods would be castoff or developed. Different communication networks in many SG components, thus IoT devices need to support the required communication protocols, which make the transfer of information from sensitive meters to essential system possible, and since SG IoT devices take limited properties and capacity, they like batteries and computing power.

Information storing or measurement and then knowledge integration processes need to be trained to compress and aggregate payload data so that information and data sorting can be energetically and economically utilized. Latency and packet loss are key metrics that test healthy tape performance. Because congestion roots delays and packet loss, it reduces structure routine as IoT devices and or IoT entries have to resend information, resulting in long delays and increasing the likelihood of congestion, and SG cannot meet the needs expected, such as it is necessary to reduce delays, augment the network style by outcome the best possible range of IoT Associates in the portals and nursing devices, and reduce the quantity of networks to each gateway. Subsequently, a normal network comprises numerous gateways and alternative IoT devices with diverse characteristics and resources; the ability to exchange information between these devices is extremely important that IoT devices must provision completely diverse communication protocols and designs. Sensors, smart meters, and various like strategies that live and gather information on a highly intellectual grid generate vast information that can consume large amounts of energy and other resources and act as an obstruction.

The requirement is to design a sensible grid in order to competently stock and progress this enormous quantity of accumulated information. There are several discrete morals for IoT devices, but there is no single standard for SG IoT devices. This can cause security, reliability, and capacity issues for SG IoT strategies. Consequently, a concerted calibration effort is needed. To monitor and control IoT strategies in SG, it must constantly custom a very sensitive network, and attackers manipulate the measured data with smart sensors and meters, resulting in huge economic Thus, to design a secure communication for IoT devices on a SG, taking into account the resource constraints of IoT devices and testing about safety procedures for these devices, i.e., there are compute and storage limitations on IoT devices. Therefore, always design or apply security solutions to support IoT devices. From insights gleaned from sane accountants, a taste of what can be learned habits of the user, e.g., waiting times, it is therefore important to ensure that such personal data are not used without the user's consent. Adequate security measures should also be developed, such as trust management between IoT devices belonging to completely different parties, such as clients and devices, authentication, authorization, integrity information theft, confidentiality, and identity in police investigations.

3.3   Conceptual Model of Smart Grid

Bilateral IEDs, analogous to sensors, actuators, well devices, and good meters, provide broad domain and applicability of the capacity line, cumulative reliability, and quality, preserving the time balance among production and production, energy consumption [8], consistent and economical power supply, optimal use of resources, energy saving, distributed production of renewable energy, and reduction of losses and reduction of greenhouse gas emissions through sanctions.

Smart grid system corresponds to several components, corresponding to regional dispatch centers, power generation and distribution facilities, sub-stations, clients, exchange offices, ICT devices, periodic metering units (PMUs), log servers, connected terminal units (RTUs), equipment, distribution boards, protections, IEDs, Human machine Interfaces (HMIs), circuit breakers, protocol entries, and health meters [9]. The same parts are linked to a good operating, monitoring and flow network, as well as to the main electricity meters. Current cybersecurity techniques may not be sufficient to meet the need for good networked cybersecurity [9]. Hence, good networked systems have unique goals, milestones, and opportunities for a reliable communication structure and a reliable power source. Good networking applications have resources that need to be considered for a cost-effective implementation.

Supervisory Control and Data Acquisition (SCADA) ensures clear scheduling and compliance of the power distribution network. It is commonly used in immense gauge environments [10]. By locally controlling the automation and equipment of the medium voltage stations, this will help everyone to ensure the consistency of the energy offered and diminish the costs of network maintenance and operation. Distribution Management System (DMS) and Energy Management System (EMS) are sub-systems linked to SCADA. It provides values intended for power dominance, compliance, and performance in industrial procedures. A SCADA scheme involves four components [11], as illustrated in Figure 3.3:

1. Information interface devices such as an RTU and a Programmable Logic Controller (PLC).
2. Communication net equivalent to satellite, radio, telephone, and cable TV.
3. Main Central Processing Unit.
4. HMI code or computer system, collecting or changing the state of information compensations the network. Remote and mechanical control processes can be realized with RTU and PLC. Several technologies are used to secure SCADA networks, including VPN, IPSec, firewalls, handler and device validation, and Intrusion Detection Systems (IDS).

In addition, access logs and distribution control instructions stay extremely important to a SCADA scheme. Network time information must be coordinated to effectively confirm the consistency and safety of the SCADA system [12]. Consequently, customers must obtain an Association Agreement with their utilities in order to use an equivalent standard reference time. GPS with date and time synchronization to generate log and time files, and all controls are safe and accurate. Therefore, DER can be used to control the load. Advanced Metering Infrastructure (AMI) is the incorporation of numerous telecommunication that offer enhanced connections

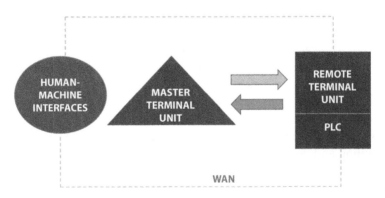

Figure 3.3 Architecture of SCADA.

among the control center and the associated meters [13] A virtuous IoT created mesh makes AMI easy to apply. AMIs are also known to be good indicators [14]. A good OLD counter, an active input, and a counter data organization scheme remain the core elements of the AMI [14]. AMI is liable intended for assembling, analyzing, loading, and delivering dimension information sent by meters to sanctioned parties.

Then, it processes the information to forecast demand and manages discounts and billing. It helps clients to make the most of their energy by knowing how long they are using it. In addition, it helps to collect valuable information about customer service usage to preserve the reliability of your skill system. AMI initially fetches by sending computer code updates, orders, inquiries, and pricing information from approved parts to existing service points [15].

A technological solution can be a good measure. Good accounting includes new instrumentation, telecommunications infrastructure, and central information analysis systems. In addition, it enables bi-directional information flow, optimizes electrical grids, and helps improve the protection, consistency, and quality of service (QoS); they need to meet performance, energy, and security [16]. Meters provide two-way communication among the central system and meters. Good meters record valuable information equivalent to energy consumption for control or charging [17]. It will from time to time provide information upon demand or in response to firm incidents of the efficacy company. They will jointly respond to needs related to power failures, load shedding, period estimation, and computer code updates to the two-way communication capability. In addition, they will act as an EMS zone that monitors the energy consumption of well-equipped home appliances, equivalent to oven, refrigerators, air conditioners, and electric vehicles. The IoT-based grid is a type of standard power line with IoT technologies. The IoT is one of the punitive ideas that play an essential role in a good web. A good mesh is considered in combination with a shape.

Implementing the IoT on a good network enables large-scale, bi-directional flow of information and properties throughout the network infrastructure for remote control and monitoring of the power system. With the IoT, you can efficiently view and manage your desired devices over the Internet. Each device on the network is considered a connected entity and contains a completely diverse IP address that can be castoff to control strategies on the network, therefore linking the various devices into an intelligent and autonomous system. This helps to transfer large amounts of information to the Internet. Communication is likely to the massive availability of alternative sensors, actuators, and good objects on board the entire system, as well as the use of good alternative meters and smart objects from the client's point of view. It also allows you to reschedule energy consumption and demand, helping customers monitor their consumption and change their behavior.

Plug-in Hybrid Electric Vehicle (PHEV) helps reduce CO_2 emissions and reduce dependency on fossil fuels by supporting DER in good networked applications [18]. PHEV works with hydrocarbons and electricity. PHEV batteries can be charged at a customer check-in counter or elsewhere. Subsequently utmost PHEV batteries are intended to discharge quickly, PHEVs will deliver power to the grid [19]. The installation of the automobile network will expand reliability and surge the capacity of the electrical network. Still, the trade-off among margins and prices remains distorted. For start-ups, DER, RES, and communication gears are alternative key features for a good network. Capacitive line communications are available over wireless, wired, fiber optic, microwave, and local area networks wherever good bandwidth differences are used.

The SG can be an idea that fit in ICT with grid-connected power systems to provide economical and smart production and consumption of energy [20]. It is categorized by a two-way movement of all electricity and information. Sensitive network techniques include new solutions that will effectively use the current electrical system to reduce or eliminate failures, sags, and overloads. Utilities can take advantage of this as it will reduce the need for goods for important things. If demand exceeds an entire generation, then these systems can prevent network outages or major power outages and increase the responsibility, quality, safety, and security of network bandwidth. Sensitive network solutions are commonly used in all parts of the network: production, transmission, and distribution. Lately, the common component of the sensitive network, the sensitive home, has become an important (general) topic of analysis and interest in SG applications. A sensitive home denotes to the use of ICTs in home control ranging from dominant devices to automation of home options windows, lighting, etc. A key element of a safe home is the use of intelligent energy planning algorithms that can enable residents to maximize a priori choices on how to use electricity to reduce energy consumption.

Additional frequently used term is home automation or home mechanization. The combination of advanced information, communication technologies, and detection systems creates the proliferation of new potential applications. Cutting-edge new ideas, the ubiquitous or ubiquitous love of computers [21], wherever the computer looks everywhere and everywhere, has great potential for application in a sensitive network [22]. Sensitive devices or objects can communicate and process data, from easily discoverable nodes to sophisticated home devices and sensitive phones. Assorted network of such objects is underneath the umbrella of a rapidly evolving quality scheme called the network of objects (IoT). IoT is a global network of consistent objects that have unique access. According to [23], IoT is a "nurse's assistant" that combines discovery and causation devices that enable information exchange between platforms through a single structure, a typical effective picture for additional advanced applications. This can be achieved through ubiquitous discovery, information analysis, and knowledge mapping in cloud computing because they weave structure. Thus, the object network aims to increase comfort and strength through selective interactions between sensitive objects. IoT quality typically includes multiple wireless sensor networks (WSNs) and radio frequency identification (RFID) devices. WSN can be an excellent example provided by the analytic community over the past 20 years.

WSN includes sensitive sensors that communicate via through radio communication. RFID devices remain not that thin. It mostly consists of two parts: a tending assistant computer circuit with certain machine abilities and an antenna for communication.

3.4 Building Computerization

Structure computerization is essentially a unified management scheme for all activities in a construction such as shopping center and marketable offices. Examples are temperature regulator in all departments, water treatment structure, automatic door control system, and lighting regulator. It consumes a proportion of electricity if do not do it right. The IoT is a platform available to the largest companies in the world. It is a server situated anywhere in the world. It has the ability to talk to diverse things on the Internet. It assumes that the user has received the login information. They will log in, analyze, and organize their activities remotely. For example, a user can access workplace air conditioning from anywhere—a boon to the IoT. The IoT platform has enough space to store and analyze all information. In addition, the automatic control can be controlled via software or coding. This coding can be useful for building mechanization managed by the SG and its activities by the IoT platform. Load analysis is urgent, possible with SG and IoT. At the same time, these buildings have a large area of electricity production from renewable sources, to this system.

The idea of the IoT combined with insightful dimensions could lead to the renovation of homes, homes, and offices in energy sensitive environments. The analytical community is increasingly interested in integrating the IoT paradigm into the idea of a sensitive network, especially in sensitive home solutions. Web search quality trends for the terms "web of things", "smart grid", and "smart home" since 2004 shown in Figure 3.4. According to Google statistics, the trends may increase further for terms "clean things" and "smart home". The notice over time is in line with Google's trends since 2004 for the Web of Things, the SG, and the smart home. In this article, its aim is to offer a general approach to the integration of innovative IoT solutions in a fragile home, taking into account all the challenges of household energy management as well as security challenges and solutions, on the computers, networks, and the possibilities of sensitive protocols at home; to discover the gift of the IoT framework in the literature; to analyze these innovative solutions; and to outline the problems for future analysis. NIS describes the methodology that is used in this paper to identify the latest relevant changes, in line with the literature dealing with hr enamels topics, SGs, and the fragile home.

An analysis is carried out in three directions. First, potential and existing IoT applications, as well as IoT-related applications, which are visible from various components of a sensitive network, are analyzed wherever these solutions are located and or used, often, with special emphasis on the sensitive home. The current decisions are then summarized in a new comprehensive framework that includes key options from review known methodology. The analysis concludes by examining the overall responsive

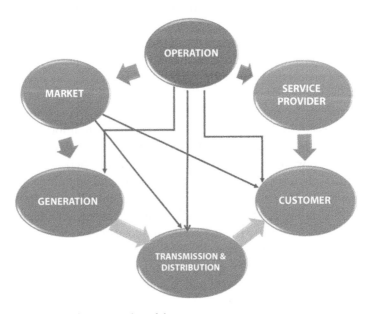

Figure 3.4 Smart grid conceptual model.

home management model for the most holistic structure based on IoT to address its integral layers and core activities as defined in innovative solutions. The fourth section covers IoT resources energy, memory, and process performance, as well as networks, skills, information analysis, security, and privacy. It presents helpful tips and solutions needed to resolve these issues. Various structures are introduced around the world and commercially to explain the IoT construction [41], especially for sensitive web applications. Currently, the structure most used is the National Institute of Standards and Technology (NIST) [24]. The areas of consumption, distribution, transport, and production are accountable for the distribution, transport, and production of energy. Market areas, activities, and service providers are responsible for the provision of services, the management of energy distribution, and the management of the energy market [25]. The areas of generation, transmission, and distribution include power plants. In addition, the industry means that SCADA loves management systems.

3.4.1 Smart Lighting

In support of Directive 20-20-20, optimizing the power of street lighting is an important function of nursing associates. In particular, this service maximizes the luminosity of streetlights according to the time of day, the weather, and the occurrence of community. For such a service to function properly, it must integrate traffic lights into the city's sensitive infrastructure. Alternatively, you can use twice as many connected access points to get voters to join Wi-Fi. Plus, the fault detection system is simply applied to City Energy Conservation's light road managers: in addition to the air quality monitoring service, IoT gatekeeper can deliver city-wide energy monitoring service so it is not necessary authorities and voters to ensure that the expanse of energy essential for the various services is quantified clearly and precisely traffic lights, public lighting, control camcorder, air conditioning of public buildings, etc. This in succession can increase its ability to identify and prioritize most sources of energy consumption in order to optimize their behavior.

To provide this service, energy management devices must be integrated into the city's power supply system. In addition, it will also be possible to extend this service with the functions of executive management of own power generation structures, for example, panels of electrical phenomena.

3.4.2 Smart Parking

Smart parking amenity relies on street sensors and smart displays to guide drivers to the finest parking in the metropolitan [21]. The aids of this facility remain manifold: earlier parking search means less carbon emissions from the car, fewer connections, and happier voters. Reasonable parking is often direct integrated with the city's IoT infrastructure. In addition, through harassment, short-range communication technologies, frequency identification, or near-field communication (NFC), electronic parking permits verification system in areas reserved for residents or people with disabilities can use the services, thereby providing more quality services to citizens who will use them legally. This aids and is a cost-effective tool for quickly detecting wrongdoing.

3.4.3   Smart Buildings

The evolution of a rational city is that there is a claim of these ideas with commercial building environments, possibly with multi-building campuses [22], and corporate structures have a wide spread variety of asset monitoring, management, and improvement needs, and many object networks, smart city applications, and smart city applications are used to accomplish assemblies; some of these applications comprise but are not imperfect to video police investigations, investigation, traffic access control, energy management with lighting, indoor air quality or comfort control, and home exposure [23–26]. The following list outlines the common components and systems that use power and all benefit significantly from enhanced detection, automation, and control (IoT-based) (list incomplete): Heating, Ventilation, and Air Conditioning (HVAC); standard boilers, air compressors, and chillers; server zone; uninterruptible power supplies (UPS); air conditioners for the laptop area (CRACS); medium-sized wardrobes; racks and blade/virtual servers [27–29]; light-emitting diode (LED) lighting; daylight sensors; thermostats (used in general heating, ventilation and air conditioning systems, and power consumption); demand response devices; cooling system fundamentals amplification unit (RTU); and cooling towers and heat pumps. In total, the main components of electricity consumption are: cooling: fourteen, 9%; ventilation: fifteen, 8%; lighting 17.1%; cooling: fifteen, 8%; work equipment, 4.1%; and a new computer. Building management systems (BMS) have always been used to control various functions linked to buildings. BMS can be an extended platform to monitor and control the mechanical and electrical apparatus of a building. BMS is commonly castoff to control masses and increase power, thereby decreasing the energy required for lighting, heating, cooling, and ventilating a building.

The BMS interacts with the control equipment through several mechanical/electrical subsystems to accommodate the prevailing time frame and energy consumption, commonly used to fulfil request-response (DR) contracts. While a BMS for power generation is usually focused on electricity consumption, a future BMS should cover altogether energy sources subsidiary a building, with gas, sustainable energy, water, and steam schemes. Opportunities for interior environment and airborne eminence stay too significant. BMS has recently migrated to an IP network. This permits remote monitoring through a central operations center. Intelligent interior lighting not only provides central (and/or remote) intelligent control and increases passenger comfort but also reduces energy consumption. The IoT can take the functionality of this BMS to the next level. Low-cost sensors and simple applications are increasingly obtainable, usually as a software package as a facility provided by the SaaS cloud. HVAC and Smart Enhancement Dedicated Applications for Vulnerable Cities are just two key areas accelerated by the IoT. They now bring IoT ready to build applications in the wider framework of city-centric claims.

3.4.4   Smart Grid

The advantage of smart cities is that they are aided by sensitive grids (SGs). SG is committed to providing real estate in an economical and efficient way, providing reliable and safe power. A reliable and cheap energy supply is undoubtedly important for cities. Therefore, SG maintains a healthy city model. M2M/IoT technology is intended for automatic exchange of information between devices, so it is relevant to SG. M2M communication takes place between two or more mechanical objects, healthy specific cities, and applications that generally evade direct human interference. With M2M technology, organizations track and accomplish resources; stocks; transport fleet; oil and gas ducts; coalmines; extensive substructure; usual spectacles, *viz.*, weather, agricultural invention, biological surroundings, and the watercourse; and, as mentioned, an analyst. Wireless can be the backbone of M2M. These wireless technologies include unlicensed native properties (questionable fog) and LEO (Low Earth satellites). All these aids are required by SG.

The equipment gradually began to support higher-level M2M regulator and data acquisition systems SCADA via wireless and satellite connections; these communication skills are applied to the SG for urban and rural environments, one-to-one, mainly for the space transmission and distribution (T&D) sector.

SG intelligently integrates knowledge about the activities of consumers interrelated to the network: consumers, producers, and therefore the distribution network. Efficient, unique, economical, and safe feeding are the main objectives of SG. SG covers the numerous phases of energy production, distribution, and consumption. The area is to harness the power of computerization to increase distribution control, environmental efficiency, and consumption. SG control skills are critical to solving these problems as well as energy management problems. The exchange of capabilities increasingly seeks to integrate ICT in general and the IoT in particular in its operations, as well as in the periphery; electrical networks improved in this way are called SG.

Interesting three core issues in:

1. rural transport compliance,
2. receipt control, and
3. specialized automatic readers.

Well-known examples of the use of IoT for energy interaction and SG/AMI include the following: sensitive thermostats; smart devices that can work with DR-based SG power administration device level actuators; manage power storage at the plug-in level, wherever low-cost devices are often elated or off remotely; IoT solid state illumination with LEDs and daylight sensors for smart lights that not solitary provide intellectual unified control or remote but also reduce energy consumption by increasing residence; and the ability of consumers to obtain and resell inexperienced renewable energy to SG.

Many of the key challenges in delivering large-scale IoT amenities in urban environments comprise: lack of generally accepted IoT standards, particularly at higher levels; consumers are forced to choose a provider system and not just to "get stuck"; however, this provider cannot expand and connect to alternate systems. Different applications like traffic management, infrastructure management, energy management, police investigations, and public transport are nowadays and for the foreseeable imminent, complete keys, and disparate technology archives: administrators had to implement separate and fragmented systems, alternately the whole scheme, which will exchange information between individual subsystems.

The practice of wireless networks, particularly in busy urban environments, can increase the radio frequency range and new frequency bands can be devote; 5G technologies are designed to address many of these problems. Despite these challenges, many hope that this technology will gradually emerge in urban materials. Various known technology issues are under scrutiny to resolve outstanding issues. For example, IoT researchers and developers have recognized the importance of standards for the successful

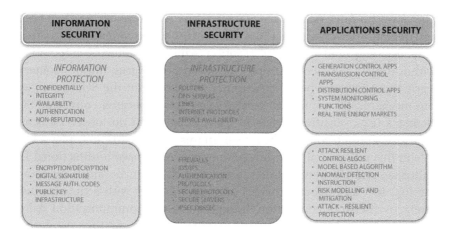

Figure 3.5 Smart grid security.

implementation of vulnerable cities. The classic benefits of standardization include capacity, repeatability, reusability, and low cost. Research has shown that faster preparation and lower cost of actual payments by city agencies are often achieved (30% reduction by 2025 compared to limited supplier status) (Machina technical documentation analysis, 2016). Therefore, it is extremely significant to endure to develop existing values that will cover core, fog and possibly even analysis [30].

The new 5G analysis is predictable to bring about essential changes in the project of cellular systems, creating added value for measuring information that is effective and therefore useful in IoT applications and vulnerable cities. The massive storage medium will also support IoT-sensitive multimedia urban claims. Technologies that could lead to any field and partly to wild change include advanced device intelligence, built-in support for M2M communication, device-oriented architecture, massive MIMO, and even millimetre waves for microwave properties [31]. Cybersecurity analysis is likewise important for sensitive urban applications, particularly in the state of affairs of infrastructure administration, e.g., electricity, water and wastewater, traffic, and management [32, 33] as illustrated in Figure 3.5. How the vast information generated by the system is processed at the city level should be clear and independent [34].

3.4.5   Integration IoT in SG

SG has already been widely used to discover, transmit, and process information, and IoT skill now plays an important part in building networks.

The powerful force behind the SG enterprise is to recover creation, keep and operation by confirming that all elements of the competence grid are in a "listening" and "speaking" position, while also allowing automation within the SG [35]. For example, in an old power grid, utilities solitary learn about failure when the customer requests it. In the SG, the utility can mechanically respond to service interruption because connected SG elements (e.g., sensitive meters in the affected area) no longer transmit information received from the sensor. In this case, the IoT may play a key role in this setup, as all network components must have bi-directional IP addresses and communication capabilities. This can be aided by using the IoT. IoT technology provides users and devices with a time-limited interactive network connection through numerous communication skills, power tools through numerous IoT sensitive devices, and then the necessary collaboration to understand the era, a two-way high-level information exchange. Bandwidth between multiple applications increases the overall power of SG [36, 37]. SG IoT applications are often categorized into three, supported by a three-tier IoT architecture [38, 39].

Classification of IoT aided SG diagram is illustrated in Figure 3.6. First, the IoT is used to deploy various sensitive devices in the IoT to suit the equipment conditions, i.e., IoT perception level. Second, the IoT is used to gather information from devices with its sensitive IoT devices connected through multiple communication technologies. Third, the IoT is useful to the dominant SG across application interfaces in the IoT application layer. Sensitive IoT devices typically include wireless sensors, RFID, M2M devices, cameras, infrared sensors, optical sensors device scanners,

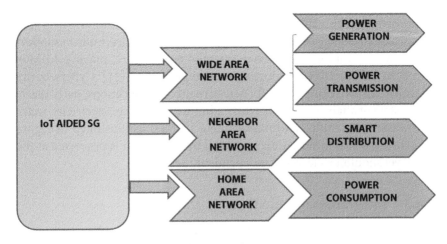

Figure 3.6 Classification of IoT-aided smart grid.

GPS, and many data collection devices. The search for data in Associate in Nursing SG is often strongly supported and enhanced with IoT expertise. Together, IoT skill plays an important part in the implementation of ICT and transmission infrastructure for SG, supporting network building, perception and transmission for the SG, aiding in network construction, process, safety supervision, conservation, safety observance, info assortment, measurement, user interaction, and so forth. Additionally, the IoT conjointly permits the mix of data currently, power currently, and distribution owing a SG [40, 41]. In addition, existing SG architectures in the main consider the requirements of power distributors to accomplish the entire power grid [42]. The shoppers are retrieved with a net of smart meters by implies that of General Packet Radio Service (GPRS) or various portable systems.

The novel authenticity wherever customers could now have other sensible home setups being Wi-Fi has not so far stayed combined within the net communications of prevailing SG architectures [43, 44]. Whereas almost architectures do deliberate present sensible home infrastructures, they are not intended for measurability in giant arrangements [45, 46].

Procedures explicit to IoT and SG schemes thus cannot be head on applied to IoT-aided SG schemes, as they solitary deliberate the discrete features of either the IoT or the SG structures that is not enough for Associate in tending unified IoT-aided SG structure. A SG is incorporated with four cores of subsidiary station: power generation, transmission, distribution, and operation. IoT are usually functional to all or any or any these subsystems and seems as an optimistic account augment them, creating the IoT a significant part for SG. Among the house of power generation, the IoT are typically adopted for the observance along with dominant of energy expending, components, energy storage, and power association, equally as for dealing disseminated power strategies, PV power plants, pumped-up storage, wind power, and biomass power [47, 49]. In the dwelling place of power transmission, the IoT are often castoff for the observance and management of transmission lines and subsidiary stations, moreover for transmission tower guard [47, 48].

In the space of power distribution, IoT is often castoff for distributed computerization, similarly as within the supervision of processes and instrumentation. Within the space of power operation, the IoT are often castoff aimed at sensible homes, automatic meter reading, electrical vehicle charging and discharging, for assembling statistics concerning home appliances energy consumption, power load dominant, energy potency monitoring and management, power demand administration, and multinetwork consumption [47, 48]. In the remainder of this segment, a tendency to define the quality of IoT technology then most popular communication technologies aimed at numerous roles of the 3 SG layers like WAN, NAN, an HAN, as represented in Figure 3.7.

1. Home Automation Network is the primary layer; it accomplishes the users' as required power needs including sensible devices, home appliances such laundry machines, TV, AC, fridge and micro ovens, EV, and renewable resources. HAN is positioned at intervals built-up elements, in industrial plants and in business structures too links electrical utilizations by sensible meters [50].

2. HANs could take either a mesh or star topology the well-liked communication skills for HANs are wired expertise, ZigBee, Bluetooth, and radiocommunication skills. A family contained a diversity of IoT wise strategies and appreciated a home entryway, sensible meters, detector and mechanism nodes, sensible home-based applications, and electrical automobiles. A home entree links to sensible meters and intermittently assembles power consumption data of the house utilizations [51].

3. HANs accomplish dual roles, authorization, and control. The authorization performs identities and new strategies and achieves the devices. The operation permits communication among sensible strategies by creating the links and completes consistent act for the numerous SG layers. A dynasty customs two-way communication for claim response management services [52, 53].

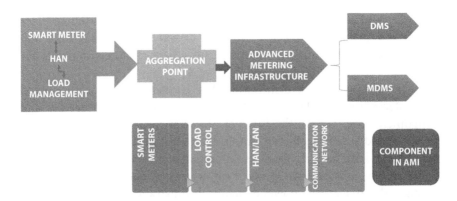

Figure 3.7 Advanced metering infrastructure.

4. Within the advancing communication path, the sensible meters' load and time period power consumption info of the house instrumentation, connected to IoT sensible devices, are composed by home entries and communicated from the buyer facet to the NAN to be forwarded to a utility center. Among the recessive statement path, the house entree performs as a central node and accepts active electricity rating data from the NAN, which is then provided to smart meters or IoT smart strategies for prompting the specified act for home-based appliances.

3.5   Challenges and Solutions

- The nonexistence of extensive IoT standards realization, particularly on the higher layers, operators are leftward by taking to elite a vendor's system and not solely be "wedged", thereupon retailer, however, unable to enlarge a lot of broadly and interrelate with an alternative system.
- Measurability relics a concern: As the urban user grows higher, the architecture, proprieties, and analytics schemes will be ready to sustain or grow effortlessly.
- The diverse applications such as power management, surveillance, traffic management, infrastructure management, and public transference are presently then aimed at the predictable future complete resolutions and technology silos: executives need to arrange separate and uneven systems, instead of one wide system, a scheme that would part information and knowledge amid the separate sub-systems; ability remains evidently an issue.
- Security, privacy, and discretion problems will develop more persistent because the IoT types itself are additional insistent in peoples' lives. Any IoT device poses an occurrence exterior that may end in a security risk, a lot of therefore than the common laptop on a system.
- Current investigations have revealed that solely a section of IoT strategies consume strong security devices designed into them: most items within the new linked world are established with negligible security structures, creating them terribly weak end-points. It is therefore mandatory upon the upright town net to produce a high level of security required aimed at every object.

- In spite of those contests, many are excited that the technology can more and more realize its approach into the material of a city. Issues identified higher than are being sharply researched so as to resolve residual concerns.
- New analysis interested in 5G is predicted to guide to basic changes within the style of cellular systems, creating information measure a lot of value effective and therefore functioning for IoT and smart town applications and provision the multimedia-oriented IoT smart metropolitan claims.
- Cyber-security investigation is additionally important for smart city claims, particularly in the setting of structure organization.

Abundant applications associated prospects are afforded by IoT preparation in provision of smart capitals. The potential occurs toward enhance source organization: the flow of properties, people, and automobiles; SG is an evolving mission. Its execution will lead to various edges for the society. Nevertheless, it is to face a number of challenges and issues once it involves security. Cyber security is a vital a part of the grid's security concern, because the grid develops and expands within the future, the number of nodes that may be not vulnerable to cyber-attacks will surge, so as to create the SG a lot of popular, it ought to be free after any security drawbacks and threats so as to own a higher future. The building computerization and energy protection through "SG and IoT" is coming advance knowledge to establish, monitor, and management electric happenings.

This mechanism normalizes energy with efficiency and overall promotes inexperienced energy. The scheme works on web and IoT server so schedules of watching and dominant may be manageable from any a part of world. There is excellent extension to applications in extreme climate wherever tough for human to try to electrical distribution, controller and monitoring. There are some trials like security of building data and user corporate info.

There are some hitches in building; this mechanism for risky space wherever severance is essential factor. In fact, whereas the variety of style choices for IoT schemes is very wide, the set of open and consistent etiquettes is suggestively slighter. The facultative machineries, also, have stretched level of maturity that enables aimed at the sensible recognition of IoT descriptions and services, fluctuating since field trials that may expectantly enable to clear the uncertainty that also averts a huge implementation of the IoT pattern.

As the globe continues to urbanize, property development challenges are progressively targeted in cities, notably within the lower-middle financial gain countries wherever the pace of urbanization. IoT can sway be an essential tool to deal with these several developing urban challenges.

3.6 Conclusions

Foremost trials in SG technology are renewable incorporation, data supervision, solidity, cybersecurity, and so forth; though there is no extermination found, multiple methods from researches are underneath trial implementation through many preliminary projects. Socio-economic problems are predominant however being resolute through joint efforts. Awareness programs are set across numerous platforms to bring a better understanding and collaboration. Different issues like discretion, regulations, policies, power larceny, and plenty of other issues are being known and determined. Reduced cost, increased consistency, enhanced power organization, self-healing grid substructure, inexperienced and clean power, and so forth are the foremost effects that inspire SG. The sensible grid may be a vast, interconnected system, with several new and rising elements and applications, which needs a radical investigation on the ability problems as well. In spite of many issues, clients are willing to adopt sensible distribution network. Clearly, various technical challenges and issues related to effective and secure communication and data process should be resolved before realizing the vision of a smarter power grid.

References

1. Caragliu, A., Bo, C.D., Nijkamp, P., Smart cities in Europe. *J. Urban Technol.*, 18, 2, 65–82, 2011.
2. Minoli, D., *Building the Internet of Things with IPv6 and MIPv6*, John Wiley & Sons, Inc, New York, 2013.
3. Alvi, S.A., Afzal, B. *et al.*, Internet Of multimedia Things: vision and challenges. *Ad Hoc Netw.*, 33, 87–111, 2015.
4. RWS, *RWS-150002 Views on Next Generation Wireless Access 3GPP RAN Workshop on 5G, September, Lenovo, Motorola Mobility*, 2015.
5. Kaur, K., Garg, S., Kaddoum, G., Bou-Harb, E., Choo, K.-K.R., A big data-enabled consolidated framework for energy efficient software defined data centers in iot setups. *IEEE Trans. Ind. Inf.*, 11, 2613, 2019.
6. Meneghello, F., Calore, M., Zucchetto, D., Polese, M., Zanella, A., IoT: Internet of Threats? A Survey of Practical Security Vulnerabilities in Real IoT Devices. *IEEE Internet Things J.*, 6, 5, 8182–8201, Oct. 2019.

7. Kolias, C., Kambourakis, G., Stavrou, A., Voas, J., DDoS in the IoT: Mirai and other botnets. *Computer*, 50, 7, 80–84, Jul. 2017.

8. Kimani, K., Oduol, V., Langat, K., Cyber security challenges for IoT-based smart grid networks. *Int. J. Crit. Infrastruct. Prot.*, 25, 36–49, 2019.

9. Rawat, D.B. and Bajracharya, C., Cyber security for smart grid systems: Status, challenges and perspectives, in: *SoutheastCon, 2015*, pp. 1–6, 2015.

10. Mrabet, Z.E., Kaabouch, N., Ghazi, H.E., Ghazi, H.E., Cyber-security in smart grid: survey and challenges, Comput. *Electr. Eng.*, 67, 469–482, 2018.

11. Liu, J., Xiao, Y., Li, S., Liang, W., Chen, C.L.P., Cyber security and privacy issues in smart grids. *IEEE Commun. Surv. Tutor.*, 14, 4, 981–997, 2012.

12. Tan, S., De, D., Song, W., Yang, J., Das, S.K., Survey of security advances in smart grid: a data driven approach. *IEEE Commun. Surv. Tutor.*, 19, 1, 397–422, 2017.

13. Aouini, I. and Azzouz, L.B., Smart grids cyber security issues and challenges. *Int. J. Electr. Comput. Energ. Electron. Commun. Eng.*, 9, 11, 1263–1269, 2015.

14. Ghosal, A. and Conti, M., Key management systems for smart grid advanced metering infrastructure: a survey. *IEEE Commun. Surv. Tutor.*, 21, 3, 2841–2848, 2019.

15. Liu, J., Xiao, Y., Li, S., Liang, W., Chen, C.L.P., Cyber security and privacy issues in smart grids. *IEEE Commun. Surv. Tutor.*, 14, 4, 981–997, 2012.

16. Bekara, C., Security issues and challenges for the IoT-based smart grid. *ProcediaComput. Sci.*, 34, Supplement C, 532–537, 2014.

17. Xu, L.D., He, W., Li, S., Internet of things in industries: a survey. *IEEE Trans. Ind. Inf.*, 10, 4, 2233–2243, 2014.

18. Waraich, R.A., Galus, M.D., Dobler, C., Balmer, M., Andersson, G., Axhausen, K.W., Plug-in hybrid electric vehicles and smart grids: investigations based on a microsimulation, Transp. *Res. Part C*, 28, 74–86, 2013.

19. Colak, I., Sagiroglu, S., Fulli, G., Yesilbudak, M., Covrig, C.-F., A survey on the critical issues in smart grid technologies. *Renew. Sustain. Energy Rev.*, 54, Supplement C, 396–405, 2016.

20. Iyer, G. and Agrawal, P., Smart power grids. *42nd Southeastern Symposium on System Theory (SSST)*, IEEE, pp. 152–155, 2010.

21. Moreno-Cano, V., Terroso-Saenz, F., Skarmeta-Gomez, A.F., Big data for IoT services in smart cities. *Proceedings of the IEEE 2nd World Forum on Internet of Things (WF-IoT)*, Milan, Italy, December 14–16, 2015, p. 418, 2015.

22. Kyriazis, D., Varvarigou, T., White, D., Rossi, A., Cooper, J., Sustainable smart city IoT applications: heat and electricity management & eco-conscious cruise control for public transportation. *2013 IEEE 14th International Symposium and Workshops on a World of Wireless, Mobile and Multimedia Networks (WoWMoM)*, June 4–7, 2013.

23. Corna, A., Fontana, L., Nacci, A.A., Sciuto, D., Occupancy detection via iBeacon on Android devices for smart building management. *Proceeding*

of DATE '15 Proceedings of the 2015 Design, Automation & Test in Europe Conference & Exhibition, Grenoble, France, pp. 629–632, March 09–13, 2015.

24. Ghayvat, H., Mukhopadhyay, S., Gui, X., Suryadevara, N., WSN- and IoT-based smart homes and their extension to smart buildings. *Sensors*, 15, 5, 10350–10379, 2015.

25. Keles, C., Karabiber, A., Akcin, M., Kaygusuz, A., Alagoz, B.B., Gul, O., A smart building power management concept: smart socket applications with DC distribution. *Int. J. Of Electrical Power & Energy Syst.*, 64, 679–688, 2015.

26. Lizzi, L., Ferrero, F., Danchesi, C., Boudaud, S., Design Of antennas enabling miniature and energy efficient wireless IoT devices for smart cities. *Smart Cities Conference (ISC2), 2016 IEEE International*, September 12–15, 2016.

27. Mauser, I., Feder, J., Müller, J., Schmeck, H., Evolutionary Optimization of Smart Buildings with Interdependent Devices. *Applications of Evolutionary Computation, vol. 9028, Lecture Notes in Computer Science*, Springer, pp. 239–251, 2015.

28. Oti, A.H., Kurul, E., Cheung, F., Tah, J.H.M., A framework for the utilization of building management system data in building information models for building design and operation. *Automation Construction*, 72, 2, 195–210, 2016.

29. Srivastava, S. and Pal, N., Smart cities: the support for internet of things (IoT). *Int. J. Comput. Appl. Eng. Sci.*, VI, II, 5–7, 2016.

30. Moreno, M.V., Zamora, M.A., Skarmeta, A.F., User-centric smart buildings for energy sustainable smart cities, Transactions on Emerging Telecommunications Technologies, vol. 25, no. 1, pp. 41–55, 2014.

31. Boccardi, F., Heath, R.W., Jr., Lozano, A., Marzetta, T.L., Popovski, P., Five disruptive technology directions for 5G. *Commun. Mag., IEEE*, 52, 2, 74–80, 2014.

32. Cerrudo, C., *Keeping Smart Cities Smart: Preempting Emerging Cyber Attacks in U.S. Cities*, ICIT (Institute for Critical Infrastructure), 2015, Whitepaper, June. https://icitech.org/wp-content/uploads/2015/06/ICIT-Smart-Cities-Brief1.pdf

33. Chakrabarty, S. and Engels, D.W., A secure IoT architecture for smart cities. *Consumer Communications & Networking Conference (CCNC), 13th IEEE Annual*, January 9–12, 2016, 2016.

34. Hu, J., Yang, K. *et al.*, Special issue on big data inspired data sensing, processing & networking technologies. *Ad Hoc Netw.*, 35, 1–2, 2015.

35. Waraich, R.A., Galus, M.D., Dobler, C., Balmer, M., Andersson, G., Axhausen, K.W., Plug-in hybrid electric vehicles and smart grids: investigations based on a microsimulation, Transp. *Res. Part C*, 28, 74–86, 2013.

36. Colak, I., Sagiroglu, S., Fulli, G., Yesilbudak, M., Covrig, C.-F., A survey on the critical issues in smart grid technologies. *Renew. Sustain. Energy Rev.*, 54, Supplement C, 396–405, 2016.

37. NIST, *Computer Security Division*, Computer Security Resource Centre.

38. Al-Fuqaha, A., Guizani, M., Mohammadi, M., Aledhari, M., Ayyash, M., Internet of Things: A survey on enabling technologies, protocols and applications. *IEEE Commun. Surv. Tuts.*, 17, 4, 2347–2376, 4th Quart., 2015.

39. Yaqoob, *et al.*, Internet of Things architecture: Recent advances, taxonomy, requirements, and open challenges. *IEEE Wirel. Commun.*, 24, 3, 10–16, Jun. 2017.

40. Liu, J., Li, X., Chen, X., Zhen, Y., Zeng, L., Applications of Internet of Things on smart grid in china, in: *Proc. 13th Int. Conf. Adv. Commun. Technol. (ICACT)*, pp. 13–17, Feb. 2011.

41. Zaveri, M.A., Pandey, S.K., Kumar, J.S., Collaborative service oriented smart grid using the Internet of Things, in: *Proc. Int. Conf. Commun. Signal Process. (ICCSP)*, pp. 1716–1722, Apr. 2016.

42. Samarakoon, K., Ekanayake, J., Jenkins, N., Reporting available demand response. *IEEE Trans. Smart Grid*, 4, 4, 1842–1851, Dec. 2013.

43. Khan, A.A. and Mouftah, H.T., Web services for indoor energy management in a smart grid environment. *Proc. 22nd Int. Symp. Pers. Indoor Mobile Radio Commun. (PIMRC)*, pp. 1036–1040, Sep. 2011.

44. Benzi, F., Anglani, N., Bassi, E., Frosini, L., Electricity smart meters interfacing the households. *IEEE Trans. Ind. Electron.*, 58, 10, 4487–4494, Oct. 2011.

45. Hu, Q. and Li, F., Hardware design of smart home energy management system with dynamic price response. *IEEE Trans. Smart Grid*, 4, 4, 1878–1887, Dec. 2013.

46. Viani, F., Robol, F., Polo, A., Rocca, P., Oliveri, G., Massa, A., Wireless architectures for heterogeneous sensing in smart home applications: Concepts and real implementation. *Proc. IEEE*, 101, 11, 2381–2396, Nov. 2013.

47. Shu-Wen, W., Research on the key technologies of IOT applied on smart grid, in: *Proc. Int. Conf. Electron., Commun. Control (ICECC)*, pp. 2809–2812, Sep. 2011.

48. Wang, Y., Lin, W.M., Zhang, T., Ma, Y.Y., Research on application and security protection of Internet of Things in smart grid, in: *Proc. Int. Conf. Inf. Sci. Control Eng. (ICISCE)*, pp. 1–5, Dec. 2012.

49. Basit, A., Sidhu, G.A.S., Mahmood, A., Gao, F., Efficient and autonomous energy management techniques for the future smart homes. *IEEE Trans. Smart Grid*, 8, 2, 917–926, Mar. 2017.

50. Deng, R., Yang, Z., Chow, M., Chen, J., A survey on demand response in smart grids: Mathematical models and approaches. *IEEE Trans. Ind. Informat.*, 11, 3, 570–582, Jun. 2015.

51. Mashima, D. and Chen, W.-P., Residential demand response system framework leveraging IoT devices, in: *Proc. IEEE Int. Conf. Smart Grid Commun. (SmartGridComm)*, pp. 514–520, Nov. 2016.

52. Aburukba, R.O., Al-Ali, A.R., Landolsi, T., Rashid, M., Hassan, R., IoT based energy management for residential area, in: *Proc. IEEE Int. Conf. Consum. Electron.-Taiwan (ICCE-TW)*, pp. 1–2, May 2016.

53. Mortaji, H., Hock, O.S., Moghavvemi, M., Almurib, H.A.F., Smart grid demand response management using Internet of Things for load shedding and smart-direct load control, in: *Proc. IEEE Ind. Appl. Soc. Annu. Meeting*, pp. 1–7, Oct. 2016.

4

Industrial Automation (IIoT) 4.0: An Insight Into Safety Management

C. Amuthadevi[1] and J. Gayathri Monicka[2]*

[1]Department of Computer Science and Engineering, SRMIST, Kattankalathur, India
[2]Department of Electrical and Electronics Engineering, SRMIST, Ramapuram Campus, India

Abstract

Industry 4.0 is the recent revolution in automotive and manufacturing industries for the production of smart devices to make the complete digitalization. One of the significant applications of IIoT is predictive maintenance. In hazardous places, prediction about disaster is helpful to manage the people's safety and reduction of damages. Machine Learning (ML) approaches are very useful for prediction. ML develops a mathematical, trainable model to analyze the data and apply with different kinds of existing methods for interrogating data. In this chapter, it is going to be discussed about how the advanced and automated data processing is connected with the new types of Computer Vision (CV) applications which influences directly with the human lives and safety of physical assets in hazardous places. The activities such as disaster early warning, recovery, and reconstruction system are to be studied. Also, some of the practical issues in the planning and recovery processes will be discussed.

Keywords: IIoT, predictive maintenance, Machine Learning, optimization, disaster safety management

4.1 Introduction

Earlier industry revolutions in 1980s and 1990s herd innovative in manufacturing technologies. Industry 4.0 is the recent revolution in automotive and manufacturing industries for making the smart devices by combining

*Corresponding author: monigaya5281@gmail.com

R. Anandan, Suseendran Gopalakrishnan, Souvik Pal and Noor Zaman (eds.) The Industrial Internet of Things (IIoT): Intelligent Analytics for Predictive Maintenance, (89–118) © 2022 Scrivener Publishing LLC

wide range of computing technologies such as cloud, networking, Big data, fog/edge computing, Internet of Things (IoT), Machine-to-Machine Communication (M2M), Machine Learning (ML), and Cyber Physical Systems (CPS). Industry 4.0 is also called as Industrial IoT (IIoT). A crucial facade of Industry 4.0 is autonomous construction of approaches drove by the concept called IoT, the impression that by binding a connected physical/virtual objects, devices, and machines which can communicate each other. Thus, the revolution is integration of computing and manufacturing [1].

To make the applications as intelligent, ML algorithms are useful and also improve the cognitive ability. ML is a kind of Artificial Intelligence (AI); once algorithm/model is trained with data samples, the model is able to get the test data and makes the output, based on the training. So, it is possible to mimic the human decisions in real-time situations based on the past experience (data driven reasoning). The most common real-time applications can be built by combining IIoT and ML algorithms. The pattern that is matching with new real-time (test) data should be identified with trained data, to classify the test data [2].

Figure 4.1 illustrates how the different domains are connected to make the functionality of IIoT. Different kinds of communication devices send the raw data to the connected nodes which may aggregate and respond immediately. Even though the decision is made in nearby nodes, the data along with solutions are updated in the cloud server. In few situations, specific alarm will be notified based on the nature of the application.

Smart city, smart vehicles management, smart positioning, manufacturing, and self-driving cars are some of the common applications of IIoT.

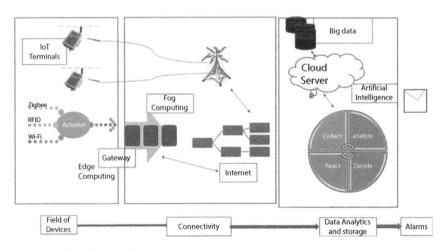

Figure 4.1 Working of IIoT.

The smart decision-making used in these kinds of applications can be utilized in decision-making. There are two types of disasters: natural and man-made. Natural-disasters are triggered owing to many reasons alike soil corrosion, seismic activity, tectonic actions, air pressure, and also ocean currents.

Some of the natural disasters are:

(i)   volcano,
(ii) tsunami,
(iii) flood,
(iv) earthquake,
(v)   landslide,
(vi) forest fires, and
(vii) hurricane.

Among these, few of them can be predicted earlier and used to save many lives. The prediction also will be helpful to the government to make the necessary actions and alert the people to migrate to safer places.

Some of the man-made disasters are listed in the following:

(i)   hazardous material spills,
(ii) fires,
(iii) contamination of groundwater,
(iv) accidents in transportation,
(v)   structure failures,
(vi) mining accidents,
(vii) blasts and performances of terrorism.

Many times, the data to be collected from various kinds of sensors and all are battery-based devices. To conserve the energy, reduce the complexity, and improve the security, fast data processing is needed. Caching is one of the useful techniques that avoid the redundant transmissions of data and reducing the latency. Complexity can be reduced with increasing efficiency, because of emerging ML and evolutionary algorithms with large instances of data. IoT with analytics finds the valuable information from the raw data that will be sent to multiple analytics pipelines and may create the security breaches.

4.1.1   Fundamental Terms in IIoT

The different domains interconnected in IIoT are explained in the following.

4.1.1.1   Cloud Computing

Cloud computing is a distributed computing technology that offers all the heterogenous resources as on-demand services [3]. The major advantages of clouds are reliability, cost savings, and unlimited data storage capacity. It provides the following services:

(i)   Infrastructure-as-a-service (IaaS): This provides physical machine, virtual machine, storage, and memory.
(ii)   Platform-as-a-service(PaaS): This provides run time environments, development, and deployment tools.
(iii)   Software-as-a-service (SaaS): This provides licensed software to the customers.

The deployment methods are private, public, hybrid, and community based. The important aspect is that the customer can utilize the resources as long as the need and pay only for what actually they used. One of the important cloud service providers is Google that many users are using in world wide.

4.1.1.2   Big Data Analytics

As massive growth of sensors and mobile devices are connected via internet, big data encompasses huge datasets [storage exceeds one terabytes (TB)] and will be useful to analyse the real-time data to make decisions. In IoT, data arrives from heterogeneous devices/events and in the form of Complex Event Patterns (CEP). Most of the events are interrupted quickly for immediate decision-making and applying in the current situation. Decision-making needs pre-processing, and correlating with what happened in near-time events from various data sources and need to create rules to predict the future events [4]. These allow establishments to shape real-time solutions using the concept of IoT and excerpt the information after the big data causes to arise the insights on or after millions of actions in nominal period.

The data collected may be structured, semi-structured, unstructured, and combination of more than one type. Some of the popular analytical tools are Yarn, MapReduce, HDFS, and Spark. They can be used to do clustering, classification, and prediction. Big data processing pipeline includes collection of data, training, and querying by big data tools.

4.1.1.3   Fog/Edge Computing

Many applications in IoT need quick response either because of critical kind of application or cost reduction. Therefore, the latency (duration of raw data transmission to actuator and receiving output from the actuators) should be minimal. If the cloud is used, then the cost will be lower, because of the shared resources, but the latency will be significant because of round trip time between sensor nodes to remote servers. Fog and edge computing are two kinds of solutions to solve this. The difference is where the computing happens. In edge computing, for sensitive applications, most of the processing such as aggregation and computation are done at the edge/local gateway but the data and other resource intensive operations should be reached to centralized data collection server [5].

In edge computing, all the data collection nodes should be connected with local gateway. In fog computing, the processing is moved to nearby Local Area Networks (LANs) which are somewhat situated far away when comparing to gateways in edge computing. Fog computing offers low-latency computing facilities at the LAN that is an enabler for the evolving IoT systems [6].

4.1.1.4   Internet of Things

Internet of Things (IoT) is an organization of interconnected physical/virtual devices/objects which are given Unique IDentifiers (UIDs) and all are able to communicate over a network without the need of either Man-to-Man or Man-to-computer interaction. Smart vehicles, smart watches, home automation, and remote healthcare monitoring are some of the real-time examples

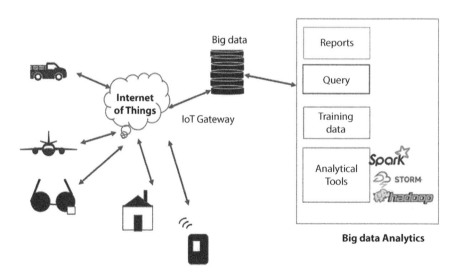

Figure 4.2 Big data analytics with IoT.

of IoT applications. The working of IoT devices along with analysis is represented in Figure 4.2. All the data produced by IoT devices are not having the analytical power. The data may be noisy and heterogeneous. To solve this issue, preprocessing is required. After pre-processing, big data analytics can be combined with IoT devices to identify the hidden or unobserved patterns and innovate into useful information [7]. This will be helpful for the companies, organizations, or individuals to manage the large amounts of data and extract useful information by big data-mining to make important decisions, and to identify the trends and make predictions.

4.1.1.5   Cyber-Physical-System

CPS is an innovative concept of digital system by combining "computing, interaction and controlling" as a single system by closed control feedback systems. CPS has two important concepts:

(i) It has fast connectivity to acquire the real-time data (such as temperature and humidity with the help of low-cost sensors) in the physical environment and make useful information from the cyber space.

(ii) Managing the data and using the advanced computation ability, it creates the cyber-space [8].

Therefore, CPS pairs the sensors and actuators to interact with real-time environment/physical world and systems can able to react to changes in the environments for automating or controlling some tasks.

The aim of CPS is to use in large-scale systems, to automate the tasks with improving the efficiency, reliability, usability, and safety. In future developments in CPS, the human control/intervention will be fewer and core control will be more, based on intelligence-based cores developed in automated systems. CPS differs from embedded system; embedded system focuses on devices embedded in single/stand-alone system, but CPS focuses on large number of connected physical and computational devices [9]. CPS uses many evolving technologies and given in the following:

(i) Multi-Agent Systems (MAS) for intelligence and version over de-centralized segmental systems,

(ii) Service-Oriented Architecture (SOA) for interoperability,

(iii) Big Data for large data mining,

(iv) Cloud for sharing remote resources,

(v) M2M for interconnectivity amongst devices, and

(vi) Augmented reality to allow the human inside the process.

4.1.1.6   Artificial Intelligence

To make the devices as "smart", the devices need intelligence [10]. Different disciplines such as philosophy, computer-science, statistics, sociology, and psychology have different definitions for AI. AI is one of the technologies that make the system with reasoning power like human's traditional decision-making. Still, it is arguable that which decision is best under some specific scenarios in specific domains. Sometimes, AI lacks with creativity in decisions, but humans can do correctly by taking long time. AI should like human's intelligence to take the rationale decisions at appropriate times. Initially, AI algorithms were developed for playing board games with humans. Then, it was applied in symbolic reasoning. After that, because of popularity and success, AI becomes interdisciplinary approach. Intelligence can be improved by adding more domain specific knowledge, data, and analysis. Based on the need of applications, only certain tasks can be automated and this is called as narrow-AI.

AI highly relies on data-science methods and may need tools, because of voluminous and real-time data. Data science deeply gives broader insights of data [11] and analyzes and predicts the uncertainty. The origin of the data science is Knowledge Discovery process (KDD) and statistics. The analysis includes data exploration, hypothetical testing, regression, and time series analysis, as given in the following:

(i)   Exploration of data does pre-process,
(ii)   Hypothesis testing: questions arrive from the explored data is converted into statements called as hypothesis that may be proved as true or false
(iii) Regression finds the relationship parameters between the data and target information, and
(iv)   Time series analysis is useful for temporal structured data where prediction of future values is the most challenging task.

4.1.1.7   Machine Learning

ML is one of the sub domains of AI; it focuses on developing a set of algorithms to make the components or computing devices to learn automatically and improve their performance based on the experience (given as data samples). Algorithms used in ML are iterative to discover the hidden or natural patterns available in the data samples and use it for reliable and better predictions or decisions. After training, when these algorithms are exposed to unseen data, they are able to adapt independently.

ML is one of the most trending method and used almost in all the domains with the intersection of more technologies such as AI and data science. There are many emerging algorithms are being developed to process the data faster and make accurate predictions [12]. The applications of ML are tremendous in speech recognition, Natural Language Programming (NLP), healthcare applications, financial modeling, recommendation systems, face detection, and object recognition (Computer Vision) etc.

Learning phase of ML contains the following steps:

(i)   Collection of training data,
(ii) Pre-processing,
(iii) Feature selection or extraction,
(iv) Model training with selected features.

There are three major kinds of ML algorithms and given in Figure 4.3.

(i)   Supervised learning,
(ii) Unsupervised learning, and
(iii) Reinforcement learning.

(i) Supervised Learning
Supervised learning has n-number of data samples as input-output pair (labeled data). The learning task is to find the function of mapping from input to output. Input is a vector and output is a single value/categorial label. If the prediction is categorial label, then it is called as classification, and in case of continuous value, it is called as regression. The mapping function may be linear or non-linear. Some of the supervised

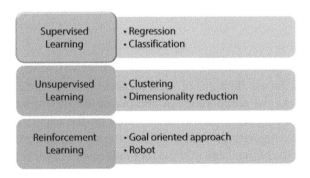

Figure 4.3 Types of ML.

learning algorithms are Decision Trees (DT), Support Vector Machines (SVM), linear regression, Naive Bayes, logistic regression, K-Nearest Neighbor algorithm (k-NN for classification) and Neural Networks (Multilayer perceptron). Based on the algorithm selected, the parameters must be learned to improve the prediction accuracy. Parameters are significant in ML algorithms. In semi-supervised learning, most of the data samples are labeled and few are unlabeled.

Nowadays, Deep Learning (DL) algorithms are more popular, because it solves complex problems even though the data samples are varying, unstructured, and also interconnected. DL has multiple layers of neuron (similar to Artificial Neural Networks), along with one input layer, one output layer and multiple number of hidden layers are available. Algorithms like Back Propagation (BP) are used to learn the weights of interconnected neurons automatically by using the inputs such as images, text, or sound. There is no need of feature extraction because of convolution operation and pooling. Convolution does repeated filtering on input to get the feature map. Pooling operation makes down sampling and also dimensionality reduction.

(ii) Unsupervised Learning

In unsupervised learning, the data set is not labeled. The hidden pattern among the given data is identified and based on the similarities of features, and the given datasets are grouped into multiple numbers of clusters. Then, it may be labeled as Group 1, 2, ..., n. There are different kinds of distance measures such as Manhattan distance, city block distance, and Euclidean distance, which are used to find the similarities between data samples. The usage of unsupervised learning is exploratory analysis and dimensionality reduction.

Figure 4.4 illustrates the difference between supervised and unsupervised learning using the same kind of data samples.

Fuzzy and K-means clustering are most commonly used for clustering. The objective of clustering is to reduce the dissimilarities within a cluster and increase the dissimilarities in inter-clusters. Dimensionality reduction reduces the feature set in the ML algorithms to take away only the useful and relevant features either for classification or clustering.

(iii) Reinforcement Learning

Reinforcement Learning (RL) is a goal-oriented approach and has multiple agents who interact with the real-world environment to make decisions. It may use either supervised or unsupervised learning to build the model. The agent reacts to the environment. It may be a hardware, software, or

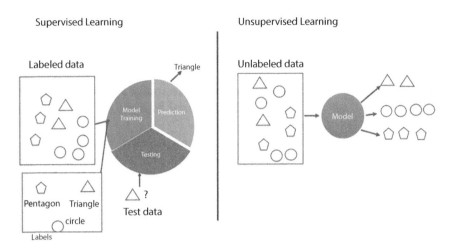

Figure 4.4 Supervised and unsupervised learning.

combination of them. When correct decision is made, the reward (positive score) will be given, in case of incorrect decision, penalty (negative score) will be given. The ultimate aim of RL is to get the highest cumulative score. In the nonappearance of a training sample-dataset, it is destined to learn from its experience. In robotics, RL behaves novel by using "Trial-and-Error" concept.

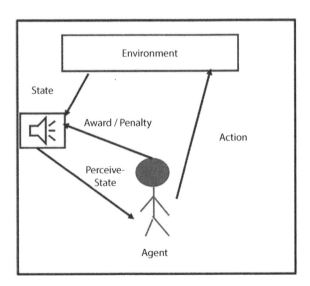

Figure 4.5 Reinforcement learning.

The elements of RL are given in the following:

(i)   Policy: It is a way of agent's behavior based on the current situation. It is like stimulus-response.

(ii) Reward function: Increasing reward is the goal of RL. If the action taken in the current state is toward the goal, then a positive value is awarded and called as award.

(iii) Value function: It defines how much award the particular agent can get from the current state to the goal state. It is the impression of the behavior of the environment.

(iv) Model of the environment: Model predicts the next state and corresponding reward. The working of a simple agent is represented in Figure 4.5.

4.1.1.8   *Machine-to-Machine Communication*

M2M is a communication technology protocol for remote processing. The communication type may be serial, Power-Line-Connection (PLC), and wireless communication by IoT. It may also use LANs and Wide Area Networks (WANs) along with the Internet. To structure the IIoT environment, all the devices such as sensors, actuators, and gateways should be integrated and communicated autonomously without the intervention of human [13]. M2M can translate the data and activate based on the pre-programmed procedures. Most of the challenges are faced in M2M, because of heterogeneous networks, connectivity issues, computing machines, and policies [14].

4.1.2   Intelligent Analytics

As increasing numbers of connected sensors are used, they create voluminous data periodically. They should be aggregated before sending to remote server. To avoid the redundant and non-useful data, big data mining can be used. This helps the headache of data transmission.

Intelligent analytics helps to understand, analyze the data, and identify useful information which will be helpful to the organizations for making well-formed decisions and inform to the respective people in the organization at right time. It uses the concepts of big data, AI, and data science. Data visualization from different view point is to be taken care based on the needs of an application. By using appropriate tools, collection of current data, and history of information, analytics should result in accurate results. The mature predictions lead to optimization.

The intelligent analytics are categorized into three types. They are descriptive, predictive, and perspective using the mining, AI, and statistics [15].

(i)   **Descriptive analytics**: used in streaming the context. It will answer for the following queries: "What and why a particular event has happened?" and "what is happening now?"
(ii) **Predictive analytics**: used to replying for the following queries: "What and why some event will happen in the future?"
(iii) **Prescriptive analytics**: answering for the following queries "What and why should be done now". It is attracting to the researchers, because it is a matured data analytics and lead to reach the optimal solutions.

4.1.3   Predictive Maintenance

The integration of sensed data with predictions is used in IIoT applications to find the significant relationships with predictions and the procedures of maintenance. In manufacturing industries, the objective is to assure the maximum throughput in the manufacturing line and to improve the production with reduction of cost and throughout the life cycle of an equipment. The data driven approaches are used to make the predictive maintenance. In any organization, each equipment is an important asset. To avoid the complete shut-down, prediction of faults is vital. Complete monitoring of each and every device may be useful to predict about when the servicing is required to avoid the fault and decide on when to back up the data. There are three kinds of maintenance procedures used in industries [16].

(i)   **Predictive maintenance**: where the component is restored or substituted after wear, fault, or break down.
(ii) **Preventive maintenance**: customs sensor data for continuous monitoring of a system and evaluates it in contradiction with historical events to predict the failure before it happens.
(iii) **Corrective maintenance**: recognizes the faults by a result of walkthroughs or inspections.

Based on the specific needs of applications, the guidance can be designed about how to utilize the streaming technologies and big data analytics tools for the use cases of predictive maintenance [17]. Each domain and application has different requirements, based on the requirements, the suitable analytical tool is chosen. While automating the complex operations, one of the challenges is reliability and safety of devices and data [18] which may have great impact on decision-making.

In this chapter, predictive maintenance is taken for assets safety during the hazardous events.

4.1.4   Disaster Predication and Safety Management

Natural disaster is beyond the human being's control and unavoidable. Many countries faced different kinds of disasters and some are very deadly.

World Health Organization (WHO) stated that during the year 1900 to 2018, nearly 14 million disasters happened [19] in world wide.

4.1.4.1   Natural Disasters

Our country faced wide range of natural hazards such as flooding, drought, cyclones, extreme heat waves, landslides, wildfire, and earthquakes. The assets which need safety are listed in Table 4.1, according to the priority. Few of the unfortunate events happened in India are listed in the following:

(i)   Uttarakhand Flash Floods in the year 2013, because of the heavy rainfall and enormous Landslides.

(ii)   Kashmir Floods disaster in the year 2014, because of unremitting torrential rainfall and swelling of river Jhelum.

(iii)   Bihar flood disaster in the year 2007, because of five times more rainfall when comparing to the monthly middling of 30 years.

(iv)   The Indian Ocean Tsunami in the year 2004, because of Tsunami, it originated on Indonesia and affected 12 countries.

Table 4.1 Types of assets needs safety [50].

S. no.	Type of asset	Example
1.	Humanity	Human lives
2.	Physical asset	Buildings, roads, and gateways and devices
3.	Software	System and application software
4.	Communication	Networks, clouds
5.	Data	Sensor, big data

    (v) Gujarat Earthquake in the year 2001, because of earthquake.

  (vi) Super Cyclone, Odisha in the year 1999.

 (vii) Great Bengal Famine in the year 1770, because of Drought or Famine.

4.1.4.2   Disaster Lifecycle

The systematic way of representation of disaster lifecycle is represented in Figure 4.6.

    (i) The preliminary phase is disaster identification that is based on the earlier catastrophes which will be useful to forecast the occurrences in future. It will be helpful for arranging the needed resources in a timely manner for rescuing in appropriate time [20].

  (ii) Prediction is carried for the forecasting disaster events based on the history of data, community experience, and analysis of environmental and geographical data. Based on the previous history, some wireless nodes can be deployed in the disaster occurred in places for effective monitoring.

 (iii) Mitigation process is similar to prediction. Mitigation helps to save the human lives and reduce the economy loss

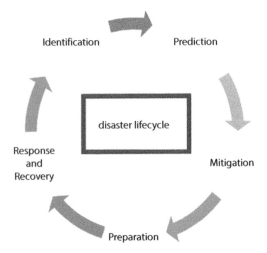

Figure 4.6 Disaster lifecycle.

because of disaster events. Some of the approaches used in mitigation are preventive maintenance, goal-oriented evaluation, land use, and regulation preparation for building standards.

(iv) Preparation involves planning a set of procedures to manage the emergency situations. It includes creation of awareness and ensuring that necessary essentials are available. Preparation ensures the timely response.

(v) Response and recovery: Response executes the plan immediately as per well-defined preparation to save lives, efficient and timely communication to the people with coordinated way. Recovery is a follow-up procedure acceptable for rehabilitation.

4.1.4.3   Disaster Predication

It is very difficult to predict the natural disasters like earthquake; it needs lot of activities, coordinated effect to save the people, and also manage the economic loss. Effective management needs collection of data to get previous situations during and after earthquake, making coordination and effective decision-making [21]. Even though the disasters are non-avoidable, the approach called disaster reduction can be done by the method using prediction.

Over the data collected for long times, many algorithms or approaches supports in prediction. Big data analytics combined with ML algorithms are useful to visualize (finding the common and hidden patterns, not identifiable easily by human) and to analyze disaster prediction.

This analysis can be useful in six major disaster management applications [22]. They are as follows:

(i)   Early alarming about damage,
(ii)   Assessment of damage,
(iii) Monitoring and detection,
(iv)   Forecast and predict,
(v)   Post-disaster organization and response,
(vi)   Long-term assessment of risk and reduction of risk.

Some applications like prediction of landslide are required in the mount areas. Landslide is a dynamic and very complicated structure. It needs to process the continuous monitoring of time series data to forecast the landslide displacement [23]. The displacement leads to landslide.

For cyclone prediction, the exact positioning of high- and low-pressure areas are to be tracked to predict how heat in these areas are migrating in the tropical areas using satellite images and computer technologies. The model can predict 5 to 7 days in further from the starting date of prediction. Using the storm monitoring and the rainfall amount, floods can be predicted. Topography, moisture of the soil, and characteristics of river basin can be considered for flood prediction. Sometimes, the wireless sensors deployed in the water bodies give the water levels, and this data will be used for forecasting the flood.

Satellite images and remote weather prediction are used to predict the forest fires and aids to decrease the numbers of forest areas burned per annum. Forest fires may source the tripping of multiple transmission lines concurrently, making a most sever threat to the safety of power grid. The amount of risk may not be competently estimated and it is very difficult to lead the optimization of fire extinguishing equipment allocation.

4.1.4.4   Safety Management

In each country, the government is making different policies on safety management. The motivation of these policies is that the government wants to pool the resources from the humanity to identify the uncertainty of extreme disaster events. The mitigating role is recovering the people as early as possible based on the mitigation plan that was framed by the government already. Safety related policies are differing from one location to another. The disaster damage, loss, and number of people in the surrounding area will be used to give the priority about safety management policies. The disasters are vulnerable events and the assessment should be reshaped based on the social, physical, and economic issues [24].

While constructing in disaster happened place, it needs perfect planning because it involves multiple safety considerations and, in that task, multiple experts must be involved to make decisions. The group of experts examine and apply fuzzy theory to consider multi attributes and consider all the risk factors for analyzing the safety concerns. This technology will be helpful to planners and emergency responders to converge all the experts view in safety planning of reconstruction [25]. Safety confirmation system [26] suits for evacuation center operations. The headquarters consolidate the risks and analyze the operations given by operations suggested by evacuation center operations. In the safety confirmation system, it uses some communication to inform the details of refugee's to relatives who are in remote locations from the government's local website.

Emilio Tissato [50] suggested the phases of risk assessment.

Phase 1: Risk calculation context
Phase 2: Points of attack detection
Phase 3: Mapping of threat
Phase 4: Privacy, safety and security and reliability mapping
Phase 5: Detection of vulnerability
Phase 6: Estimation of probabilities
Phase 7: Estimation of impacts
Phase 8: Calculation of risk matrix
Phase 9: Prioritization of security controls
Phase 10: Action plan

4.1.5 Optimization

For any problem solving, multiple feasible solutions may be available. In each solution, it has different impact on the real-time scenario. Some of the nature-inspired optimization algorithms are Genetic algorithms (GA), Particle Swarm Optimization (PSO), Ant Colony Optimization (ACO), and Memetic Algorithms (MA). Selecting proper method improves the effectiveness. Efficient forecasting and scheduling operations play a vital role in the relief of saving people and lowering the damages in the event of disasters. These operations come under evolutionary and optimization problems. Response phase needs the concept of optimization to make selection of the location, allotment of medical tents, and evacuation in simultaneous manner [27]. The critical nature of scenarios must be considered to make the choices. Some of the approaches like Monte Carlo simulation and dynamic p-robust approaches are used to find the different scenarios and formulate the new paths for safety reliefs. Identifying various parameter values will be useful for robust reliable optimization. The rapid support decisions improve the response and recovery.

During emergency period the goal should be supplying the emergency services to the people with the goal of transport unit loss using the optimization model in the crowded conditions [28]. Bayes model theory with some optimization algorithms such as ACO for finding the efficient path from one place to another is needed to manage the congested conditions.

The remaining sections in this book chapter are organized in the following way. Section 4.2 describes the different methods/technologies related to predictive maintenance and safety management. Section 4.3 explains the issues of research work in this domain. Section 4.4 explains the new ideas found in this domain, and final section concludes and directions of research in future.

4.2   Existing Technology and Its Review

Many of the disasters are unpredictable, and their unexpected occurrences will cause unbelievable damages to human lives. Under these situations, active disaster management needs very rapid response and activities must be taken. This is a crucial task to mitigate the belongings of disasters. Efficient information management and fast communication recovery are vibrant mechanisms for disaster response and relief. In this section, some of the existing technology in IoT environment and the natural disaster management are going to be outlined.

4.2.1   Survey on Predictive Analysis in Natural Disasters

Hasegawa *et al.* [28] introduced a device called as QUEST (Q-shu University experiment with steady-state spherical tokamak) to originate the large current of 50 KA. To minimize the operational costs and reducing the danger of unexpected failures, the contact resilience of multiple ohms was evaluated in order to make the predictive maintenance. Predictive maintenance was achieved, by monitoring the occurrences of problems, the failure was blocked and maintenance was executed as a planned manner. The alarm system was built and the experimental information was shared among the systems by building a network. For few devices, static Internet Protocol (IP) was assigned. For control devices, it had static IP and Media Access Control (MAC) addresses to evade the wasting of resources of network.

W. Gao [29] used ANN to predict the landslide using Grey System. Monotonously increasing characteristics and displacement of landslide need to be analyzed the time series data in the specific area where landslide happened frequently. Grey system combined with Evolutionary Neural Network (ENN) was proposed for prediction system. Composition of displacement and time series trend were used by ENN architecture. Backpropagation algorithm (BP) was used in ENN and applied in landslide Xintan. The results proved that this method was better in landslide prediction.

Matthews [30] applied Decision Theory to analyze about how earthquake were predicted accurately and reliably. Even though several optimistic estimates are used to identify the key parameters, the reliable function for the action should be used. He identified the self-organizing behavior of earthquakes prediction was based on two key factors.

(i)   the base rate of severe-quakes on the time scale of precursor, and

(ii)   the qualified costs of disregarding perfect predictions and answering to false alarms.

Even though with common values of these factors, the resultant least accuracy taken by the likelihood ratio needed to meet the correct predictions of significant earthquakes is not perfectly achieved in state-of-the-art methodologies.

G. Molchan and Romashkova [31] worked in the earthquake prediction and the quality of space related to time by using two-dimensional error diagram (n, τ) in which n represented the fraction of "failures-to-predict" and τ represented local-rate of alarm (averaged) in the space. The earthquake events during 1985 to 2009 (which had higher magnitude between 8 and 8.5) were taken as data samples and the M8 algorithm was used for prediction. The upper estimates were taken to handle the uncertainty.

Takahashi et al. [32] developed a network in the ocean floor to predict the earth quakes and tsunamis in the Japan Trench. By deploying seismometers and pressure sensors, the magnitude above 8 were collected. Based on the sensor details, the arrival time, tsunami height, and duration were predicted. They observed that the prediction accuracy depends on the height of tsunami and target point. But using seismometers, real-time prediction was done with buoy system and proved that estimation of target area was strongly correlated with target point.

Voigt et al. [33] used capabilities of earth observation used in the national and international level services, relief efforts, and security issues considered during the situations of disasters using the multi-source satellite images. Image analysis algorithms were used to map the tasks of resource lifecycle events to management support. These algorithms were used for rapid mapping of disaster response in tsunami, landslide, and forest fires.

Nico et al. [34] in Canada and Rauste et al. [35] in Finland used the thermal images to map the areas into wild forest fires using Advanced Very High Resolution Radiometer (AVHRR). Raw thermal data from satellite was taken as input about the amount and the number of truly burning fires was predicted.

4.2.2   Survey on Safety Management and Recovery

Hanna *et al.* [36] discussed the various issues regarding Discovery Recovery Planning (DRP). This includes recovering the damaged computers, connected to the hospital groups. The planning assured about healthcare applications to reach the people affected during the disaster without interruptions with the goal of hospital and nursing functions.

Alabdulwahab [37] implemented some technology-based support to business to recover from the disaster. The data, hardware, and software are the major assets to the IT companies. Different strategies to recover the data were framed out.

Sanderson *et al.* [38] examined the one of the essential needs called as transitional shelter that was used in Haiti, analyzed some of the decision-making process could be used for making the adoption policy and making T-shelters. Based on the decisions, the results were compared with different responses planned in urban areas, post-disaster recovery, and redevelopment skills.

Barnes *et al.* [39] developed a novel method for classification and detection of structures using high-resolution satellite images. The features of images in near shore area were used for response planning during emergency. Both the storm impacted and non-impacted features were extracted from the images especially in blocked routes and used to automatically finding the discovery and rescue areas. The σ-tree template structures were used to reduce the time needed for training and it did not use high amount of computing resources.

Harris and K. Laubsch [40] surveyed different kinds of the airships at different height level from the earth to capture the live videos to enable the agile response. Flight ceilings of airships are designed depending on the tallest buildings in disaster affected area.

Moore [41] identified the different issues by interactions with electrical workers, managers in corporate, and professionals in safety management in a national hospital facility. The challenges in the recovery processes were identified to explore the electrical safety and disaster preparedness. Few case studies were done and the following were identified.

(i)   Elaborated challenges when handling the recovery project afterward an electrical disaster what affects employers and pendant legal action.

(ii)   Energized work plan to be noticed by safety professionals and executives.

(iii)   After the hazardous event, maintenance and safety culture to be followed by employers.

Slinn [42] proposed recovery system for railway management. After the interlocking failure happened, the communication between the sensors and control point the pictures were shared. From that picture, the details of train, states were identified to decide about what trains should be removed. To get the reliable pictures in railway management, COT technology was used. To assure the display the remote fail-safe image, encryption was suggested. For enforcing image lifetime, embedded image read-back was used.

4.2.3   Survey on Optimizing Solutions in Natural Disasters

Shao [43] surveyed the potential threats to the IT-based companies and proposed a discrete optimization model to use the redundancy mechanism for critical functions in recovery planning phase of recovery management. The overall objective of the author was maximizing the survivability of the IT functionalities in the organization. Each function was allocated with different level of redundancy based on priority. Dynamic probability–based programming was applied. In case of no redundancy, the model reduced the reliability related problems and lead to fault-tolerance.

Lu *et al.* [44] suggested the optimization method in urban places for disaster prevention using Geographic Information System (GIS) technology. He worked for optimal (by fast estimation) fire extinguishing equipment in a power grid during fire-disasters. The quick calculation method was proposed for identifying risk index in the transmission line. Hunan provincial power-grid was taken as case study. By using the computing resources, risk index was calculated soon to deploy the fire extinguishing equipment. The time of calculation was less than five minutes because 30 trillion operations were performed per second.

Unmanned Aerial Vehicle (UAV) was used by Zhang and J. Liu [45] because of wider coverage and low-vast, fast deployment in post-disaster environments. Two cooperative UAVs were used: one for downlink transmission and another one on rescue vehicles for emergency response. The data were sent as packets transmitted from an UAV to a vehicle, if time duration for the truck enclosed, UAV is more than the stated average network access delay. Performance metrics given for the network and this method gave good numerical results. Optimal setting of network parameters achieved optimal performances in the post-disaster areas.

Cheng-fang Wang and Yi-min Sun [46] analyzed different types of disaster in urban areas. Several case studies were done to identify the basic correlation between the urban morphology optimization and corresponding disaster prevention. The parameters such as location of the urban place or city, environment, size of the urban, structure, and the direction of the development of urban were used as parameters to analyze. The spatial information from GIS was used to optimize the locality of urban toward disaster direction.

Yuan *et al.* [47] proposed Resilient Distribution Network Planning Problem (RDNP) for coordinating and distribution of resources. The objective was to minimize the damage of the system. Hurricanes create huge losses economically and casual life of humans. The problem was formulated as two stage strong optimization model. Uncertainty was solved by *N-K* contingency method. The system was validated using micro-grids and proved that resilience was good during natural disasters. Yuan *et al.* [48] worked to improve the grid resilience during hurricanes, and the consequences such as physical and cyber-attacks can be reduced by optimal plans. One of the optimal solutions is planning the decisions to coordinate the DG replacement, distribution of the power flow model, and hardening.

Changfeng *et al.* [49] developed optimization based on Bayes risk function for managing emergency resources in the transportation network using a case study to direct the composite association between supplies distribution and selection of path, using the factors such as travel time uncertainty and the lasting capacity of road during distribution. Emergency logistics structure of the network was taken and total loss of disaster area was predicted using Bayes risk function. ACO algorithm was used in crowded situations and proved that the optimization model behaved in better manner during the congested conditions.

4.3   Research Limitation

Limitations are impacts which cannot be controlled by the researchers. They may be the deficiencies, situations, or influences that cannot be measured by the investigators. They influence the restrictions on the methodology to be applied and impacts on the conclusions.

4.3.1   Forward-Looking Strategic Vision (FVS)

The International Data Corporation (IDC) analysts identified that in most situations, most of the real-time environments are yet to deploy the sensors for data collection. So, many of the IoT applications are suffering to collect the real data. Based on the applications even though sensors are deployed and communications are done properly, huge data are collected, the users of IoT may not get satisfaction because of lacking data analytics skills and security concerns, because of not having or developing an FSV.

Many mathematical models of statistics and ML (sometimes combined as hybrid) approaches are needed with big data to get the scientific and quantifiable results. If suitable approaches are used with optimal parameters, then the goal can be attained. If the data set collected is biased, then for new kind of data, the result may be incorrect. The balanced interplay of insights of data analysis gives informative and successful solutions.

4.3.2   Availability of Data

The benefits of disaster management depend on the available and appropriate data. The data collected may not have the sufficient information, not in the structured format, and aggregated from different locations. Sometimes, the data may be irrelevant. False and incomplete data leads to uncertain outcomes. Sometimes, mathematical models have to be used for identifying missing and incorrect values in the collected data. Therefore, to make the data to be usable directly, some pre-processing methods are to be applied.

4.3.3   Load Balancing

There are four layers in IoT. They are sensor and actuator layer (sometimes, these two layers are combinedly called as perceptual layer), network layer, data processing, and application layers. Sensor and actuator layer have the direct access to gateway. In edge computing, most of the data processing work is done in the gateway. Most of the computing resources are needed at the local gateway.

In fog computing, data should be transferred to the data processing layer that is far away from the sensors. Therefore, based on the type of computing, allocation of resources is a challenging task. Dynamic scheduling model with priority based one should be selected, because of the nature of the application. Based on the scheduling method selected with real-time situation, the available resources should be balanced. Therefore, the resource allocation task makes the computing as distributed computing.

4.3.4   Energy Saving and Optimization

The overall energy consumption is calculated as the summation of autonomous consumptions created by machining, transfer of data at all the stages of hazardous events, and mining algorithms. In edge computing, much energy will be consumed at the local gateway and in the fog computing much energy will be consumed in devices at the data processing layer. Most of the real-time devices are battery based and rechargeable, so the energy-saving mechanism is to be considered. The different kinds of modes like sleep and wake up can be used and a particular event can be used for triggering sleep mode to active mode to save the energy.

Efficient allocation of computing resources is a challenging task because of

(i)   Processing power limitation,
(ii) Rapid computationally intensive applications,
(iii) Energy consumption analysis needs the complex system by consideration of spatial attributes.

Optimization algorithms can be utilized to identify the threshold level for each kind of sensor about, under what values the switch over between wake up and sleep mode should be done.

4.3.5   Cost Benefit Analysis

Sometimes, the real cost benefit may not be identifiable in accurate way. Few applications can be done only in simulation, but not in the real world. It may be because of the cost of real-time implementation, nature of the event. It should not be trial-and-error effort.

Before going to real implementation, simulations can be done. Based on the success of simulation prototypes can be created to analyze the real-time risks and improve the efficiency. The task of identifying idea, simulation, prototyping, and evaluation should be iterative tasks until all the stakeholders get satisfaction.

4.3.6   Misguidance of Analysis

Many attempts can be done to find the approaches for predicting the major earthquakes, and sometimes, they are misguided because of the dynamic nature of the event. This may be created because of false alarms, device hacking, inefficient communication, and coordination lacking. The output of the ML algorithms depend on the based on the data samples fed into the algorithm. If some data collected has incorrect values, then misguidance may happen.

4.4   Finding

The principle outcomes of a study in this chapter give what are suggested in the literature and from this what are revealed or indicated.

4.4.1   Data Driven Reasoning

In many real-time problems, it is possible to find all the possible solutions beforehand and select the suitable one. Safety and recovery during disaster is such a kind of problem. But in the data driven approaches, multiple data sets in history can be collected, and experiences of them can be utilized to provide the solution in the basis of evidence-based approach. Problem solution can be created by rule based that gives solution similar to real prediction. Using advanced technologies for data collection and analysis techniques (with reasoning), effective recovery and reconstruction plans can be done and executed.

4.4.2   Cognitive Ability

Cognitive ability is a general rational ability that involves reasoning, solving problems, preparation, abstract thinking, comprehension of complex ideas, and self-learning using the experience. It needs more attention. Even though enough guidance were given to the people, the police, emergency handlers, NGOs, and others involving in the reconstruction may experience cognitive disruption and this can affect their response in rescue-related tasks. This may happen because of the unexpected scenarios faced by all the responding people. Based on the cognitive skills trained in the system, trained system (or algorithm) should make clear decisions to guide in stressful situations.

4.4.3   Edge Intelligence

Using edge intelligence, the sensing device takes the control of its data and communications organization, improves the accuracy and quality, and reduces the time delays. Intelligent edge algo enlarges set of associated systems closer to the users. The intelligent algorithms are used either in the device or in the edge of a network with particular coverage of locations should be used for more critical applications. Safety applications in disaster response got real-time experiences and insights, deliverable in a context aware manner.

4.4.4   Effect of ML Algorithms and Optimization

ML algorithms have better attainments than human beings, using the algorithms like regression and classification. Using optimization methods, the minimal resources would be utilized or minimal time can be taken and the better solutions can be found. Therefore, the overall execution cost can be less with user defined time. There may be multiple feasible plans for response and recovery generated. But based on the real-time scenario, optimal plan must be selected by using meta-heuristic optimization algorithms.

4.4.5   Security

The data collected and the decision made under different scenarios should be shared within the people or authorities who involved in the safety management application. The security for data, network, and data storage devices must be provided to avoid the active and passive attacks which are planned by the hackers. The risk should be predicted in earlier and standard encryption and corresponding decryption algorithms can be used to enhance the security. Based on the use cases, the appropriate algorithms can be utilized.

4.5   Conclusion and Future Research

4.5.1   Conclusion

Disaster management is as the group of activities, management of resources, and tasks for managing with all humanitarian features of emergencies, preparedness, response, and also recovery in direction to reduce the impact of disasters. Proper analysis and prediction on a time scale of decades makes the planning and response arrangements. During the planning and response, the factors such as safety of the people, safety of physical assets, and providing food, medicine, and temporary shelters must be taken care.

Based on the experience, the construction ideas, development in urban areas, green spaces, and the municipal affairs provide multi-discipline power to make the safe city. Different countries have different kinds of natural disasters based on the region in terms of latitudes, climate changes, industrialization and other conditions of nature.

4.5.2   Future Research

For further research, the assets can be categorized into essential, shelters, companies' infrastructure, communication lines, vehicle track, road, and standing water, train track, based on that priority can be applied. Based on the category, appropriate plan can be applied to reduce the damage of assets. Different security levels can be defined based on the different use cases. Based on the use case types, recovery plans can be generated.

References

1. Chen, B., Wan, J., Lan, Y., Imran, M., Li, D., Guizani, N., Improving Cognitive Ability of Edge Intelligent IIoT through Machine Learning. *IEEE Netw.*, 33, 5, 61–67, Sept.-Oct. 2019.
2. Mallapragada, P.K., Jin, R., Jain, A.K., Liu, Y., SemiBoost: Boosting for Semi-Supervised Learning. *IEEE Trans. Pattern Anal. Mach. Intell.*, 31, 11, 2000–2014, Nov. 2009.
3. Rodriguez, M.A. and Buyya, R., Deadline Based Resource Provisioningand Scheduling Algorithm for Scientific Workflows on Clouds. *IEEE Trans. Cloud Comput.*, 2, 2, 222–235, 1 April-June 2014.
4. Akbar, A., Khan, A., Carrez, F., Moessner, K., Predictive Analytics for Complex IoT Data Streams. *IEEE Internet Things J.*, 4, 5, 1571–1582, Oct. 2017.
5. Di Pascale, E., Macaluso, I., Nag, A., Kelly, M., Doyle, L., The Network As a Computer: A Framework for Distributed Computing Over IoT Mesh Networks. *IEEE Internet Things J.*, 5, 3, 2107–2119, June 2018.
6. Shah-Mansouri, H. and Wong, V.W.S., Hierarchical Fog-Cloud Computing for IoT Systems: A Computation Offloading Game. *IEEE Internet Things J.*, 5, 4, 3246–3257, Aug. 2018.
7. Marjani, M., Nasaruddin, F., Gani, A., Karim, A., Hashem, I.A.T., Siddiqa, A., Yaqoob, I., Big IoT Data Analytics: Architecture, Opportunities, and Open Research Challenges. *IEEE Access*, 5, 5247–5261, March 2017.
8. Hong, C., Applications of Cyber-Physical System: A Literature Review. *J. Ind. Integr. Manag.*, 02, 1750012, 2017.
9. Barbosa, J., Leitão, P., Trentesaux, D., Colombo, A.W., Karnouskos, S., Cross benefits from cyber-physical systems and intelligent products for future smart industries. *2016 IEEE 14th International Conference on Industrial Informatics (INDIN)*, Poitiers, pp. 504–509, 2016.
10. Ghosh, A. and Chakraborty, D., Law, A., Artificial intelligence in Internet of things. *CAAI Trans. Intell. Technol.*, 3, 4, 208–218, 2018.
11. Weihs, C. and Ickstadt, K., Data Science: the impact of statistics. *Int. J. Data Sci. Anal.*, 6, 189–194, 2018, https://doi.org/10.1007/s41060-018-0102-5
12. Jordan, M.I. and Mitchell, T.M., Machine Learning: Trends, Perspectives, and Prospects. *Science*, 349, 6245, 255–60, 2015.

13. Esfahani, A., *et al.*, A Lightweight Authentication Mechanism for M2M Communications in Industrial IoT Environment. *IEEE Internet Things J.*, 6, 1, 288–296, Feb. 2019.

14. Moustafa, N., Adi, E., Turnbull, B., Hu, J., A New Threat Intelligence Scheme for Safeguarding Industry 4.0 Systems. *IEEE Access*, 6, 32910–32924, 2018.

15. Lepenioti, K., Bousdekis, A., Apostolou, D., Mentzas, G., Prescriptive analytics: Literature review and research challenges. *Int. J. Inf. Manag.*, 50, 57–70, February 2020.

16. Carvalho, T.P., Soares, F A. A. M. N., Vita, R., Franciscob, R.d.P. Basto, J.P., Alcala, S.G.S., A systematic literature review of machine learning methods applied to predictive maintenance. *Comput. Ind. Eng.*, 137, 1–10, September 2019.

17. Sahal, R., Breslin, J.G., Ali, M.I., Big data and stream processing platforms for Industry 4.0 requirements mapping for a predictive maintenance use case. *J. Manuf. Syst.*, 54, 138–151, December 2019.

18. Yan, J., Meng, Y., Lu, L., Li, L., Industrial Big Data in an Industry 4.0 Environment: Challenges, Schemes, and Applications for Predictive Maintenance. *IEEE Access*, 5, 23484–23491, 2017.

19. *Number of reported disasters by type*, Hannah Ritchie and Max Roser, National Geophysical Data Center, 2019 [Online]. Available: https://ourworldindata.org/natural-disasters.

20. Johnson, G., *Solving disaster management problems using ArcGIS*. Nov. 9, 2003. http://campus.esri.com

21. Samaad, T., Tahir, G.A., Mansoor-ur-Rahman, Ashraf, M., Comparative Performance Analysis Between Agent-Based And Conventional Diaster Management System. *2018 International Conference on Smart Computing and Electronic Enterprise (ICSCEE)*, Shah Alam, pp. 1–6, 2018.

22. Arinta, R. and Andi, E., Natural Disaster Application on Big Data and Machine Learning: A Review, Researchgate publications, 2019.

23. Gao, W. and Zheng, Y.R., Study on Some Forecasting Methods in Geotechnical Engineering, in: *Proc., 6th Conf. of Chinese Rock Mechanics and Rock Engineering Society*, Beijing, Science Press, vol. 1, pp. 90–93, 2000.

24. Comfor, L., Risk, Security, and Disaster Management. *Annu. Rev. Polit. Sci.*, 8, 335–356, 2005.

25. Wang, W. and Zhang, Y., Group decision making in safety planning for earthquake disaster area reconstruction. *2011 Second International Conference on Mechanic Automation and Control Engineering*, Hohhot, pp. 6552–6555, 2011.

26. Ishida, T., Sakuraba, A., Sugita, K., Uchida, N., Shibata, Y., Construction of Safety Confirmation System in the Disaster Countermeasures Headquarters. *2013 Eighth International Conference on P2P, Parallel, Grid, Cloud and Internet Computing*, Compiegne, pp. 574–577, 2013.

27. Fereiduni, M. and Shahanaghi, K., A robust optimization model for distribution and evacuation in the disaster response phase. *J. End. Int.*, 13, 117–141, 2017.

28. Hasegawa, M., Hanada, K., Idei, H., Kawasaki, S., Nagata, T., Ikezoe, R., Onchi, T., Kuroda, K., Higashijima, A., Predictive maintenance and safety operation by device integration on the QUEST large experimental device. *Heliyon*, 6, 1–7, June 2020.

29. Gao, W., Predication of Landslide Based on Grey System and Evolutionary Artificial Neural Networks. *2010 International Conference on System Science, Engineering Design and Manufacturing Informatization*, pp. 64–67, 2010.

30. Matthews, R.A.J., Decision-theoretic limits on earthquake prediction. *Geophys. J. Int.*, 131, 3, 526–529, Dec. 1997.

31. Molchan, G. and Romashkova, L., Earthquake prediction analysis based on empirical seismic rate: the M8 algorithm. *Geophys. J. Int.*, 183, 3, 1525–1537, Dec. 2010.

32. Takahashi, N., Imai, K., Sueki, K., Obayashi, R., Emoto, K., Tanabe, T., Real-Time Tsunami Prediction System Using Oceanfloor Network System. *2019 IEEE Underwater Technology (UT)*, Kaohsiung, Taiwan, pp. 1–5, 2019.

33. Voigt, S., Kemper, T., Riedlinger, T., Kiefl, R., Scholte, K., Mehl, H., Satellite Image Analysis for Disaster and Crisis-Management Support. *IEEE Trans. Geosci. Remote Sens.*, 45, 6, 1520–1528, June 2007.

34. Nico, G., Pappalepore, M., Pasquariello, G., Refice, A., Samarelli, S., Comparison of SAR amplitude vs. coherence flood detection methods— A GIS application. *Int. J. Remote Sens.*, 21, 8, 1619–1631, May 2000.

35. Rauste, Y., Herland, E., Frelander, H., Soini, K., Kuoremaki, T., Ruokari, A., Satellite-based forest fire detection for fire control in boreal forests. *Int. J. Remote Sens.*, 18, 12, 2641–2656, Aug. 1997.

36. Hannah, K.J., Ball, M.J., Edwards, M.J., Disaster Recovery Planning, in: *Introduction to Nursing Informatics. Health Informatics (formerly Computers in Health Care)*, Springer, New York, NY, 2006.

37. Alabdulwahab, M., Disaster Recovery and Business Continuity. *Int. J. Sci. Eng. Res.*, 7, 3, March-2016.

38. Sanderson, D., sharma, A., Kennedy, J., Burnell, J., Asian Journal of Environment and Disaster Management. *Asian J. Environ. Disaster Manag.*, 6, 131–151, 2014.

39. Barnes, C.F., Fritz, H., Yoo, J., Hurricane Disaster Assessments With Image-Driven Data Mining in High-Resolution Satellite Imagery. *IEEE Trans. Geosci. Remote Sens.*, 45, 6, 1631–1640, June 2007.

40. Harris, M. and Laubsch, K., Disaster recovery. *Eng. Technol.*, 4, 7, 26–29, 25 April-8 May 2009.

41. Moore, M., Case study: Electrical disaster recovery operations for a hospital. *2013 IEEE IAS Electrical Safety Workshop*, Dallas, TX, pp. 69–76, 2013.

42. Slinn, J., Innovative technologies in disaster recovery: the big picture, in: *Railway Safety Assurance. Management and Method in a Safe Network,* pp. 1–22, 2014.
43. Shao, B.B.M., Optimal redundancy allocation for information technology disaster recovery in the network economy. *IEEE Trans. Dependable Secure Comput.,* 2, 3, 262–267, July-Sept. 2005.
44. Lu, J., Guo, J., Jian, Z., Xu, X., Optimal Allocation of Fire Extinguishing Equipment for a Power Grid Under Widespread Fire Disasters. *IEEE Access,* 6, 6382–6389, 2018.
45. Zhang, S. and Liu, J., Analysis and Optimization of Multiple Unmanned Aerial Vehicle-Assisted Communications in Post-Disaster Areas. *IEEE Trans. Veh. Technol.,* 67, 12, 12049–12060, Dec. 2018.
46. Wang, C.-f. and Sun, Y.-m., Optimization of urban morphology for comprehensive disaster prevention supported by GIS. *2011 International Conference on Multimedia Technology,* Hangzhou, pp. 1136–1138, 2011.
47. Yuan, W., Zhao, L., Zeng, B., Optimal power grid protection througha defender-attacker-defender model. *Rel. Eng. Syst. Saf.,* 121, 83–89, Jan. 2014.
48. Yuan, W., Wang, J., Qiu, F., Chen, C., Kang, C., Zeng, B., Robust Optimization-Based Resilient Distribution Network Planning Against Natural Disasters. *IEEE Trans. Smart Grid,* 7, 6, 2817–2826, Nov. 2016.
49. Zhu, C., Fang, G., Wang, Q., Optimization on Emergency Resources Transportation Network Based on Bayes Risk Function: A Case Study. *Math. Probl. Eng.,* 4, 1–9, 2016.
50. Nakamura, E.T. and Ribeiro, S.L., A Privacy, Security, Safety, Resilience and Reliability Focused Risk Assessment in a Health IoT System: Results from OCARIoT Project, *Global IoT Summit (GIoTS),* pp. 1–6, 2019.

5

An Industrial Perspective on Restructured Power Systems Using Soft Computing Techniques

Kuntal Bhattacharjee, Akhilesh Arvind Nimje*, Shanker D. Godwal and Sudeep Tanwar

Department of Electrical Engineering, School of Engineering, Nirma University, Ahmedabad, Gujarat, India

Abstract

The application of computational approaches in the past has yielded appreciable results. The increased system complexity causes difficulty in system modeling. Analytical tools were vastly employed, including areas such as biology, medicine, humanities, management, and engineering. Soft computing techniques evolved as a result of inspiration from biological process occurring in nature; hence, performance is based on a probabilistic approach. As a result, global optimum solutions cannot be always expected for all the optimization problems, especially for multi-modal objective function. The solution determined by applying soft computing technique can be global optimum or local optimum. The ability of soft computing techniques to reach global optimum solution for maximum number of times out of certain number of trials depends on their ability "to explore search space" and "to exploit good solutions", during optimization process. Not all soft computing techniques have the same ability "to explore" and "exploit". Since early 20th century, many soft computing referred as classical soft computing techniques have been developed so far for solving the issues concerned with deregulated power system. The introduction of nonlinear devices such as thermal units with multi-valve steam turbines, Heat-Recovery combined cycle Steam Generators (HRSG), contributed in uplifting the energy efficiency of the power system. Therefore, it furthers the complexity in the mathematical model of the system. To account for increased mathematical complexity, certain approximations needed to be considered while

---

**Corresponding author*: akhilesh.nimje@nirmauni.ac.in

R. Anandan, Suseendran Gopalakrishnan, Souvik Pal and Noor Zaman (eds.) The Industrial Internet of Things (IIoT): Intelligent Analytics for Predictive Maintenance, (119–148) © 2022 Scrivener Publishing LLC

applying classical soft computing techniques. Due to approximations, the results determined by these methods turned out to be sub-optimal. The implementation of such sub-optimal results could have resulted into a huge annual revenue loss. Therefore, the primary purpose of implementing the techniques was not fulfilled. Technological advancements led to increased storage capability and improved performance of the digital computers. This helped to combat the limitations of the classical soft computing techniques and encouraged researchers to develop more soft computing techniques. The precise system modeling along with appropriate objective function can offer optimal solutions along with financial implications. The current trend is to focus on improving the operational efficiency of the system, thereby slowing down the rate of depletion of fossil fuel and saving huge amount of money.

Keywords: Restructured power system, optimization, genetic algorithm, fuzzy logic, optimization in power system

5.1   Introduction

Lotfi A. Zadeh was the first to introduce the concept of soft computing in 1981. Soft computing techniques have an integrated approach. It combines the usage of computational methods used in artificial intelligence, machine learning, computer science, engineering, and other disciplines to solve an optimization problem. It works by identifying the problem, defining it, formulating constraints, and finding the appropriate solution by employing various techniques. To determine an optimal solution, the best solution that fulfills the defined purpose should be selected amongst the other possible solutions. A soft computing technique mimics the biological process to arrive at the optimal solution. The techniques such as artificial neural network (ANN), fuzzy logic, and genetic algorithm can be applied to a problem having interdisciplinary nature. The genetic algorithm has been derived from inspiration from Charles Darwin in theory of natural evolution. It gives optimal solution using the biological operations such as selection, crossover, and mutation. It has proved its merits several times whenever applied to a complicated problem. Fuzzy logic implemented in both hardware and software. It is a simple technique used for solving problem and giving flexible control to the systems spanning from small embedded devices to large network of computers. It offers a simple way to reach at a certain decision based on indefinite, unclear, imprecise, missing, or noisy input information. Fuzzy logic approaches to control problems and mimics how a person would make a decision faster.

Fuzzy logic model is based on generation of the binary logic. Fuzzy logic works by generating binary logic. Each variable is assigned a value that can range from 0 to 1. The technique of ANN is a form of data processing encouraged by methods such as the biological nervous system modeling the brain function. The inspiration came from the structure and information device management of neurons. It is made up of a large number of highly integrated computing elements (neurons) that work together to solve the particular working function. It is constructed in different domain through a learning process such as data classification or pattern recognition. To change the structure of neuron requires the changes of synaptic through the training process.

5.2   Fuzzy Logic

"Degrees of truth" is the main computational-based approach in fuzzy logic rather than "true or false". It is a very different approach from binary logic (0 or 1) or traditional logic; it is something between "yes and no" or "0 and 1". From the beginning of humanization, human development is based on approximation. In modern days, use of fuzzy logic has proven its importance in many fields such as forecasting, soft computing world, optimization, neural networks, and many more. Generally, in the modern era, fuzzy logic is widely used in medicines, power system, energy sector, and many more.

5.2.1   Fuzzy Sets

A fuzzy set is represented as a class of object which has a band of degrees or grades of membership. This membership function is different for different sets. So, the fuzzy sets are unique as their membership function assigns different values from 0 to 1 to each object. The properties like intersection, union, inclusion, convexity, and complement are applicable to these sets. The features of these properties are generally used to show connection between fuzzy sets [1]. The objects in the real world are categorized in a general form. They do not have a unique or precisely defined class. For an example, there are various creatures included in the animal class like dog, cat, horse, and lion. But creatures like bacteria, fungi, and yeast may or may not be included in animal class. There are many such examples such as "class of beautiful women".

5.2.2   Fuzzy Logic Basics

Now, suppose X as a Space-of-Points (Objects), where each component is represented by x. Therefore, $X = \{t\}$. There exists a fuzzy set or class m in X whose involvement (characteristic) function is $F_m(x)$. This membership function relates each element in X fits within the interval $(0, 1)$. The assessment of $F_m(x)$ at x represents the "grade_of_membership" of x in m. It means that if the assessment of $F_m(x)$ is close to unity, then the "grade_of_membership" of x in m is high. When set m is defined in normal wisdom, then membership function $F_m(x)$ either 0 or 1. If x fits to m, then $F_m(x) = 1$ and if x does not fits to m then $F_m(x) = 0$. In this case, the function $F_m(x)$ becomes an ordinary one. So, the set having only two values of characteristic function is defined as ordinary set or simple set. Let X remain the actual line R and m be the number of fuzzy set which are much greater than 1. Now, precise depiction of m can be done by stipulating $F_m(x)$ as a function on R. The different values assigned to function $F_m(x)$ can be $F_m(0) = 0, F_m(1) = 0, F_m(5) = 0.01, F_m(10) = 0.2, F_m(100) = 0.95$, and $F_m(500) = 1$. It is observed that membership function has similarities to probability function when X is a countable set. The variances between them will be clear when rubrics of grouping of membership functions and their elementary possessions are defined. In fact, fuzzy set has nothing to do with statistics. There are several properties of fuzzy sets which are similar to the properties of ordinary sets like a fuzzy set is blank contingent upon its "membership function" is zero on X. For two fuzzy sets m and n to be equal, the condition $F_m(x) = F_n(x)$ is necessary to be satisfied for all x in X. The condition $F_m(x) = F_n(x)$ can be more simply written as $F_m = F_n$. The accompaniment of set A can be expressed as A'.

5.2.3   Fuzzy Logic and Power System

Power system operation, utility, and scheduling are daily important activity. These activities are further complicated by considering with system wise constraints like transmission line capacity constraints and system demand. Several classical and soft computing approach have been used to handle different power system objectives like cost and transmission loss in terms of single as well as multi-objective function with system wise constraints. Fuzzy logic application is also one of the mathematical approaches which can help to handle power system operation. Different types of fuzzy logic approach like fuzzy mixed integer programming problem [2] have been used in these regards.

5.2.4   Fuzzy Logic—Automatic Generation Control

Fast energy storage devices can reduce the frequency and fluctuation of linear power caused by small load disturbances to avoid equipment damage, reduce loads, and avoid potential interference in electrical systems [3]. AGC plays a key role in providing power with quality standards in today's fast-moving world. For making operational decision of AGC, fuzzy logic is widely used. A wide range of literatures are available for fuzzy logic and automatic generation control. Use of new optimal fuzzy TIDF-II controller in load frequency control using feedback error learning approaches [4] of a restructure power system can guarantee to stabilize the system. Fractional order fuzzy proportional-integral-derivative (FOFPID) controller integrated with bacterial foraging optimization is proposed in AGC of a power system to get intelligent and efficient control strategy. AGC of two area control having thyristor controlled capacitor can sufficiently improve the stability using conventional integral and fuzzy logic controller [5–7]. From all the above methods, it has proven that the use of fuzzy logic has given superior results compared to most of the other efficient techniques.

5.2.5   Fuzzy Microgrid Wind

Fuzzy logic used to stabilize the microgrid by controlling frequency in wind based powered microgrid [8]. In standalone micro-networks, slight variations in wind power generation and demand cause variations in system frequency. This difference is caused by the periodic environment of the wind or abrupt variations in demand. The gap between making and demand can be overwhelmed using Battery Energy Storage System (BESS). When demand is higher than production, BESS is forced to work as a source, while BESS is forced to work as a burden when production is higher than demand. Appropriate management strategies must be developed to consider battery conditions. This decision was made efficiently using FLC when the frequency changes. This resolves the charging or removal fraction of BESS based on battery charging status and power incongruity.

5.3   Genetic Algorithm

Genetic algorithm is one of the most popular algorithms among other, and because of improvising method based on Darvinn's method, it has given surprising solution. Genetic algorithms, which are based on natural mechanisms and natural genetic, are more reliable because there is no limitation for decision making process. It uses historical information structures from previous decision assumptions which increase the decision making quality of the algorithm. The programmer needs to determine objective functions and coding techniques only because GA contains probabilistic transition rules, and it is possible to see entire solution space.

In GA algorithm, the biological term does not change with the steps. It supports several parameters set solution as well as replicates entire set. A set of problem parameters is represented by fixed character which includes their environment, input, output, etc. A chromosome, which is the single solution point of the problem space, contains genetic material. Genes, which are the symbols or series of symbols, will get values called alleles. Decoding of the encoded characters and calculation of the objective function for the problem is used to estimate chromosome strings. These results are used to calculate string values. String fitness value, the raw value of chromosome string can also be calculated. To transmit information between chromosome chains effectively and efficiently, the good coding design is a must.

Mutation, crossover, and reproduction are the key three hands to carry out movements in simple genetic algorithms. The chromosome chain is chosen from the previous generation in the probing cycle and it is possible to spread it to the next generation. The crossover, which works concerning reproduction, will select special positions in the two-parent strings and gene information will be sent to the end of the string. The random values of the allele are changed during the replication crossover phase between the mutation operators. At the run time, both probabilities of crossover and mutation actions can be selected. To explore the entire decision space, choice of performance parameters is important. In the first generation, unbound search in the decision space occurs. The initial population utilizes a random number generator. By the help of original population information, the next generation will be formed. To provide enough genetic structure, population size must be chosen large which will allow for the search for an infinite space of solutions.

5.3.1   Important Aspects of Genetic Algorithm

GA is basically consequent with a population genetic prototypical. The three main key hands linked with GA are mutation, crossover, and reproduction. Reproduction is essentially an operation in which, according to its fitness value, the old chromosome is copied to a "group of pairs". A more complete chromosome (i.e., better fitness function value) will receive more duplicates in the next cycle. Depending on their fitness level, copying chromosomes means that high-level chromosomes are more likely to contribute to one or more next generation offspring. Crossover is another very significant part of GA. This is an organized combine operation. This information has been shared by two scientists. The researchers have found an innovative crossover method known as uniform crossover. Below is shown that the speed of the uniform crossover convergence is quicker than the standard "single-point" and "two-point" crossovers. Single-point crossover may be designated as a crossover point on the string of the parent organism. Any data beyond that point is exchanged between the two parent species in the string of the organism. As a specific case of an N-point crossover strategy, two-point crossover can be described. On the individual chromosomes (strings), two random points are chosen and the genetic material is exchanged at these points. Uniform crossover can be defined when randomly selecting each gene (bit) from one of the parent chromosomes' corresponding genes. Uniform crossover is shown as below [11].

Single-Point Crossover: Two vectors Parent1 and Parent2 are selected with having string length 16. Opffspring1 and Offspring2 are the results of crossover site which is 5.

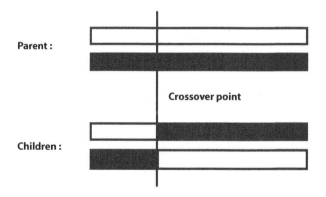

Parent1	11011 / 00100110110
Parent2	11011 / 11000011110
Offspring1	11011 / 11000011110
Offspring2	11011 / 00100110110

Two-Point Crossover: This technique can be termed as N-point cross over technique. In two-point crossover, randomly two points are selected and genetic material is transferred. Two vectors Parent1 and Parent2 are selected with having string length 16. Opffspring1 and Offspring2 are the results of crossover which are 5 and 5.

Parent1	11011 / 00100 / 110110
Parent2	11011 / 11000 / 011110
Offspring1	11011 / 11000 / 011110
Offspring2	11011 / 00100 / 110110

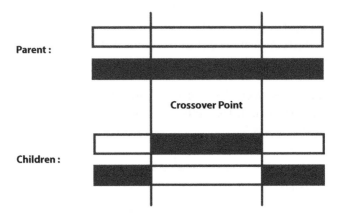

Uniform Crossover: Single bit selected from parent's string and transferred to the children string.

Parent	0 0 0 0 0 0 0 0 0 0 0 0 0 0 0 0 0 0 0 0 0 0 0 0
	1 1 1 1 1 1 1 1 1 1 1 1 1 1 1 1 1 1 1 1 1 1 1 1
Children	1 0 1 0 0 1 0 1 0 1 0 0 0 0 0 1 1 1 0 0 1
	0 1 1 0 0 0 1 0 1 0 1 1 0 1 1 0 1 0 0 1 0

5.3.2   Standard Genetic Algorithm

Step 1: Create initial population.
Step 2: Estimate fitness of population members.
Step 3: If solution found among member of population, then stop. Otherwise, go to Step 4

Step 4: Select and make copies of individuals.
Step 5: Perform reproduction using crossover and mutation operators.
Step 6: Create a new population and go to Step 2.

5.3.3   Genetic Algorithm and Its Application

Researchers and engineers have used genetic algorithm in many applications. By using genetic algorithm, extraordinary and superior outputs and results are achieved. Many literatures are available. Specifically, genetic algorithm is used in energy sector, power system, forecasting, pricing, and many problems.

5.3.4   Power System and Genetic Algorithm

Energy network is a package of energy generation, transmission, and distribution. During these generation, distribution, and transmission, power system struggles from different problems such as economic dispatches, optimal power flow, feeder reconfiguration stability, and many more. In the era of deregulated power system, price forecasting and load forecasting become necessary. In these scenarios, genetic algorithm plays a vital role to solve power system problems. By considering different aspects and constraints such as valve point loading, equality, and inequality, it prohibited operating zone, operating range limit, etc. In the directional search GA, there are two execution of directional search in GA. In first implementation, prohibited operating zones with other constraints have been considered. If all the constraints satisfy for their operating zones, then the attained solution is optimal generation. If any deficiency occurs in units, then set it to the upper or lower limits required. Most GA approaches better compared to other traditional methods and supports maximum unit value [9–16]. The approach cultivates a precise optimal solution for large-scale system [13]. In addition to the losses of the transmission network [14], the adaptability of real coded GA in meeting any number of constraints was also demonstrated by taking into account prohibited operating areas, power balance, and ramp-rate limits. The generating units' cumulative fuel-cost curves are extremely non-continuous and non-linear inherently. GA is an effective tool for real world problems of optimization. In various fields, it has been used to solve various problems [17]. When finding the high-presentation field, GA is quicker but shows difficulties when local searching for complex problems. This results in premature convergence and also has an unfortunate fine tuning of the final response. GA has been paired with SQP to solve these issues. This approach is used to solve the EDP with incremental fuel-cost functions, considering the valve point results. SQP shows itself as a best non-linear programming method to different optimization problem. The SQP can discover the search space speedily with a gradient direction and assurance a local optimum solution [18]. It is beneficial to advance the presentation of the SQP that the cost function of EDP is approached by using a "smooth and differentiable function" based on the maximum entropy principle [19]. The performance of the results is also compared with [20].

5.3.5   Economic Dispatch Using Genetic Algorithm

Step 1: Randomly created input data as unit data, load demand, etc.
Step 2: Population chromosome initialization.
Step 3: Assess all chromosomes.
Step 4: Rank chromosome rendering to their fitness.
Step 5: Select "best" parents for reproduction.
Step 6: Apply crossover and maybe mutation.
Step 7: Calculate new chromosomes and supplement preeminent into population and displacing weedier chromosomes.
Step 8: If the result converges, otherwise go to Step 5.

5.4   Artificial Neural Network

How does the brain solve all specific aspects in a few milliseconds? This question allows us to create machine vision which initially allows our brain to recognize and process disparate data. The power of our brain can be emphasized by the small size which the smallest supercomputer approaching the processing power of the brain is the size of a football stadium. The work of the human brain is quiet anonymous however some features of this extraordinary mainframe are known. The most basic elements of the human brain are certain cell types that do not seem to regenerate differently from other body parts. It is believed that these cells give us the opportunity to remember, think, and apply past experiences in our every action. One hundred billion of these cells are called neurons. The power of the human mind comes from neurons. Single neurons are complex. They have numerous fragments, sub-systems, and controls. They send data over many electro-chemical paths. Depending on the way used, there are hundreds of different modules of neurons. ANNs are synthetic networks that mimic biological neural networks found in living organisms. In the course of the study, it has been found that there were many differences between architecture and between artificial and natural neural network capabilities. This, in turn, is caused by the limited knowledge shared with the brain. ANNs include ways to regulate synthetic neurons to solve the same difficult and complicated problems that we expect from the so-called human processor the brain. While computers allow for slow and tedious tasks that can be done quickly and accurately compared to human performance, many common tasks are trivial to humans, but formulations that are very difficult to easily complete a computer can. This includes the following:

- Processing signal processing such as image processing, sound processing, and others.
- Data compression.
- Recognition and classification of detection models, including voice and optical character recognition, etc.
- Reconstruction reconstructs and returns data when some data is lost.
- Mining data extraction.
- Simplification of data.

5.4.1   The Biological Neuron

The basic unit of communication of incentive in the nervous system is neurons. Neurons are thought to have three main parts: axons, dendrites, and soma. Soma is part of neurons that contain nucleus, organelle, and cytoplasm. The axon is an extended portion of the nerve where signals (or impulses) travel to the next neuron. Dendrites are small branched projections from catfish that receive impulses from other neurons. Biological neuron is shown in Figure 5.1. When neurons transmit signals to other neurons, signals are transmitted through small spaces called synapses. Synapses act as a gateway between two neurons and connect axons from presynaptic neurons to the dendrites of postsynaptic neurons. The electrical signal produced by presynaptic neurons stimulates the release of chemicals (neurotransmitters) that diffuse through synapses to dendrites and then to soma from postsynaptic neurons. Neurons always maintain potential in their membranes. When postsynaptic neurons receive neurotransmitters, the membrane potential of the neurons changes. When neurons are sufficiently stimulated, the membrane potential near the axons achieves a threshold. After reaching the membrane potential threshold, impulses (potential action) are communicated laterally with the action to the next

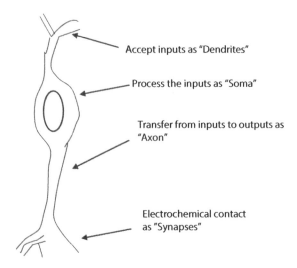

Figure 5.1 Construction of biological neuron.

neuron. Biological neurons can be connected to other neurons and accept connections from other neurons, and therefore, we have a tissue basis. In short, neurons receive information from other neurons, concoct it, and pass that information on to other neurons. Neurons integrate incoming pulses, and when this integration exceeds a certain limit, neurons send pulses in a term. The exact processing that occurs in neurons is unknown.

5.4.2   A Formal Definition of Neural Network

There is no generally accepted definition of neural networks, i.e., ANNs. But, perhaps most people in the region agree that neural networks are very simple processor networks ("neurons" or "nodes"), each of which has a small amount of local memory. A communication channel connects units that normally transmit numeric data. Nodes only work with their local data and the input they receive via the link. Neural networks are systems that can perform complex calculations, perhaps "intelligent" similar to those routinely carried out by the human brain. Most neural networks "learn" to carry out such intelligent tasks through some form of training, adjusting the weight of the connection based on some training data. In other words, neural networks learn from examples and can generalize outside of training data. In short, neural networks are massively distributed processors that inherently tend to store and expose experienced knowledge to use. In two ways, it looks like a brain: Through the learning process, the network acquires knowledge. The strength of interneuron, called weights, is used to store knowledge gained during training.

5.4.3   Neural Network Models

Mcculloch-Pitts Model
The most uncomplicated model for neurons is the McCulloch-Pitts model, as shown in Figure 5.2. Here, input to neurons is routed through several nodes of the input layer. Inputs are scaled and added by connection weights. Then, the output node produces output by applying the nonlinear function f (.). The three most generally practiced nonlinear functions are the signum, ramp, and sigmoid.

5.4.4   Rosenblatt's Perceptron

The Rosenblatt basic perceptron model is the same as the single McCulloch-Pitts deviation model, which in this case regulates connection weight through training. The important significance of neural networks lies not only in the way in which neurons are manifested but also in the way in which connections are made (usually referred to as topology). One of the calmest forms of this topology is the multi-layer perceptron, which consists of three layers.

- Input layer (network inputs)
- Hidden layer
- Output layer (network outputs)

There are several layer of neural network. From any one layer, any one neuron is connected to all other neurons in the next layer. This forms of the whole network with fully interconnected. An example of such a network

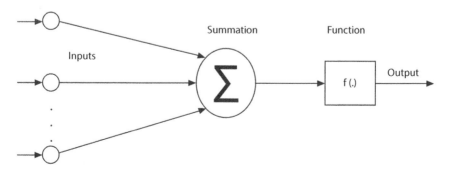

Figure 5.2 McCulloch-Pitts model.

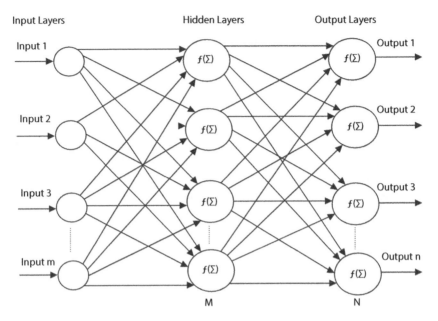

Figure 5.3 Multi-layer perceptron structure.

topology is illustrated in Figure 5.3. Inputs (usually digital values) stimulate input levels. Any node can be inserted into the network which can be formulated mathematically. For each input node, this value can be assigned a dissimilar valve liable on the type of input. From all the input nodes, the values are passed to the hidden layer node sideways with the link. The "strength" or "weight" of the link changes the value of the input node by scaling. Each link is given a different weight depending on how important or less important the information presented in this context. The hidden layer node receives information from all connected input nodes [21]. This value, in turn, is passed along with the new link to the output layer in a similar way as the information passed from input to the hidden layer.

5.4.5   Feedforward and Recurrent Networks

Feedforward and feedback are two main forms of network topology.

Feedforward Network
In a moving neural network, links between units do not form cycles. Feedforward networks generally return very quickly to input. Most cellular networks, in addition to the algorithms invented by neural network

researchers, can be trained with various effective conventional numerical methods, such as conjugate and gradients. The network topology for the multilayer perceptron shown above is an example of a simple type of feed-forward network. More complex power grids are made possible by developing the multiple hidden layers.

5.4.6   Back Propagation Algorithm

The backpropagation algorithm is the main central work for continuous work on studying in neural networks. The algorithm instructs to change the weight of the W_{pq} in each redirection network to learn several partners I/O training. Because the maximum control application uses two-layer MLN, we provide an algorithm for backpropagation. The network is shown in Figure 5.4. x is the $n \times 1$ input vector. y is the $m \times 1$ diagonal output vector. The hidden level consists of unit h, which represents the typical weight connected amongst the source level and the hidden level, while W_{jk} represents the typical weight connected amongst the hidden level and the input level.

5.4.7   Forward Propagation

The forward response of such a network is given as follows:
j^{th} hidden layer input can be expressed as

$$S_j = \sum_{k=1}^{n} W_{jk} x_k$$

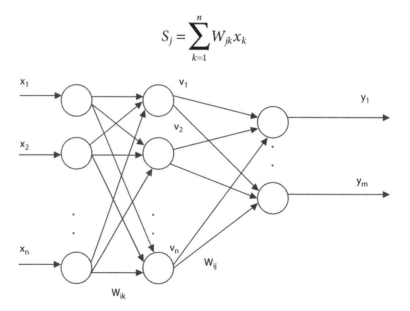

Figure 5.4 A two-layered network.

j^{th} hidden layer output can be given as

$$v_j = f(S_j)$$
(5.1)

where f is the squashing function, generally taken as sigmoidal activation

$$f(x) = \frac{1}{1+e^{-x}}$$
(5.2)

Finally i^{th} output layer input is

$$q_j = \sum_{i=1}^{h} W_{ij} v_j$$
(5.3)

Output y is given as

$$y_i = f(q_i)$$
(5.4)

Backward Propagation

The instantaneous error w_{pq} of back propagation algorithm is resultant as follows:

$$w_{pq}(m+1) = w_{pq}(m) - \gamma \frac{dE}{dw_{pq}}$$

where γ is the learning rate and $E = \frac{1}{2}(y^d(m) - y(m))^2$ is the error function to be minimized.

5.4.8   Algorithm

Backpropagation algorithm given as follows:

1. Initially, all weights are assigned to random values lies [0, 1].
2. Formulate input layer x_k, where $k = 1,2,..., n$.
3. Signal forwards the propagate through the network using

$$S_j = \sum_{k=1}^{n} W_{jk} x_k \tag{5.5}$$

$$v_j = f(S_j) j = 1,2....h \tag{5.6}$$

$$q_j = \sum_{i=1}^{h} W_{ij} v_j \tag{5.7}$$

$$y_i = f(q_i) \quad i = 1,2, ..., m \tag{5.8}$$

4. Calculate δ_i for the output layer

$$\delta i = f(q_i)(y_i^d - y_i) \tag{5.9}$$

Pattern x_k is considered by tallying the actual outputs y_i with the desired ones y_i^d.

5. Calculate the Δ_j for the "hidden layers" by propagating the errors backwards

$$\Delta_j = f(S_j) \sum_{i=1}^{n} W_{ij} \delta_i \tag{5.10}$$

6. Update weight as

$$W_{ij}(m+1) = W_{ij}(m) + \gamma \, \delta_i \, v_j \tag{5.11}$$

$$W_{ik}(m+1) = W_{ik}(m) + \gamma \, \Delta_j \, x_k \tag{5.12}$$

To update all connection.

7. Return back to Step 2 for repetition and to find the next pattern.

5.4.9   Recurrent Network

With feedback or a recurrent neural network, a cycle occurs in connection. In some feedback networks, each moment, an input is offered, a neural

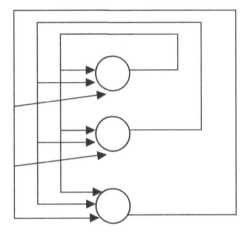

Figure 5.5 A recurrent network.

network repeats itself long before a response is generated. Feedback networks are more challenging to train than feedforward networks. Figure 5.5 shows the network topology with feedback. Some examples of this type of network are Hopfield models and Boltzmann machines.

5.4.10   Examples of Neural Networks

The following are few examples of neural networks that perform Boolean logic operations AND, OR, and XOR.

5.4.10.1   AND Operation

The network structure for implementing AND operations with the McCulloch-Pitts model is shown in Figure 5.6. The two input variables a

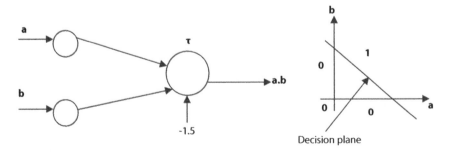

Figure 5.6 AND network.

and b are binary values and the third input is a constant called the threshold. Processing the node, labeled τ involves the sum of all inputs to the node and then determining its threshold. The threshold determination node function returns 1 if the summation exceeds zero if not 0. Network input can be mapped into 2D space and the threshold defines the portion of the plane as shown in the figure so that the output on one side is level 1, while the output on the other side is 0, i. H. Airplane is the level of solution. Thresholds must be chosen accordingly. In this case, we take −1.5. Connection weights are all 1.

5.4.10.2   OR Operation

In Figure 5.7 the OR operation differs from the AND operation only by the position of the decision plane in the 2D inputs space. Therefore, alteration in the threshold value realizes OR operation. Here, we take threshold value equal to −0.5.

5.4.10.3   XOR Operation

However, XOR operation cannot be realized using the simple McCulloch-Pitts model. This is because the outputs here are not linearly separable as in Figure 5.8. It needs two decision planes, and hence, a multiplayer network can only realize the situation. The connection weights, unless otherwise mentioned, are 1. The processing at the hidden and the output nodes, denoted by τ, include summation and thresholding as explained earlier.

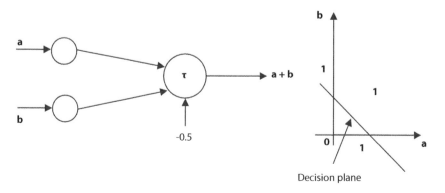

Figure 5.7 OR network.

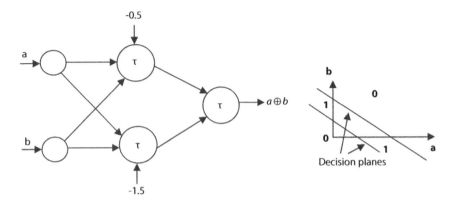

Figure 5.8 XOR network.

5.4.11   Key Components of an Artificial Neuron Network

Each segment describes an artificial neuron network's seven major components. Both components are efficient when there is one hidden layer in the neural network: one output layer and one input layer at-least.

Segment 1. Weighting Factors: An artificial neural neuron network needs a lot of inputs. Every input has its individual weight which helps to better assess the giving out unit's "summation function". These weights have the equal purpose as biology's neurons. Both inputs are not so efficient and the weights are therefore a superior influence on the processing factor because they converge to generate a neuronal response and provide more value to the effective inputs. In the network, weights are generally termed as adaptive coefficient specifying the amplitude of the artificial neuron input signal. They are a quantity of the connection power of an object. Both abilities can be strengthened through the use of different training systems and the conferral of learning guidelines to a network.

Segment 2. Summation Function: At the start of the process, the weighted sum of all inputs is determined. Inputs and their respective weights are represented arithmetically in the form of a matrix: i_1, i_2, ..., i_n and w_1, w_2, ..., w_n, respectively. As the sum of these two vectors, the whole input signal is represented. The entire signal input function comes from multiply each input I vector component by the corresponding w weight vector component and then summarize all products. Input(1) = $i_1 \times w_1$, input(2) = $i_2 \times w_2$, etc., are added as input(1) + input(2) + ... + input(n). The outcome is obtained as a single number, not a vector of multiple components.

Geometrically, a measure of their similarity can be called the inner product of two vectors. If the vector is pointing in the same direction, the internal product is maximal if the internal product is considered small, as if the vector is pointing in the 180 degrees out of phase, i.e., opposite direction. The sum function may be more complex than just the number of data sum and weight products. Until switching to the transfer function, multiplying the inputs and calculating the coefficients can be performed in different ways. The addition function may select the minimum, maximum, majority, feature, or some standardization algorithm in addition to simple product addition. The architecture and paradigm of the selected network will determine the basic algorithm to integrate neural inputs. Before it is transferred to the transfer function, several summation functions apply an additional method to the output. This mechanism is sometimes referred to as the "activation function". "Activation function" is use to permit the final output to change with time. Apparently, the "activation functions" are quite limited to science. Most existing network configurations use an "activation function" called "identity", which is similar to "not having one". Moreover, feature is probably to be a section of the entire system rather than just a component of each of the processing unit's individual components.

Segment 3. Transfer Function: By an algorithmic procedure known as the "transfer function". The product of the summary function is equal to weighted sum, is transformed into work output. In the transfer function, to evaluate the neuronal output, the summation number can be compared to a certain threshold. If the sum approaches the threshold value, a signal is produced by the processing element. If the input and weight output sum are lesser than the threshold, zero signal or some inhibitory signal is formed. The threshold is commonly non-linear or transition function. Linear functions are constrained as the output is strictly proportional to the input. It is not very good for linear functions. That was the difficulty in the initial models of the network, as stated in the book Perceptrons by Minsky and Papert. Depending on the outcome of the "summation function" is +Ve or −Ve, the transfer function might be something so simple. Zero and one, one and minus one, or other binary variations could be generated by the network. So, a transition function is a "hard limiter" or phase function. Another type of transmission mechanism, the threshold or ramp function, may replicate an area's input and is still stored as a rigid barrier outside that area. This is a linear function which is set to min and maxvalues, rendering it non-continuous. A sigmoid or S-shaped curve would still be another choice. The curve follows the asymptotes with a minimum and maximum value. This scale is generally referred to as sigmoid if it ranges between −1 and 1 within the range of 0 to 1, an interesting feature of this curve is the continuousness of the mathematical properties and their derivatives. This option works well and is often a transferring selection feature. For different network architectures, other transfer functions have been described and will be conferred future. Before the transfer function is implemented, even circulated arbitrary noise can be introduced. The mode of network paradigm training provided specifies the source and noise level. This noise is usually called artificial neuron "temperature". The name, "temperature", comes from the physical phenomenon that affects their ability to think when people become too hot or cold. This method is replicated mechanically by incorporating noise. Indeed, more brain-like transfer functions are evaluated by augmenting disturbance levels to the summation result. To mimic the features of nature more precisely, some experimenters use a source of "Gaussian noise". "Gaussian noise" is equivalent to randomly dispersed noise although in the temperature range the distribution of random numbers is through a bell curve. Temperature utilization is a field of continuing research and is not used in many technological presentations. "NASA" has just revealed a "network topology" that uses a "temperature coefficient" in a new reproductive training feature. This temperature factor, however, is a worldwide term used to get the function of the gain. This should not be confusing to the more familiar word temperature, simply adding noise to the neurons. In comparison, the "global temperature coefficient" causes the meaning of transmission to have a knowledge variable comparable to the weights of "synaptic input". This idea is believed to produce a system that has a much higher learning rate (by several orders of magnitudes) than other "feedforward" and "backpropagation networks" and produces more accurate results.

Segment 4. Scaling and Limiting: Completing the transfer feature of the processing unit, the result moves through added processes that scale and restrict. This scaling essentially multiplies the transfer value by averaging a size factor and adding an offset. Limiting is the technique that ensures that no upper or lower bound exceeds the scaled result. This limit is in adding to the hard limits that may have been performed by original transfer function. This method of scaling is used in several configurations to analyze biotic neuron models, namely "brain-state-in- the-box of James Anderson".

Segment 5. Output Function–Competition: For each processing unit, an output signal is allowed that can be sent to hundreds of other neurons. It is like the biochemical brain, with lots of inputs and just one result. The result is functionally equivalent to the value of the transfer function.

Nevertheless, few system configurations change the outcome to accommodate struggle between adjacent processing components. Unless they are strong, neurons can interact with each other, inhibiting processing elements. Competition can occur in one or two stages. Next, the competition will have to decide which artificial neuron or performance will be involved. In addition, competitive feedback helps to assess which factor in development will be involved.

Segment 6. Error Function and Backpropagated Value: In most training grids, there are variations between actual and expected outcomes. This fresh mistake is converted by an "error function" to a specific grid design. Such errors are used by the simplest architecture, but while quadratic error points, cube errors, and other paradigms are retained, they change raw errors to achieve the predefined objectives.

"Artificial neuron error" is usually spread to another processing unit's learning mechanism. Often the present error is called this type of error. The current error is usually transmitted back to an earlier layer. Nonetheless, this "backpropagated" value may be either the "current error" or the "current error" somehow multiplied.

Segment 7. Learning Function: The learning method aims at modifying variable relationship weights based on a neural algorithm on each unit's input. This method of regulating the weights of the input connections defined the "adaptation function" and the "learning mode" to achieve some desired results. The learning methods are "supervised" and "unsupervised". An instructor is required for "supervised learning". The instructor can be a collection of data training or a viewer who scores the results of the system performance. This method, learning by training, is to have an instructor. When there is no external instructor, certain internal requirements built in the network will structure the program itself. By doing this, it is thinking.

5.4.12   Neural Network Training

A neural network usually has more than two numbers of input nodes and any number of connections between nodes. Once a neural network is built with nodes and some functions to be performed at the nodes, a network can be trained. The networks are trained by changing the weight of links between nodes. Initially, all weights selected randomly. Typically, computer programs generate connection weights at random. The network then receives input and can process information about its node to produce output. Suppose the input is letters and you want from the network to confirm whether the letter "M" or the letter "N". Primarily, this problem will occur pretty often. The connection weights have to be altered and the network repeat again. Over hundreds of experiments and small variations in connection weights, networks can learn to identify letters very accurately. The whole training setup must be shown multiple times on the network to get satisfying results. Many examples are needed for networks. A common type of neural network training is retransmission. Backward creates a program that automatically changes the link weight if the results are wrong and reinforce the links if the results are correct.

5.4.13   Training Types

Training or learning algorithm can be divided in two parts: (i) Supervised and (ii) Unsupervised.

5.4.13.1   Supervised Training

In the controlled training, the correct result (target value or desired result) is known and communicated to the neural network during exercise so that the neural network can adjust its weight and try to match the results with the target value. After training, it tests the neural network, not the target value, and sees how near it is to get the precise goal value.

5.4.13.2   Unsupervised Training

In case of unsupported training, correct results during training of neural networks are not provided. Unmanaged neural networks usually do some type of data compression, e.g., B. resize or group. The difference between controlled and unsupported methods is always clearly defined. Unsupported methods can study summaries of probability distributions, and these summary distributions can then be used to make predictions.

5.4.14   Learning Rates

The rate of learning from ANNs depends on a number of factors which can be controlled. Many trade-offs need to be considered when choosing the solution. Clearly, a less rate means that much extra period is consumed on off-line learning in order to create a properly trained program. In comparison, with higher learning speeds, a slower learning system could not allow the network to make perfect discrimination possible. Commonly, when addressing the off-line training mission, characterized as "tiresome", many considerations have to be addressed in addition to time. Network complexity, paradigm range, architecture, learning rule type or rules used, and anticipated correctness need to be taken into consideration. These features play an important role in defining how extended it will take for a network to train. Varying any of these aspects can either prolong the duration of the training to an excessive span or uniform contribute to inappropriate accuracy. Most functions of learning have some facility for a "rate of learning" or "constant learning". The word is usually positive and varies from zero to one. If the "learning rate" is advanced than one, the learning algorithm can easily override the weight correction. Great rate of "learning" is not precise the prevailing inaccuracies as soon as possible; however, high actions are taken to correct errors, and the best minimum convergence is likely to be reached.

5.4.15   Learning Laws

There are many common applications of learning laws. Most of these rules are some kind of variation in Hebb's Law, the best recognized and oldest rule of learning. Research into diverse learning mechanisms remains as new ideas surface in commercial journals on a routine basis. Many scholars have the primary objective of modeling biological learning. Some try to adapt their understanding of how nature approaches learning. Any way, it is very minimal that man understands how neural treating essentially works. To be sure, learning is difficult than the simplifications described by the currently defined learning laws. Some of the most important rules are mentioned below.

Hebb's Rule: Donald Hebb implemented the well-known learning law. The definition appeared in 1949 in his book, "The Organization of Behavior: A Neuropsychological Theory". His basic rule is: "if a neuron receives an input from another neuron and both are highly active (mathematically having the same sign), the neuron weight should be reinforced."

Hopfield Law: It is analogous to Hebb's law, except that it defines the strength or weakening magnitude. It says, "if both the desired output and the input are active or inactive, increase the relation weight by the learning rate, otherwise the learning rate will decrease the weight."

The Delta Rule: This law is another "Hebb rule" variant. This rule is very popular and most extensively used. The rule is stand on the plain principle of constantly adjusting the input connection intensity to the difference (delta) among the desired output value and the meting out unit's actual output. To minimalize mean square error, this rule changes the synaptic weight. It is often called as the "Widrow-Hoff Learning Rule" and "Least Mean Square (LMS) Learning Rule". The Delta method suits in the way such that transfer function derivative converts the delta error in the output layer and is then used to change the input relationship weights in the previous neural layer. In other words, one layer at a time propagates the error back to previous layers. The process of replication of system in accuracies continues until entering the initial layer. The system created is termed as feedforward, and Backpropagation derives its name from this error term computing process. Ensure the input data set is correctly randomized when being used.

The Gradient Descent Rule: This rule is analogous to "delta rules" where the "transfer function" derivative is used to adjust "delta errors" earlier than applying to the ratio weights. Nevertheless, here, an added proportional constant linked to the learning rate is affixed to the weight-acting final amending element. The strategy is extensively applied, although it manages to converge very slowly. Diverse learning stages for diverse level of a network have been shown to help the process of learning converge more quickly. The learning levels for all those near-output layers were set lower in these experiments than near-input layers. The method is particularly vital for users, which is a strong underlying model that does not extract the input data.

Kohonen's Learning Law: Teuvo Kohonen developed the technique with inspiration of biological systems. The elements strive to evaluate or alter the weighting factor in this method. The processor unit with the highest production is avowed the winner and has the potential to both inhibit its rivals and excite its neighbors. A production is allowed only to the winner and his adjacent are endorsed to change their weights of contact. In addition, during the training period, the size of the vicinity can fluctuate. The normal paradigm is to begin with a broader neighborhood definition and narrow down as the training progression goes on. Kohonen networks are modeling the input distribution according to the idea of the winning variable as the one with the nearby contest to the input prototype. Mentioned thing is useful in modeling numerical or topological data and is often associated with it as maps or topologies that are self-organized.

5.4.16   Restructured Power System

After the invention of ANN, use of ANN has become more important in modern era. Many literatures are available citing ANN applications in medical science, space science, energy system, etc. Here, we discuss ANN application with respect to restructured power system. Since last 25 years, power utility companies are moving toward from monopoly-based system to deregulated system [22]. The electricity market has become more competitive day by day. In restructured power system, different aspects such as transmission congestion management, locational marginal prices, and ancillary service management have become more important. Due to increasing competition, load forecasting and price forecasting become a tedious task for utilities [22].

5.4.17   Advantages of Precise Forecasting of the Price

The correct estimate of the price of electricity helps to create an operative risk management plan for companies contributing in the energy market. At present, market contributors need to use various tools to regulator and diminish risks arising from price volatility in opening markets [23]. If the accuracy comes from the electricity market price, then GENCO and LSE, as the key players, can reduce risk and maximize production. Day time forecasting or hour time forecasting is best example for understanding prediction of forecasting in restructured power system. The power generation from the hydrothermal is considered with "Generation Rate Constraint (GRC)" [24]. "Hybrid Neuro Fuzzy (HNF) controller" is used for testing of control structure. Other effective soft computing techniques are also tested in deregulated power system are "Hybrid Particle Swarm Optimization (HCPSO)", "Real Coded Genetic Algorithm (RCGA)", and ANN controllers [25].

5.5   Conclusion

Main objective of chapter was to focus on various soft computing techniques which are based on restructured power system. GA, fuzzy logic, and ANN are major three techniques which are mostly used by electrical engineering researcher. Out of three, neuro fuzzy system is generally used for hybrid system. The widespread application of efficient soft computing techniques is therefore increasing. It has been observed that researcher, those who used SC-based approaches, reported good and positive results, which are encouraging. The main benefit of said approaches is that the results obtained are the clear estimates rather than the unique solution. The techniques described in this chapter assist the end user to take quick decision under the circumstances of uncertainty. The allied areas including science and engineering management are finding soft computing as an essential tool for dealing with the complex problems, and it is very simple to modeling and prediction of the said behavior problems.

References

1. Zadeh, L.A., Fuzzy sets *Inf. Control.*, 8, 3, 338–353, 1965.
2. Yan, H. and Luh, P.B., A Fuzzy Optimization Based Method for Integrated Power System Scheduling and Inter Utility Power Transaction with Uncertainties. *IEEE Trans. Power Syst.*, 12, 2, 756–763, May 1997.
3. Arya, Y., Impact of Hydrogen Aqua Electrolyzer Fuel Cell Units on Automatic Generation Control of Power Systems with a New Optimal Fuzzy TIDF-II Controller. *Renew. Energy*, 139, 468–482, 2019.
4. Sabahi, K., Ghaemi, S., Pezeshki, S., Application of Type-2 Fuzzy Logic System for Load Frequency Control using Feedback Error Learning Approaches. *Appl. Soft Comput.*, 21, 1–11, 2014.
5. Arya, Y. and Kumar, N., BFOA-Scaled Fractional Order Fuzzy PID Controller Applied to AGC of Multi Area Multi Source Electric Power Generating Systems. *Swarm Evol. Comput.*, 32, 202–218, 2017.
6. Nanda, J. and Mangla, A., Automatic Generation Control of an Interconnected Hydro-Thermal System using Conventional Integral and Fuzzy Logic Controller. *Proceedings of IEEE International Conference on Electric Utility Deregulation, Restructuring and Power Technologies*, Hong Kong, China, vol. 1, pp. 372–377, 2004.
7. Chandrashekar, M.J. and Jayapal, R., Design and Comparison of I, PI, PID and Fuzzy Logic Controller on AGC Deregulated Power System with HVDC Link. *Proceedings of International Conference on Circuits, Controls and Communications (CCUBE)*, Bengaluru, pp. 1–6, 2013.
8. Jayapriya, M., Yadav, S., Ram, A.R., Sathvik, S., Lekshmi, R.R., Selva, K.S., Implementation of Fuzzy Based Frequency Stabilization Control Strategy in Raspberry Pi for a Wind Powered Microgrid. *Proc. Comput. Sci.*, 115, 151–158, 2017.
9. Goldberg, D.E., *Genetic Algorithms Search, Optimization & Machine Learning*, Addison-Wesley, MA, 1989.
10. Austin, S., *An Introduction to Genetic Algorithms*, vol. 5, pp. 48–53, Computer Science, March 1990.
11. Chen, P.-H. and Chang, H.-C., Large Scale Economic Dispatch by Genetic Algorithm. *IEEE Trans. Power Syst.*, 10, 4, 1919–1926, 1995.
12. Adhinarayanan, T. and Sydulu, M., A Directional Search Genetic Algorithm to the Economic Dispatch Problem with Prohibited Operating Zones. *2008 IEEE/PES Transmission and Distribution Conference and Exposition*, Apr. 21–24, 2008, pp. 1–5.

13. Orero, S.O., Economic dispatch of generators with prohibited operating zones: a genetic algorithm approach. *IET Digital Library*, 143, 6, 529–534, 1996.
14. Ram Jethmalani, C.H., Simon, S.P., Sundareswaran, K., Srinivasa Rao Nayak, P., Padhy, N.P., Real Coded Genetic Algorithm Based Transmission System Loss Estimation in Dynamic Economic Dispatch Problem. *Alex. Eng. J.*, 57, 3535–3547, 2018.
15. Damousis, I.G., Bakirtzis, A.G., Dokopoulos, P.S., Network-Constrained Economic Dispatch using Real-Coded Genetic Algorithm. *IEEE Trans. Power Syst.*, 18, 1, 198–205, February 2003.
16. Subbaraj, P., Rengaraj, R., Salivahanan, S., Real-Coded Genetic Algorithm Enhanced with Self Adaptation for Solving Economic Dispatch Problem with Prohibited Operating Zone. *International Conference on Control, Automation, Communication and Energy Conservation -2009*, 4th - 6th June 2009.
17. Luk, P.C.K., Lai, L.L., Tong, T.L., GA Optimisation of Rule Base in a Fuzzy Logic Control of a Solar Power Plant. *DRPT2000. International Conference on Electric Utility Deregulation and Restructuring and Power Technologies.* Proceedings (Cat. No. 00EX328), 4–7 April 2000, 221–225.
18. He, D.-k., Wang, F.-l., Mao, Z.-z., Hybrid Genetic Algorithm for Economic Dispatch with Valve-Point Effect. *Electr. Power Syst. Res.*, 78, 626–633, 2008.
19. Chiang, C.-L., Improved Genetic Algorithm for Power Economic Dispatch of Units with Valve-Point Effects and Multiple Fuels. *IEEE Trans. Power Syst.*, 20, 4, 1690–1699, November 2005.
20. Tippayachai, J., Ongsakul, W., Ngamroo, I., Parallel Micro Genetic Algorithm for Constrained Economic Dispatch. *IEEE Trans. Power Syst.*, 17, 3, 790–797, August 2002.
21. Podvalnya, S.L. and Vasiljev, E.M., The Principle of Multi-Alternativity in Intelligent Systems: Active Neural Network Models. *Proc. Comput. Sci.*, 103, 410–415, 2017.
22. Xiao, L., Shao, W., Yu, M., Ma, J., Jin, C., Research and Application of A Hybrid Wavelet Neural Network Model with the Improved Cuckoo Search Algorithm for Electrical Power System Forecasting. *Appl. Energy*, 198, 203–222, 2017.
23. S, B.S., Kamaraj, N., Hybrid Neuro Fuzzy Approach for Automatic Generation Control in Restructured Power System. *Electr. Power Energy Syst.*, 74, 274–285, 2016.
24. Shayeghi, H., Shayanfar, H.A., Malik, O.P., Robust Decentralized Neural Networks Based LFC in a Deregulated Power System. *Electr. Power Syst. Res.*, 77, 241–251, 2007.
25. Vahidinasab, V., Jadid, S., Kazemi, A., Day-Ahead Price Forecasting in Restructured Power Systems using Artificial Neural Networks. *Electr. Power Syst. Res.*, 78, 1332–1342, 2008.

Recent Advances in Wearable Antennas: A Survey

Harvinder Kaur[1]* and Paras Chawla[2]

¹University Institute of Engineering and Technology, Panjab University, Chandigarh, India
²Chandigarh University, Gharuan, Mohali, India

Abstract

The body-worn antennas have become the emerging area for the research as it can be wearable and can be easily embedded into the clothing. The requirements of wearable antenna are increasing due to the miniaturization process and the use of flexible devices. This chapter elaborates the comparative survey of different designs of wearable antenna design technology. The substrates used for antenna designs include different textiles or conventional substrates. The textile wearable antennas are useful in body-centric communication systems and they are light in weight, flexible, and easy to integrate into the clothing. The wearable antenna covers the large span of application areas which include IoT, medical applications, UWB, telecommunications, defense applications, computing, and wearable electronic.

The different textile materials that are used in the designing of the wearable antennas are cotton, foam, jeans, polyester, nylon, silk, fleece, felt, curtain cotton, contura fabric, nylon, Kevlar fabric, etc. The different substrates have different electromagnetic properties, so the selection of the substrate material is an important parameter for consideration in the design of textile antennas. These textile antennas are fabricated using different textile substrates for the wireless systems including Bluetooth, Wi-Fi, WiMax, LAN, WLAN, medical, IoT, and broadcasting applications. Electrically conducting materials are used for ground plane and microstrip patch fabrication of wearable antennas. The conducting material is placed on the upper part of the substrate as patch and the ground is made of

---

Corresponding author: harvinderkang29@gmail.com

R. Anandan, Suseendran Gopalakrishnan, Souvik Pal and Noor Zaman (eds.) The Industrial Internet of Things (IIoT): Intelligent Analytics for Predictive Maintenance, (149–180) © 2022 Scrivener Publishing LLC

conducting material at the bottom of the textile substrate. These conducting materials should have a low electric resistance to minimize the losses. The shape of the rectangular patch can be rectangular, square, circular etc. Therefore, conducting properties play important role in the performance of these textile antennas.

The different antenna designs are investigated and the detail examination of the variation in the design, use of metamaterials, itching of ground, and their consequences on the antenna performance is summarized here. The effect of the change in the substrate material on the resonant frequency, bandwidth, gain, SAR, and radiation efficiency is presented. The antenna performance is highly afflicted in the vicinity of the human body and the location of the antenna on the human body. So, these effects are studied by analyzing the SAR parameter in different antenna designs. This survey is helpful in providing the insight knowledge of the antenna designs which can further help in the future wearable antenna design research to fulfill the requirements of best wearable electronics.

Keywords: Wearable antennas, SAR, textile antennas, fractal, IoT

6.1   Introduction

Nowadays, wearable antennas have become the important area of research. The wearable antennas requirement is increased due to the miniaturization process and the use of flexible devices. The wearable antenna is defined as the miniature antenna which can be worn by the wearer [1]. The wearable antenna allows the cloth or any other device to be a part of the communication system [2] and they are light in weight, highly flexible, and can be easily integrated with the clothes and they are comfortable to wear. The wearable antenna is used in different applications which include medical applications, defense applications, computing, and wearable electronic and IoT. There is a vast research utilizing the UWB frequency band. UWB band can be used for broadband transmission. The antennas with fractal geometry and conventional antenna structures are applicable for RFID tags [3].

The IoT usually refers to a group of devices which can sense, accumulate and switch information using internet as a medium besides any human intervention. Recently, wearable units are swiftly rising and forming a new segment--"Wearable IoT (WIoT)" using wearable material antennas due to their functionality of sensing, computing and communicating [4]. The wearable IoT technology helps the person to interact and communicate with the network through the clothes or other wearable devices via the application and the network layer. For wearable textile IoT systems, integrating antennas into textile materials helps the clothes end up a smart interface between the consumer and the network.

Internet of Things technology is useful in each and every aspect of the today's world which includes smart cities, smart homes, and connected health systems. Wearable technology is playing an essential role in enhancing the features of the smart projects by interconnecting the smart devices with the networks. So, IoT wearable technology smart devices will be highly approached devices in the coming years. It aims to enhance the living standards of the IoT users with the help of smart devices.

Wearable IoT devices can be helpful in the medical systems with the use of heart rate measurement, etc. These devices make use of the sensors which can sense and collect the required information and interact with the user and the network.

Wearable technology helps in living the smart and the healthy life. By the collaboration of the wearable and IoT technology, the smart devices can behave as most reliable devices for the IoT technology users.

Another feature of the wearable technology is the smart clothing. Wearable technology-based clothing is applicable in medical, defense, lifestyle, sports, security system, etc. Therefore, nowadays, IoT technology is working with different textile brands for developing the smart textile wearable IoT devices.

The antenna is the main component of the wearable devices. The various researches have been done in improving the antenna designs. It includes the use of metamaterials, EBG, defected ground planes, reconfigurable antennas, electro-textile antennas, etc. The main emphasis is on the textile and the fractal antennas so that the advanced wearable multiband antennas can be designed. The antenna geometries of different types of antennas highly affect the performance behavior of the antenna.

The flexible antennas' requirement has paved a way for the antenna designs with the textile materials. The different types of textile materials are used as a substrate in designing the wearable antennas like cotton, foam, jeans, polyester, and nylon. These textile antennas are fabricated using different textile substrates for the wireless systems including Wi-Fi, WiMax, BAN, Bluetooth, and WLAN applications [5]. The human body behaves as a lossy medium which affects the performance behavior of wearable antenna. So as to plan a body wearable antenna, the structural parameters and diverse electromagnetic properties of substrates ought to be wisely considered [5]. It is also required to take care of the SAR values of the wearable antenna so that back radiation cannot harm the human body. In the textile antenna designs, there is use of textile material as a substrate material and electrically conducting materials are used for ground plane and microstrip patch. These conducting materials should have a low electric resistance to minimize the losses [6]. Thus, for achieving the necessary performance of these antennas, electromagnetic properties of the materials should be taken into consideration. There is possibility that many researches may come into existence in the near future which may cause many electronics to be built into the clothing. The idea to be taken into consideration, the embroidered antenna came into existence. The embroidered antennas are also more comfortable and highly durable design for the smart clothing [7].

In 1988, first fractal antenna was worked by Dr. Nathan Cohen. Fractal antennas have self-comparable and self-repetitive qualities. The thought behind fractal antennas originated from designs existing in nature. They have space filling properties that used for structuring antennas for wideband behavior. Fractal antennas are the mix of antennas that are working at various frequencies with a compact size [8]. The miniature antennas can be integrated into smart clothing for various telecommunication-based applications. The hybrid antennas came with the advanced features with highly promising results in the field of fractal antenna technology. In hybrid fractal antennas, the various fractal geometries are fused together to design an antenna.

This chapter provides insight information about the wearable antennas. The wearable antenna system is fast growing field in various wireless and health monitoring applications and paves the way for upcoming technology. To achieve the wider bandwidth and multiband characteristics, the different fractal antennas with the textile substrate can be designed as multiband wearable antennas. A multiband antenna is an antenna which is manufactured to operate in different range of frequency bands. The design of multiband antenna is such that the different parts of the antenna are working for different frequency bands, respectively. The multiband antennas are useful for different applications like RFID (0.924 GHz), GSM (1,710–1,785 MHz and 1,805–1,880 MHz), GPS (1.575 GHz), Wi-Fi (2,400 MHz), ISM (2.4–2.4875 GHz), WLAN (2.45 and 5.8 GHz), Wi-MAX (3–3.63GHz), UWB (3.1–10.6 GHz), two-band MBOFDM (3.1–4.8 GHz), SWB (4.3–29.6 GHz), and DS-UWB (6–8.5 GHz) [4, 5, 8]. The multiband antennas gain is low and they are physically large as compared to single-band antennas to accommodate the multiple bands. It is required to study different geometries of fractal antennas, conventional antennas, hybrid fractal antennas, and textile antennas. By understanding in depth the behavior of such antennas, new correlation can be achieved about the geometry and performance of the antenna to design advanced wearable textile antennas.

6.2   Types of Antennas

Wearable miniaturized antennas are a fundamental component of each and every wearable 5G, IoT, and Medical applications. Antenna converts RF frequency into electrical signals and vice-versa. There are various types of antennas depending upon the transmission and the reception requirements.

6.2.1   Description of Wearable Antennas

6.2.1.1   Microstrip Patch Antenna

The microstrip patch antennas are having low profile and high FBR. But microstrip patch antennas have inherent narrowband property, higher loss, poor isolation between adjacent lines, and inadequate radiation properties. These antennas can be used in microwave frequencies, portable wireless devices, wearable devices, and medical applications [9].

6.2.1.2   Substrate Integrated Waveguide Antenna

Substrate integrated waveguide antenna enables high-performance and miniaturization [10]. The textiles fabrics cannot be easily integrated into electronic manufacturing processes with the use of substrate integrated waveguide antenna. It can be used for frequency scanning, beam steering, and short-range dedicated communication applications.

6.2.1.3   Planar Inverted-F Antenna

It has low profile structure and appreciable electrical characteristics, compact, and small in size as compared to monopole [11]. The bandwidth can be adjusted by varying size of ground and intermediate feed point. The height of the PIFA should be less than 10mm for efficient impedance bandwidth. The radiation pattern is dependent on antenna location and it provides narrow bandwidth. It can be used in handheld radios, smart glasses, GSM, IoT, and 5G applications.

6.2.1.4   Monopole Antenna

The monopole antenna has wide bandwidth, can easily tune and integrate with the system, and the efficiency is greater than 76%. It is less efficient in due to anti-phase image induced, their omnidirectional patterns needed to be modify in on-body applications [12]. It can be applicable in WLAN, RFID, GSM, Bluetooth, and UWB applications.

6.2.1.5   Metasurface Loaded Antenna

In metasurface loaded antenna, AMC can be located near to a reflector, dual-band EBG can decrease back radiation, and the antenna can be tolerant against the positions on the human body and improved radiation efficiency [13]. The operation bandwidth of illusion devices is limited. This antenna can be used for UHF and microwave, WiMAX, RFID, and WLAN applications. There is a great demand for the adjustable electronic designs used for wearable devices [14]. The antenna design for wearable electronics requires special focus and has several utilizations especially for health monitoring and commercial wireless communication systems [15]. Several frequency allocations have been appointed to different applications [16–18].

For achieving the desirable characteristics of antenna, it is required to have proper selection of antenna according to the application. Microstrip patch is easy to incorporate into the clothes of the human body. Wearable antennas are reported in various literatures using jeans substrate, cotton substrate, Flectron substrate [19], silk, etc. Wearable electronics are useful for various frequency bands for different applications. The double fractal antennas and air cavities are used for achieving miniaturization and broadband operations.

6.3   Design of Wearable Antennas

There is an intense work and research has been done in the field of wearable electronics. So, there is a great demand for the adjustable electronic designs. These designs require special focus and they have several utilizations especially for health monitoring and commercial wireless communication systems. Several frequency band allocations have been allocated for different applications. Table 6.1 describes the chronology for the wearable antennas which considered the advancements in the antenna designs and the intense research work being done in the area of wearable technology.

There are different techniques being used for designing the antennas based on the requirements. The structure of the antenna adversely affects the functioning of the antenna. So, while designing the antenna, the geometry of the design plays a vital role. There are various methods are described as follows.

6.3.1   Effect of Substrate and Ground Geometries on Antenna Design

6.3.1.1   Conducting Coating on Substrate

The antenna performance is affected by the conductive parts of the substrate. Using the immensely conductive coating on textile substrate

Table 6.1 Chronology for the wearable antennas.

Year	Antennas used
2004	A Novel Circularly Polarized Textile Antenna [19]
2006	Textile Patch Antenna [20]
2007	Aperture- Coupled Patch Antenna [21]
2008	Electro-Textiles Wearable Antenna [22]
2009	Body-worn E-textile antennas [23]
2011	Sierpinski Carpet Fractal Antenna [24]
2012	Terahertz Microstrip Antenna on Photonic Bandgap Material [25]
2013	Dual resonant shorted patch antenna [26]
2014	Metamaterial-based wearable microstrip patch antennas [27]
2015	Wearable Rectangular Patch Antennas with Partial Ground [28]
2016	Wearable Antennas applicable for Tele-Medicine [29]
2017	EBG-based Textile Antenna [30]
2018	Textile Antenna Arrays for smart clothing applications [31]
2019	Wearable Antenna with Circular Polarization using NinjaFlex-Embedded Conductive Fabric [32]
2020	Wearable EBG-Backed Belt Antenna [33]

causes the reduction of losses. In [34], the dielectric substrate consists of Polyamide lossy (Nylon-6) while the of nickel-copper-nickel coating was used as coating on the textile substrate for the conductive parts, i.e., patch and ground plane as shown in Figure 6.1. The design worked on the description of fives layer of human body model which consists of textile, air, skin tissue, bone, and fat layer as shown in Figure 6.2. The antenna provided good bandwidth by working descriptively on the five-layer model.

A multiband antenna designed with magnetic properties applicable in medical field, RFID, WLAN, and wireless monitoring. In [35], the conducting material was applied on the patch and the ground plane, while the antenna substrate was non-conducting textile. The human body has lower conductivity and permittivity values, so when the antenna is brought closer to the human body, the electric field's electrical impedance is reduced while there is increase

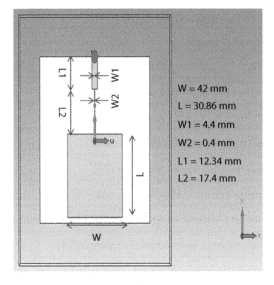

Figure 6.1 Schematic of single patch on textile substrate [34].

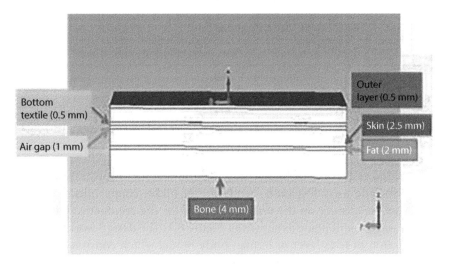

Figure 6.2 Side view of the five-layer model [34].

in magnetic field. Therefore, magnetic type antennas are very suitable for close to the body applications. The antenna performance parameters like gain, bandwidth, resonant frequency, and radiation pattern are not changed in the closeness of the human body due to the magnetic properties of the antenna design. Table 6.2 describes the SAR values that are measured at different distances

Table 6.2 SAR values of the antenna with varying distance [35].

Distance from human body	SAR value (W/kg)		
(mm)	Freq. 0.923 GHz	Freq. 2.44 GHz	Freq. 5.81 GHz
0	0.11	0.41	0.52
5.12	0.03	0.40	0.10
10.2	0.01	0.33	0.09
20.5	0.00	0.22	0.03

from the phantom in order to investigate the change in the SAR value by positioning the antenna at near and far positions from the body [35].

6.3.1.2 Ground Plane With Spiral Metamaterial Meandered Structure

In various researches, different implementations of the MTM design structures have been demonstrated. In [36], the design was introduced with the use of spiral metamaterial meandered structure in the ground plane, to decrease the SAR of the antenna. The antenna is fabricated by using photolithography technique. The use of MTMs greatly helped in decreasing the SAR value and getting the results according to international safety standards (FCC and ICNIPR). Figure 6.3 describes the antenna design with MTM cells.

Table 6.3 explains the SAR values with the change in distance from the human body. With the increase in the distance from the human body, SAR value is decreasing. The specific absorption rate (SAR) value describes the absorption rate of radiation by the human body on their exposure to radio waves.

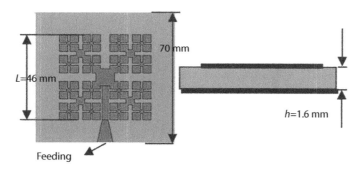

Figure 6.3 The antenna geometry with MTM cells [36].

Table 6.3 Max average SAR values at different distances from human body [36].

Resonance frequency (GHz)	SAR(W/kg)				
	10 mm	20 mm	30 mm	40 mm	50 mm
1.57	0.452	0.321	0.241	0.1914	0.155
2.7	1.1	1.02	0.898	0.786	0.662
3.4	0.67	0.532	0.398	0.294	0.218
5.3	0.75	0.5318	0.407	0.303	0.278

6.3.1.3   Partial Ground Plane

There are various design techniques for ground plane which can be adopted. The antenna can be designed with the full ground plane or the defected ground plane and the antenna behaves differently for different ground geometries. In [37], the antenna was designed on denim material with partial ground plane and rectangular patch with triangular cut as presented in Figure 6.4. The partial ground plane can alter the antenna performance parameters into the

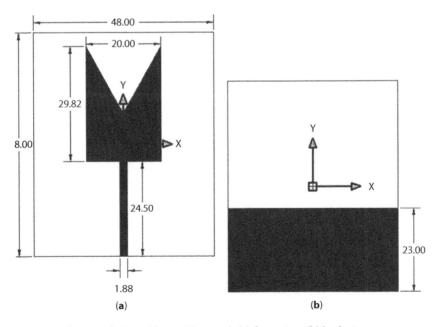

Figure 6.4 Antenna design with partial ground: (a) front view; (b) back view.

Table 6.4 Impedance characteristics of proposed denim antenna [37].

Parameters	Antenna's bending (cylindrical diameter)				
	Flat dimension ∞	10 mm	20 mm	30 Mm	40 Mm
Resonant Frequency in GHz	2.4	2.11	2.16	2.18	2.17
Impedance Bandwidth in %	68.9	72.7	72.9	72.4	72.3

desirable measurements. The antenna was designed to work on the frequency of 2.4 GHz. The measured impedance bandwidth ranges from 1.948 to 4 GHz. The antenna design was tested at different bent angles as shown in Figure 6.4.

The comparison of impedance bandwidth at different bending positions is described in Table 6.4. It is proved that the impedance bandwidth changes with the change in the bent conditions. If the cylindrical diameter was increased, then the resonance frequency also increased accordingly [37].

6.3.2 Logo Antennas

The wearable antennas can be used for an anti-theft tracking provision to the materials. In [38], the antenna design included the logo in the embedded form using non-woven fabric on a leather material as shown in Figure 6.5. With the help of positive-intrinsic-negative (PIN) diodes, the G1 and the GSM-1800 bands can be configured using a single radiating element. The PIN diodes can help in reconfiguring the resonating frequency of the antenna. In [39, 43], the logo was designed on the shoes with the patch radiator. The measured bandwidths were 60MHz with gain of 0.8 dBi and 180 MHz with gain of 3.2 dBi.

6.3.3 Embroidered Antenna

Another form of antenna geometry is embroidered conductive yarn antenna with wearable electronics. In the embroidered antennas, there are two types of loss which includes the loss with the vicinity of the human being and the loss due to conductive yarn like Silverpam. In [40, 41], the antenna design included the different sewing patterns. The measured

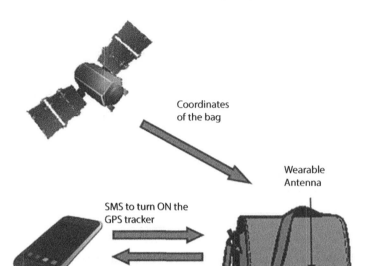

Figure 6.5 Logo-based tracking system [38].

radiation efficiency is same as that of referred copper antenna. Using these sewing patterns, radiation efficiency can be increased and the conductive yarn usage can be reduced which further help in reducing the losses.

While constructing the embroidered antenna, firstly, the embroidery is done on the textile material and then the embroidered part is cut and pasted on the dielectric material with the help of adhesive sheet. The embroidery is done using the SWF MA-6 machine. The stitches pattern and the density of the stitches make a big difference in the behavior of the antenna characteristics.

6.3.4   Wearable Antenna Based on Electromagnetic Band Gap

The electromagnetic band gap (EBG)–based wearable antenna design describes the compact and unremarkable method to fulfill the need of the wearable technology. To avoid losses due to presence of human body, the EBG structure is used as it reduces back radiations. The EBG material acts as a resonant cavity. The quality factor Q increases the gain of the antenna with EBG patches. There are various methods by which the EBG patches can be designed. Some designs include EBG with FSS which consists of cuboids, slotted cylinders, cones, etc. The antenna design using

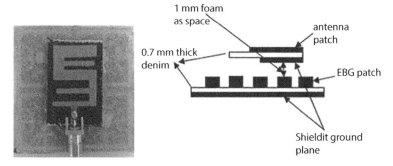

Figure 6.6 Antenna with EBG structure [41].

EBG patch is shown in Figure 6.6. This antenna resonates at frequency of 2.4 GHz and used for medical applications. There is 95% improvement in SAR value due to the effect of EBG [41]. The antenna simulation results in 7.8 dBi gain, 2.17–2.83 GHz impedance bandwidth. In [42], wearable coplanar antenna was designed which was combined with an EBG surface and it operated at 2.45 and 5.5 GHz frequency bands. Even the small EBG-based structure is helpful in the reduction of back radiations and SAR values.

6.3.5   Wearable Reconfigurable Antenna

An antenna with reconfigurable feature is able to change its performance dynamically, in a controlled method. Reconfigurable antennas can be

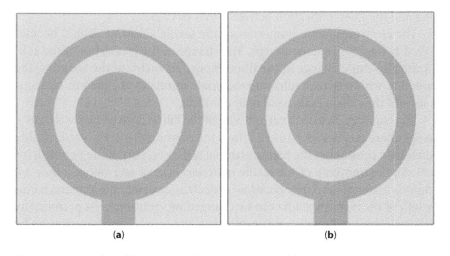

Figure 6.7 Reconfigurable Antenna of O-shape: (a) OFF; (b) ON [43].

designed by integrating PIN diodes or MEMS devices into the geometry of the antenna. In [43], the O-shaped antenna design used a small
slot structure with dimensions of 11 mm × 11 mm, so it was helpful
for on-body application due to its small structural design. The copper
was used as a conducting plane which is integrated with foam. Steps 1
and step 2 are, respectively, considered as the ON and OFF mode which
works at different frequency bands as shown in Figure 6.7. The ON mode
resonated at 2.38 to 2.52 GHz, and for OFF mode, antenna resonated at
5 to 5.5 GHz.

6.4   Textile Antennas

The textile antennas are the antenna designs which uses textile material
as a substrate and the conducting and the ground plane are designed with
any conducting materials. The antenna should be of small size and low
weight. The antenna should be capable of providing wide bandwidth and
the proper radiation pattern meeting the requirements of the application.
Textile materials that are used as an antenna's substrates are of two types:
natural and man-made fibers.

In [44], the three patch antennas with rectangular patch were designed
using different textile substrates. One antenna design which used cotton substrate measured a reflection coefficient of −15 dB, antenna using
jeans substrate showed reflection coefficient of −17 dB, and antenna with
silk substrate measured reflection coefficient of −12 dB at 2.44 GHz. The
proposed antennas are useful in medical applications for patient monitoring and the interconnection between PAN devices.

The electromagnetic properties of the textile substrate should be analyzed before the antenna design. The change in the properties of the substrate also cause change in the dimensional geometry of the antenna. The
antenna with different substrate materials resonates at different frequencies and thus changes its band of application.

The complex dielectric permittivity of the fabric is given by $\varepsilon = \varepsilon o (\varepsilon r1 -$
$j\varepsilon r2)$ where $\varepsilon o = 8.854 \times 10-12$ F/m is the permittivity of the vacuum. The
dielectric constant of the textile material is the real part of the permittivity,
$\varepsilon r1$. The permittivity of the textile materials is close to 1 because they are
porous materials and they have low dielectric constant. The antenna bandwidth of the textile antenna can be changed by variation in its permittivity
but by lowering the substrate permittivity, the resonance frequency can be
increased.

The different textile substrates with their electromagnetic properties are listed in Table 6.5.

In textile wearable antennas, there are different textile materials which can be used as the substrate. Textile materials that are used as an antenna's substrates are of two types: natural and man-made fibers. The antenna should not be affected by the near field effects of the human body. If the antennas are insensitive to the body effects, then it reduces detuning and improves the battery life time.

The impacts of addition of layers of cloth on the behavior of wearable electro-material UHF RFIDs was studied [45]. Figure 6.8 presented the wearable dipole antenna design dimensions. The electro-textile label antennas were pressed on the cotton T-shirts with the help of hot-melt adhesive and covered with a stretchable defensive encapsulant. The behavior of the labels was assessed on-body in different conditions. Two kinds of winter covers on the T-shirts were studied to analyze the impacts of wearing over the RFID tags. It has been proved that including a thick layer of coat on the shirt also does not prevent the tag from working yet diminishes the top read extend from 7 to 5 meters. The manufactured electro-material tags can be read from distance of 2 to 5 meters, all over the range of UHF-RFID

Table 6.5 Different textile materials with their dielectric constant values.

Textile material	Dielectric constant	Loss tangent
Felt	1.38	0.023
Curtain Cotton	1.57	0.01395
Polyester	1.44	0.01
Jeans	1.67	0.01
Polycot	1.26	0.01386
Fleece	1.17	0.0035
Panama	2.12	0.018
Silk	1.75	0.012
Tween	1.69	0.0084
Perspex	2.57	0.008
PTFE	2.05	0.0017
Leather different	1.8-2.4	0.049-0.071

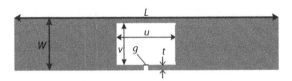

Figure 6.8 UHF RFID tag antenna design [45].

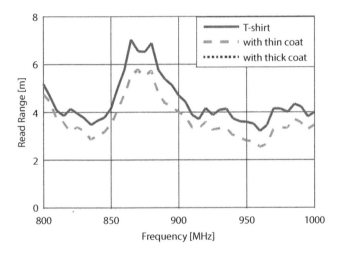

Figure 6.9 UHF RFID tag read range measurements vs. frequency [45].

frequency band. Figure 6.9 describes that the thick winter coat had the same impact on the readable distance as the thin coat.

Textiles are able to communicate with the outer world without any requirement of costly equipment. These textile antennas are small in size and flexible antennas, so they can be integrated in any type of sensors and accessories. Therefore, the textile wearable antennas can be applicable for the IoT systems. Textile antennas embedded into clothes provides wireless interface for the IoT applications.

The wearable antennas are the antennas which are easy and comfortable to wear. The antenna designs use different materials as a substrate in their designs. If the substrate material used is the textile antenna, then it proves to be the comfortable wearable antennas. Based on the various textile antenna designs, the description of effect of the substrate materials on the antenna performance is described in Table 6.6.

The textile materials have the permittivity and loss tangent values which are not readily available. The textile materials are also more inhomogeneous materials than the other high-frequency counterparts. The antennas which

Table 6.6 Description of textile materials.

Objective/Purpose	Material used	Merits	Demerits
UWB All-Textile Antenna [25]	Shield it Super (conductor), Felt (substrate)	Gain of 7.75 dB at 10 GHz, UWB application, return loss (48.8 dB)	Bandwidth of Felt substrate is 0.98 GHz
(GPS-GSM)–based tracking system for anti-theft operations [41]	Conductive non-woven fabric (nylon) on leather substrate	Non-woven conductive fabrics are not expensive and free from frazzle, desirable reflection coefficient and radiation pattern, features of elctro-textiles, return loss (27 dB) for GSM down link	Permittivity and loss tangent of leather require proper tuning to obtain good matching in scattering parameters, return loss (15 dB) for GPS
Wearable fractal antenna for wideband application (4.3 to 29.6 GHz) [47]	Polyester substrate	Increased impedance bandwidth, Polyester material with dielectric constant 3.2, gain is 6.5 dB, covers 4.3 to 30 GHz, works at UWB and SWB	The gain and gain is very low at lower frequencies (3–4 GHz) of UWB band.

(Continued)

Table 6.6 Description of textile materials. (*Continued*)

Objective/Purpose	Material used	Merits	Demerits
Wearable textile antenna using EBG as a substrate [42]	Woven conductive fabric, Zelt for patch, ground and feedline	62% Efficiency, Zelt fabric has high durability, high tear resistance, and easy handling. Zelt is unlikely to shrink. At 2.45 GHz, gain is 6.4 dBi and at 5.8 GHz, gain is 7.6 dBi and bandwidth of 660 MHz at lower frequency.	The bandwidth at higher frequency is approx. 12% which is a challenge for a dual-band EBG antenna designs.
Bluetooth patch wearable antenna [44]	Goch, Jeans, and Leather substrates	Return loss obtained from jeans is 36.9dB.	The Goch textile material is generally having hairy and fluffy properties, provides very low return loss of −11.8 dB.

(*Continued*)

Table 6.6 Description of textile materials. (*Continued*)

Objective/Purpose	Material used	Merits	Demerits
Embroidered conductive yarn wearable antennas [40]	Conductive yarn (silver thread)	Radiation efficiency is same as copper antenna in human vicinity, UWB bandwidth, efficiency 80% for 4 (yarns/mm).	The amount of conductive yarn is required to be minimum, behaves differently with yarn density
On-body communications [33]	Silk, cotton, and jean substrates	The permittivity for jean material is high. The jean materials are thick material which can act as a good insulator between the human body and the radiating material, max. gain for jeans (8.25 dB), max. gain for silk (3.07 dB)	Due to reflective property of silk material, it provides return loss of 12 dB, low bandwidth (0.288 GHz)

are made up of textile/foam substrates offer high flexibility but introduce additional losses. To reduce losses, the electric resistance of the conducting materials is required to be low and stable. The increase in impedance bandwidth is due to increase in spatial waves. Textile fabrics' thickness and density are variable with the low pressure as the textile materials are porous and compressible materials. Textile fabrics' thickness is also an important parameter, so the thickness of the fabric material should also be precisely chosen while designing the textile antennas.

6.5   Comparison of Wearable Antenna Designs

A comparative description of the various wearable antenna designs is presented in Table 6.7. The wearable antenna design required to be adhering with FCC standards regarding the safety of the human body by the wearable electronics. Hence, while designing the antennas for wearable applications, the interfering effects should be taken into consideration. As seen, energy antenna performance parameters like bandwidth, gain, and return loss distinguish the various antenna designs from each other. Some antenna designs used textile material as a substrate; others used non-textile material like copper and bronze. The textile materials are popular among them.

6.6   Fractal Antennas

The numerous researches have been done in the field of wearable antennas which are applicable in different areas. The fractal antenna designs came into being in which single antenna is useful in different frequency bands. The fractal antenna refers to the self-similar structures. Fractals are usually utilized to review natural objects. Fractals are the space fillers; hence, this property helps in accurately packing into small size. The powerful packing technique is helpful in the miniaturization if the antenna. The scaled geometry of fractal antennas help in designing antenna to resonate at different frequency bands. Fractal antennas have many applications in wireless communication system. Fractal antennas can be designed using various shapes. For example, a quarter wavelength monopole can be transformed into a similarly miniaturized antenna by using the Koch fractal shape.

Wearable antenna can be designed using a microstrip antenna which is used in Body Area Network. The different antennas are designed using fractal geometry but using different textile substrate and keeping same

Table 6.7 Comparison of wearable antenna designs.

Antenna type	Material used	Applications	Merits	Demerits
Tunable 433 MHz (ISM band) antenna [27]	Wearable Material	Wearable wireless sensor applications, health-related applications	Improvement in the power deliver to the antenna, reduction in consumption of current, long battery life span, less repeaters	Power loss of 0.84 dB, work is focused only on the 433 MHz band
Pattern-reconfigurable wearable antenna [14]	Textile Material	Impedance bandwidth operates in 2.4-GHz band	Gain is 3.9 and 2.0 dB at the +1 and ZOR mode, resp. SAR values are well satisfied for both the modes.	Efficiencies about 38% and 45% for the two modes, bending dependence
Microstrip Antenna, Koch Snow Flake Fractal curve [8]	Curtain cotton and Polycot	Multiband Applications	Return Loss > 16 dB	Limited Bandwidth
Metamaterial Fractal Antenna [27]	Metamaterial spiral	Wireless applications such as GPS, IoT, Wi-Max, and Wi-Fi	SAR value calculated is 0.925 W/Kg	Efficiency average 40%

(Continued)

Table 6.7 Comparison of wearable antenna designs. (*Continued*)

Antenna type	Material used	Applications	Merits	Demerits
EBG structure Antenna [30]	EBG Patch	Medical Applications	Reduced back radiation, less impact of frequency detuning, gain enhancement of 7.8 dBi	Electrically large, poor FBR
Microstrip Fractal [24]	Polyester substrate	UWB and SWB applications (4.3 to 29.6 GHz)	High peak gain	Less impedance bandwidth
Upper and lower layers having fractal structures, microstrip patch antennas [47]	Microstrip patch fractal antenna	Ultra-wide bandwidth (4.1 to 19.4 GHz)	Average gain of 6 dBi	Asymmetrical Geometry
Flexible PIFA Antenna [25]	Copper-bronze etched conductor	WBAN Applications	SAR is 1.75 W/kg	Efficiency 9%
Fractal Antenna [46]	Low-cost textile material-denim and felt fabric	Wireless Applications	Highly durable, comfortable to wear, save environment	Bending performance not observed

dimensions for antennas. The antenna designs used different textile materials as a substrate. These antennas provide the multiband operations at different resonant frequencies. There are various researches have been done in the field of fractal wearable antennas. The different papers published on wearable antenna designs using fractal geometries.

Low profile antennas play important role in the development of 5G communication systems and IoT. There is a need of the development of miniaturized antennas with high efficiency and large gain values for 5G and IoT applications. The antenna designs with the metamaterials and fractal geometries are helpful in gaining high efficiency than the other antenna geometries.

6.6.1 Minkowski Fractal Geometries Using Wearable Electro-Textile Antennas

In [46], the Zelt and Flectron two electro-textile materials, and the polyester fabric material as a dielectric medium were used. For 132 MHz, the gain provided by Flectron-based antenna was 6.54 dB and the Zelt antenna provided 7.4-dB gain with 104 MHz of impedance bandwidth. The gain efficiency for Zelt antenna is described in Figure 6.10. The miniaturization was achieved by using Minkowski structure for the antennas. The first iteration antennas were applicable for WiBro frequency band and the next iteration antennas were more miniaturized and tuned to GSM 1900 applications. Zelt-based antenna provided far better results than the Flectron-based antenna.

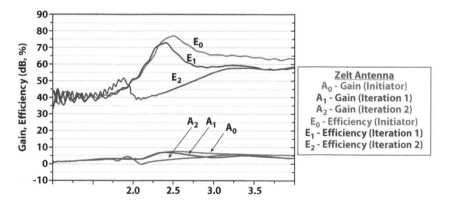

Figure 6.10 Gain, efficiency vs. frequency for Zelt antenna [46].

6.6.2   Antenna Design With Defected Semi-Elliptical Ground Plane

The antenna design included the defected semi-elliptical ground plane which works on the frequencies 4.3 to 29.6 GHz [47]. The proposed antenna was used for UWB and SWB applications. The impedance matching was not there for all the three iterations as it covered only limited bands from 0.1 to 30 GHz. In the second iteration, to increase the impedance bandwidth, the slot was designed in the feeding point in the ground plane of the antenna. The antenna design structure with slot for providing different iterations is shown in Figure 6.11.

6.6.3   Double-Fractal Layer Wearable Antenna

The antenna design employs the properties of the fractal structure on the top and lower layers of the antenna. The antenna is designed with double fractal layer which enhances the features of the antenna. The antenna characteristics have been improved to the great extent with the help of double-layer fractal geometry. The antenna provides wide bandwidth of frequency ranging from 4.1 to 19.4 GHz [48].

6.6.4   Development of Embroidered Sierpinski Carpet Antenna

In fractal geometry also, various embroidered antenna designs have been developed. In [49], the embroidered antenna design included two different

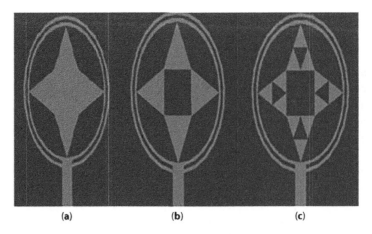

(a)   (b)   (c)

Figure 6.11 Wearable fractal antenna with different iterations: (a) 0th; (b) 1st; (c) 2nd iteration [47].

textile materials as substrate materials. The geometry of the antenna is based on the Sierpinski carpet with successive iterations as shown in Figure 6.12. The silver-nylon yarn conductive threads were used in radiating and the ground planes as described in Figure 6.13. Both antennas showed miniaturization effects, flexibility, and omnidirectional pattern. The Felt antenna showed gain of 7.9 dB and 90.47% efficiency, whereas the jeans material showed 7.1 dB gain and 89% efficiency.

This exploration work will open a way for planning fractal antennas by using other fractal geometries. According to the requirements of the wearable systems, fractal antennas are useful in multiband frequencies for different areas of wireless applications and IoT market [51]. The wearable fractal antenna technology helps us to design miniaturized, comfortable to wear, and multiband antennas with large bandwidth into a single device.

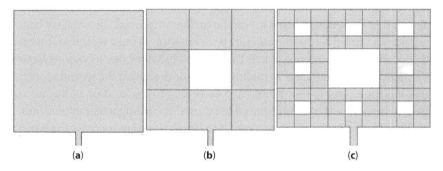

(a)   (b)   (c)

Figure 6.12 Wearable fractal antenna with iterations: (a) 0th; (b) 1st; and (c) 2nd [49].

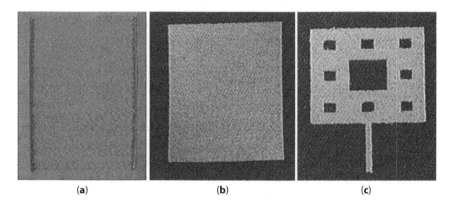

(a)   (b)   (c)

Figure 6.13 The embroidered Sierpinski carpet antenna: (a) substrate material; (b) back side; (c) front side [49].

6.7   Future Challenges of Wearable Antenna Designs

The process of designing wearable antennas has to face various challenges as these antennas have a direct touch with the human body. The lower the value of SAR of Multiband Magnetic Type Wearable Antenna, the lesser the quantity of radiation is absorbed by body tissues. There are some threshold values above which the SAR values are not safe for the human exposure [50]. The standard values for SAR are 2 W/kg for 10 g and 1.6 W/kg for 1 g of body tissues. As the antennas come nearer to the human body, antenna performance parameters' responses get changed. In wearable antennas, omnidirectional radiation patterns are desirable so that the antennas can be placed at any position on the human body. The antenna should be flexible and of small size so that the sensors can be integrated in the antenna. Although the antenna is required to be efficient and immune to be detuned by the human body effects, the antenna can be incorporated with re-configurable feature also so that the antenna behavior can be further improved. The angle of bending plays a crucial role in the antenna performance. Being a wearable antenna, the location of the antenna affects the antenna behavior due to various factors like bending, twisting, and wrinkling. So, while designing the wearable antennas, it is important to test the antenna according to the location of the human body where the antenna is required to be used according to the application.

The efficiency of the antenna ought to be improved to increase the battery life span of the wearable antenna. By decreasing re-transmissions, the battery life can be increased. The higher gain and pattern diversity is linked with the link budget. The rise in the link budget improves the battery life of the antenna. Antenna performance parameters aside from electrical resistance, like radiation efficiency, gain, and radiation patterns, are also adversely influenced by human body existence in the nearby vicinity [10]. It is needed to compare the free space which is zero absorbing material with that of the antenna efficiency within the presence of an absorbing material like human body.

6.8   Conclusion

Based on the survey, it has been predicted that there are numerous performance parameters for concern in designing the antennas which includes bandwidth, return loss, bending performance, radiation characteristics, and gain. It has been predicted that the geometry of the antenna design also affects the performance behavior of the antenna. The substrate height, material properties, and the design dimensions are the main parameters to be taken into consideration while designing the wearable antennas. The geometry of the antenna design specifies the resonance frequency and the application bands for the specific antenna design. From different antenna designs, it has also been observed that the SAR values reduced as the distance of the antenna increases from the human body.

Textile antennas act as a vital part in today's wireless communication in the areas of tracking, navigation, medical, IoT, and computing application. Due to the low dielectric constant value of textile material, there is an increase in the spatial wave which causes increase in the impedance bandwidth of antenna. The textile antenna can be embedded into the clothing, easy to wear, comfortable, and light weight antennas which proves them to be a quite helpful in the wearable antennas market. There are large number of fractal antennas which are helpful in multiband frequency applications like medical, UWB, SWB, WiFi, WiMax, Bluetooth, 5G, IoT, WiBro, and GSM. The fractal antenna has an advantage that the single antenna can be used for multiple frequency band applications. The different hybrid fractal antenna design geometries and other conventional antenna designs studied so far can be redesigned as textile wearable antennas by using the textile materials as substrates. A comparative description of the different textile substrates and wearable antenna designs is presented in a categorized way with the expectation of providing guidance for concerned researchers.

References

1. Jain, S.K., Baviskar, N., Golait, N., Jain, S., Design of Wearable Antenna for Various Applications. *Antenna Test & Measurement Society (ATMS India-18)*, pp. 2–6, 2018.
2. Al-Ashwal, W.A.M., Ramli, N.K., Mohamud, S., Performance of ultra-wideband wearable antenna under severe environmental conditions and specific absorption rate (SAR) study at near distances. *ARPN J. Eng. Appl. Sci.*, 10, 4, 1613–1622, 2014.
3. Chen, X., He, H., Ukkonen, L., Virkki, J., The Effects of Added Clothing Layers on the Performance of Wearable Electro-Textile UHF RFID Tags. *2nd URSI AT-RASC*, Gran Canaria, 28 May – 1 June 2018.
4. Alase, J., Sakhare, V., Kamble, S., Athane, A., Textile Antennas for Wearable IoT Applications. *J. Textile Clothing Sci.*, 2, 2, 7–15, 2019. Retrieved from https://www.jtcsonline.com/index.php/jtcs/article/view/20
5. Elbasheer, M.K., Osman, A.R., Abuelnour, A., Rahim, M.K.A., Ali, M.E., Conducting materials effects on UWB wearable textile antenna. *Proceeding of the World Congress on Engineering 2014*, vol. 1, WEC 2014, July 2-4 2014.

6. Lovika, and Jyoti, Calculation of Specific Absorption Rate(SAR) of Patch antenna on Human Brain and Design of Low SAR value Microstrip Patch Antenna. *IJISET - Int. J. Innov. Sci., Eng. Technol.*, 5, 4, 2348–7968, April 2018.
7. Sabban, A., Small New Wearable Antennas for IOT, Medical and Sport Applications. *2019 13th European Conference on Antennas and Propagation (EuCAP)*, Krakow, Poland, pp. 1–5, 2019.
8. Singh Bhatia, S. and Singh Sivia, J., A Novel Design of Wearable Fractal Antenna for Wideband Applications. *International Conference on Advances in Human Machine Interaction (HMI - 2016)*, March 03-05, 2016.
9. Wang, H., Zhang, Z., Li, Y., Feng, Z., A dual resonant shorted patch antenna for wearable application in 430 MHz band. *IEEE Trans. Antennas Propag.*, 61, 12, 6195–6200, Dec. 2013.
10. Agneessens, S. and Rogier, H., Compact half diamond dual-band textile HMSIW on-body antenna. *IEEE Trans. Antennas Propag.*, 62, 5, 2374–2381, May 2014.
11. Soh, P.J., Vandenbosch, G.A.E., Ooi, S.L., Husna, M.R.N., Design of a broadband all-textile slotted PIFA. *IEEE Trans. Antennas Propag.*, 60, 1, 379–384, Jan. 2012.
12. Oraizi, H. and Hedayati, S., Miniaturized UWB Monopole Microstrip Antenna Design by the Combination of GiusepePeano and Sierpinski Carpet Fractals. *IEEE Antennas Wirel. Propag. Lett.*, 10, 67–70, January 2011.
13. Tumsare, K.V. and Dr. Zade, P.L., Microstrip Antenna using EBG Substrate. *Int. J. Recent Innov. Trends Comput. Commun.*, 4, 12, 73–76, 2016.
14. Saeed, S.M., Balanis, C.A., Birtcher, C.R., Durgun, A.C., Shaman, H.N., Wearable flexible reconfigurable antenna integrated with artificial magnetic conductor. *IEEE Antennas Wirel. Propag. Lett.*, 16, 2396–2399, 2017.
15. Hussain, S., Hafeez, S., Memon, S.A., Pirzada, N., Design of Wearable Patch Antenna for Wireless Body Area Networks. *(IJACSA) Int. J. Adv. Comput. Sci. Appl.*, 9, 9, 146–151, 2018.
16. Bharadwaj, R., Parini, C., Alomainy, A., Experimental investigation of 3-D human body localization using wearable ultra-wideband antennas. *IEEE Trans. Antennas Propag.*, 63, 11, 5035–5044, 2015.
17. Song and Rahmat-Samii, Y., A Systematic Investigation of Rectangular Patch Antenna Bending Effects for Wearable Applications. *IEEE Trans. Antennas Propag.*, 66, 5, 2219–2228, 2018.
18. Priya, A., Kumar, A., Chauhan, B., A Review of Textile and Cloth Fabric Wearable Antennas. *Int. J. Comput. Appl.*, 116, 17, 975–8887 April 2015.
19. Klemm, M., Locher, I., Troster, G., A Novel Circularly Polarized Textile Antenna for Wearable Applications. *Wirel. Technol.*, 1, 137–140, 2004.
20. Locher, I., Klemm, M., Kirstein, T., Troster, G., Design and Characterization of Purely Textile Patch Antennas. *Adv. Packaging, IEEE Trans.*, 29, 4, 777–788, 2006.

21. Hertleer, C., Tronquo, A., Rogier, H., Vallozzi, L., Van Langenhove, L., Aperture-Coupled Patch Antenna for Integration Into Wearable Textile Systems. *Antennas Wirel. Propag. Lett.*, 6, 392–395, 2007.
22. Ouyang, Y. and Chappell, W.J., High Frequency Properties of Electro-Textiles for Wearable Antenna Applications. *IEEE Trans. Antennas Propag.*, 56, 2, 381–389, February 2008.
23. Kennedy, T.F. and Fink, P.W., Body-Worn E-Textile Antennas: The Good, the Low-Mass, and the Conformal. *IEEE Trans. Antennas Propag.*, 57, 4, 910–918, April 2009.
24. Oraizi, H. and Hedayati, S., Miniaturized UWB Monopole Microstrip Antenna Design by the Combination of GiusepePeano and Sierpinski Carpet Fractals. *IEEE Antennas Wirel. Propag. Lett.*, 10, 67–70, January 2011.
25. Ranjan, K., Singh, G., Jha, K., Analysis and design of terahertz microstrip antenna on photonic bandgap material. *J. Comput. Electron.*, 11, 364–373, 2012.
26. Wang, H., Zhang, Z., Li, Y., Feng, Z., A dual resonant shorted patch antenna for wearable application in 430 MHz band. *IEEE Trans. Antennas Propag.*, 61, 12, 6195–6200, Dec. 2013.
27. Joshi, J.G. and Pattnaik, S.S., Metamaterial based wearable micro strip patch antennas, in: *Handbook of Research on Wireless Communications and Networking-Theory and Practice*, pp. 518–556, IGI Global, USA, February 2014, Chapter 20 Information Science Reference (an imprint of IGI Global).
28. Budhiraja, I., Khan, M.A.A., Farooqui, M., Pal, M.K., Multi- band stacked microstrip patch antenna for wireless applications. *J. Telecommun.*, 16, 2, 8–11, October 2012.
29. Christina, G., Rajeswari, A., Lavanya, M., Keerthana, J., Ilamathi, K., Manoranjitha, V., Design and Development of Wearable Antennas for Tele-Medicine Applications. *International Conference on Communication and Signal Processing*, India, April 6-8, 2016.
30. Ashyap, A.Y.I. and Abidin, Z.Z., Compact and Low-Profile Textile EBG-Based Antenna for Wearable Medical Applications. *IEEE Antennas Wirel. Propag. Lett.*, 16, 2550–2553, 2017.
31. Chin, K.-S., Wu, C.-S., Shen, C.-L., Tsai, K.-C., Designs of Textile Antenna Arrays for Smart Clothing Applications. *Autex Res. J.*, 18, 3, 2018.
32. Li, J., Jiang, Y., Zhao, X., Circularly Polarized Wearable Antenna Based on NinjaFlex-Embedded Conductive Fabric. *Hindawi Int. J. Antennas Propag.*, 1–8, 2019, 8 September 2019, Article ID 3059480.
33. Pei, R., Leach, M.P., Lim, E., Wang, Z., Song, C., Wang, J., Zhang, W., Jiang, Z., Huang, Y., Wearable EBG-Backed Belt Antenna for Smart On-body Applications. *IEEE Trans. Industr. Inform.*, 16, 11, 7177–7189, 2020, https://doi.org/10.1109/TII.2020.2983064
34. Rano, D. and Hashmi, M., Design and Analysis of Wearable Patch Antenna Array for MBAN Applications. *2016 Twenty Second National Conference on Communication (NCC)*.

35. Purwanto, H., Rakhmadi, A., Basari, A Multiband Magnetic Type Wearable Antenna for Wireless Patient Monitoring Applications. *2016 Progress In Electromagnetic Research Symposium (PIERS)*, Shanghai, China, 8–11 August, 2016.

36. Subramaniam, S. and Dhar, S., Miniaturization of Wearable Electro-textile Antennas using Minkowski Fractal Geometry. *2014, IEEE International Symposium on Antennas and Propagation & USNC/URSI National Radio Science Meeting.*

37. Marzudi, W.N., Zainal Abidin, Z., Dahlan, S.H., Ramli, K.N., Majid, H., Kamarudin, M.R., Rectangular patch with partial ground wearable antenna for 2.4 GHz applications. 2015 *IEEE International RF and Microwave Conference*, pp. 104–109, 2015.

38. Monti, G., Corchia, L., Benedetto, E.D., Tarricone, L., Wearable logo-antenna for GPS–GSM-based tracking systems. *IET Microwaves, Antennas & Propagation Research Article*, 31st May 2016.

39. Saha, P., Mandal, B., Chatterjee, A., Parui, S.K., Harmes Paris Logo Shaped Wearable Antenna for Multiband Applications. *Proceedings of the Asia-Pacific Microwave Conference*, 2016.

40. Yoshikawa, T. and Maeda, T., Radiation Efficiency Enhancement Based on Novel Sewing Patterns for Embroidered Wideband Wearable Slot Antennas. *IEEE Antennas Wirel. Propag. Lett.*, 1–3, January 2016.

41. Ashyap, R.Y.I., Abidin, Z.Z., Dahlan, S.H., Majid, H.A., Shah, S.M., Kamarudin, M.R., Alomainy, A., Compact and Low-Profile Textile EBG-Based Antenna for Wearable Medical Applications. *IEEE Antennas Wirel. Propag. Lett.*, 16, 2550–2553, 2017.

42. Zhu, S. and Langley, R., Dual-Band Wearable Textile Antenna on an EBG Substrate. *IEEE Trans. Antennas Propag.*, 57, 4, 926–935, April 2009.

43. Sivabalan, A. and Jothilakshmi, P., Micro Strip Wearable O-shaped Reconfigurable Antenna for Medical Applications. *Int. J. Recent Technol. Eng. (IJRTE)*, 8, 1, 318–324, May 2019.

44. Skrivervik, A.K., Bosiljevac, M., Trajkovikj, J., Design Considerations for Wearable Antennas. *2016 URSI International Symposium on Electromagnetic Theory (EMTS).*

45. Chen, X., He, H., Ukkonen, L., The Effects of Added Clothing Layers on the Performance of Wearable Electro-Textile UHF RFID Tags. *2nd URSI AT-RASC*, Gran Canaria, 28 May – 1 June 2018.

46. Subramaniam, S. and Dhar, S., Miniaturization of Wearable Electro-textile Antennas using Minkowski Fractal Geometry. *2014 IEEE Antennas and Propagation Society International Symposium (APSURSI).*

47. Bhatia, S.S. and Sivia, J.S., A Novel Design of Wearable Fractal Antenna for Wideband Applications. *International Conference on Advances in Human Machine Interaction (HMI – 2016)*, R. L. Jalappa Institute of Technology, Doddaballapur, Bangalore, India, March 03-05, 2016.

48. Christina, G., Rajeswari, A., Lavanya, M., Keerthana, J., Ilamathi, K., Manoranjitha, V., Design and Development of Wearable Antennas for Tele-Medicine Applications. *International Conference on Communication and Signal Processing*, India, April 6-8, 2016.

49. Ahmad, S., Saidin, N.S., Chelsa, C.M., Development of embroidered Sierpinski carpet antenna. *2012 IEEE Asia-Pacific Conference on Applied Electromagnetics (APACE 2012)*, Melaka, Malaysia, December 11 - 13, 2012.

50. Ahmed, M.I., Ahmed, M.F., Shaalan, A.A., SAR Calculations of Novel Wearable Fractal Antenna on Metamaterial Cell for Search and Rescue Applications. *Prog. Electromagn. Res. M*, 53, 99–110, 2017.

51. Loss, C., Gonçalves, R., Lopes, C., Pinho, P., Salvado, R., Smart Coat with a Fully-Embedded Textile Antenna for IoT Applications. *Sensors*, 16, 938, 2016. https://doi.org/10.3390/s16060938

7

An Overview of IoT and Its Application With Machine Learning in Data Center

Manikandan Ramanathan* and Kumar Narayanan

Department of CSE, Vels Institute of Science, Technology and Advanced Studies, Chennai, India

Abstract

Internet of Things (IoT) enables the gadgets, tools, machines, computers, instruments, or any devices that are associated to the internet and controlled through the internet from anywhere. Consequently, an unimaginable amount of data is generated, and this needs to be monitored and processed, and actions are needed to be taken. In this regard, through data centers, along with IoT, AI, and machine learning techniques, and through implementing edge computing, we can achieve the required high-speed computation. This chapter describes the IoT protocols, surveys IoT in the data center, and edge computing with machine learning techniques.

Keywords: IoT, AI, data center, machine learning, edge computing

7.1 Introduction

The Internet of Things (IoT) is the interconnection of devices, instruments, tools, vehicles, home utilities along with sensors, actuators, and software over the network. The data is collected from these devices and transferred over the internet network, and also, it receives the data from the external world through internet. IoT means making the device as internet-aware [8].

---

*Corresponding author: maniramphd@gmail.com

R. Anandan, Suseendran Gopalakrishnan, Souvik Pal and Noor Zaman (eds.) The Industrial Internet of Things (IIoT): Intelligent Analytics for Predictive Maintenance, (181–202) © 2022 Scrivener Publishing LLC

IoT applications [9] can be as follows:

1. Mobile devices
2. Smart meters and objects
3. Washing machine
4. Health care implementations
5. Smartwatches
6. Fitness devices
7. Interconnected automobiles to achieve automatic car
8. Home automation systems: lighting, home security, cameras, AC control, media control, etc.
9. Sensors to measure: weather, traffic, ocean tides, road signals, gas appliances

IoT protocols with OSI standard is mapped in Figure 7.1.

Figure 7.2 and Table 7.1 can be referred for various IoT protocols [14].

Internet: IPv6 over Low Power Wireless Personal Area Network (6LoWPAN) is the first and most standard. Refer Figure 7.3 for various IoT packet headers [9].

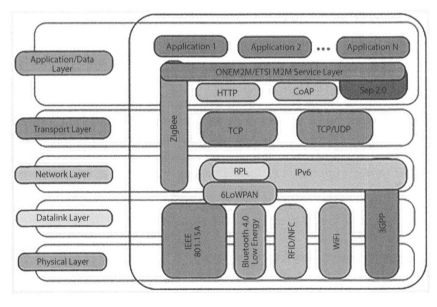

Figure 7.1 IoT protocol with OSI standard.

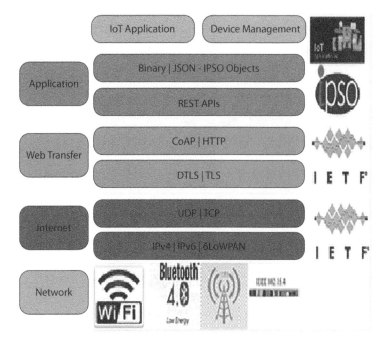

Figure 7.2 IoT layers and protocols.

Table 7.1 IoT protocols.

Infrastructure	IPV4/IPV6, 6LowPAN
Identifier	RFID, EPC, IPv6, URIs, uCode
Communication	Bluetooth, Wi-Fi, LPWAN
Data Exchange	CoAP, MQTT, Rest API, HTTP
Service Discovery	DNS-SD, mDNS
Semantics	JSON
Management of Device	TR-069

7.1.1 6LoWPAN

- 6LoWPAN is IPv6 over Low Power Wireless Personal Area Networks defined in RFC 6550.
- 6LoWPAN layer lies between data link and network layer.

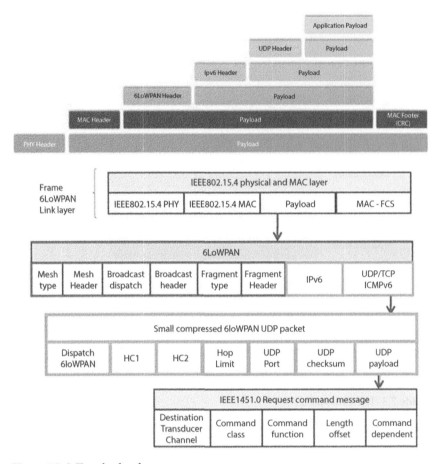

Figure 7.3 IoT packet headers.

- This provides a method to transfer the data with respect to IPV6 over IEEE 802.15.4 networks. It can have direct connection to internet or any kind of network [2].
- This protocol encapsulates long IPV6 headers in to IEEE 802.15.4, not beyond 128 bytes.
- IEEE 802.15.4 handles the MAC layer and drivers.
- 6LoWPAN sites on top of WPAN devices and acts as adaptation layer to be used by the normal IPv6 stack.
- 6LoWPAN transparently handles the fragmentation and reassembly between different MTUs.
- Frames in 6LoWPAN are of four types and they are as follows:

- No 6loWPAN header (00)
  - ✓ Any frame which is not following 6LoWPAN specifi-
    cations will be discarded.
- Dispatch header (01)
  - ✓ This header is used for compression of multicast and
    IPV6 header.
- Mesh header (10)
  - ✓ This header is used for broadcasting.
- Fragmentation header (11)
  - ✓ Break the IPV6 long headers to fit in the fragment size
    of 128 bytes length.

7.1.2   Data Protocols

There are few data exchange protocols that are followed in IoT, in which
major data protocols of IoT are CoAP [2], MQTT [2], Rest API, etc.

7.1.2.1   CoAP

CoAP is a simple IoT protocol; CoAP is Constrained Application Protocol.
This protocol is mainly developed for small smart devices designed for
constrained devices and networks, which are made up of microcontrollers.
This protocol is used to transfer data between end points, and it is designed
same like HTTP.

CoAP has two kinds of message passing between server and client. Server
and client are also called as end points. They are nothing but the smart
devices connected to the network. Each message is embedded with message
ID which is unique ID and it is used to detect the duplicate messages.

Two types of messages are as follows:

1. Confirmable Message (CON): This is a message where the
   sender gets the acknowledgement of each message with
   respect to mapping the key or ID for each message. For each
   confirmable message, if the receiver is not able to process
   and if its CPU or controller is busy, then it can send RST
   (Rest) message to sender to stop sending for some specified
   time. Each CON message has token ID embedded in it; this
   token identifier is used to match with the acknowledgement
   of messages. Refer Figure 7.4 for message sequences of confirmable messages.
2. Non-Confirmable Message (NON): Sender sends the message to receiver, and it will not wait for any acknowledgement.

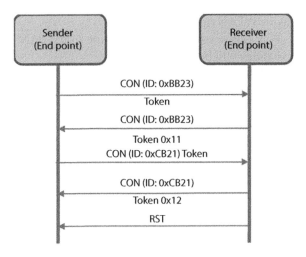

Figure 7.4 Confirmable message passing mechanism.

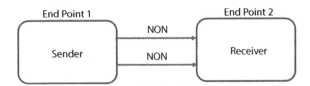

Figure 7.5 Non-confirmable message passing mechanism.

This is called as non-confirmable messages. Refer Figure 7.5 for non-confirmable message sequence.

CoAP Features

1. Synchronous message
2. Asynchronous message exchange
3. Simple parsing mechanism
4. URI and content-type support
5. Caching support

CoAP Security
Datagram TLS over UDP is used for securing mechanisms in CoAP. Datagram TLS supports RDA, AES, etc.

7.1.2.2   MQTT

MQTT is Message Queuing Telemetry Transport; it is an IoT data protocol. It uses publish/subscribe messaging mechanism. This also acts on client/server mechanism. The client is a sensor that "publishes" the information to server and it sends to all the subscribers of that server. The communication mechanism is based on TCP. Refer Figure 7.6 for MQTT subscriber-publisher model.

Comparison of CoAP and MQTT is discussed in Table 7.2.

7.1.2.3   Rest APIs

Rest API is representational state transfer application programming interface (API). Rest is used to publish the requests of controller to an

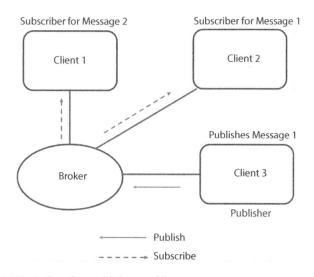

Figure 7.6 MQTT subscriber-publisher model.

Table 7.2 Comparison of CoAP and MQTT.

S. no.	CoAP	MQTT
1	It uses Request-Response method	This protocol uses Publisher-Subscriber
2	One-to-one protocol, sending message	Uses Central Broker to dispatch messages from publisher to clients
3	State Transfer Protocol	Event-Oriented Protocol

application. Rest API is used as communication mechanism between controller and application. A secured TCP connection is established between controller and associated network elements (NEs).

Representational State Transfer (REST) is an architecture framework and methods with set of guidelines used to create web services. Rest API supported systems uses HTTP (Hypertext Transfer Protocol) to communicate with HTTP defined methods such as GET, PUT, POST, and DELETE. These operations are used to retrieve the webpages by web browsers, and it sends data to servers which are present in remote. These are mapped to read, create, update, and delete operations with respect to HTTP methods. These operations are referred as CRUD.

- The HTTP server running on port 80 receives all REST request.
- If the server finds a "/rest/" in the URL, then it redirects that request to the REST server running on local loopback interface.
  GET
  The GET method is used to retrieve the data of a resource or group of resources of the system.
  POST
  A resource is created by sending the HTTP POST method to the URI of the collection in which the resource will reside. The body of the request is used to send either a representation of the object to be created or a list of parameters providing information necessary for the creation of the resource.
  PUT
  The PUT method is used to perform complete replacements on pre-existing objects.
  DELETE
  The DELETE method is used to remove resources.
  REST RESPONSE CODES
- HTTP_METHOD uses different response codes depends on command.
- 200OK is SUCCESS RESPONSE CODE.
- 404 Not Found—non-existent resource.
- 500 Internal Server Error.
- 201 Created—for POST SUCCESS.
- 400 Bad Request—incorrect parameters.
- 405 Method Not Allowed—unsupported HTTP_METHOD.
- 204 No Content.

Standards-based protocols are used to provision the application-based network's NEs.

7.1.3 IoT Components

IoT has three major elements; these are as follows:

- Hardware
  a. Physical devices—sensors and actuators
- Middleware
  a. Data acquisition
- Visualization
  a. Application and representation

IoT components [1] are depicted in Figure 7.7.

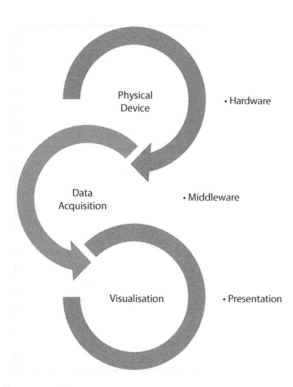

Figure 7.7 IoT components.

7.1.3.1   Hardware

This layer is a physical layer consisting of physical devices such as sensor and actuators. Any device which is going to get monitored and controlled over the internet will be part of hardware elements. The communication among them is depicted in Figure 7.8.

- Sensors

Sensor is a device which is used to monitor and detect the events and converts one form of energy to another form in our IoT to digital form from electrical transmission signals. Based on these readings, data needs to be interpreted and sent to control center. There are different group of sensors such as mechanical, thermal, gas, and voltage. We must select the sensors based on the IoT applications [13].

- Control Center

Control center gets the signals from sensors and converts them to digital signals and sends the messages to actuators.

- Actuators

Actuators convert the certain form of energy to motion. Any device which gets the message from control center and acts upon it is called as actuators. In gas monitoring system, cylinder is the actuator [13].

- Transducer Interface

Transducer interface [13] is through electronic data sheets which are embedded in sensors and actuators through TEDS sheet (Transducer Electronic Data Sheets); these are stored in embedded memory. XML-based mechanism can be used which is popular among various manufacturers. The parameters it may contain are device identifiers, data attributes, sensor measurement parameters, etc.

7.1.3.2   Middleware

Middleware is the data exploration and acquisition. It generates the messages; each message is stored and computed, and based on the results of the computation, the events have to be generated [12, 13].

Figure 7.8 IoT communication architecture.

7.1.3.3   Visualization

Visualization component is the representation or application which should GUI displays to understand the control and management of IoT devices over the internet through these user interfaces.

7.2   Data Center and Internet of Things

7.2.1   Modern Data Centers

Data center can be used to compute, process, and store data from various end users of the systems like insurance, banking, educational universities, colleges, government offices, and private offices. The data processed in the data centers are extremely large, and the high latency or service disruption is not acceptable for the customers.

Day by day, the usage of internet increases, network bandwidth increases, number of users increments, and work load increases; in addition to this introduction to IoT, all such factors would affect the data center when everything has to be computed at data center. With respect to IoT environment, any device will be connected to internet and it will be managed for anywhere which might affect the speed and latency and this will also become an overload to the data center when all transactions are stored in data center [6].

Data center is connected across the core network and backbone by connecting the end users to access devices, access devices connected to distribution side of the network [16]. The distribution network consists of distribution or aggregation switches and routers. The distribution switches are connected to core-switches. The core switched will have uplink which will be connected to cloud or WAN. High availability and backup is achieved at all the three levels. At each level, there is a backup device at core, distribution, and access devices to ensure the availability and avoid disruption to the end users. This is depicted in Figure 7.9.

There is a backup path at all levels; disaster recovery mechanism is important for any data centers to take care of the highly valued data of customer data and communication between them.

7.2.2   Data Storage

Over the years, the internet working of devices makes the data volume very high and the data passed between devices needs a very less latency in the response. The increase of small devices and electronic devices in industries, home, hospitals, road traffic and signal, automobiles, etc., increases the data with high volume.

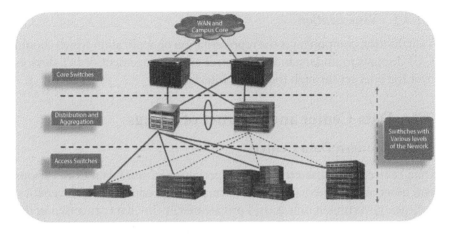

Figure 7.9 Data center architecture.

IoT is the emerging technology, and because of the huge smart devices, the amount of data becomes very high. So, it becomes a critical issues and challenging on maintenance of data storage, data analysis, and computation. Data centers will face highly challenged environment in terms of energy efficiency, reliability, and availability of data.

Artificial intelligence and machine learning techniques such as supervised learning, unsupervised learning, neural network, and genetic algorithms need to be applied to make automatic decision-making. There should also be a distributed environment to access the top of rack in data center to access the data storage devices. Distributed and modular architecture in both software and hardware design is required to reduce the latency.

7.2.3   Computing Process

Another important factor of IoT is method of processing the IoT data; various frameworks of computing [3] are as follows:

1. Fog Computing
2. Cloud Computing
3. Edge Computing
4. Distributed computing

7.2.3.1   Fog Computing

In this computational framework, computation is held at edge servers; this filters the data to data center. All data will not be sent to data center. The

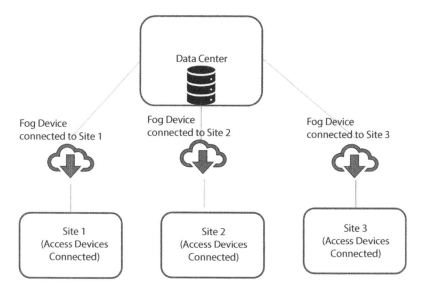

Figure 7.10 Fog computing.

load of data center is reduced by offloading the computation, network services, and storage to servers at the edge. Fog computing architecture will do limited operations, computations, services, and storages at edge servers [4, 5]. This is majorly implemented in military and health applications.

In Table 7.3, pros and cons of fog computing is discussed.

Table 7.3 Pros and cons of fog computing.

Pros	Cons
Amount of data sent to cloud is reduced	Physical location takes away from anytime, anywhere any data benefit of the cloud
Bandwidth of the network is conserved	Lot of security issues seen, by spoofing the IP address
Latency is less, response time is quick	Issues in privacy
Data is very closer to edge, the data in edge is secured rather than issues seen while sending to data center	Availability of the device is a challenge
Simplifies the network and CPU load is reduced	Security concerns in wireless network

Each site in the access side is connected to the fog device or fog computer. Each fog device is connected to data center. When there is a local processing and storage that happens, it happens in fog device and it will only contact cloud data center only based on the special services and data storage. This method of computing increases the speed while it processes and computes at fog devices itself. Fog computing deployment can be referred in Figure 7.10.

7.2.3.2   Edge Computing

Data is processed at the edge of the internet connecting device, processing the data where the sensors of the device are connected. This device is called as edge device. This is far away from the internet backbone; some of the data needs processing at the edge itself where the redundant data copy is required at edge and other layers. Edge computing deployment can be referred in Figure 7.11. But still, the enhancement of security implements the speed in data computation. Action will be taken in nanoseconds. Edge computing is achieved with smaller networks where the edge servers connected to IoT data; this becomes a distributed architecture. Single point of failure can be avoided in this method. Edge computing solves the bandwidth issue which is visible in cloud computing. Bulk data pushing to cloud data center is not required in edge computing. This computing is suitable for less latency and real-time applications. All the IoT devices are connected to IoT gateways which will perform computation and storage.

7.2.3.3   Cloud Computing

In cloud computing, the data is sent to data center for further processing; big data is sent and processed at data center. Cloud computing involves

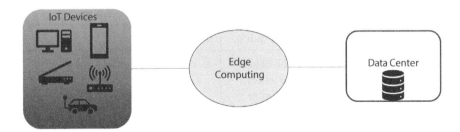

Figure 7.11 Edge computing.

high latency and speed cannot be achieved as like other computing frameworks. Considering the huge data generated by IoT, the load of the CPU will also be high. The following are the different types of computing: cloud computing is a centralized way of processing the data, lot of chances for single point of failure. Sending the huge data of IoT to cloud will increase the bandwidth and the cost.

Cloud architects mapped the degree to common service types [10]:

1. Software as a Service (SaaS)
   a. Application itself is shared as a service.
   b. Examples: GoTo meetings, Cisco Webex Meetings, Zoom Meetings, Google Meet, and Google Apps.
2. Platform as a Service (PaaS)
   a. It provides a framework or environment for development which is shared as a service, which can be used to build customized development or application.
   b. Examples: Google Application Engine, Windows Azure, Amazon AWS Elastic, Notebook Jupyter, and Google Code collaborator.
3. Infrastructure as a Service (IaaS)
   a. Services offered for computation, storing along with network deployments.
   b. Examples: Google Compute Engine, Microsoft Azure, and Amazon AWS.

A huge amount of data moves to cloud computing, and it adds more pressure on the data center. Data center needs to be a central management platform and should have ability to perform quickly and easily.

7.2.3.4   *Distributed Computing*

Distributed computing architecture is mainly developed for handling huge amount of data. The major challenges are faced when IoT application generates huge data by sensors and actuators. In this architecture, data is partitioned to packets and each partitioned packet is assigned to different central processing units for computation. Hadoop and Spark are examples of such frameworks. Advantages of this architecture are as follows:

1. Low latency
2. High processing speed

3. Able to handle voluminous data
4. Saves energy
5. Reduced CPU load

7.2.3.5   Comparison of Cloud Computing and Fog Computing

Table 7.4 compares the cloud and fog computing with respect to IoT attributes of application and its processing.

7.3   Machine Learning Models and IoT

Big data generated by IoT connected devices to be interpreted and takes decisions within microseconds. Machine learning models can be utilized to learn the model based on the data and predict the action. Also, big data analysis can be quickly interpreted based on the machine learning models. Various machine learning models can be used with IoT, and major machine learning models such as Supervised Machine Learning, Naïve Bayes Method, and K-Nearest Neighbor can be used. Also, neural networks and deep learning techniques can also be used. Figure 7.12 can be referred for various machine learning phases.

Table 7.4 Comparison of cloud and fog computing.

Requirement	Cloud computing	Fog computing
Latency	Low	Huge
Server node is placed at	Within the core internet and backhaul	Edge device of the network
Security	Spoofing attack is possible	Can determine a method
Geographical distribution	Centralized	Distributed
Real-time interactions	Supported	Supported
Delay in response	High	Low
Interconnection between client and server	Multiple nodes interconnected across the device and data center	Immediate next hop

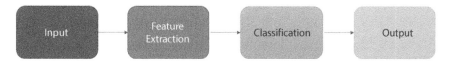

Figure 7.12 Stages of machine learning.

Identifying the best machine learning models to be applied for IoT application is based on the following factors.

1. The type of application in which IoT is implemented.
2. IoT parameters and attributes that get generated from the IoT device.
3. Machine learning algorithm based on data driven mechanism.

Main IoT data characteristics are amount of data, accuracy, redundancy, dynamicity, velocity, completeness, noisy reduction, etc. These data characteristics play an important role in choosing the machine learning model. Machine learning algorithms and IoT together can achieve high speed response, better communication, accuracy in data, better decision-making [11], etc. To solve the real-world complex issue, along with IoT, machine learning also plays an important role. Both IoT and machine learning together analyze the data to its depth and help for critical decision-making from the huge sensory data generated by IoT.

7.3.1   Classifications of Machine Learning Supported in IoT

Different types of machine learning algorithms [3] that are supported with IoT framework are depicted in Figure 7.13.

7.3.1.1   Supervised Learning

In supervised learning, the learning model is trained with "labeled data". Outcomes can be predicted for unforeseen data as input. The label can be a True or False, Yes or No, Positive or Negative, etc., i.e., either binary value of "1" or "0". The following machine learning algorithms are part of supervised learning.

1. Decision Tree
2. Naïve Bayes
3. Support Vector Machines

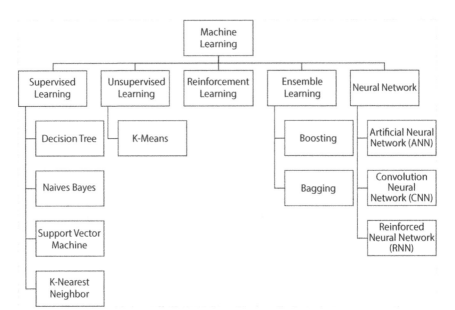

Figure 7.13 Classification of machine learning that can be supported in IoT.

4. K-Nearest Neighbor

Supervised learning collects the data and provides the data output from the previously learnt data. This learning method is used to solve real-world problems.

7.3.1.2 Unsupervised Learning

In unsupervised learning, the learning model is trained with "unlabeled data". Outcomes can be predicted for unforeseen data as input. The input data can be random, no systematic pattern, and there will not be any associated labels. K-Means algorithm is an example of this learning method.

7.3.1.3 Reinforcement Learning

In reinforcement learning, reinforcement agent decides on what action to be performed on the given data. It learns from experience when training data set is not present. This method maps the actions to rewards to suit the best possible rewarding action by trial-and-error method.

7.3.1.4   Ensemble Learning

The ensembling method is combining the prediction of various predictions of various models. This kind of combined prediction is to increase the accuracy. This model can be used for classification and regression algorithms. Weighted average is used in bagging, whereas weighted voting is used in boosting. Gradient Boosting, Random Forest, and Bagging are the examples of ensemble learning.

7.3.1.5   Neural Network

Neural network model is designed based on the simulation of biological neurosystem. Each active unit is called "neuron". Each neural network is designed with neuron, network architecture, and learning method. Neuron is a unit, and the main purpose is for computational component. The input signals are multiplied with weights and the signals are aggregated. Aggregated signals are compared with threshold, and it is called bias. If the aggregated signal is higher than bias, then the neuron is activated using an activation function.

7.4   Challenges in Data Center and IoT

7.4.1   Major Challenges

The following are the major challenges of IoT [2] and data center; this is also depicted in Figure 7.14.

1. **High Availability:** All devices in the network should be highly available, and if any device restarts or switched off, then the recovery mechanism or backup communication path should be defined and should be in operational condition.
2. **Speed:** With high speed, latency should be less. It should also achieve high speed in processing the data and computational speed [7].
3. **Data Storage:** IoT system should have required data storage, since it generates huge amount of data. Any disk repository failures should be identified well in advance; currently, we have RAID (Redundant Array of Inexpensive Disks). To be more effective IoT systems, identify machine learning models and predict the failures well in advance to reduce the downtime of the data center [15].

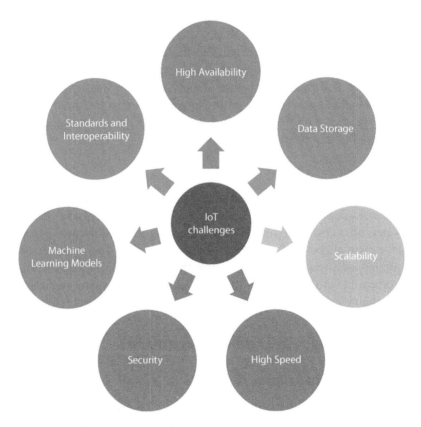

Figure 7.14 Challenges in IoT and data center.

4. **Machine Learning Methods:** Proper machine learning models to be identified to make decision automatically. If the machine learning techniques are not proper and learning is not performed properly, then the automatic decision-making in IoT will become risky.

5. **Scalability:** Architecture should support high scalable numbers of devices in IoT network. All the applications and computational mechanisms should be highly scalable.

6. **Security:** Unsecured devices can block the services. The network traffic should be monitored to detect the malicious traffic. It should detect the suspicious behavior in the IoT environment [10].

7.5   Conclusion

IoT is playing a significant role in the smart technology world. IoT along with machine learning and AI techniques becomes the world's giant powerful communication between smart devices. IoT can connect any small devices over the internet and it can be controlled from anywhere in the world through this technology. The processing of data in the network along with IoT, data center, edge computing, and AI techniques will be an optimistic environment for smart control and automation. Advantage of big data analysis can also be utilized. In this chapter, we have discussed IoT, IoT protocols, handling IoT in modern data centers, various IoT applications, and major challenges.

References

1. Gubbi, J., Buyya, R., Marusic, S., Palaniswami, M., Gubbi, J. *et al.*, Internet of Things (IoT): A vision, architectural elements, and future direction. *Future Gener. Comput. Syst.*, 29, 1645–1660, 2013.
2. Salman, T., Networking Protocols and Standards for Internet of Things. Internet of Things Protocols and Standards (wustl.edu).
3. Mahdavinejad, M.S., Rezvan, M., Barekatain, M., Adibi, P., Barnaghi, P., Sheth, A.P., Machine learning for internet of things data analysis: a survey. *Digital Commun. Networks*, 4, 161–175, 2018.
4. Aazam, M. and Huh, E.-N., Fog computing micro datacenter based dynamic resource estimation and pricing model for iot, in: *2015 IEEE 29th International Conference on Advanced Information Networking and Applications*, IEEE, pp. 687–694, 2015.
5. Shi, Y., Ding, G., Wang, H., Roman, H.E., Lu, S., The fog computing service for healthcare, in: *Future Information and Communication Technologies for Ubiquitous HealthCare (Ubi-HealthTech), 2015 2nd International Symposium on, IEEE*, pp. 1–5, 2015.
6. Turing, A.M., Computing machinery and intelligence. *Mind*, LIX, 236, 433–60, 1950.
7. Jouppi, N.P., Young, C., Patil, N., Patterson, D., Agrawal, G., Bajwa, R. *et al.*, In datacenterperformanceanalysisofatensorprocessingunit, in: *Proceedings of 2017 ACM/IEEE 44th Annual International Symposium on Computer Architecture*, Toronto, ON, Canada, 2017 Jun 24–28, pp. 1–12, 2017.
8. *Big Data in IOT*, Available from:https://mindmajix.com/big-data-in-iot.
9. Atzori, L., Iera, A., Morabito, G., The Internet of Things: a survey. *Comput. Networks*, 54, 15, 2787–2805, 2010.

10. Botta, A., de Donato, W., Persico, V., Pescape, A., Integration of cloud computing and Internet of Things: a survey. *Future Gener. Comput. Syst.*, 56, 684–700, 2016.

11. Bottou, L., From machine learning to machine reasoning. *Mach. Learn.*, 94, 2, 133–149, 2014.

12. Gama, K., Touseau, L., Donsez, D., Combining heterogeneous service technologies for building an Internet of Things middleware. *Comput. Commun.*, 35, 4, 405–417, 2012.

13. Liu, C.H., Yang, B., Liu, T., Efficient naming, addressing and profile services in Internet of Things sensory environments. *Ad Hoc Netw.*, 18, 85–101, 2014.

14. Miao, W., Ting-Jie, L., Fei-Yang, L., Jing, S., Hui-Ying, D., Research on the Architecture of Internet of Things. Paper presented at the *2010 3rd International Conference on Advanced Computer Theory and Engineering (ICACTE)*, 20–22 Aug. 2010.

15. Nastic, S., Vögler, M., Inzinger, C., Truong, H.L., Dustdar, S., rtGovOps: A Runtime Framework for Governance in Large-Scale Software-Defined IoT Cloud Systems. Paper presented at the *2015 3rd IEEE International Conference on Mobile Cloud Computing, Services, and Engineering*, March 30, 2015–April 3, 2015.

16. Liu, Y., Muppala, J.K., Veeraraghavan, M., Lin, D., Hamdi, M., *Data Center Networks*, Springer Briefs in Computer Science, 2013.

8

Impact of IoT to Meet Challenges in Drone Delivery System

J. Ranjani*, P. Kalaichelvi, V.K.G Kalaiselvi,
D. Deepika Sree and K. Swathi

Sri Sairam Engineering College, Chennai, India

Abstract

The emergence of Artificial Intelligence, and subsequently, Internet of Things (IoT), has given rise to tech conversations, which otherwise might have been, a feat impossible to achieve. This enhances connectivity and, therefore, is vital in having brought about a change which is necessary to help the growth of the world. The aviation sector has also implemented this coming of age technology. The main objective of this paper is to bring up the IoT technology into the lights and to emphasize on its successful wide ranged applications in aviation sector. During the investigation, the author found how IT sector interacts with the users by commonly sharing many features of a city. Thus, on further surveying the City-as-a-Platform past researches, both airports and cities are considered as platforms for systems related to IoT, like levels of service performance indicator the management of airport lacks.

The implementation of IoT in the aviation industry includes IoT precursors like Radio Frequency Identification (RFID) labels and sensors. The IoT has spread its evolving technological applications to many other industries also. The airlines IoT victory and its competitive challenges have afforded itself to keen inspection, by up to date upgradation to produce high success rates in present and future digital world. Collaborating with the excellent exposures of her colleagues serving the connected aviation domains, the author has split the lifecycle of this technology into three divisions, namely, 1. the technological possibilities, 2. the technological deployment, and 3. the technological refinement and functioning. So concerning the efforts and works of every individual employee is the pre-eminent

Corresponding author: ranjani.it@sairam.edu.in

R. Anandan, Suseendran Gopalakrishnan, Souvik Pal and Noor Zaman (eds.) *The Industrial Internet of Things (IIoT): Intelligent Analytics for Predictive Maintenance*, (203–228) © 2022 Scrivener Publishing LLC contribution to its well-defined success rates. The "Implementation of IoT and Digital Transformation within the Airport Industry" is developed for the airport IoT professionals.

Keywords: IoT, CAAS (City as a Service), integration of aviation, technology, levels of service (LOS)

8.1   Introduction

With the inclusion of digital technologies, the airline industry has now been able to deliver exclusive customer experiences, simplify essential process, and most drastically increase the output of the workforce. Succeeding stride in leveraging Internet of Things (IoT) can cause the journeying of newer dimensions within the aviation industry [1]. Altogether with other technologies like AI and robotics will produce opportunities connected with service relief development. Additionally, the IoT ecosystem can start all the particular entity and resources together within the industry value chain and make it appear as if it is the new normal.

8.1.1   IoT Components

Components are linked to connecting and managing people on the basis of the data and resources that they come forth to choose, interact, and decide, which are as follows:

- Components allied to information
- Components allied to processes
- Components allied to things

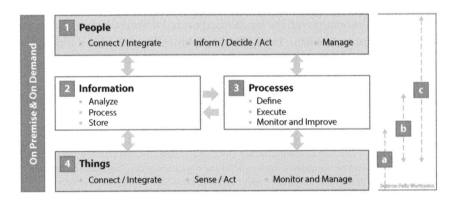

8.1.2   Main Division to Apply IoT in Aviation

Organization should follow the underlying strategy to test the full potential of IoT in aviation:

1.   Hyper-personalization: The usage of IoT in an aviation sector will pave the way for making the flight experience a better one, by providing data at a regular basis, at all interaction points, whether in flight or off it.

2.   Tracking passengers: Luggage carrying and consequent loading on and off is not quite pleasant for some of the passengers due to some reasons, and in order to eliminate that, the digitalization becomes necessary, and here is where IoT comes to action. The usage of this coming of age technology will help the passenger track their packages on a real-time basis, thereby giving them lesser reasons to worry with regard to the safety of their valuable goods. During this process, virtual auto-generated messages will be displayed to the owner of the package, with regard to where it is and also of its proximity to the passenger and alerting in time about unexpected luggage accidents.

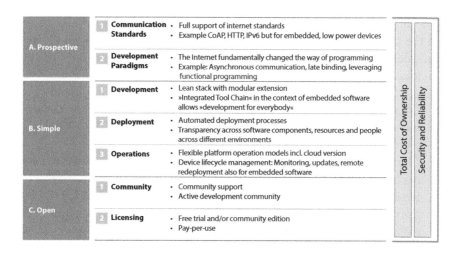

3.   Alerts and actions: As technology sees a rapid advancement, it becomes necessary to incorporate its advantageous nature and makes best use of its abilities in order to achieve a level of satisfaction like no other. Airlines can now use IoT

to be aware of any kind of problems or discomfort caused to the passenger and finds a suitable solution for it beforehand. This will mean that the cabin crew and anyone who is involved in customer welfare can ensure that no stone is left unturned in order to make their experience memorable and hassle free.

4. Monitoring: With the influence of linked networks, the aviation industry procures the opportunities and induces the enhancements in primary and secondary services. The advantageous sensor signals afford to sell especial incentives like fast lane and lounge. The assimilation of enterprise statements with IoT will assist airlines to efficiently detect the functioning of these extra welfares.

5. Operational efficiency: Real-world application is frequently used to improve the performance of aircraft. IoT provides lot of facility for navy consumption, diminishing performance costs and identifying task in advance. Practical technique assists in reorganization tasks and proficient development of continuation actions.

8.1.3   Required Field of IoT in Aviation

IoT introduces lot of new techniques to deliver precision in all aspects, in the upcoming future. The effect of using IoT in the aviation industry includes reduction of time period, enhancement of passenger comfort, and increase in security levels.

- Data sensors: Sensors entrenched the linked substance assist to monitoring and group accurate real-time information. The modern world we need to have frequent data sensor.
- Cloud computing: The IoT is used in cloud computing for utilizing information sharing.
- Smart airports: By applying the latest technologies, the local and global airlines can reproduce the idea of smart cities to procure realistic information. Industries need to assimilate, strengthen, and research multiple data that are about to develop a smart service benefitting passengers as well as industries.

A customer chooses to travel in flight, when compared to other cheaper modes of transport because of the services and added advantages. Due to the kind of comfort which is provided on air, and an experience that is second to none, by the end of the journey, the customer is left wanting for more. And to satisfy their needs, to a greater extent, the airport and airlines should take more steps.

Smart, an airport is said to be, when the customer has zero issues with regard to the fulfillment of his needs and wants. We can make that happen by incorporating technologies that help the customer to exactly find out details like luggage safety, boarding details, where he stands in a queue on a real-time basis. This will be a time saving experience.

- Gateway: The best technology for IoT gateways is Beacon. The admonition is associated with the following: A boarding card display on time, boarding pass, flight status, or passenger's mobile screen.

This way, travelers get précised data time to time. Furthermore, the airline will also be notified of how far the travelers are. This helps make better decisions, such as how long you should attend before a particular start.

- Smart baggage: The usual concern of passengers is about whether their bags are stocked on the plane. Airports can utilize smart baggage tags to help the travelers track their baggage with the help of a mobile app. Communication networks such as cellular networks or Wi-Fi are not a cost-effective option and have no scope, mainly for long-haul airlines.

Additionally, they will be informed about the specific carousel where they can take their luggage from, as well as what it will take.

To unlock the full potential of the IoT, it is necessary to have a stable, secure network that can provide power to multiple connected devices.

- Low investment: IoT is capable of working at short range Wi-Fi networks and works on ISM frequency bands. This will prove as an effective cost cutting method as it has low deployment costs.

8.1.3.1 Airports as Smart Cities or Airports as Platforms

As a multi-sided network, smart cities are considered to include the interest of the public and their participation, commercial viability, and various market opportunities.

These four variables create an environment that is similar to the smart city environment. This is for the general public of each participant. Smart technology enables smart city business activities that are data-driven and benefit citizens. The design of airports to create the city is significantly different. Airports have data such as silos and other large corporate structures.

Between logistics rules and operations with other parts of the airport, there may be a rock. In order to identify airports as a market that is multisided, it is important to take into consideration that airport revenues come from multiple directions.

This helps us to regard as the airport as a platform for interconnecting passengers and cargo or airlines. By internalizing the network effects between these categories, the airport industry adds value to all.

8.1.3.2   Architecture of Multidrone

The way of getting video films with flying vehicles in a self-sufficient way is being tested. It forces a progression of challenges related to robot situating and route, smooth control of the camera, crash evasion, and so forth, principally when the application is outside.

8.1.3.3   The Multidrone Design has the Accompanying Prerequisites

The framework ought to have the option to replicate ordinary shots from cinematography administers self-luringly, shooting static and portable targets.

- It ought to likewise guarantee smooth advances along the shots while simultaneously executing impact shirking and monitoring no-fly zones, security, and crisis circumstances.
- Finally, it ought to consider the restricted assets of the robots, for example, the battery life.

We propose a design (Figure 8.1) where arranging can occur at various stages and with various modules. For example, figuring a sheltered way to an arrival spot or to a particular shooting position can be viewed as arranging, yet appropriating distinctive shooting assignments among the colleagues and organizing them is likewise arranging.

Arrangement can prove to be useful, and industrious, provided the chief is ready to make the changes. Nonetheless, during the execution of the arrangement, the first conditions may differ, making that underlying arrangement not, at this point helpful. Envision, for example, that a few

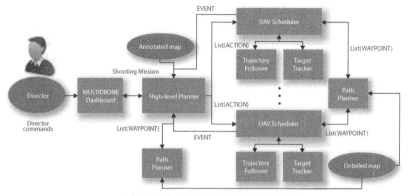

MultiDrone architecture for autonomous cinematography

Figure 8.1 Multidrone architecture for autonomous cinematography.

pieces of the arrangement were not effectively cultivated (vulnerabilities in robots' activities or targets' developments), that there were new orders from the chief or that unforeseen crisis functions occurred. Every one of these circumstances can trigger another arranging stage at a more significant level.

In the framework, there will exist a high-level planner accountable for deciphering significant level orders from the cinematography chief (indicated through the dashboard), make an interpretation of them into various assignments (e.g., positions to visit and explicit shots to be taken), and circulate them among the robots of the group.

The entire arrangement of elevated level orders indicated by the chief will be signified as the Shooting Mission, which will be part into consecutive or equal Shooting Actions to be performed by the various robots in the group. Consequently, each robot will fuse the important functionalities to play out its relegated Shooting Actions. The scheduler will deal with the errands appointed and will send low-level orders to follow arranged directions or track targets, utilizing extra way organizers relying upon each activity. As expressed over, the significant level organizer will be utilized for pre-arranging before the flight, yet additionally for rethinking after sudden functions or new chief's orders.

8.2   Literature Survey

Highly equipped and fully functional systems are made use of, by allowing the user to link his data to a cloud where the information can be stored for a considerably long time and retrieved as and when he needs it. The status of the aircraft received from the Flight Management System (FMS) indicates the after-flight report. The data is redistributed against the reference manual, which is the original minimalist tool. The system is designed to speed up the post-flight inspection response time and again.

The traveling is the placement of our life as an important one. It may be local, national, or global. In prolonged journals, our priority is to succeed within the holiday spot and fasten the maximum amount of artwork needed. The airplane lets in this touring smooth and absolutely fast. With the arrival of the era, the touring through airplane advanced to supply greater protection and conform to their passengers. This article is to find out the ultra-modern development of IoT and their usability within the improvement of the airport. These studies look at several articles alongside the ultra-modern research taking place. The technological improvement within the airport has incredibly increased nowadays. In this paper, smart airport device has been implemented and designed as a prototype using internet web server, database, and hardware Node MCU ESP8266 and RFID playing cards.

The app is developed using block coding and the implementation and consequences suggest that the code and format device worked perfectly without any errors. The check-in device is coming less difficult and character nice with smart gambling playing cards RFID. If there is any baggage misplacement, then net web website online can guide with vicinity and details.

Flight industry is one of the zones which have a solid potential to profit by RFID and the IoT. The most widely recognized escape clauses experienced in the aviation industry for baggage handling are misplaced stuff, lost things, and harm to possessions. So, for giving a superior and secure framework to the travelers, we have proposed a plan of staff following and taking care of a framework utilizing savvy RFID labels and IoT which depends on cloud workers. We have planned a model in two areas having both registration and registration measures.

A more made sure about calculation is utilized for creating labels that are connected to printed stuff names with the subtleties of traveler and aircraft put away in it. RFID peruses in the registration regions encourage step following of things which forestall stuff misfortune.

The things' constant position is followed and put away in a cloud utilizing IoT and interesting ID can be recovered by the travelers any place and at whatever point is important. A similar ID can be utilized while gathering sack at registration counters. The framework guarantees less utilization of time and security for stuff, is conservative, and thus gives consumer loyalty.

The future vision of the web is to interface everything, for example, with elements such as transport organizations, and correspondence organizations. This would turn into a suitable source of inspiration to include a more capable vehicle frame. Shrewd air terminal innovation will prompt numerous developments in the aeronautics area, which thus will build the effectiveness and profitability of the whole air terminal administration framework.

This engineering will offer customized types of assistance and substance to various voyagers at the air terminal and ensures that every single explorer who enters the air terminal will get a definitive client experience and fulfillment.

8.3   Smart Airport Architecture

As of now voyagers are associated with the web more often than not as a matter of course, and they completely expect the accessibility of cooperation is identified with them to work consistently. The purpose of this exploration paper is to propose engineering in asset the executive's application for the usage of air terminal administrations offered to the voyagers. Brilliant airports will give a clever application the combination of RFID innovation, IoT, and Google indoor guides onto the current framework of the air terminals so as to decide all the more decisively the utilization of air terminal administrations accessible to explorers.

In a perspective on late turns of events, there are different parts of aeronautics areas that should be thought of, for example, remote correspondence and systems administration of the air terminal exercises. Through the utilization of RFID innovation with IoT and installing a little versatile application into a wide assortment of extra devices and hardware that are utilized in everyday tasks; this will empower new types of correspondences and do different activities easily.

The significant quality of RFID innovation and IoT, particularly in the flight business, is the high effect that it has on lion's share of the activities that are done in the air terminals.

The effect of RFID with IoT will improve the day by day activities of this area. Concerning the improvement of the keen air terminals individuals will discover better offices at the air terminals. Likewise, even the representatives working at the air terminals will have improved efficiency at every one of their working levels.

During the advancement of use need to worry with various libraries fluctuates to a working framework for the fruitful defeat of web issues and conventions. The application will run on shrewd electronic contraptions utilizing working framework offered types of assistance and will assist the travelers with arranging their excursions effectively and appreciate the excursion with application.

Nor *et al.* [15]: They wrote a piece on customer fealty and service standards in Domestic affordable Aviation Services, Malaysia. This paper ambition is to increase a philosophical shape on great provider and its patron fealty dating among the customers of Malaysia's home for least price aviation amenities. Reliability, tangibility, sensitivity, reliability, and empathy are regarded to be vital elements of the level of provider and can offer medical records approximately patron pride. Thereafter, the patron pride implications are extra mentioned in this text too. The effects of this evaluation are supposed to help the organization in offering an excessive level of provider to customers and enhancing loyalty with clients in addressing their wishes and wishes.

Aruna & Nisha [16]: They share information on smart automated airlines and potential analysis of airport functionalities. This study emphasizes generally on technology for smart aviation within side the improvement of passenger terminals. Scattered literature on unique references has been compiled to demonstrate the traits of clever airport with sensible instances in an international sense. Empirical recommendations on clever airport generation deployment are addressed primarily based totally on sensible elements of airport operations. Significant emphasis is paid to the instances of Asia, Middle East, and Europe's maximum appearing local airports. This observation contributes to the educational and business quarter with the aid of highlighting the benefits of integrating clever airports inside key regions of aviation stability, passenger comfort, operating productivity, and resource management limited. This paper explored extra techniques of implantation below traveler, bags handling, and regulatory controls.

Samia *et al.* [17]: They wrote an essay concerning smart airport: an airport management program targeted on IoT. Air journey has been one of the important components of globalization, as indicated with the aid of using them. The increase has been explosive for decades, transferring on from aviation technical improvements on the only facet and men's tendency to journey on the other.

Yu-Hern and Chung-Hsing [18]: They study providers for home airways. This paper affords an essential technique for comparing the level of provider thru patron surveys of home passenger airways. Crisp survey effects are represented and processed as fuzzy units to mirror the inherent subjectivity and obscure perceptions of the clients to the great ranges supplied with the aid of using airways with respect to more than one provider attributes. To formulate the evaluation query a complicated multicriteria evaluation (MA) version is used. The version is solved with the aid of using a powerful set of rules incorporating the attitude or preference of the selection maker on standards weights and overall performance scores for assessments of the clients. To display the effectiveness of the approach, an empirical observe is conducted of home airways on a relatively aggressive path in Taiwan.

I-Shoo (2016): His studies targeted the airline enterprise in Taiwan. The goal is to pick parameters for the Taiwanese airline enterprise for enhancing the standard of airline offerings. Numerous elements along with low rail rates, high-velocity rail growth, better petroleum prices, better global airline opposition, and the current monetary disaster have led many Taiwanese airways to enjoy economic problems or even closures. Researchers have begun out to outline vital necessities for reinforcing the standard of operation, with the goal of developing airways' strategic advantages. However, numerous of the selected metrics are afflicted by a great technical problem: all the metric measurements are exceptional, contributing to insufficient requirements for calculating the extent of operation. In order to efficiently rank and choose our parameters, their estimates understand the interrelationships and consequences of the measurements and necessities of the evaluation.

Khader and Abdul (2016): Their study on standard of carrier determinants within side the airline marketplace. The aim of this is to research the stages of pride and the significance attributed to the general first-rate airline carrier and to pick attributes of Tiruchirappalli Airport air passengers. With flight frequency, the diploma of price assigned to airline offerings increased. Airline carrier expectancies can range throughout diverse nationalities and exceptional socio-monetary classes. There can also be versions among short- and long-haul routes, as well as nearby and overseas offerings. Airline executives should sell loyalty via ways of maximizing airline enjoyment for tourists. This may be completed via way of means of differentiating airline offerings into segmented consumer categories.

Michael (2003): Competition and performance product research within the US airline industry. This looks at exploring capability linkages among the two via a way of reading whether or not the lack of opposition in a specific direction contributes to worse consequences on time. The United

States Consequences Bureau of Transportation Data in 2000 displayed that on routes in which the simplest one provider gives direct operation; each the frequency and length of flight delays are substantially greater. Better on-time overall performance is correlated with extra opposition. Environment, noise, and routing selections frequently offer a major contribution to know-how flight delays. The findings on this paper propose that flights are, in common, much less normal on time on routes functions via means of simply one airport having a market exchange and better in conditions in which airways have a marketplace proportion on the airports functioned. Scheduling accounting suggests that the actual carrier presented is plenty worse; on their proprietary routes, the airways plan longer flight times, all else is equivalent.

Mehran and Mostafa (2009): They write of the carrier first-rate elements of Ranking Airlines the usage of a flimsy approach. Objectives of this paper are comparing the airline enterprise's carrier performance variables and score positive variables in Iranian society to enforce a Fuzzy TOPSIS solution. The article calls the studies population of graduate college graduates. While college college students are a community of capability clients of airways, the paper consequences could not be applicable to different airline consumer agencies and greater studies needed to see whether or not the equal score of carrier first-rate measurements may be visible among positive consumer agencies of exceptional activity backgrounds. The paper helped in permitting coverage makers' within side the airline enterprise to pick out key carrier first-rate elements in Iranian clients' eyes.

Gour and Theingi (2009): They write an essay on standard of operation, retention and behavioral cause. The cause of this paper is to take a look at the relationships in passengers of three low-fee carriers (LCCs) presenting airline offerings in Thailand among the constructs of carrier first-rate, pride, and behavioral intent. The evaluation notes that the order of priority of the servicing performance measurements evaluated right here is flight schedules, flight attendants, tangibles, and floor staff. Passenger interplay with those aspects of carrier performance is taken into consideration very great in describing behavioral intentions. The time table in large part impacts glad tourists. These customers take pleasure in successful word-of-mouth touch and feature plans to buy lower back big. Unhappy passengers choose to alternate airways in preference to supplying the LCCs with feedback.

Shoo et al. (2014): They share their perspectives on instrumentation and fitness tracking of smart airport pavements. This document provides a quick assessment of many current studies on the growth of ingenious superior detection and surveillance structures for the highway pavement community, along with a viable program for long-term pavement protection and surveillance at airports offers. Examples of these executable programs include the use of Wi-Fi RFID tags to assess the temperature gradient of the pavement layer. The self-powered MEMS/NEMS sensors with abundant of real-time operation over local pressure, temperature, and moisture content objects on an airport pavement. This will eventually blow up and prevent catastrophic disasters.

8.4   Barriers to IoT Implementation

Despite having the right resources and knowledge, implementing IoT solutions can be a major undertaking for even the most technologically advanced companies. Let us look at some of the major trouble areas below.

1. Defense, security, and privacy [2]: Safety is a billing standard in the aviation industry. Any new technology, whether effective or inexpensive, can be implemented if it constitutes a security threat. When physical objects are linked digitally, the arrangement of digital data can have real-world implications. As the acceptance of IoT defines, cyber security and data privacy are highly related.

2. Framework and technology: Large IoT implementations encompass a variety of controls and tools, all of which need to be interconnected and coordinated. There are very few ready-to-use airport IoT solutions currently on the market. It can be hard to find what the IoT ecosystem needs.

3. Talent: As IoT is highly welcomed, the duties of employees may differ from time to time due to continuous tech up gradations. To address this trend, the airport has introduced mastering programs for existing operators, expanded the recruitment of young employees, and improved management leaders and coordinate talented associates. Addressing the skills gap should be a priority. This is a compelling business case. One of the biggest barriers to IoT adoption in any industry is concerns about return on investment (ROI).

4. Financing and financing: Even with a strong business deal that provides a transparent and appropriate ROI, airports struggle to find the first funds needed to launch the project.

As the margins of airline operated is limited, extra money to fund an IoT project can be a source of dread for any airline managerial.

A systematic approach to identifying funds and funding opportunities by raising questions about project priorities, deadlines, and stakeholders can help reduce confusion and promote IoT adoption.

8.4.1   How is the Internet of Things Converting the Aviation Enterprise?

The IoT is getting used an increasing number of, or even worldwide giants are already the usage of optimization or facts accumulating answers. All this to enhance current procedures, acquire system and document extra statistics, or maybe introduce new offerings for his or her clients, thereby growing income revenue. How is the IoT converting the fact of the aviation enterprise? We will provide an explanation for the lot with inside the textual content below.

Airlines are more and more seeking out answers in order to permit them to introduce extra expenses and thus growth income. It regarded that the acquisition of a favored seat, large baggage, or precedence boarding is the maximum; however, it seems that contemporary-day technology permits enforcing extra offerings that, on the identical time, increased consolation of the traveler and provide him the acquisition of more facilities also.

8.5   Current Technologies in Aviation Industry

Digitized Security: Today, advanced technologies are being developed to minimize passenger waiting time to implement advanced concepts such as "safe passage". Biometrics is often used to simplify the verification process, thus reducing the burden on staff. As they are equipped with the latest security system for security purposes, security systems [5] are slowly becoming a staple technology trend in airport terminals (Figure 8.2).

- VR for Last-Minute Changes: A leading global airline is exploring a latest way to upgrade their tickets for passengers by allowing 13 them to use VR for premium seats. The passengers were asked to upgrade at the last minute. The airline stated that VR could be used to see the advantages of a premium economy with extra legroom and seat pitch.

- Biometrics: It has probably been used by the airlines for some while and is gaining popularity. Some of the world's largest airports have invested in fingerprint and facial addresses. The aviation says that facial recognition is used to make up a new passport for the costumers. Biometric identification is introduced at the lounge and openings in many airports and the technology is combined with a data display flight system to provide advanced personal details to the travelers.

8.5.1 Methodology or Research Design

In designing and administering the survey, the authors selected a target audience of experts who were able to respond honestly to a survey and better uncover the real mechanics of the technology implementation world: avionics are active in the aviation industry and colleagues in the aviation

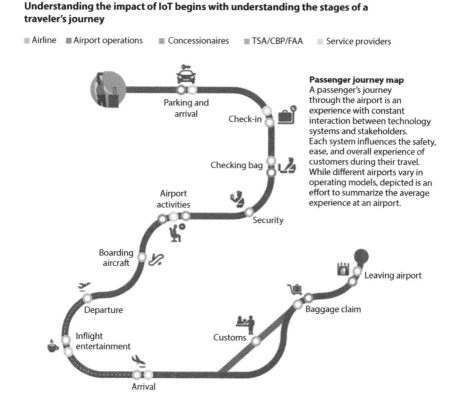

Figure 8.2 Current technologies in aviation industry.

industry. Colleagues of "Aviation Community" are a multinational network of experts working on a project-specific basis "at the site" and at technology companies associated with the airport.

The authors have provided a great variety of alternatives and characteristics for each question rather than increasing the amount of data. Microsoft type applications were used to develop, manage and evaluate the SP survey.

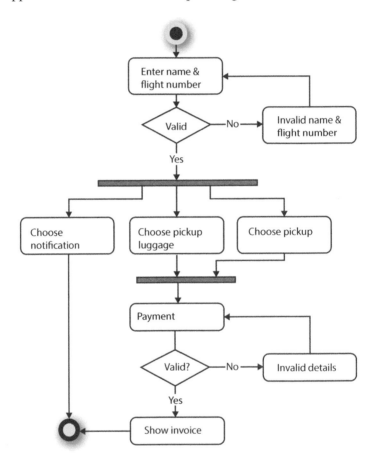

8.6   IoT Adoption Challenges

8.6.1   Deployment of IoT Applications on Broad Scale Includes the Underlying Challenges

- There are many contributors in the airlines and each of these contributors possesses their own environment with controls and automations. Meantime, most of the stakeholders rely on each other for smoother functionality to be carried out. As IoT adoption increases, it becomes needed by the airlines to expand the scope further than restricted companies and to collaborate with those stakeholders who share a common IoT vision.

- Operations of airline industries are multifariously spreading across the globe along different geographical areas. Each of which will have their own technical tractability. The evolving IoT focuses on fulfilling all this varied ethnic inclusiveness [5].
- The airline sector works with high level security. This extraordinary encryption, security and privacy would be the key factors for someone to opt IoT-based technology in aviation industry. Since privacy is considered as a sensitive issue nowadays, the IoT emphasis on deploying many advanced technologies such as facial recognition to manage large passenger's private data.

8.7 Transforming Airline Industry With Internet of Things

IoT highly focuses on providing satisfying travel experience for the passengers. Using beacon technology, educating airline workers to use wearables and introducing remote maintenance solutions, businesses are provided with a wide variety of possibilities for IoT to obtain battering. In rapidly transforming digital world, the traditional and low budget careers must incorporate new game plans for attaining excellence in this sector. Commercial aviation is actively evolving competitive trade.

Balancing between the establishments of high-level loyalty for the costumers and offering the travel ease services at lesser budget is a continual challenge experienced by this sector. Up to a minute, data-driven cooperation is facilitated by the evolving digital era in the aviation industry. An information analysis and real-time apprehension helps the aviation sector to relevantly serve the target audience [6].

The key objective of this paper is to emphasize that IoT is a top-notched effective and efficient technology used in unique sense of airport.

8.7.1 How the IoT Is Improving the Aviation Industry

Aviation companies have made the usage of the IoT a part of their entire phase of digital transformation. Digital transformation process includes the required amendments to the industries and its potential to offer the solution in which the industry works and does business. Digital transformation not only affects where our activities are focused or where we concentrate and where we behave, but it must also shake up the organization's internal processes itself and provide them with the required technical resources and adjust them wherever necessary to make the most of the possibilities of the digital world. Airline companies work under high specifications. This sector is a strong illustration of state-of-the-art tech [7]. They operate with a huge quantity of passenger info, then preserve privacy, and then transfer it through assistants who use Agito address customer queries for example.

8.7.1.1   IoT: Game Changer for Aviation Industry

Computerized innovations are invoking latest possibilities for airline domains to exclusively offer delightful user experience. For instance, social networks monitor the customer's emotions about the services that they offer. Innovations like boarding card vestures, virtual addresses, and instrumental paying at the departure venue has been introduced [8]. The utilized advancements create a wholesome and a wide real-time view for costumers and it initiates airline campaigns on the basis of transaction status. Computerized world can make this process simpler and easier which as a result will improvise the travel experience.

Earlier, boarding process constitutes the efforts of human labors and cabin crew members to manage the underlying works, but now on implementation of advanced technologies, the cabin crew is relieved from these tasks and is promoted to directly serve their passengers in a better way. Amalgamating IoT with other advanced automations like AI, big data analytics, robots, and cloud computing improves the day to day service standards in aviation industry.

8.7.2   Applications of AI in the Aviation Industry

8.7.2.1   Ticketing Systems

AI and IoT are being practiced more in ticketing systems. Aviation ticket pricing is affected by the elements such as flight distance, oil expense, seasonality, reputation etc. it has complex fare market governance. IoT airlines uses AI uses AI-based algorithms to minimize price point and manages better revenue. Tools like expected marginal seat revenue (EMSR) and ancillary price are enhanced by AI [9]. It achieves the goal to provide better service to the costumer and also to bring up the industrial economy.

8.7.2.2   Flight Maintenance

Aeronautical sustentation is quite a difficult piece of work. Mechanical parts have to be maintained periodically. In order to establish an effective maintenance, airlines take immense effort to plan their maintenance schedules. Maintenance violation can cause flight cancellation which in turn results in expensive losses.

Aircraft parts are maintained with AI-based predictive analysis that is done regularly. Failure of mechanical parts can be predicted beforehand. Repairing tasks also makes use of AI tools. The IBM Watson TV commercial about aviation gives a glimpse into the longer term of such AI-powered maintenance.

8.7.2.3   Fuel Efficiency

For an airline industry, Jet fuel is the main operational cost. Also, airplanes produce 2% of entire human induced CO2 emission which reduces the fuel wastage. In order to examine the data about aircraft mass, distance, altitude, passenger count, fuel amount, etc., machine learning algorithms are used [10]. For example, partnership is established between southwest and GE aviation Digital solutions to implement big data an AI to reserve $100 million on fuel.

8.7.2.4   Crew Management

The success of this industry is determined by the collaborative efforts of every individual. Many key elements such as availability, certificates, qualifications, and scheduling delays have to be managed. Thus, machine learning automation takes up the role of human labor. One such example is "Jespersen" which is an AI dependent crew roistering network that is assigned to maintain and manage crew assignments.

8.7.2.5   Flight Health Checks and Maintenance

Rolls Royce is considered to be the premium manufacturer of aircraft engines. Azure IoT solutions has partnered with Rolls Royce to use cloud platforms to maintain racks of data for predictive maintenance. Health status of engines is also examined with the help of IoT gadgets [11]. Every aeronautical constituents of their Boeing 787 to the planes wireless network are linked through IoT devices by virgin Atlantic.

8.7.2.6   In-Flight Experience Management

With economic IoT innovations, the in-flight experience is improved since now. For ex: the Easy Jet has facilities of fixed microphones and IoT LEDS in their uniforms [12]. Emergency guidelines are displayed in LEDS with flight numbers for the passenger to contact the crew during the times of exigencies.

8.7.2.7   Luggage Tracking

Monitoring over passenger's luggage are the important features of air transport. Instead of paper tags, Lufthansa is making use of IoT for the same purpose [13]. Development of RIMOWA tag displays the details electronically. The costumers can link their digital tags and trackers to their Bluetooth devices thereby traveling peacefully.

8.7.2.8   Airport Management

Five hundred beacons are utilized by the Miami International Airport for indoor navigation. Similarly, London City Airport has firstly deployed IoT technology to monitor airport traffic [14]. Cam coders and sensors can also be used for security objectives.

8.7.2.9   Just the Beginning

The aviation sector has just begun applying the AI and IoT in their domains. Utilizing the immense advantage of emerging technologies in scheduling, revenue management, etc., to enhance the user's comfort will eventually rise up the trends of applying AI and IoT within the airline industry.

8.8   Revolution of Change (Paradigm Shift)

"The Change from a model in setback from which a replacement tradition of ordinary science can evolve is way from a collective process, one achieved by an articulation or extension of the old paradigm. Rather it is a reconstruction of the world from new fundamentals, a reconstruction that changes various of the field's most straightforward theoretical generalizations and also many of its paradigm methods and applications. During the transition period there'll be an outsized but never complete overlap between the issues which will be solved by the old and by the new paradigm. But there will also be a difference in declarations in the means of solution. When the transformation is over, the industry would have altered its dimensions of the sector, its methods, and its objectives" Created a reference implementation called the Drone Delivery application for explore the challenges of implementing the IoT App [15]. Some of the businesses manage a fleet of drone aircraft, and also customers requiring drone can request it to select up goods for delivery. There are two types of telemetry send by drone:

- Flight data: Latitude, longitude, altitude, velocity, and acceleration. For every 5 seconds once, each drone sends this data.
- Operating status: Engine temperature and battery level. For every 20 seconds, each drone sends this data.

We assume the drones support IP protocol and MQTT, so the drones are mostly-connected devices. That is, they send a continuing stream of knowledge while on the wing, instead of batching data at intervals.

8.9 The Following Diagram Shows the Design of the Application

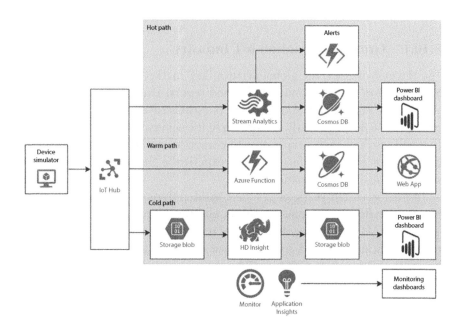

The architecture includes numerous data streaming paths performing different functions:

- Hot path: The hot path monitors the drones' operating status to detect anomalies in the engine temperature. It uses Azure Stream Analytics to compute the typical temperature of engine of every drone over a 2-minute window. Anomalous readings are stored in Cosmos DB which triggers an alert. The sample application includes stub code for the alerts. These stub codes can be modified accordingly to send an SMS message or a push notification to a mobile app.
- Warm path: The latest positioning information of all the drones to cosmos DB are written by Warm path using Azure functions.
- Cold path: Every raw telemetry are grabbed and then processed by the cold path using Hindsight. The sample application includes a Hive query that summarizes the pickup and drop-off times for each delivery, on the basis location from the drones. You can then use Power BI to explore and picture the results.

8.10   Discussion, Limitations, Future Research, and Conclusion

8.10.1   Growth of Aviation IoT Industry

"By the end of 2025, the global aviation IoT market is appraised to reach $25.13 billion", says an online published report. During the forthcoming years from now, the aviation market is estimated to show a remarkable growth of 16.36% in CAGR. According to the survey, the significant factors that will result in such a rapid growth comprises of the developing a smart airport by granting satisfactory client experience plus providing compensations in business declinations.

In the forecasted years, as per the considerations of part wise enhancements, the fleet management part is estimated to show an increase of 16.08% at CAGR. The essential zones of market improvements that include datacenters, devices, and communicatory services are estimated to progress with the rate of 15.67% CAGR by the year of 2023.

With respect to the area, the boundaries of Asia pacific will be the rapidly outgrown region for the future years. The thriving CAGR appraisal is to be at 18.6% and the basic aspect of enhancement in this region holds the expanding stipulation of in-flight linkage along with the connected electrical equipment, and notably the high funding is in IoT outcomes by airline officialdom.

8.10.2   IoT Applications—Benefits

The three basic beneficial objectives from utilizing an IoT application are as follows:

- Operational efficiency
- Strategic differentiation
- New revenue

Having all these effective features into the account, airlines can accomplish big in near future. We know that aviation industries are earlier deploying IoT applications, but operating them even more efficiently, we could achieve more by provoking security effectiveness, can improve the travel lines for peaceful travel experience also called as differentiation [16]. By installing geofencing on rideshares, IoT can also generate high revenues.

8.10.3   Operational Efficiency

Operational efficiency is one of the foremost IoT classes that is already being implemented in many airports. For example, many airports use inspection system with the help of internet and GPS proficiency to examine the ground crew levels of airport. One such airport has invoked the idea of a smart bathroom system, where various sensors will be installed in bathroom assets like toilets, faucets, air dispensers, and soap dispensers. These sensors transfer the data by checking the shortage or damage of the assets to the maintenance department hence promoting both cleanliness and user-friendly travel circumstances. The airports may also include autonomous vehicles, tenders, and baggage carts. Also using IoT applications in schedules, gate numbers and on other large data sources will improve the traveling experience thoroughly automating human labors.

8.10.4   Strategic Differentiation

A smart airport can provide a more differentiated product than a non-smart airport. However, the differentiation is a quite tedious process. Differentiation includes a large group but the customer preference for an ease filled travel becomes more significant. Smart IoT products can collects customer preferences regarding this and can intimate us with what differentiates the travel options and what does not. Apart from passenger's contentment, the differentiation also focuses on various stakeholders or can also go more than that, targeting the environmental factors. Heathrow Airport is one such example.

Their main concern is to reduce the nitrogen dioxide levels in the surrounding in order to improve the quality of air locally. They analyzed that the problems were due to the airlines that were parked near the gates using auxiliary power unit (APU) instead of plugging into the power grid and solved this issue by using microphones to check the sounds of a running APU and then by comparing with the schedule of the airline it reminds the airline regarding when it need to plug-in onto the power grid instead of using an APU, thereby saving money and improving the quality of air locally.

8.10.5   New Revenue

Nowadays, the latest advancements in IoT can generate high revenue sources. This is accomplished generally by creating new products and user-friendly services for the customers. Improvising the pre-existing solutions with the help of IoT not only simplifies the deployment process but is also recognized by lot of market stake holders [17]. However, this revenue generation requires a large group of stakeholders and thus considered to be an arduous task. In spite of the fact that implementing new revenue techniques are considered to be hard, it is not completely impossible to deploy.

One airport to prove this right simply used WIFI APs (Access Points) as sensors to collect distances and frequencies of the traveler's movement. Hence, by identifying the places travelers visit more often they placed advertisements at those frequent points and the advertisements reached the travelers at a pretty good level when compared to the other airports, thereby increasing the operator's landside revenue.

8.11   Present and Future Scopes

IoT has special objectives in using sensor communications in internal management and costumer services, as follows:

8.11.1   Improving Passenger Experience

Temperature sensors are installed across the cabins to predict and control the climate around. Similarly, costumers are provided with a well-organized flow of data to guide through the entire airport processes.

8.11.2   Safety

Varied constituents of aircrafts possess different sectors that are interconnected with each other, with the central system and mainly to the ground phases. This helps them to attain more security and process real-time diagnosis, offering value to both industry and the costumer. Example: Boeing 787 fleet follows the same.

8.11.3   Management of Goods and Luggage

RFID labels are applied by Delta airlines to properly track luggage in their destinations [18]. Shipping industry also uses them to track their commodities. Adding to it, tracked data can be monitored by the users via their smart phones also.

8.11.4   Saving

Optimizing the fuel consumption along with taking an effective route results in lower expenditures, thereby increasing the profits. These features are already implemented by Air Asia which is predicted to save 30–50 million dollars over five years.

8.12   Conclusion

The application of IoT has just come to light in the sectors of aviation industry. These evolving automations possess greater abilities in transforming different units in airlines like predictive maintenance, revenue management, and scheduling to provide excellent costumer experience. Thus, in the forthcoming years, as the needs increase, the deployment of emerging technology will be executed in a much-accelerated approach. IoT overall aims to fulfill all the requirements that airline needs today. The significance of IoT applications in aviation industries is envisaged to create a benchmark by transforming it into a super-cognitive sector in the future digital world.

References

1. Martin Bugaj, D., Aircraft Maintenance- New Trends in General Aviation. *Technol. Manag. Traffic*, 17, 231–234, 2005.

2. Pate, J. and Adebola, T., AMELIA: An application of the Internet of Things for aviation safety. *15th IEEE Annual Consumer Communications & Networking Conference (CCNC)*, 2018.
3. Gupta, N., Sengupta, S., Naik, V., A Firewall for Internet of Things. *9th International Conference on Communication Systems and Networks (COMSNETS)*, pp. 411–412, 2017.
4. Masutti, A. and Fernandez, I.O., ECJ on Contractual Protection for Airlines' Online Databases. *Aviat. Space J.*, 7, 35–37, 2015.
5. Paterson, A.C., Safety Data Collection, Analysis and Exchange. *Aviation J. Channel Islands*, 9, 13, 2017.
6. Clay, *The Paper vs Electronic Flight Logbook Showdown*, 2017, February 22, Retrieved from Clayviation: http://clayviation.com/2017/02/22/paper-vs-electronic-flight-logbook/.
7. Cain, A., *Introduction ToPhp/Mysql I*, 2011, May, Retrieved from Slide Player: https://slideplayer.com/slide/6295191/.
8. Watt, A., *Chapter 13 Database Development Process*, n.d, Retrieved from BC Open Textbooks: https://opentextbc.ca/dbdesign01/chapter/chapter-13-databasedevelopment-process/.
9. Shankar, P.S., *Streaming My SQL tables in real-time to Kafka*, 2016, August 1, Retrieved from yelp Engineering: https://engineeringblog.yelp.com/2016/08/streaming-mysql-tables-inreal-time-to-kafka.html.
10. Airbus, *Getting to Grips with MMEL & MEL*, Blagnac, France, 2005, August.
11. Schofield, J., From Pdf Files to Excel Spreadsheets, 2010, February 15, Retrieved from The Guardian: https://www.theguardian.com/technology/askjack/2010/feb/15/convertpdf-to-excel.
12. Safi, M., Chung, J., Pradhan, P., Review of augmented reality in aerospace industry. *Aircr. Eng. Aerosp. Technol.*, 14, 2019.
13. Singh, A., Meshram, S., Gujar, T., Wankhede, P.R., Baggage tracing and handling system using RFID and IoT for airports, in: *2016 International Conference on Computing, Analytics and Security Trends (CAST)*, IEEE, pp. 466–470, 2016, December.
14. Novo, O., Blockchain meets IoT: architecture for scalable access management in IoT. *IEEE Internet Things J.*, 5, 2, 1184–1195, 2018.
15. Nor, S.N.M.Y., Jamil, B., Wan, E.W.R., Service Quality towards Customer Loyalty in Malaysia's domestic Low-Cost Airline Services. *Int. J. e-Educ., e-Bus., e-Manag. e-Learn.*, 3, 4, 2013.
16. Aruna, R., Nisha, J., Smart Airport: A Review on Future of the Airport Operation. *Glob. J. Manag. Bus. Res.: Adm. Manag.*, 20, 3, 2249–4588, 2020.
17. Samia, B., Abdelkader, B., Wassila, G., Smart airport: an IoT-based Airport Management System. *ICFNDS*, 19, 20, 2017.
18. Yu-Hern, C. and Chung-Hsing, Y., A survey analysis of service quality for domestic airlines. *Eur. J. Oper. Res.*, 139, 166–177, 2002.

9

IoT-Based Water Management System for a Healthy Life

N. Meenakshi[1]*, V. Pandimurugan[2] and S. Rajasoundaran[2]

[1]Department of Information Technology, Hindustan Institute of Technology and Science, Chennai, India
[2]School of Computing Science & Engineering, VIT Bhopal University, Madhya Pradesh, India

Abstract

Water is a fundamental asset forever, and its administration is a central point of contention these days. Quality of water is important to live a healthy life and make the strong community against the communicable disease prevention and precaution of the water spread diseases. Drinking water could be horribly valuable for all individuals as water utilities face more difficulties. These difficulties emerge because of high populace, less water assets, and so on. Thus, various techniques are utilized to screen in the constant water quality. To ensure that protected dispersion of water is done, it ought to be observed progressively for new methodology in IoT-based water quality has been anticipated. In the contemporary world, Water contamination is one of the key reasons for various assortments of water-borne illnesses like dengue fever, plague cholera, and numerous diseases. For individuals, 43% of passing in the whole world is brought about by water contaminations. Thus, the nature of the drinking water is investigated continuously using Internet of Things (IoT) [14]. The IoT applications utilizing sensors for sewer and storm water observing across arranged scenes, water quality evaluation, treatment, what is more, feasible administration is presented. The investigations of rate impediments in biophysical and geochemical measures that help the biological system administrations related to water quality are introduced. The utilizations of IoT arrangements dependent on these disclosures are additionally examined.

Corresponding author: nmeenakshi@hindustanuniv.ac.in

R. Anandan, Suseendran Gopalakrishnan, Souvik Pal and Noor Zaman (eds.) The Industrial Internet of Things (IIoT): Intelligent Analytics for Predictive Maintenance, (229–248) © 2022 Scrivener Publishing LLC

Keywords: Deforestation, IoT, water sensor, reservoirs, quality metrics, data analysis

9.1   Introduction

Life, as we are aware, could not exist without fresh water. Water gives oil for living cells, the very structure squares of life. Water circulates through living creatures, moving materials, for example, supplements to our organs, encouraging the synthetic responses that drive life's capacities, and eliminating waste materials [5]. Water performs comparative capacities for whole biological systems as it accomplishes for person creatures. It circles far and wide, moving supplements and building materials to environments, encouraging the substance correspondence between biological systems, and also purifying biological systems so they can keep up ideal execution. In addition, the solid arrangement of great water for human employments relies upon the sound working of environments, especially freshwater biological systems. Water and rock appear and transform into different structures as an element of the sceptical material science of the Universe.

9.1.1   Human Activities as a Source of Pollutants

The survival of water is important for human as well as all living things in the earth. How the water is polluted and spoiled in the natural as well as artificial, however artificially means 90% of the pollutants by humans and remaining may be some other living things. Naturally, how the water is polluted by means of broken trees, animal, mammal, and other living things life cycle, it is polluted 10%. Rapid population and industry development are the main sources of water pollutants. Human population is the main reason of water pollutant in the earth, because they put all the wasted and unused things in the river, pond, well, etc.

- In 2015, Chennai flooded reason also due to occupying the pond and blocked the small reservoirs, stream by the humans, they build the houses and industries, etc., we wasted the natural water source like rain water, and it is not maintained properly. Due to improper maintained of the resources, we suffered drinking water especially quality water not only humans and other living things also suffered due to lack of water.

- Improper infrastructure and lack of knowledge about the water spreading disease, many of them not to worry about the water resource and it proper planning management. Because of that, containment of water and its quality is spoiled.
- Deforestation is also the important factor for climate change and water resource lagging reasons [16]. Due to cutting tree, going for artificial, the nature nowadays show the impact to the humans like heavy rain, flood, sunny, and no drinking water.
- The impenetrable surfaces in metropolitan and mechanical territories are another factor that impacts the quality and amount of water. These surfaces are commonly covered with impervious black-top or solid materials [22]. These additionally cause disturbances characteristic hydrology and causation of expanding top stream and flooding. Appropriately, the turbidity and supplements are affected which bring about an expansion in residue and toxins which lessen supplement cycling.

9.2   Water Management Using IoT

IoT in water treatment utilizes the idea of reasonable sensors put in at various focuses inside the water framework. These sensors gather data and send it back to the perception frameworks. This information may incorporate, water quality, temperature changes, pressure changes, water spill location, and synthetic break discovery. In the Figure 9.1 shows the water quality

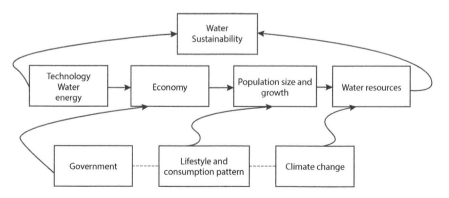

Figure 9.1 Water quality factors.

factors and main structure, IoT in water treatment lies a dependable correspondence innovation that is acclimated send information from actual articles over a remote channel to a PC with shrewd investigating programming. Cell phones and tablets will have applications that interface with the cloud or be incorporated with an EAM CMMS framework to get to the IoT detecting component information continuously [2]. This innovation can encourage experts, designers, and elective office the board labourers to ask experiences where they are or places designs ordinarily cannot reach.

An IoT-empowered reasonable water sensor can follow quality, weight, and temperature of water. Indeed, a sensor goal can live fluid stream and may be used by a water service organization to follow the stream over the whole treatment plant. This could even be a convenient instrument to incorporate with an EAM CMMS subsequently you will follow all the information for the plant in one clear arrangement. Specialists would then be able to get to this information, decipher the information, and make recommendations and ship off the force supervisor. IoT can even play an occupation in break location and send an on the spot receptive to a distant dashboard. These notices are prompt any place as though an architect needed to look at the sum by hand or by walking it could take hours for a retardant to be recognized. IoT has a few edges and can expand the efficiency of staff, keep them out of danger, and decrease supererogatory costs for office the executives.

9.2.1   Water Quality Management Based on IoT Framework

Water pollution is a serious social problem that affects all living beings including human community. Due to the gradual development of industrial wastages and the development of population rate, water scarcity and water pollutions are increasing uncontrollably. Water pollution means that the consumable water contains harmful minerals and chemicals. The polluted water creates lot of medical illnesses to animals and human beings. This cause either immediate or long term serious health issues of the living being those who consume the polluted water. Water pollution spreads around various water resources such as rivers, reservoirs, and ground water [1]. In this situation, finding the quality water and managing the water quality for the healthy life is really important.

Technology gives various solutions to for water purity issues. There are several techniques as given below.

- Water Thermal Testing
- Water pH Level Testing

- Water Chloride Testing
- Materials and Metal Consolidation Testing
- Other Mineral Testing

Mostly, these testing methodologies are executed in various chemical and testing laboratories. In this case, this testing setup requires more development costs and space. To make this testing simple, recent researchers are using Internet of Things (IoT) technology and efficient sensor units [11].

IoT is an emerging technology that is applied and experimented through various applications and platforms. IoT architecture and the internal functions are easily customized for supporting resource management systems, industrial control systems, home automation systems, intelligent transportation systems, public support systems, and other systems. The main benefit of using IoT platform for water quality management system is reducing the man power, development cost, and experiment time.

This chapter discusses the effective way of water quality management system with the help of IoT facilities and devices.

9.3   IoT Characteristics and Measurement Parameters

IoT is a term indicates the inter connection of more than one heterogeneous physical components such as computing devices (processors), hardware units like sensors, relays, software modules, and any internet elements. This kind of IoT is considered as completely heterogeneous networks with multiple functionalities. IoT framework has been designed and developed based on the solutions we need for real-time problems.

This chapter needs an efficient solution for finding the quality of various water samples collected from different residential places. This effort helps the people to consume good quality water in future days [8]. At the same time, the IoT-based water quality management system can be implemented at any house itself. Therefore, the water consumers are able to check their water quality daily to take care of their health. This IoT framework saves the individuals from suffering with water related diseases.

Water contains many minerals or chemicals. In addition, water has several types of characteristics such as tastiness, appearance (color), odor, and the ingredients with it. Based on the characteristics, a few water types are consumable directly for daily life. Water cannot be identified in completely pure state but it contains more chemical and biological substances. Among these substances, a few are not harmful for health but others are toxic to living beings.

Water is collected from various resource units. All water resources are gradually polluted due to sewage water, dusts, and other industrial junks. Pollution control authorities use various water quality measurement techniques as follow.

- Physical measurement validations
- Chemical quantity validations
- Bio measurement validations

Among these techniques, physical test reveals the sensed contents of water sample collected from particular resource. It delivers the physically observed water characteristics such as color, odor, temperature, conductivity, and dissolved substances. Particularly, physical testing or any other water quality monitoring technique needs valid sample measurement threshold values for checking the quality of water [12].

Chemical test reveals the water contaminants such as pH levels, potassium, sodium, chlorine, and other chemical contents that affect the quality of water. In the same manner, biological particles are identified using various bio-instruments. However, most of the tests are conducted at specialized scientific labs. This kind of water substance analysis is useful for giving suggestions to improve the water quality. At the same time, IoT devices such as sensor and other water quality detecting devices help the common people to ensure the quality of daily water.

IoT elements and the architecture can be designed with appropriate functions that to be activated with in the computation devices (processors). The following devices and sensors are advised to create IoT-based water quality management system.

- Processor or controller units
- Water quality measuring sensors
- Relays and indicators
- Power units
- Quality fixing algorithms
- Reports and analytical results

This IoT system uses to create sequence of water substance measurements in daily basis. This helps to detect the water quality improvement or degradation.

Figure 9.2 illustrates the standard framework of IoT-based water quality management system. In this framework, tiny processor or controller units, power sources and water quality sensor modules are incorporated [15]. These sensors are developed by various manufacturers such as Yosemite, Myron, Aquas, Van Walt, and others. In the same way, IoT-based

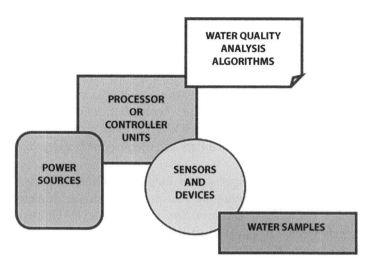

Figure 9.2 Water quality management framework.

prototypes are mainly developed using notable hardware units like, Arduino, Raspberry Pi, NodeMCU, and other platforms.

In the scenario, various water samples are taken for quality measurements. These samples are evaluated with the help of quality analysis algorithms or data analysis algorithms. Each water sample has its unique chemical and physical characteristics. The sensors used in IoT architecture extracts the quality measurements of different water samples that are collected from multiple water resources.

Water quality sensors, hardware platforms, and the technical specifications are described with proper comparison. This analysis helps to build efficient water quality management system [17].

The water quality management systems are expected to produce minimal errors in the detection of water quality characteristics at any cost. This is attained with the help of necessary evaluation procedures and the suitable sensors. In addition, the water quality evaluation algorithms give more accurate results than manual predictions. These computations are carried out in the IoT processor units or controller units. In IoT platform, both microcontrollers and microprocessor are frequently used based on the hardware requirements.

9.4   Platforms and Configurations

Arduino is a free and license-free platform for developing IoT environments used to create any applications. Arduino has many controller versions and programming packages that are useful for various device management activities such as sensor readings, actuators' output manipulation, generic input management, generic observation management, and supporting for project oriented library packages [4]. A real-time water quality management system can be developed using the Arduino hardware and software packages. Arduino hardware modules (controller) are enabled with many General Purpose Input and Output (GPIO) pins for managing I/O activities. At the same time, tiny controllers and memory units are giving sensor data manipulation facilities.

Table 9.1 gives the comparison of various Arduino versions and the characteristics. There are multiple Arduino versions are available other than these versions such as micro, flora, and menta [1]. However, these denoted versions are mostly suggested by many IoT developers.

In each version, different board types are released with notable features for supporting various IoT applications. Analyzing the needs for water quality measurements and data validations, Arduino Due shall be identified for handling multiple sensor data inputs. At the same time, Arduino helps to develop tiny prototypes with limited constraints [21]. In this case, the other IoT platform provides more vibrant water quality management solutions with inbuilt processor units and Linux-based operating system

Table 9.1 Arduino specifications.

Arduino board	Adaptability	Configurations
Arduino Uno	Moderate prototype development and applications	Controller-ATMega-328- 8 Bit AVR, 5V, 16MHz, 32KB, 14 Pins I/O
Arduino Mega	Highly active IoT environment and more data handlings	Controller-ATMega-2560- 8 Bit AVR, 5V, 16MHz, 256KB, 54 Pins I/O
Arduino Due	Very high processing and memory capabilities. Support for analog and digital applications	Controller-ARM-SAM-8 Bit, 3.3V, 16MHz, 512KB, 54 Pins I/O
Wi-Fi and other shield compatibilities are varying for different versions		

services. These hardware and software solutions are provided by Raspberry Pi modules.

Raspberry Pi boards and inbuilt applications are more flexible and faster than any Arduino boards. In this comparison, Raspberry Pi boards are equipped with multiple processor cores and efficient memory modules. In addition, they are having Linux-based Raspbian operating system services. These board editions are more suitable for real-time sensor data analysis processes than Arduino-based microcontrollers.

Generally, Arduino controllers are used to develop project prototypes rather than real implementations. For implementing IoT-based water quality management system, the need for more memory and high processor speed is inevitable at any cost. In this regard, various Raspbian operating system versions and board models are invented. Most of the Raspberry Pi boards offer more sophisticated software environments for installing additional package. This kind of facility helps to build sensor dependent data analysis programs and algorithms inside the IoT computation units (processors).

In addition, Raspbian operating system supports for program interface and hardware interface operations. In this environment, water quality measurement sensors can be installed and operated easily.

Comparably, Raspbian Pi is highly proficient to handle real-time sensor events and process the events with the help of preconfigured data analysis algorithms. In addition, most of the Raspbian Pi modules are enabled with camera input slots that are helpful to detect water qualities based on image analysis (physical test). At the same time, these modules are having more resilient transmitter blocks for transferring the water quality results from one place to another place. This helps to implement remote quality monitoring tasks.

According to these hardware and software environments, water quality sensors are identified to detect the water particles and the physical conditions. In the same way, chemical qualities can be detected with the help of appropriate sensor units [23].

Water quality sensors are manufactured by multiple companies and they are marketed by various shops (online and offline) [3]. Table 9.2 gives the details of Raspberry Pi and Arduino specifications for water quality sensors. For example, the following sensors are needed to generate daily data on successful water quality observations. The appropriate sensor values help to extract the correct water contents and characteristics. This work advises for implementing intelligent algorithms (Machine Learning and Deep Learning) for classifying accurate water characteristics based on physical, chemical and biological measurements. In this regard, the sensors need to be selected and planted on input pins of processor units.

Table 9.2 Raspberry Pi and Arduino.

Specifications	Raspberry Pi Model 2-B	Raspberry Pi Model 2-B+	Raspberry Pi Model 3-B	Arduino due
Processor	Broadcom BCM-2836	Broadcom-BCM-2835	Quad-BCM-2837	ARM-SAM
Number of Cores	4	1	4	1
RAM	1 GB	512 MB	1 GB	512 KB
I/O	40 Pins	40 Pins	40 Pins	54 Pins
Clock Speed	900 MHz	700 MHz	1.2 GHz	16 MHz
Operating System	Linux Distributed Editions	Linux Distributed Editions	Linux Distributed Editions	None
Company	R-Pi Foundation			Arduino LLC

9.5   Water Quality Measuring Sensors and Data Analysis

Many sensor manufacturing companies are available to produce different types of water quality measurement sensors that are adaptable to IoT environment. However, the following sensors are identified to provide multidimensional data from integrated sensor equipment.

Aqua-400 Probe (Six in One)

- Water conductivity, resistivity, liquefied solids, and actual salinity
- Total rate of disbanded oxygen content
- Rate of oxidation reduction potentiality
- Range of pH
- Water temperature (Fahrenheit and Celsius)
- Water pressure/level

Aqua-400 Probe is a kind of multi-sensor panel that can be inserted into any water type. This holds totally six sensors used to measure physical qualities and chemical qualities as listed above. This sensor unit has active and inactive modes of operations with accessories such as cables and user interface tools. In this units, sensor replacement slots are available that are covered by stainless steel planes. The water quality sensors shall be permanent or plug-in type. The later one is more reliable to deal with more frequent water quality measurement analysis tasks. For connecting purpose, this sensor unit has RS-232 and Modbus components are provided. In addition, this module gives 36V (Variable DC) power source. This kind of sensor units is really reactive and cost effective to check the quality of any type of water that is collected from various resources.

In the same way, the extensible version of aqua quality sensor is aqua 500 model. This sensor unit has multiple sensors to check both physical and chemical characteristics of water. At the same time, this has mobile application supported software and telemetry unit to transmit the sensor data to various locations. This sensor unit support for remote monitoring processes that is more reliable than on location monitoring tasks. Even though these sensor units help to measure the quality of water contents, there is need to improve the quality of results [7]. Nowadays, ML and DL techniques are widely used in decision making systems that are implemented for various applications.

This chapter suggests for the development for supervised and unsupervised classification techniques for analyzing the continuously producing water quality measurements. These ML and DL techniques increase the accuracy rate of water quality-based sensor data. There are notable techniques such as Support Vector Machine (SVM), Random Forest (RF), Deep Neural Networks (DNN), Recurrent Neural Networks (RNN), and other techniques [9]. These techniques are usable for analyzing the sensor data with trained datasets (standard water quality measurements). This produces home-based intelligent IoT-based water quality management systems that can be used by anyone. The basic block diagram of Intelligent IoT system for checking the quality of water contents is given below in Figure 9.3.

This kind of extensive data analysis algorithms is implemented and can be imported in to any IoT processors, controllers, or operating system services. This ML approaches minimizes the quality detection error rates that are happen due to manual analysis [18].

Water quality measurement frameworks are developed using various architectures and multiple components [6]. Among the various frameworks, IoT-based water quality analysis model gives more simple and effective real-time solutions. This model can be updated and modified using various water quality sensors and integrated sensor units. In addition, the IoT environment is supporting for both software components and hardware-based assistance. In this regard, ML and DL techniques are encouraged to analyse the real timer water sensor data patterns.

The analysis on these values provides flawless water quality ratings compared to any other manual techniques. In addition, these analyzed results can be processed for providing more statistical range of water quality databases. This helps for any person or any government that needs for improving water quality ratings [10]. This continuous practice supports for healthy life of any living beings getting water from various resources.

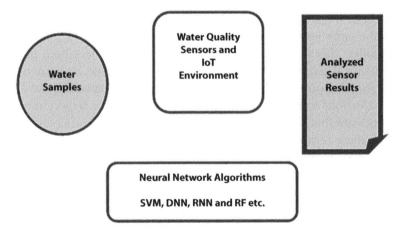

Figure 9.3 Intelligent IoT-based water quality management framework.

9.6   Wastewater and Storm Water Monitoring Using IoT

9.6.1   System Initialization

It is assessed that by 2028 practically 40% of the metropolitan populace will live in water-focused on regions as this valuable ware is turning out to be scant quickly [19]. Along these lines, IoT shrewd water the executive's arrangements are must to keep away from a pre-foreseen water emergency.

Till now, the water business was fundamentally relied distinctly upon Supervisory Control and Data Acquisition (SCADA) framework which could not screen the whole water conveyance framework because of the handy restriction of its establishment focuses [22].

Smart system, an End-to-End IoT arrangement, guarantees improved brilliant water the executives through IoT water sensors which are introduced at different areas in the IoT water framework to detect any spillage or different glitches.

Smart system as of now has pre-designed total IoT Business Solution for water industry which can be executed for different business cases in weeks rather than months.

The IoT savvy water the board strategies can lessen water cost by up to 20%, bringing about better incomes with lower costs. IoT shrewd water the executive's framework likewise gives occasions to regions to diminish operational expenses around development, support, and that is only the tip of the iceberg. Smart system out of the case arrangement coordinates with in excess of 150 water sensors including keen water meter, shrewd water system regulator, IoT water stream meters, and IoT water valve.

9.6.2   Capture and Storage of Information

Water quality data is acquired by sensors and collected by IoT devices. The IoT devices add spatial and temporal information to the data. The information is transmitted to the message broker using the thing Send operation.

9.6.3   Information Modeling

For the storm water and wastewater management, the city and urban areas are properly maintained and well-designed water flow structure to be followed. In the city limit wastewater are collected and it should be reprocessing and reusable in the different ways [13]. If city have good control and, maintaining system for the wastewater flow and drainage system means there is no way to contiguous spreading disease to water. Figure 9.4 illustrates information modeling of smart wastewater management.

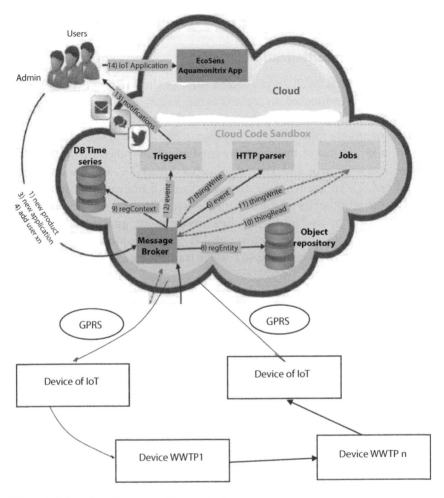

Figure 9.4 Smart wastewater quality monitoring system.

- Most of the cities do not have strong water flow, monitoring system to maintain a good water reservoir in the earth. Due to that, many of the natural resources are wasted and so much water to be polluted unknowingly.
- In the information modeling, we can place sensors to be the monitoring device to control the wastewater and storm water decentralized. Many places plotting sensor and getting information building infrastructure is very tricky task for to maintain the quality and monitoring the water resource.
- In the system consist of many databases like DB time series, object repository, and message database. How it is connected

to the HTTP server via some events like think write, think even, and triggers based on the signal passed through it. RegEntity is connected between the object repository and message broker of the system [16]. N number of devices we can connect through the GPRS signal and it will have passed through the wireless sensor.

- The various contaminants like chloromethane, trichloroethylene, Tetrachloroethylene, and dichloromethane are more important of the water particles and if it is affected by the pollutants then it will become as unusable stage.

- The path loss analysis is also important for water management using IoT, and it will be calculated by the mathematical term like propagation medium of layer, free space loss, and dispersion of supress layers of the soil [20].

- The model may have evaluated by the thickness of the soil layer, asphalt layer, frequency, noise floor, soil moisture, and asphalt temperature.

9.6.4   Visualization and Management of the Information

The information and result are displayed in many forms of images and graph representation for the water management system. Here, we may use the interface consists of web service and protocols to pass the information authentically and secularly [9]. The various inputs from the water sensors it will communicate to the data repository and also have alert message if any mishap happened in the containment level of water supply. Web of Things enables the water business to arrive at all the recorded targets. Besides, on account of IoT, we idea of Internet of Water arises. It infers associating all the frameworks and major parts in the water gracefully chain—crude water, treatment plants, conveyance pipes, service organizations, organizations and customers, and so forth—and enabling chiefs with significant experiences on the condition of water assets and gear utilized in this area [25].

Relatively few advances can beat IoT in the water enterprises because of its sufficient chances and wide application. For instance, IoT empowers the following:

- Straightforwardness to the cycles in the water flexibly chain.
- Ongoing checking and the capacity to promptly address recognized issues.

- Mechanization and increase of human force.
- Economical practices on account of decreased waste.
- Forward-arranging water protection procedure dependent on information investigation and expectation calculations.

9.7   Sensing and Sampling of Water Treatment Using IoT

As of late, perhaps the greatest test confronting mankind is guaranteeing an adequate flexibly of value water. From food creation to living space rebuilding, drinking water to sterilization, clean water is the most searched after resource of the human populace. Table 9.3 shows the different sensors and it company for maintaining the water quality.

Table 9.3 Water sensors.

ABB	Eureka environmental engineering	Mena water
ADS Environmental Service	Eutech*	Meter Master
Advanced Measurements & Controls	GE	METTLER TOLEDO
Anacon	Georg Fischer	Multitrode
Analytical Sensors & Instruments Ltd	Global Water Instrumentation, Inc.	Oakton Instruments
Analytical Technology	Hach	OI Analytical
AquaMetrix	Hanna Instruments	Omega Engineering, Inc.
Arjay Engineering	HF Scientific	Process Instruments (Pi)
ASA Analytics	Honeywell	ProViro Instrumentation

(*Continued*)

Table 9.3 Water sensors. (*Continued*)

ABB	Eureka environmental engineering	Mena water
Banner Engineering	Horiba	Real Tech
BeLink	Icx Technologies (FLIR)	RMS Water Treatment
Cambell Scientific	In USA Inc.	Rosemount*
Chemical Injection Technologies, Inc. (Superior)	Inficon	Scan Measurement Systems
Cole-Parmer	Innovative Components	Severn Trent Services
Control Micro Systems	Innovative Waters	Siemens
Datalink Instruments	*In-Situ* Inc	Stedham Electronics
DEVAR Inc.	Invensys	Stevens Water Monitoring Systems, Inc
EMEC Liquid Control Systems	Itron	Thermo Scientific
Emerson	ITT Water and Wastewater	Vega Controls
Endress + Hauser	JMAR	Wedgewood Analytical
Entech Design	Keco Engineered Controls	YSI

The blast of our populace as of late has squeezed this significant resource. Adequate, top notch water is basic for human, creature, vegetal, and financial life, and observing water is the initial step to overseeing it. The different contaminants in need of sensing are shown in Figure 9.5.

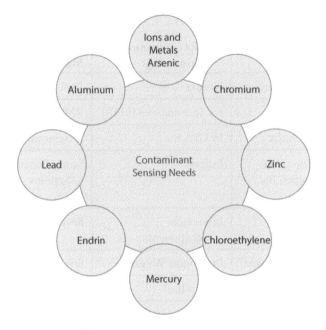

Figure 9.5 Containments of sensing in water.

References

1. Casanova, J., Devau, N., Pettenati, M., Managed aquifer recharge: An overview of issues and options, in: *Integrated groundwater management*, Springer, Cham, 2016.
2. Catarci, T., Dix, A., Kimani, S., Santucci, G., User-centered data management. *Synth. Lect. Data Manag.*, 2, 1, 1–106, 2010.
3. Chen, J., Broussard, W.P., Borrok, D.M., Speyrer, F.B., A GIS-based frameworkto identify opportunities to use surface water to offset groundwater withdrawals. *Water Resour. Manag.*, 10, 1–11, 2019.
4. Cromwell, J. and McGuckin, R., Implications of climate change for adaptation by wastewater and stormwater agencies. *Proc. Water Environ. Fed.*, 2010, 15, 1887–1915, 2010.
5. DeZellar, J. and Maier, W., Effects of water conservation on sanitary sewers and wastewater treatment plants. *J. Water Pollution Control Fed.*, 52, 1, 76–88, 1980.
6. Dhasmana, A., Uniyal, S., Kumar, V., Gupta, S., Kesari, K.K., Haque, S. *et al.*, Scope of nanoparticles in environmental toxicant remediation, in: *Environmental Biotechnology: For Sustainable Future*, pp. 31–44, Springer, Berlin, 2019.

7. Dong, X., Vuran, M.C., Irmak, S., Autonomous precision agriculture through integration of wireless underground sensor networks with center pivot irrigation systems. *AdHoc Netw.*, 11, 7, 1975–1987, 2013. https://doi.org/10.1016/j.adhoc.2012.06.012.

8. Li, S., Xu, L., Wang, X., Wang, J., Integration of Hybrid Wireless Networks in Cloud Services Oriented Enterprise Information Systems, *Enterp. Inf. Syst.*, 6, 2, 165–187, 2012.

9. Heinzelman, W.R., Kulik, J., Balakrishnan, H., Adaptive protocols for information dissemination in wireless sensor networks. *Proceedings of the 5th annual ACM/IEEE international conference on Mobile computing and networking*, pp. 174–185, 1999.

10. Sharma, H. and Sharma, S., A Review of Sensor Networks: Technologies and Applications. *Recent Advances in, Engineering and Computational Sciences (RAECS)*, pp. 1–4, 2014.

11. Godavarthi, B. and Nalajala, P., Design and Implementation of Vehicle Navigation System in Urban Environments using Internet of Things (IoT). *IOP Conf. Series: Materials Science and Engineering*, vol. 225, 2017.

12. Jing, M., The Design of Wireless Remote Monitoring System of Water Supply Based on GPRS. *International Symposium on Computer Science and Society (ISCCS)*, pp. 29–31, 2011.

13. Purohit, A. and Gokhale, U., Real Time Water Quality Measurement System based on GSM. *IOSR J. Electron. Commun. Eng.*, 9, 3, 63–67, 2014.

14. Chen, S., Xu, H., Liu, D., Hu, B., Wang, H., A vision of IoT: Applications, challenges, and opportunities with china perspective. *IEEE Internet Things J.*, 1, 4, 349–359, 2014, [8] Nalajala, P., Godavarth, B., Lakshmi, Raviteja, M., Simhadri, D., [15] Morse code Generator Using Microcontroller with Alphanumeric Keypad. *International Conference on Electrical, Electronics, and Optimization Techniques*, pp. 762–766, 2016.

15. Backer, L. and Moore, S., Harmful algal blooms: future threats in a warmer world, in: *Environmental pollution and its relation to climate change*, A. Nemr (Ed.), 4, pp. 485–512, 2010.

16. Bakker, K., Water security: research challenges and opportunities. *Science*, 337, 6097, 914–915, 2012.

17. Balci, P. and Cohn, A., NYC wastewater resiliency plan: Climate risk assessment andadaptation, in: *ICSI 2014: Creating infrastructure for a sustainable world*, pp. 246–256, 2014.

18. Bellar, T.A., Lichtenberg, J.J., Kroner, R.C., The occurrence of organohalides inchlorinated drinking waters. *J.-Am. Water Works Assoc.*, 66, 12, 703–706, 1974.

19. Benskin, J.P., Li, B., Ikonomou, M.G., Grace, J.R., Li, L.Y., Per- and polyfluoroalkylsubstances in landfill leachate: patterns, time trends, and sources. *Environ. Sci.Technol.*, 46, 21, 11532–11540, 2012.

20. Bogena, H.R., Herbst, M., Huisman, J.A., Rosenbaum, U., Weuthen, A., Vereecken, H., Potential of wireless sensor networks for measuring soil water content variability. *Vadose Zone J.*, 9, 4, 1002–1013, 2010.

21. Bredehoeft, J., Monitoring regional groundwater extraction: The problem. *Groundwater*, 49, 6, 808–814, 2011.

22. Menzel, L., Globale Entwicklung—Wasser als limitierender Entwicklungs-faktor, in: *Wasser—Grundlage des Lebens. Hydrologiefür eine Welt im Wandel*, G. Strigel, A.D.E. von Eschenbach, U. Barjenbruch (Eds.), pp. 82–88, Schweizerbart, Stuttgart, 2010.

23. Menzel, L. and Matovelle, A., Current state and future development of blue water availability and blue water demand: a view at seven case studies. *J. Hydrol.*, 384, 245–263, 2010.

24. Michelsen, G., Bildung für nachhaltige Entwicklung. Meilensteine auf einem langenWeg, in: *Berufliche Bildung für nachhaltiges Wirtschaften.Konzepte—Curricula—Methoden—Beispiele*, E. Tiemeyer and K. Wilbers (Eds.), pp. 17–32, Bertelsmann, Bielefeld, 2006.

25. Salganik, L.H. (Ed.), *Key competencies for a successful life and well-functioning society*, pp. 63–107, Hogrefe, Cambridge, 2009.

10

Fuel Cost Optimization Using IoT in Air Travel

**P. Kalaichelvi[1]*, V. Akila[2], J. Ranjani[1],
S. Sowmiya[1] and C. Divya**

[1]Sri Sairam Engineering College, Chennai, India
[2]Gokaraju Rangaraju Institute of Engineering and Technology, Hyderabad, India

Abstract

Numerous hot research topics in airline industries such as optimal aircrafts speeds, increasing flight engine efficiencies, weather forecasting for finding optimal flight route, and cost optimization in fuel consumption and in reduction of flight weight by means of cutting edge design, reducing baggage weight, and so on, where airline industries are using Internet of Things (IoT) technology effectively to eliminate the safety, security issues. To diminish the engine weight, a system with a gearbox, or some other shaft speed decrease device, is proposed. Main goals of this paper were to bring the concepts that would be able to increase the efficiency, to track the baggage, cost-effective controlling management, and to optimize the fuel consumption. The fuel consumptions in base line circumstances are appraised to analyze the variable impacts on fuel consumption. Hence, the research topic on air traffic management should take decisions on the eventual field test by reducing the validation of time and cost of the luggage checking methods.

Thus, we focus on cost reduction and fuel optimization by using IoT. Despite a projected increase in air travel in 2030 by a factor of 2.50, the emissions in 2030 are expected to rise only 125% of the 2005 level. We have proposed a method to determine that airline fuel consumption can be reduced by 38% and cost management of aviation and for passenger's satisfaction.

Keywords: Internet of Things (IoT), baggage, luggage, gearbox, cost optimization

*Corresponding author: kalai.it@sairam.edu.in

R. Anandan, Suseendran Gopalakrishnan, Souvik Pal and Noor Zaman (eds.) The Industrial Internet of Things (IIoT): Intelligent Analytics for Predictive Maintenance, (249–280) © 2022 Scrivener Publishing LLC

10.1   Introduction

The airline industries manage its multi-dimensional operations continuously by depending on IoT technology. The usage of IoT in aeronautics has taken the air industry to new elevations. It is monitoring the aircraft location and fuel consumption and checking safety parameters remotely. The implementation of Internet of Things (IoT) in aviation will frame a intercommunicate digital structure with interacting procedure for the industries that leads up to auto control and auto air vehicle by that way stakeholders could achieve their profits in the competitive world. IoT permits to condense or eradicate the greatest communal grievances in the industry. It has the ability to enhance reliability, quality, customer satisfaction, and fuel effectiveness in an industry that is predicted to rise extensively in the coming years. Basically, IoT is an integrated system consisting of autonomous sensor devices with communicating facility via internet connection to work altogether. The communications among the physical objects are associated to the internet over network devices or routers and conversation data.

The role of IoT in aviation is maintenance and efficiency. It permits objects to be precise across prevailing network infrastructure. The methods for fuel reducing is to improve engine efficiency, varying maintenance and operation practices, and enlightening weight management.

10.1.1   Introduction to IoT

As a ubiquitous framework, the IoT is the outcome of evolution in insolent networks. Sensors nodes and peripheral devices interconnect via wireless sensor network (WSN) via internetwork connection and collaboratively yield value added services in IoT. Any devices can be connected to the other and they achieve automation in respective fields yielding services. The WSN nodes are resource restricted in the usage of energy. This is because of minimal battery power in WSN nodes. This constraint has led to low memory, communication, and computation capability in WSN [4, 5].

10.1.2   Processing IoT Data

The data obtained from the connected IoT device is massive in amount and the obtained data need to be pre-processed before the data is analyzed. The data is obtained from different device and different source and hence they may be different format. The following steps are carried out in processing IoT data:

- Standardize the data format. A unique data format is followed in data collection center and the obtained data is converted into a specific format.
- Have redundant back up of the newly transformed data.
- In a dataset, filter any unwanted, corrupted, or redundant data. This is done to improve accuracy.

10.1.3   Advantages of IoT

- Remotely access monitoring device through automation process.
- Device-to-device communication made possible reducing human intervention.
- Data collection made at ease.
- Process automation enables business handling mechanisms.

10.1.4   Disadvantages of IoT

- Though IoT has proliferated to a larger extent, there is no specific international standard for IoT.
- IoT shares information online in cloud and data vulnerability is a threat.
- Handling big data is still considered as a challenge in the field of IoT.

10.1.5   IoT Standards

ZigBee is a widely used industrial standard that offers low data rate and low power wireless data communication via internetworks. The standard IEEE 802.15.4 enables smart communication sensor devices (ZigBee) to communicate with each other.

10.1.6   Lite Operating System (Lite OS)

It is a decedent of UNIX operating system for WSNs. Lite OS supports Internet of vehicles (IoV), which are connected through smart devices and enables in home and vehicle automation.

10.1.7   Low Range Wide Area Network (LoRaWAN)

It supports communication between voluminous smart devices used in smart cities.

10.2   Emerging Frameworks in IoT

10.2.1   Amazon Web Service (AWS)

It is a widely used cloud computing service developed for IoT developed by Amazon. This structure ensures secure communicating interactions between smart devices and the cloud. It ensures elastic data storage for the dynamic data manipulation mechanisms.

10.2.2   Azure

This framework is developed by Microsoft. It is designed for IoT suite and enables data storage and analysis on the cloud. The data visualizing services offered by Azure is widely used.

10.2.3   Brillo/Weave Statement

This framework structure is offering IoT applications by a Google platform. It is a combination of Brillo OS, an android OS, and Weave, which agreeing the information exchanging communication between smart devices such as actuators, mutuators, and with the main system involved in baggage checking process.

10.2.4   Calvin

This framework is from Ericson for distributed IoT applications. It is framed for application developers and for handling runtime environments.

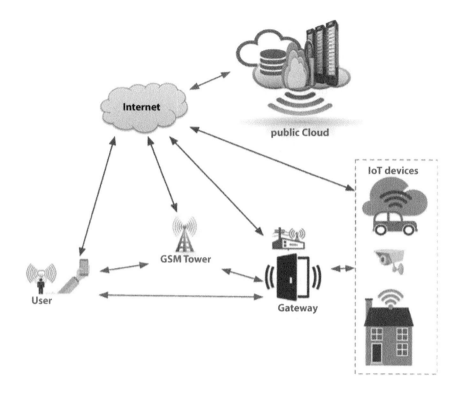

10.3   Applications of IoT

The IoT framework is premeditated to meet various applications rang-ing from home-based robotics system and industrial applications to the advanced Industrial IoT (IIoT). The important enterprise applications of IoT are Telecom, Automation, and Energy.

10.3.1   Healthcare in IoT

IoT empowers patient observing systems with benefits of distant monitor-ing and computerized data investigation. This enables better and reliable health care service. Remote methods enable Human-Computer Interaction (HCI) in health maintenance.

10.3.2 Smart Construction and Smart Vehicles

They enable automated services which reduce energy consumption, ease of operation, and advanced user-friendly features. This service also helps in securing the structure of the organization with the help of robotic automation.

10.3.3 IoT in Agriculture

Smart farming ensures nutrient management, automation in irrigation and crop harvest systems. Data collected over a period of time can be analyzed for better crop yield.

10.3.4 IoT in Baggage Tracking

The customer baggage/luggage is attached with tags and these tags are used for baggage identification and tracking in case it is lost. This is done using RFID baggage tracking technology.

10.3.5 Luggage Logbook

The important events that take place in the air travel provide a display space compliance with air safety regulations service bulletins. If the plane is in good condition, then the development of digital technology will work on time.

10.3.6 Electrical Airline Logbook

The definition of Isibaya, a new generation of electric airline log book is for those who need data input, typos, and errors, can be corrected as shown in

Figure 10.1 Aircraft monitoring system.

Figure 10.1. This is probably too big an attractive feature such as math and filtering. Many Logbook agendas can simply communicate that how many things are being said have you been in the last 90 days, or how many hours you have it flows like a time of earth falling under real metal conditions. He suggests that by having this kind of log book, it will make it easier for computer user's format with interest and soft taste of paper book.

10.4   IoT for Smart Airports

The IoT concept enhances communication from at any time, from any location, by anyone at by any human or anything. Once these things are related to the network, smart processes and services increasingly support our frugality, the atmosphere, and our well-being, where air travel or cargo will convert as the maximum significant characteristics of terrestrial use. Its advancement has been evident for eras, resulting the technical advancement of aviation on the one hand, and the tendency of men to travel on the other side. With the ever-increasing volume, current management systems and airport infrastructure need to change in order to change faster and more stable. To make passenger travel more liquid, airdromes are progressively adopting innovative technologies. In this paper, we propose an airport management system based on the IoT concept, in which passengers, luggage, planes, or rest areas are considered objects. In our airport administration system, we plan our goals to streamline air traveling passenger and air transportation and air traffic control events, improve user-friendly services, streamline airline services, and provide air travel passengers with smooth, secure, and reliable air transportation.

Nowadays, internet users and service providers are interconnecting their system with the internet facility very easy and automatic process. Similarly, the innovations and evolutionary technology and designs could access in free of cost through the above facilities. This system is estimated to propose expansion of a resource management organization strategy for use of air travel passenger and their services. Multi-dimensional parameters in airline industries are used as inputs IoT by the help of input readers such as RFID and Bluetooth to the analytical tools that are used to manage the existing system of the aviation such as infrastructure and route calculation, optimizing the flight loading system and so on to increase the stakeholders profit with the safe, secure, and reliable air transport service. This technological implementation facilitates and ensures various air travelers that they can enter the airport with pre knowledge with updated information of the flight schedules, so that they can get the ultimate safe and secure journey in their travel with optimized cost. The facilities and comforts of the various travelers at the airport also ensure that each traveler enters the airport will also get the ultimate customer experience and satisfaction with optimized flight prize. Various data observing card such as RFID and Bluetooth devices are attached with the objects such as baggage, flight engine parts, and airports. This facility enables to gather the information required for further process of data analysis and decision-making system. These process are used to improve the efficiency of the airline activity and the passengers experience and administrative process such as user-friendly baggage tracking observing apparatuses and supplementary. The three priorities are first generation of airline transaction passengers, jobs, and luggage [1].

The airline industries acquire the full advantage of IoT integrated system to innovate the complete system design such as customer satisfaction and administration activities as shown in Figure 10.2. In this field, technological innovation can reduce the traveling cost with clean and green flight travel with friendly service. However, this success will only be available if there is an international connection with supervision agencies and big deals with business industries to respond to each and every technical need accordingly. The Internet is already playing a major role drastically changed the day-to-day activities and performance of airline activities from taking passengers up to carry them into their destination location. Our study in this research incorporates the existing airline technology with the foundations of IoT perception in the aeronautical industries and practices toward the satisfaction of passengers with their baggage and belongings with sophisticated way of travel in all levels of travel.

Many research centers are currently uploaded in-depth research on new solutions that will meet these technical requirements. The main reason for our chapter is to give an extensive discussion about the current state of baggage technology and the use of IoT especially with monitor and tracking of passengers' belongings with the help of RFID and with WSN system. This ability provides the availability of passenger's belongings with portable identification and tracking gadgets variables using information from the file in central database in a simple and easy way of display the normal messages and by generate warning/alert messages to the passengers as well as to the administrative people. The reader or observer tags will be attached to various items that are needed to be tracked or monitored. So that the observed or identified data will be gathered, stored, and analyzed for further process in it. This information is collected through help of RFID readers as radiofrequency waves that will be present nearby activities of the object [2].

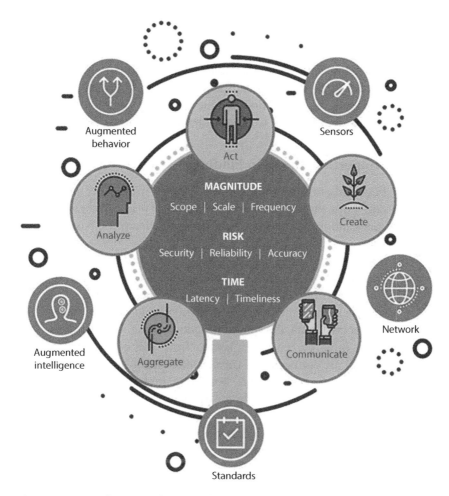

Figure 10.2 IoT information chain to collect aviation data.

10.4.1 IoT in Smart Operation in Airline Industries

IoT permits to screen the flaw of system, inform customer service experts regarding imminent responsibilities, and straight them to the correct place. The IoT not only changing the area correlated with automated logistics but also in the aerospace industry. Entirely, the fluctuations are intended to increase the profits and engine efficiency, reducing the fuel consumption. The ways aviation is helping airlines to provide better services to their customers are automated check-ins, baggage tracking, maintenance and other functional operations, in-flight entertainment, etc.

10.4.2   Fuel Emissions on Fly

When analyzing the amount of carbon dioxide emissions in the world, transparency, especially in marketable aviation through goods, or on domestic and international flights, the following findings provide details describing passenger presentation and fuel discharges in universe level are proportionally identified and to be considered.

10.4.3   Important Things in Findings

- Fuel emissions of amounted to 2.2% of from other petrol emissions among global level. In terms of prices in the aerospace industry, emissions will be higher from the past five years.
- Airlines from airports in the United States and in their areas emit about one-fourth (24%) of the world's total emissions of CO_2, maximum of which come from domestic carriers. The highest carbon and hydrogen emissions associated with passenger are China, the United Kingdom, Japan, Germany, etc.
- Forty-three percent of emissions from fuel of commercial aircraft are connected to traveler movement on slight body journeys, trailed by wide body jets, and regional flights, which are already made by a cargo car.

IoT data collection that is processed to reduce is used to increase profit and efficiency in aviation industries.

10.5   Related Work

Focusing the developments of IoT in aviation is around protection, maintenance, productivity, security, and passenger satisfaction. The capacity of IoT with actuators and commentator and sensor is communicated among them with digital transformation technologies by considering the surrounding activities of every objects, so that it allows airline industries to improve its performance in several areas, whether in passenger service or in their interior management. Further, the airport automation is one of the profits of the usage of IoT that is expected to deliver the fastest growth in worldwide spending over the 20th century. Transport is classified third among the business industries that will expend the most on IoT resolutions, after the industrialization [1].

Information from sensors creates a physical event or formal that originated object communicates the statistics to others above a network. The communication network collects different fragments of statistics from the various sources and periods. Around the late of 2030, an international wise air industries association estimates that there will be 7.2 billion air travelers, doubling the 3.8 billion passengers chalked up in 2016. The dramatic increase of passengers means airport need to be able to accommodate rise air traffic. IoT enables the industries to deliver extensive penalties in the upcoming future. Its effects on the aviation industry include reduction of travel time, enhance passenger comfort, reduce fuel consumptions, and enhance security levels. Sensors are used to monitor and collect accurate real-time data that are used to make critical decisions with the help of IoT information [2]. IoT is used to decrease fuel emissions from aircrafts which is the resolution taken by airline organizations. It will also make flying less dependent on humans for handling baggage or cargo, apart from reducing the weight of an aircraft that will decrease fuel burn.

Fuel consumption in aircraft fuel is the one of the biggest budget for any airline. Petroleum cost interprets 30% of aeronautical industry's functional costs and the worldwide air industry's total outgoings, by considering this cost, the lesser fuel habit will have an insightful impact on the productivity of airlines. For superior airlines, noteworthy cost investments can be attained through smooth small drops in fuel depletion. The collaboration of general electronic and Alitalia for the usage of IoT to improve fuel productivity through changes in flight functions procedures, wing flap positions, and adjustments in airspeed using sensor data. IoT deployment by the quarrying industry has established significant developments in safety and optimized cost [3].

Passenger's baggage loss and mismanagement demonstrate to be large problem challenged by airline companies. Airlines can use RFID tags on bags to help keep track of flyers luggage with the help of a mobile app, the user, as well as the company and can constantly monitor luggage and avoid baggage misplacement. The achievement by delta is neared 100% success level with RFID baggage tracking that is made by the superlative among the worldwide airlines during 2015.

SITA estimates the cost for IoT in 2018, that nearly partial of airports will be utilized IoT sensors to transmit luggage location information to passengers at bag droplet and luggage assertion. Hence, the stress related to checking the luggage will be reduced. Flight fuel is one of the prime operational costs for an airline industry. Human-induced wastage carbon is produced by airplanes will be around 2% of the total. Fuel burden subsidizes to the usage and upsets the lowest line, so resounding the optimal amount improves the efficiency [4].

To check and maintain the health of the aircraft engines IoT devices are used at the endpoints to check the health of the engines. The estimation of the global market in aviation is estimated near 25.13 billion dollar by the year 2020. In the mid of the period 2016–2022, the airline industry is estimated to eyewitness a healthy CAGR around 16.34%. As per the estimation report, the deployment of IoT by the smart aerodromes for providing an enjoyable customer experience along with rewarding the cost incurred in the business. Improved fuel efficiency developed for engine performance, data analytics, and foretelling maintenance can result in significant gains in fuel efficiency.

The fuel consumption of new aircraft designs is studied to deploy the new cost-effective techniques by providing remaining to operators over a long term time frame. Airline industries could reduce its cost by near 6% around the year 2030 and 30% around the end of the year 2050 compared by base case. Optimization of fuel cost by less usage also reduces fuel discharges also with less air transport operational cost [5].

The experts in the aviation industries estimated the consumption of fuel usage for emerging aircraft engine and develop designs to reduce its cost around 48% in 2030 relative to the 2,000 baseline as shown in Figure 10.3. While deploying emerging technologies in conventional airframe designs

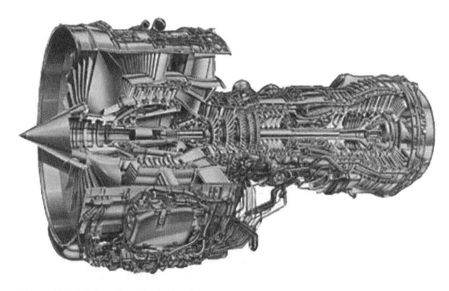

Figure 10.3 High-end engine in jet plane.

for the estimated costs and benefits, they will be purchasing new, more fuel effectiveness aeroplane around 2025 and mid of 2050. They compare the cost effectiveness with identified and emerging technology in this study to develop a new aircraft types under the manufacturers research while discusses the policies to bridge any gap [6].

The IoT will further enhance the air travel passenger's experience by agreeing that smart airports will help to speed up the passenger check-ins, customs procedures, and security. As the above facility, the aircraft fuel cost occurs around 30% of airline costs, the fuel saved around the millions of US dollars per year with emerging aircraft. It identifies fuel-saving opportunities and monitor progress. It enables smart patterns that can offer material on energy usage in aircraft production, which could lead to significant cost savings and supportable operations. Since the advanced analytics algorithms analyze the usage and propose energy-saving measures, energy consumption could be reduced by 20%. Airplane attached with cutting edge wingtip equipment is an emerging technology to reduce the fuel consumption, that achieve the optimal fuel consumption along with the cruising speed for each aircraft based on various altitudes [7].

Conventional and commercial aircraft have winged on average around 10% faster than their optimal traveling speed. IoT in fleet management provides optimization in routing, maintenance, fuel management, among others. The usage of IOT gives great control to the users, in order to reduce the weight in all direction of an aircraft, convinced electrical system bridging the aircraft can be accomplished with low fuel cost. So, once the exact fuel status is available, the refueling decisions can be taken to optimize fuel acquisition and while also considering the carrying cost of fuel in the wings for the next flight.

Fuel discharges as hydrocarbon fuel burning products and is straight related to the aeroplane fuel consumption, which, in turn, is an operation of aircraft weight, aerodynamic proposal, engine project, and operating manner of the aircraft. It is controlled by the emerging engine design as prime development, but the emissions in total could be reduced over the fuel efficiency improvement [8].

The usage of IoT gives great control to the users; they have a second to second access to the information and control over the IoT expedients, sensors, actuators, and their performance. The steps to implement IoT in aviation companies are ideation and strategy, pilot and roadmap, capture store and process, scale and deploy, and operate. It improves customers and supplier's capability to provide supplementary digital-based facilities. It holds an incredible amount of e-enabled aircraft design that rising radically and the new sensors embedded into aircraft equipment, fragments,

Figure 10.4 Fuel emissions from jet airplane.

and systems that increased merchants' ability to collect appreciated data as shown in Figure 10.4. On the operational side, sensors have been deployed in aircraft engines for some time, providing vital information on engine performance and fuel consumption. An engine can have more than 5,000 sensors generating many gigabytes of data per second [9].

The requirement of safety journey and the availability of IoT the importance of security checks are pulling from various sources. Some technologies such as biometrics and contextual information for increased levels of assurance and baggage checking security cover hundred percent of luggage security and assure unknown slips through the crashes, auto-repair, and intellectual supervision increasing the lifespan, security, and safety of air travel. A periodical succession approaches and real-time aeronautical path regulate the fuel burn and passenger comfort. Automation in aircraft vehicle administration and examination management saves fuel as well as time and reduce air traffic also. Additive manufacture plan helps in improving efficiency through demand parts [10].

Safety of passengers, crew, and the aircraft is the top priority in commercial aviation. The estimation of accurate the fuel consumption during aircraft function is key point to determine the fuel capacity, reducing the airline operational cost, and extenuating environment impacts. Aerodynamics parameters for the optimal fuel consumption used to model wind tunnel experiments and to obtain a static diagram extracted from the consequences of the study focus on the exodus uphill phase of aeroplane operation and offer a new optimal fuel consumption model. Modeling the

Figure 10.5 IoT real-time connectivity in airline industries.

optimal fuel consumption was built upon the attitude of the preservation of energy and regression exploration as shown in Figure 10.5 [11].

The improvement in emerging gas turbine engines consumes considerable chamber for to reach complete efficiencies around 30% higher than the greatest engines in facility today, with a considerable reduction in fuel emissions. Profitable aviation is extremely competitive business for which the optimization of fuel usage is major equipment. The considerations of cost reduction will be a challenge and have to be taken into version as new systems are proposed for marketable development. A revolutionary IoT in the aviation industry is the modern equipped device in aviation industry with a variety of sensors that produce several petabytes of data per flight that are combined with other in-flight data, the evidence can expand engine performance, efficiency, maintenance, and management regarding to optimize fuel costs and faster travel times [12].

To measure certain insight values, different actuate and mutate sensors are protected and used for communication and integration of raw data to information with centralized manner. All the above are used to measuring the landing process, airport management, and control activities, route planning, improve the effectiveness and security of the aeroplane during travel and real-time weather forecasting which offers the possibility of optimizing the airport maintenance and suspicious interpositions that expand the operating time of the aircraft and growth in safety, offering an additional value to the airline itself and to the passengers. Interaction between the ground system and the aircraft system will become richer and robust while exchange the information. Selecting the most efficiency route planes, at the same time optimizing the fuel cost with lesser fuel burn, leads to lower travel ticket prize and therefore exploits profits of the airline industries [13].

Fuel fraction is the heaviness of the petroleum separated by the uncultured take-off heaviness of the aircraft. Depends upon the weight of the plan, the petroleum will be consuming the fuel during aircraft operation. So, an accurate assessment of the fuel consumption during each trip will be a large share of the total fuel that can help regulate the fuel load exactly and evade necessary fuel consumption and the subsequent negative atmosphere effect. It will benefits airline industries via a less operating cost and air traffic flow optimization forecasting and more operative benefits of air traffic organization [14].

A secure environment in aviation industry in the military exercises, analyzing aircraft engine presentation and fuel organization are some of the facets that can be observed into the real time with requisite precautionary action, resulting in better management and efficiency of flight engine operations. Managing smooth and efficient flight engine operations will be a big challenge for airlines industries. Accessing information by passengers when delay of flight departure, delay, waiting time, and entrance alteration on their instantaneous and fingertips using circumstantial or location-based pursuing. Thus, the expenditure for refining on fuel competence and passengers' belongings and baggage tracing will be varying by up to 20% at different airdromes on a specified day. Thus, the real-time information on cost of fuel at different locations on the aircrafts route plan, fuel available in the aircraft, impact of carrying additional fuel on efficiency, directions for the route, and weather forecast for the most optimal refueling plan can be identified for every individual aircraft [15].

The sensitive operations in airline industries belong to the weather conditions. The development of continuously restructured flight strategies with respect to obtainable weather information concerning altering wind and overall conditions can empower aircraft to use fuel additional competently and traverse their airplanes in safer surroundings that avoid turbulence and make air flights relaxed journey to the traveling public. The precipitate literature obtainable here exemplifies to pilots and navigators and also increases the efficiency by reducing the fuel consumptions and cost management. Thus, it improves the safety and security of passengers while traveling [16].

10.6 Existing System and Analysis

Aeronautics administration resolution concentrating in reducing the fuel emissions, where IoT is enable in a position to help reduce carbon emissions from aircraft. It will also reduce the dependency on human interaction for handling baggage or cargo. Apart from reducing flight weight in the all other ways of air travel operations, weight reduction is to be achieved by reducing the usage of fuel of the aircraft. Since the growth in the aviation sector from two decades, the growth in buying power of the customer, time, and energy will be saved while communicating between different places of business or organization [17].

Deciding where to refuel and how much to refuel can now be a real-time decision and not a pre-planned manifest. Based on instantaneous information of the fuel cost at different locations during the flight travel, the aircraft's route plan as reducing the cost of aircraft fuel will impact in earning of profit for both stakeholders and passengers, where it is important that the preplanning the effective fuel cost for optimal route, to regulate the profitable route for entire locations of the world over land and overwater by considering the weather forecasting on travel of every individual aircraft [18].

10.6.1 Technology Used in the System

To determine fuel availability in the aircraft in real time, the IoT technology with data analytical methods are recommend during the period of refilling the fuel whenever it is required with the machine learning algorithm. Aircraft fuel prices in Europe vary by up to 17.5% at different airports on a given day. Some percentage of the benefit reaped out of refueling optimization will add the profit in some extent of the airline industries [19].

Pilots are in position to make a lot of conclusions during a flight operations and these choices range from taking the decision of changing velocity and changing the altitude according to change the traveling route at each travel. All these decisions are to be taken by individual of pilot that includes in fuel consumption of the aircraft on travel time, but the operations related with pre-planning decisions of the administrators, they are not independent in total. External factors such as weather conditions and aircraft weight that change for each flying journey and wind speed contribute toward a diverse outcome. Forecasting the outcome for different actions and providing them to the pilot in real time will enable them to make the right choices [20].

Here is how different technologies will come in to play for this use-case: IoT to determine real-time conditions—internal and external to the aircraft; predictive analytics to determine next best actions; peer benchmarking— employee of the month, days are behind us. Peer benchmarking is real time now [21]. Performance can be measured in real time. A study by the University of Chicago concluded that there is a positive impact pilots can make to fuel consumption. Amount of impact made was attributable to what was at stakes. Higher stakes resulted in better fuel efficiency.

If you can make information available to the pilots and also provide the benchmarks that can be possibly achieved, it is one step in the right direction.

The significant key factor for profitable airline industries is fuel consumption, so that the fuel optimization to be considered in all sides of air travel operations. From complete expenditures of airline industries, the operating cost is accounted by 20%. Hence, we have to consider the optimization of fuel consumption to make the profit in the airline industries [22].

Main benefits of the connected aircraft, lower fuel consumption and emissions, maintenance, customer baggage loss, and mishandling prove to be a big issue faced by airline companies. IoT can intervene and help solve the issue. Airlines can use RFID tags on bags to keep track of flyer's luggage. With the help of mobile app, the passengers as well as the stakeholders can constantly monitor luggage and avoid the problem of baggage during the accommodation time such as luggage misplacement. Delta's mobile sends push notifications through which passengers can see their baggage location constantly. Delta has achieved a 99.7% success rate with RFID baggage tracking, which made it the best among global airlines in the age of 2017 [23].

Baggage tracking system in airline industries is executed with the help of beacons related with baggage monitoring process. The location of baggage of passengers evaluated with the help of actuator sensors to dewdrop and claim the luggage. The integrated IoT sensors are used here to monitor passenger's luggage by the help of cell phone along with the passengers while conveyor sashes onto the luggage claim carousel as shown in Figure 10.6.

The integrated IoT technology helps to avoid the unnecessary stress and fear developed during luggage checking time and they can concentrate other activities.

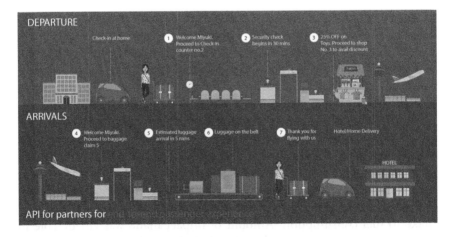

Figure 10.6 Smart luggage IoT connected tracking system.

The flight engine involved with numerous parts which are attached with IoT devices that helps to extract significant input information for investigation of flight-testing phase, when the information processed with the help of data analytical model and Artificial Intelligent models. where the neural network design involved with complicated algorithms that are helped to design an optimized economic model in aeronautical smart administration and cost of traveling prizes [24]. Economic analysis on flight safety systems required real-time data that needs more expenditures on preservation phase itself and then predictable phase that are considerable part of expenditure than caused by safety system. While compare the cost of analysis model and frame template structure of the forthcoming optimized design model, the cost for the existed safety level will cultivate exponentially with rise of the difficulty of airplane and becomes intolerable for the industry in its competitive market. Refilling the special care for safety system on tremendously dependable and decision-making system based on real-time information eradicates the participation of human influence [25].

Aircraft safety, security, and reliability system are extremely important and serious process for passengers as well as company's competing scenario. So that these systems are designed as an active practical system, to regulate safety and security on time of time of flight travel based on real-time information that are collected, aggregated, and processed by means of sensor devices and integrated system communication among them through internet connection. The basic measurement techniques are involved in the safe keeping and monitoring process for the passenger's baggage is considered here. A proper warning and alert system is followed to accomplish the weight reduction of the flight, so that the ticket prize could be reduced. The measurement taken against the airplane exploitation that leads to reliable, secure, and safety journey with passenger friendly service and with good performance of the system itself. The airplane maintenance cost, design, and production cost could be reduced by following the system model with proper real-time decision-making system accordingly. By following the above terms, the travel of airplane passengers and air traffic raised at 236.80 million during the year of 2018 [26].

The demand in the air travel in our country and volume of flights in Indians civil aviation sector has developed in spirited manner. Also, we can say that our country's international aviation marketplace has recognized that many successive years of growth during the end of 2020. A large level of commercial benefits occurred due to the significant evolution while it happens that an export product from our country become a key achievement for growth in cargo air traffic as significant percent of total trade [27]. The balance sheet of freight industries shown a most effective, unified, and real-time effective worldwide profit by the end of the next decade. In the

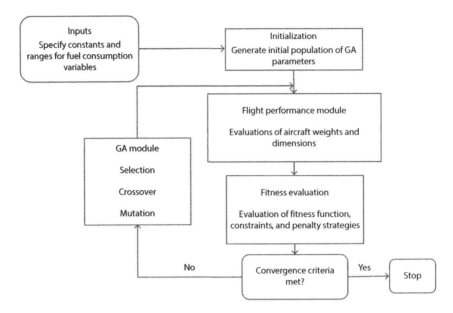

Figure 10.7 Evaluation and performance improvement.

proposed system, the integrated technology in aviation market comprises cumulative operational efficacy and improved passenger understanding is predictable to drive the IoT in aviation market as shown in Figure 10.7.

By end market, the airports section is predictable to raise at the maximum rate during the estimate period. An IoT environment consists of network-enabled smart devices that are entrenched systems such as communication hardware and sensors for effective communication of data. IoT participate data from various devices and uses analytics to share valuable information with applications built to address exact needs. With the development of digital technologies, the airline industry provides an exclusive passenger's experiences and develops the productivity of the workers. A numerous opportunities, customer services, and passengers' facilities will be enhanced by implementing IoT technologies and communication.

10.7   Proposed System

A profitable airline industries is possible by many factors, among them the optimization of fuel cost is most critical and gainful commercial factor for the same. So, any airline industry could be increase their profit through fuel evading agreements that can offer a cost-effective and secure travel with a competitive price for passenger's air travel ticket over a period of time. The alternative procedure to reduce flight cost and improve the industry profit is possible when an industry occurs the green fuel technology when it needs the refueling their aircrafts and also by offering the discounts for native flights than other flights. U.S. airlines spent $3 billion on fuel in July 2019, benefiting from a 4% decrease in the average price per gallon year-to-date relative to 2018. By this way this, model could minimize aviation fuel consumption.

The IoT developments will be focused around safety, maintenance, efficiency, security, and customer experiences and personalization. IoT promises to deliver widespread consequences in the coming future. The effects on the airline industry include reduction of travel time, enhanced passenger comfort, and enhanced security stages. This idea offerings an optimized fuel consumption model for civil air transport and also the optimized aircraft engine design. A machine learning algorithm offers real-time information as its input with the flow of the input directed to determine the minimal and optimized cost in fuel consumption based on real-time data during travel.

While simulate our aircraft model with optimal cost for fuel consumption, our idea operated with the simulated algorithm and it could employ with the following different phases: identification of status, fix the boundary for route selection, and vibrant arbitrary modification. The idea could be implemented in domestic/passengers and even in international airline industries, where fuel consumption could be decreased from 9 liters/100 Km to 3 liters/100 Km, and 10 liters/100 Km to 4 liters/100 Km during the time period from 1970 to 2013. We could decide that the fuel demands for domestic/civil air transport will be increased by a particular percentage of the economic growth in the country for every year only from the export process that is grown due to innovations in airline industries technological improvements.

While implementing our idea the growth of the airline industries could be attained according to the demand by the passengers with safe, secure, and reliable service. The expenditure to attain these three of safe, secure, and reliable with optimal cost to the passengers, similarly the revenue of the marketable airline industries with 12–15% of increment of their profits as well as total revenues. But the expenditure for the opposite account such as provision of safety, security with reliability, the second expenditure after fuel cost will be there such as IoT implementation, monitoring, tracking, and warning and alert system. So, our county decided to improve the total count of the airports up to 300 by the end of 2030. So, we are in the 7th biggest civil flight marketplace in the world and are set to become the world's 3rd main by 2030.

In-service fleet size of Indian airlines stood at 588 airplanes, as of May 2018. It is further expected to grow to 1,100 planes by 2027. The fuel emission also controlled in air travel by the implementation of ever increasing technology, the emission in worldwide will be decreased by achieving green fuel technology using bio fuel. The operating cost of flight also reduced by means of lowering fuel emission during travel, and luggage weight reduction through the help of integrated system of the sensor devices and transportations between them.

A growth in profit would certainly not only for industry players, also for the aircraft design, transport industrialists and airline industries are using smart technologies to achieve the cost-effective methods so that fuel emission could be reduced that, in turn, optimize the everything from the

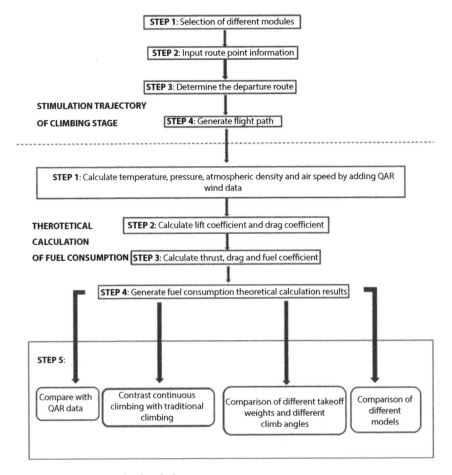

Figure 10.8 Steps involved in fuel consumption.

way of fuel consumption as shown in Figure 10.8. Unlike other traveler aeroplane, some upcoming projects will have attached wings with the tail portion of the flight that are framed by cutting edge technologies. So that the drag and thrust forces are balanced/controlled according to the altitude and speed of the flight during travel. This technical design modification melodramatically decreases the drag forces so that the flight control and fuel efficiency will be optimized drastically. If the upcoming project is aiming for a scheduled air transport and for optimized fuel consumption, then we can achieve the following plans with effective way:

- 30% reduced in fuel consumption than passenger flight;
- 40% lowering noise;
- 50% decrease in landing and take-off emission.

The assistance to the passengers during the travel given by the system, which brings people self-possessed and transports possessions in a common location, with safe and secure manner. The success of cost-effective transport technologies adding a new value over air transport speed, reliable air travel, and then flexible worldwide travel. Passengers can buy their traveling ability through the wired and wireless network, over any space, any distance with positive things on the atmosphere. Air travel agencies also provide to civilization in other life-threatening, non-transport zones such as disaster amenities, search and rescue, tragedy liberation, and climate watching. In 2030, the air traveling passenger experienced a predominant facility with the technology being implemented. IoT technology is most effective one while implementing real-time decision-making system to achieve all kinds of optimized process of airline industries. So that we can say that the technology is a heart of the air transport system with energetic, efficient, and dispersed integrated system model which leads the travelers and administrative people into a quick, smooth, and predictable air transport activities and interactions. This system offers a Quality of Services (QoS) to passengers, as well as on-board control with comfort zone of journey with valuable travel with the help of artificial Intelligence. AI offers various optimization technique to reach a potential task in airline industries.

The another great phenomena called data science is applied in optimization of flight operations that carries binary data as multi-dimensional input information for various analytical process such as machine learning algorithm, statistical analysis, and so on. Those process converts the binary data gathered from IoT as actionable flight information, where cloud storage system is used to dump and then accessed wherever needed. IoT on the technological innovation networks in aviation and aims to generate endorsements that will allow the sector to fulfil the demanding goals by the year 2030. The analysis should be repeated periodically to verify the advancement of research and innovation toward the goals of aviation in 2030. The cutting edge technology in attached wing near the tail part of the flight offers an extra benefits as protection from fuel emissions and also from turbulence noise. Fuel burn system for flight operation required more energy, so that the fuel burn technology improved by double cooler technology, so that the fuel emissions reduced directly which, in turn, reduce the fuel cost by significant amount percentage that will result in a 5% lowest cost in fuel consumption. Fuel emissions from nitrogen oxide are reduced in considerable amount of percentages that are a function of the airplane, engine, and combustor outline. The other dimension of weight reduction is also possible by lowering the weight of carbon handbrakes by the way of alternate the hand break with switches and remove hand break from an airplane which leads to reduce the flight weight. The reduction of flight weight always leads to an optimized fuel cost consumption. Another benefit here is the reduction of carbon dioxide from emissions which, in turn, causes of avoiding/reducing fuel consumption while air travel.

The provision of accessing on-board service to passengers is personalized to each passenger. All this so that airline industries can greatly adjust to the needs and favorites of the passenger. The other way of reducing the flight weight is by lowering in the passengers belongings and required food during travel. The is possible by pre-acquiring the passenger' food habit and requirements during travel time well in advance with their acceptance, so that the management can maintain the optimal food in the flight which, in turn, causes for weight reduction. The acquisition is possible by proper communication ability with the help of technological tools that are

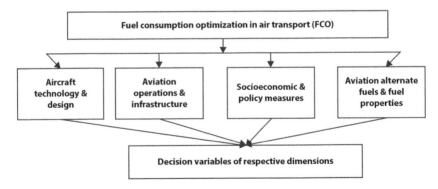

Figure 10.9 Optimization of aircraft fuel.

managed in the industries as integrated system design as shown in Figure 10.9. The implementation of the system is focusing to obtain a detailed information about their flight passengers by this way they can able to display passengers food habits with personalized business advertisements with their own foodstuffs. Decisions made through cockpit connectivity could end up saving the aviation industry annual estimation is $15 million, not to decrease fuel discharges by some extent during 2035.

Messaging in airline industries is very critical one in targeted places in airline businesses. IoT places major role in collecting and cumulating information, it is achieved that a proper communication to every individual passenger on time so that individual needs and interests are satisfied that is relevant to the improvement of profit in airline industries. Everything is promised by the communicating facilities in aerodromes by means of WSN and usage of its application that monitor the whole airport and user behavior and advertisers. The IoT application gives a solution to aircrew to accomplish the passenger service to their cabin by means of wireless communication technology. Altogether used to achieve an effective

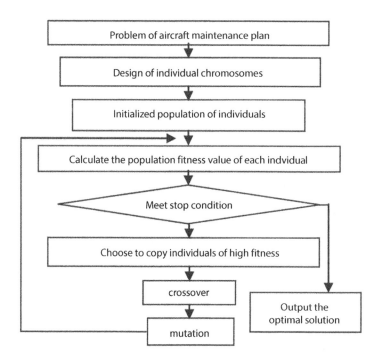

Figure 10.10 Overall idea for fuel cost optimization.

management such as passenger safety and respond to their requirements sooner as shown in Figure 10.10.

IoT is the modernized expertise addressing hazardous use cases in profitable aviation. It has the probability to advance the reliability, excellence, client gratification, and cost optimization for fuel in an airline industry that is expected to grow significantly in future. In order to maximize value from IoT investments and pro-actively auto-regulate, it is in industry's finest interest to update the present standards that share data through industry to comprise IoT data where appropriate or adapt a new standards to frame a new prototype for IoT integrated data exchange and possession ship through airlines and suppliers. With air travel and associated pollution expected to swell by mid-century, the impacts of delayed action are too bug to disregard.

Various kinds of sensors are deployed in an aircraft in wireless mode to monitor multi-dimensional parameters such as temperature sensor for weather forecasting, compression in engine while traveling, fuel deviation indicator, accelerometer to sense the speed of the flight, RADALT to indicate altitude and speed of the aircraft, nose wheel sensor to control landing speed of the flight, pilot stick sensor to control the flight lifting speed and other lifting activities, motion sensor to detect interrupted objects, and Ailerons sensor to detect turbulence problems. A microcontroller chip is attached with the sensors that will receive input from all sensors and monitor the deviations to track the scenario and record multi-dimensional parameters and then sent to cloud data storage. The wireless sensor networking technology is used to further communication among them that leads to weight reduction of the flight and also the reduction of difficulty in integrating and controlling the system model. Crew in cockpit can take the advantage of graphical user interface to view and control the multi-dimensional parameters shown from the allowed webpage. Here also, the IoT technology used in surplus way of mode and the base station could access the same information from the ground. The available parameters are stored server provided by cloud data base module or cloud memory module for further analysis that are used at the time of failure of the IoT devices or in the failure of the local memories. Suppose if there is any failure in that the real-time binary data from the aircraft health in case of worst weather climate and then failure in communication by means of radar, then the offshore available data will be guided by the base station authority by means of IoT by analyzing the available information and limitations.

We can expect the increment of worldwide aircraft travel in forth coming years up to a considered percentage and the number of airport up to a level as the same as the previous one by the year of 2030. Also the international airport estimates its passengers count up to the 8 billion by 2030. A consistent demand is grown for IoT in airline industries, so that the innovations in airline industries play a key role to improve the profit here and satisfy the customers as well as stake holders. Designing new technological and cutting edge parts of flight could be optimized through real-time data collections via satellite, so that critical decisions to be taken at even in crucial scenario. Non-critical information gathered and uploaded via WSN but critical information is processed by satellite. The landing information the aircraft, the complete critical and non-critical information at the end of travel, will be uploaded via wireless communication for further analysis of statistical data.

The capability of the IoT with mutuators, sensors, and actuators develop the interacting capacity between **devices** and **interconnect** with a system model for digitalization that have some precise goals, that allows air travel industries to improve in various zones such as passengers satisfaction and friendly service, weather forecasting to determine the optimized routes, and crew cockpit control and internal management. On the other hand, systematic checking procedures for passengers will be automated so that the waiting time will be optimized for the flight passengers.

The sensor devices also used to measure the safety system of the passengers while do an auto checking method, that are interconnect with a central scheme in the ground, so that all productivity explained in the previous steps are increased with optimal prize. The extended operating time for aircraft management also reduced with minimal cost in long term that are contributed an added value for a couple of instance in the airline

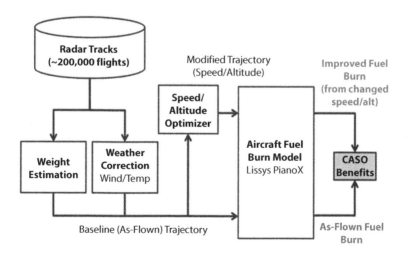

Figure 10.11 High-end platform in travel route comparison for optimization.

itself and to the client. A worthy instance of this exercise is implemented in high-end aircraft swift as shown in Figure 10.11.

Management of baggage is arranging the activities transparently to the passengers' destination and it will notify passengers instantaneously by means of RFID labels and wireless network technology being applied in airline industries. The shipping companies are also utilizing the digitalization technology for their similar activities of monitoring and tracking real-time data for passengers baggage safety so that they can really monitor at all periods via their smart display for their possessions safety and for taking the most efficient optimized traffic airline routes, at the same time as lowering the fuel intake, it outcomes in lower expenses and therefore exploits profits.

The most parameters for demonstrating fuel intake are in various altitudes, longitudinal rushing, ground speed, accurate airspeed, and rapidity engine spool rpm. The intercontinental civil flight party schemes about the fuel emissions from international aviation will triple in 2030 compared with the current trends in worldwide flying fuel emissions, including navy and universal aviation. Focusing the benefits offered for airlines and customers and reproducing both the prominence of aviation segment and the anticipation that new rules to sanctioned aircraft fuel optimization notably by fuel emission regular for new aeroplane will be accepted. Airline industries can make profit by means of the above parameters with optimal price for passengers travel over a specific period.

10.8   Components in Fuel Reduction

The components used to reduce fuel consumption are as follows:

- Drag reduction
- Engine efficiency
- Wiring
- Eng. sensors-used to show the signal for airplanes

10.9   Conclusion

Thus, flying is a heavily controlled and supervised sector. Safety cultures have increased trust and lowers cost. IoT ensuring the security of the air travel system. At the same time, it keeps tracking the luggage and maintains the cost and fuel reduction. By using the IoT, the aviation industry helps to enhance the efficiency of aircraft reducing time travel. This paper concludes that it can reduce fuel consumption up to 30%. It increases the productivity by reducing the cost and fuel consumption. The weightage of aircraft can be condensed to decrease the fuel usage. Planning the aircraft design in a better way of cutting-edge winglets and engine can also reduce the costs of aircraft passengers. Finally, IoT recovers the efficiency and maintains the safe aircraft systems and passengers for driving it to achieve more development.

10.10   Future Enhancements

For further upcoming enhancements, it needs to be quite easy to develop the airline system. In forthcoming, the efficiency of airplanes can be increased more than compared to the present. The maintenance of aircrafts, safety, and security can be enhanced to build an improved performance of aviation. The petroleum consumption could be condensed more by designing an aircraft structural design. To enhance the consumption of fuel reduction, engines and winglets can be modified to redesign by using the technology. Thus, IoT in aviation advances the aircraft industry by the way there is a 3.25% of chance that the fuel emissions can be reduced by 37.5%–50% in 2030.

References

1. Kalaichelvi, P., Akila, V., Rani, T.P., Sowmiya, C., Divya C., A closer look at a big data analytics, 1, 4, 69–109, 2021.
2. Shi, X., An, X., Zhao, Q., Liu, H., Xia, L., Sun, X., Guo, Y., State-of-the-art internet of things in protected agriculture. *Sensors*, *19*, 8, 1833, 2019.
3. Cilfone, A., Davoli, L., Belli, L., Ferrari, G., Wireless mesh networking: An IoT-oriented perspective survey on relevant technologies. *Future Internet*, *11*, 4, 99, 2019.
4. Angadi, A., Dias, R., Bagali, M.U., An Aircraft Health Monitoring System using IOT. *Indian J. Sci. Technol.*, *9*, 33, 1–5, 2016.
5. Bloem, J., Van Doorn, M., Duivestein, S., Excoffier, D., Maas, R., Van Ommeren, E., The fourth industrial revolution. *Things Tighten*, *8*, 1, 11–15, 2014.
6. Birch, N.T., 2020 vision: the prospects for large civil aircraft propulsion. *Aeronaut. J.*, *104*, 1038, 347–352, 2000.
7. Gilchrist, A., *Industry 4.0: the industrial internet of things*, Apress, 1, 1–12, 2016.

8. Chatterjee, A., Flores, H., Sen, S., Hasan, K.S., Mani, A., IoT-based algorithms for distributed location detection for flights. *Int. J. Hybrid Intell.*, *1*, 2–3, 191–210, 2019.

9. Lamb, K., *Challenges of Digitalisation in the Aerospace and Aviation Sectors*, CDBB, 1, 2018.

10. Amankwah-Amoah, J., Stepping up and stepping out of COVID-19: New challenges for environmental sustainability policies in the global airline industry. *J. Clean. Prod.*, *271*, 123000, 2020.

11. Taneja, N.K., *Re-platforming the Airline Business: To Meet Travelers' Total Mobility Needs*, Routledge, 1, 15–45, 2019.

12. Jha, K., Doshi, A., Patel, P., Shah, M., A comprehensive review on automation in agriculture using artificial intelligence. *Artif. Intell. Agric.*, *2*, 1–12, 2019.

13. Drummond, M., Great ways airlines are using internet of things. *Erişim Tarihi*, *25*, 25–30, 2018.

14. Karakuş, G., Karşıgil, E., Polat, L., The Role of IoT on Production of Services: A Research on Aviation Industry, in: *The International Symposium for Production Research*, Springer, Cham, pp. 503–511, 2018, August.

15. Uden, L. and He, W., How the Internet of Things can help knowledge management: a case study from the automotive domain. *J. Knowl. Manag.*, 1, 12–15, 2017.

16. Rapolu, B., *Internet of aircraft things: an industry set to be transformed*, 2018, Aviation Week Network. Available at:)(Published January 18, 2016. Accessed January 29, 2019) https://aviationweek. com/connected-aerospace/internet-aircraft-things-industry-set-be-transformed View in Article.

17. Lacity, M.C., Addressing key challenges to making enterprise blockchain applications a reality. *MIS Q. Executive*, *17*, 3, 201–222, 2018.

18. Marcus, J., Airbus uses IoT to fuel 'factory of the future'. *Intelligent Aerosp.*, *11*, 12–15, 2016.

19. Saraçyakupoğlu, T., Additive Manufacturing Technologies in the Aviation Industry in Pursuit of Weight Optimization, 12–15, 2019,

20. Abd Hakim, H., Ghadzali, I.F.S, Fadzil, A.I., Development of Smart Aircraft Logbook Based on IoT. *Int. J. Eng. Adv. Technol. (IJEAT)*, 9, 1, October 2019.

21. Korchagin, A., Deniskina, A., Fateeva, I., Lean and energy efficient production based on Internet of Things (IoT) in aviation industry, in: *E3S Web of Conferences*, vol. 110, EDP Sciences, p. 02124, 2019.

22. Hugbo, T., *Space enabled smart Africa (SESA)*, (Master's thesis, Engineering and the Built Environment), openUCT, 2019.

23. Badea, V.E., Zamfiroiu, A., Boncea, R., Big data in the aerospace industry. *Informatica Economica*, *22*, 1, 17–24, 2018.

24. Birudavolu, S. and Nag, B., India's Regulatory Environment and Response to International Trade Issues, in: *Business Innovation and ICT Strategies*, pp. 275–312, Palgrave Macmillan, Singapore, 2019.

25. Ramalingam, T., Christophe, B., Samuel, F.W., Assessing the potential of IoT in aerospace, in: *Conference on e-Business, e-Services and e-Society*, Cham, Springer, pp. 107–121, 2017, November.

26. Ismail, S., *Exponential Organizations: Why new organizations are ten times better, faster, and cheaper than yours (and what to do about it)*, Diversion Books, 1, 25–35, 2014.

27. Woodbury, T. and Srivastava, A., Analysis of virtual sensors for predicting aircraft fuel consumption, in: *Infotech@ Aerospace 2012*, p. 2449, 2012.

11

Object Detection in IoT-Based Smart Refrigerators Using CNN

Ashwathan R.[1], Asnath Victy Phamila Y.[1*], Geetha S.[1] and Kalaivani K.[2]

[1]School of Computer Science and Engineering, VIT University, Chennai, India
[2]Department of Computer Science and Engineering, Vels Institute of Science, Technology and Advanced Studies, Chennai, India

Abstract

With advancements in IoT, the research and development of smart homes have reached a new level. There are many instances where homes with smart technology have been built in the recent years. With the need for speed, comfort, and efficiency, smart homes are sure to make a huge impact in the future. The proposed smart fridge module is based on open-source, low-cost hardware design. The proposed framework can be added to already existing fridges. The framework has a camera that captures an image of the interior of the fridge. From this image, the different products present and their quantity are determined. The proposed system also contains various sensors that help in determining the presence of different products and their quantity. A food quality monitoring module that helps in reducing the waste generated from the fridge is also incorporated. In expansion, the framework incorporates an Android application that lets clients effortlessly check a basic need list from their mobile gadgets. The smart refrigerator module allows the refrigerator to communicate with a remote device like a mobile phone. It can determine what is present in the fridge and count the number of each object with the help of image processing. The YOLO algorithm has been used for this as it is fast and is good for real-time processing. A snap of the items in the fridge is taken every time a product is placed in or removed from the fridge. This is monitored by the PIR motion sensor. The ultrasonic sensor installed on top of the bottle measures the distance from the liquid and then the quantity of liquid can be calculated by this. The gas sensor detects if any gasses are emitted by rotten fruits. All the details are updated to the database. These can be viewed from the app. If the quantities of products are less than a predefined threshold, then a notification is sent to the mobile app.

*Corresponding author: asnathvicty.phamila@vit.ac.in

R. Anandan, Suseendran Gopalakrishnan, Souvik Pal and Noor Zaman (eds.) The Industrial Internet of Things (IIoT): Intelligent Analytics for Predictive Maintenance, (281–300) © 2022 Scrivener Publishing LLC

Keywords: Convolutional neural network, object detection, smart refrigerator, IoT, YOLO, raspberry, Nodemcu, Android app

11.1   Introduction

For the realization of smart homes, there is a need to develop smart appliances. Automated lights, fans, fridges, garages, air conditioners, etc., are just a few of these appliances that would make life very easy. A refrigerator is the most used appliance in the kitchen and is important in storing and maintaining the freshness food items at home. According to research conducted by the United Nations Environment Program, each year, more than 1.3 billion tons of food is wasted. The majority of the wastes include expired food items and rotten fruits and vegetables from refrigerators. Thus, it becomes important to make sure that the food items in the fridge are used before they expire or rot.

With the rapid growth of technology, many companies have given ideas for the development of smart refrigerators. But these refrigerators are very costly and are therefore not very popular among the middle-class families. Current smart fridges use a combination of RFID equipment managed through a desktop application that screens the items within the refrigerator and caution the client in case any things are about to run out. The problem of using RFID is that all the products should have an RFID tag attached to it. Tagging cannot be done for all products.

A module that can be added to make a smart fridge based on open-source; low-cost hardware design is developed. The proposed framework can be added to already existing fridges. The framework has a camera that captures an image of the interior of the fridge. From this image, the different products present and their quantity are determined using the YOLO (You Only Look Once) algorithm. The proposed system also contains various sensors that help in determining the presence of different products and their quantity. A food quality monitoring module that helps in reducing the waste generated from the fridge will also be incorporated. In expansion, the framework incorporates an Android application that lets clients effortlessly check a basic need list from their mobile gadgets.

According to surveys conducted by the UN, a lot of food waste comes from the household refrigerator. People can easily forget what they have in the fridge and therefore the product can remain in it for ages and when it is finally taken out it may be spoiled and thus is discarded, especially fruits and vegetables. A fridge that can detect the spoilage of food is required. In today's society, the percentage of working women has increased. They rarely check what items they have in the refrigerator. They may not know when a product may get over. Thus, a smart fridge that can automatically send a list of required products if they get over becomes a necessity. The smart fridges present in today's market are very costly and are therefore not easily available to the common man. This is the motivation behind the development of an object detecting system based on IoT in a smart refrigerator.

The existing systems have a stock counting mechanism that determines the number of items in the fridge that is not very efficient. They use high-cost items like RFID to detect every product. They also do not include a technique for measuring the amount of liquids in the bottles. Most of the existing systems need manual entry of this quantity. There are also no systems where they have combined the idea of stock counting mechanisms and a food quality monitoring system that works together.

So, the main challenge here is to develop a cost-efficient system that is really quick in detecting the objects present in the refrigerator. Also, the product quality measuring module has to be simultaneously run along with the product detection. The food monitoring system has to be accurate and must not give false notifications that may be a waste of time to the user.

Another challenge is protecting the entire smart system when it is installed in the refrigerator. It must be able to withstand the cold, and also during power shutdowns, it must be safe from the dripping water from the melting of ice in the fridge. So, it needs a protective casing.

11.2   Literature Survey

Mezgec, S., and Seljak, B. K. [1] have presented a new way to detect and recognize food and drink in images. They have developed a new CNN architecture known as NutriNet. The model had been trained with a dataset that containing 225,953 images, 512 × 512 pixels each, of 520 different items. An image containing a food item or drink acts as the input to the recognition model. The output is a text label that contains the class of the food. The performance of the developed network has been compared with other ones like AlexNet, GoogLeNet, and Deep Residual networks. The CNN that they had developed is a modified version of the AlexNet architecture. The NutriNet uses pre-trained models of some other architectures. Therefore, it has a larger input image size. It also has an additional convolutional layer that sets it apart from AlexNet. There are six layers in total. The additional layer has been used to gain more knowledge about features in images that have high resolutions.

Zhang, J., Shao, K., and Luo, X. [2] have developed a hybrid CNN-GRNN model that can be efficient with a small sample. During the training phase, the model uses a convolutional neural network (CNN) to extract the features of the image. The fully connected layer then carries out the prediction.

During the testing phase, feature extraction is done by the CNN similar to training, and the classification is done by the GRNN. The GRNN, which has better function approximation capability, replaces the BP neural network. The GRNN has only one variable which makes it better for training than BP. There is no need for the network to iterate. It is able to work with a small sample database. This increases the identification precision and expands the application scope of CNN.

Radovic, Adarkwa, and Wang [3] have given the set of procedures and parameters that need to be used to train CNNs for the efficient and automatic detection of objects on the ground in aerial images. They have used the YOLO software for adapting and testing the CNN.

Zeng, G. [4] discusses the various non-destructive methods that can be employed to detect the quality of fruits. The methods that have been discussed here include detection using optical properties, detection using sonic vibration, detection using machine vision, detection using nuclear magnetic resonance, detection using electrical properties, detection using computed tomography, and detection using electronic noses.

Gao, H., Zhu, F., and Cai, J. [5] have developed a modular electronic nose that can be fitted inside a refrigerator and detect if there is any food spoilage. The user is notified about the spoilage through an LCD display. It works by detecting gases and chemicals like CO_2, acetone, and ethanol that are produced when food items when they rot. Bluetooth module is used to enable wireless communication with the electronic nose. The sensors that they used include CO_2 sensor, alcohol/organic solvent sensor, and temperature humidity sensor. These sensors work together to provide values on the detection of the chemicals at the particular temperature and humidity setting. These inputs are fed to the microcontroller which processes then and sends signals to the Bluetooth module so that it can be transmitted. They have used an ATMega2561 MCU as the microcontroller.

Muralidaran, S., Patil, S., and Poddar, A. [6] have developed a prototype for the detection of the freshness of fruits. They have used various sensors to determine this. A Raspberry Pi has been used to process the data collected. First, they have used an open CV to detect the shape, size, and color of the fruit. They have combined this with the readings from the sensors to make it more efficient. A load cell has been used to determine weights of the fruits placed on it. A gas sensor has been used to detect the presence of gasses present or those emitted by rotten fruits. They have displayed the freshness percentage on an LCD display.

Jayasankar, Jeyashree, Deepalakshmi, R., and Karthika [7] have proposed an efficient classification system for fruits and vegetables using CNN model which extracts features of the image needed for classification. Saliency is a form of image segmentation technique. Image saliency has been used to select the important regions based on the saliency map, i.e., to segment the images in the picture. Three modules have been used for saliency extraction, namely, particular feature extraction—DKL colors, intensity, and orientations are considered as features to extract; activation—utilizing equilibrium distribution over map locations activation maps are formed; and normalization—normalized activation maps are combined into a single image as the output. The VGG model has been then used to train the items for classification. For the experiment, over 26 categories of fruits and vegetables were used and the classifying system achieved an accuracy rate of 95.6%.

Varun, K. S., Kumar, K. A., Chowdary, V. R., and Raju, C. S. K. have designed a system [8] in which an ultrasonic sensor is used to detect the level of water and is displayed as a percentage. The ultrasonic sensor has two parts: trig and echo. Trig emits a sound wave to an object. When it strikes, the object it bounces back and is called the echo. The echo part detects the reflected sound ray and measures the time taken for the sound to return. The distance can be calculated based on this time.

$$v = 2\frac{d}{t} \tag{11.1}$$

where v is the velocity of sound, t is the time taken, and d is the distance between the sensor and the water surface.

$$d = v\frac{t}{2} \tag{11.2}$$

This sensor is mounted on the roof of the tank. Therefore, based on the distance, the level of water in the tank can be determined.

Sunmonu, R., Aduramo, Sodunke, Abdulai, O., and Agboola, E. [9] have developed a cost-effective automatic pump system that turns on the pump if the level of water in the tank falls below a certain percentage. The liquid level is monitored by an ultrasonic sensor that is strategically placed in the tank. The signals from the sensor are fed to a circuit that controls the working of the pump. They have used an ATMega328P for processing the signal from the ultrasonic sensor. The Arduino Uno is not used as it is fragile. They have placed a LCD display to show the percentage of water present in the tank.

Kaner, A., and Rane, M. [10] have developed a model to automate the process of turning the motor off when the tank is filled. The model contains four probes A, B, C, and D, which are placed at four different levels in the tank. Three LED indicators, red, yellow, and green, connected to transistors have been installed at each level. Red denotes that the tank is empty, yellow denotes that it is half full, and green denotes that the tank is full. Once the green LED indicator is on, a relay switch mechanism automatically switches the motor off to avoid wastage of water.

Vargas, Ceres, Martín, and Caldero L. have developed [11] an automated system for filling of bottles based on the level and correct placement of corks. The laser and IR sensors are discarded as these were more suited for opaque and flat surfaces. Hence, ultrasonic technique is used. The knowledge of the echo signals time is used to check if the measurement is valid or not.

- $V_{max} > V_{threshold}$
- The rise time T_r, $T_1 < T_r < T_2$, where T_1, T_2 are empirical values.

Nasikkar, Kulkarni, and Kakuste [12] have developed a state-of-the-art smart refrigerator that intimates the user through an Android app if the quantity of any product is less. They have used various methods of detection of products for the different types of food. IR sensors are used to determine the presence of eggs. Load cells have been used to maintain a certain quantity of food. IR proximity sensors have been used to determine the quantity of milk and juices. The Arduino Uno has been used as the microcontroller. They have also used a GSM module that sends the list of required products to the nearby grocer on the push of a button on the mobile app.

Ringe, Dalavi, and Kabugade [13] have developed a smart refrigerator. A Raspberry Pi module has been used as the main processor. The Raspberry Pi has been used as it has Broadcom BCM2835 SoC full high definition multimedia processors with 512-mb SDRAM memory and it works on the Linux operating system. Gas sensors have been used to determine the freshness of the food. Load sensors have also been used to determine the quantity of the food present. They have used a camera that gives a real-time image of the food items present inside the fridge. An ESP32 Wi-Fi module has been used to connect the fridge to a mobile application.

Wu, H., and Chuang, Y. [14] have built a low-cost smart fridge with Raspberry Pi. They have installed two sensors, namely, the IR proximity sensor and a light sensor. They have used two cameras: one inside and one outside. They are all connected to the Raspberry Pi. The inner camera, which is triggered when the fridge is opened, is used to capture an image of the items inside the fridge. The outer camera, which is triggered when an object is placed near it, captures images of new products that are put into the fridge and adds it to a database created using firebase.

An Android application had been created for users to view food items in the fridge from anywhere at any time.

11.3   Materials and Methods

The smart system must be able to calculate the quantity of items like fruit, vegetables, milk and cartons in the refrigerator every time an object is placed or removed from the fridge. It must be able to detect a wide variety of all the commonly used items in our everyday lifestyle. The smart refrigerator system must also detect the presence of any rotten fruits or vegetables inside the refrigerator so that they can be removed by the user. This is to ensure that the other food does not go spoilt and helps to prevent food wastage. It must notify the user if any object has run out of stock or has gone empty. For this, an application connected to the system that can be accessed from the user's smart mobile phone is needed. The system must be easy to install and must be reliable.

Usability, safety, portability, reliability, extensibility, confidentiality, process integrity, and synchrony are some of the non-functional requirements considered for this proposed system. The hardware and software requirements and the sensors used in the proposed system are listed in Tables 11.1 and 11.2. The system needs two microcontrollers and an array of sensors for functional purposes.

NodeMCU is a microcontroller that was developed by the ESP8266 Opensource Community. MCU stands for micro-controller unit. It acts as an IoT platform. It has an integrated Wi-Fi module (ESP8266) which allows it to directly connect to the internet without other peripherals.

Table 11.1 Materials used in the proposed system.

Hardware	Software
i. Raspberry Pi 3	i. Android Studio
ii. NodeMCU	ii. Rasbian OS
iii. PIR Sensor	iii. Arduino
iv. Ultrasonic sensor	iv. Python IDE
v. Gas sensor - MQ-3 sensor	v. Firebase
vi. Temperature Sensor	
vii. Pi Camera	
viii. Connecting wires	

Table 11.2 Uses and purpose of sensors.

S. no.	Sensor		Uses	Purpose in the proposed system
1	PIR sensor		Automatic lighting, security applications, thermometer	Used to detect when an item is placed in the fridge or removed
2	MQ-3		It is used for detecting gas leakage and for breath analyzer. It can detect Alcohol.	Used to detect if there are any rotten fruits or vegetables in the fridge
3	Ultrasonic sensor		Distance measuring, level measurements, obstacle detection	Used to determine the quantity of milk present in a bottle

(Continued)

Table 11.2 Uses and purpose of sensors. (*Continued*)

S. no.	Sensor		Uses	Purpose in the proposed system
4	DHT11 Sensor		It is used to measure the temperature and humidity	Used to determine the temperature maintained inside the fridge
5	Pi Camera		It is used to capture the object	Used to capture the picture of the items in the fridge.

This along with its small size makes it suitable for IoT devices. It has access to 13 GPIO pins of ESP8266 with 30 pins in total [15].

Raspberry Pi is a single board computer that was developed in the UK by Raspberry Pi Foundation. The model used in this proposed system is the RPi 3. It has four Cortex-A53 processors that use the ARMv8-A 32 bit instruction set and has 1 GB memory, 4 USB ports, 1 HDMI output for video, and 1 analog 3.5-mm phone jack for audio output. It has a microSDHC slot, with USB boot mode. It is Wi-Fi and Bluetooth enabled. It has 40 pins. This module is devoted to the sensing and early detection of food spoilage, mainly fruits and vegetables. This module consists of a gas sensor and temperature/humidity sensor that is controlled by a NodeMCU. These sensors help in measuring some critical values that will help in determining whether the fruits and vegetables are fresh or not. The MQ3 gas sensor detects the presence of any alcohol of ethanol in the air. These are the main gases that fruits and vegetables emit when they start to go rotten or bad. So, when the gas sensor detects the presence of these in the air, its value changes and is notified to the user. The quantity of liquid in bottles is also measured by an ultrasonic sensor fitted in the bottle caps. It detects the level of water or any other liquid inside the refrigerator and updates the info in the database [16].

Sensors placed in the proposed system collect data and they go either to the NodeMCU or Raspberry Pi. The NodeMCU sends the data collected directly to the database. The image data in the Raspberry Pi is transferred to the processor where the objects are identified using the YOLO algorithm. It is then updated to the database. The Android app retrieves data from the database. The flow diagram of the proposed system is shown in Figure 11.1.

The main module has two microcontrollers, namely, the NodeMCU and the Raspberry Pi 3. The ultrasonic sensor, temperature sensor, and gas sensor are connected to the NodeMCU. The PIR motion sensor and the Pi camera are connected to the Raspberry Pi. Firebase is the real-time database that is used to store the data collected by the sensors. The Raspberry Pi is used to provide the 5-V power supply that the sensors require, except the temperature sensor which is powered by the 3.3 V output of the NodeMCU. All the components are connected together using connecting wires and a breadboard. Two B type cables are required to connect the Raspberry Pi and NodeMCU to the processor. The architecture diagram of the proposed system is shown in Figure 11.2. The various phases involved in the proposed system are as follows: image processing, product sensing, quality detection, and Android application.

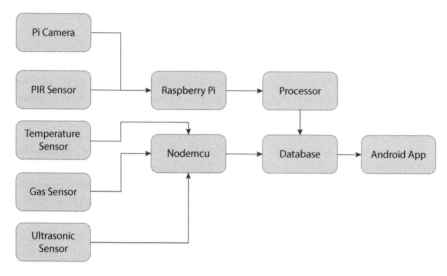

Figure 11.1 Flow diagram of the proposed system.

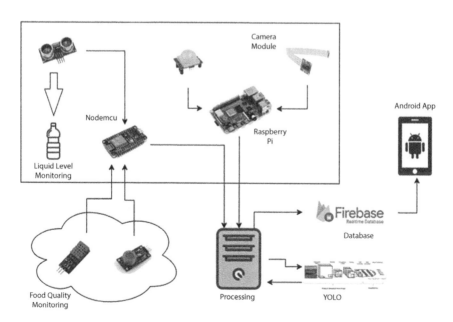

Figure 11.2 Architecture of the proposed system.

11.3.1   Image Processing

The object detection and identification is done in the main processor, here the laptop. The images that are captured by the Pi camera are sent to the processor by a client-server architecture where the Raspberry Pi acts as the server and the processor, the client. The YOLO has been used to recognize the objects. In this proposed system, YOLO has been implemented using DarkNet, an open-source neural network framework.

In order to train computer vision models, there is a need to provide the models with supervision in the form of labeled data. As there are more and more labeled data to model, the model begins to learn the underlying patterns in labeling decisions. After the training process is complete, an object detection model for automatic inference can be deployed.

The model was trained using a set of 500 images that were downloaded from Google. Before training the images have to be annotated. This was done manually using Microsoft's Visual Object Tagging Tool (VoTT).

11.3.2   Product Sensing

This module is used to detect the presence of items in the fridge, identify them, count them, and update it to the database. This module has a Pi camera attached to a Raspberry Pi. The camera takes a snap of the items in the fridge whenever an item is removed or inserted into the fridge. The items are then identified using YOLO and a count is taken. This module also has an ultrasonic sensor that is mounted near the bottle rack. This sensor is used to find the quantity of liquid inside the bottle. This value is then updated to the database.

PIR sensors are normally used to sense motion and to detect the human movement within the allowable range. These sensors are mostly used in home appliances and gadgets because of its characteristics such as low-power, small, less expensive, and do not wear out. "Passive Infrared", "Pyroelectric", or "IR motion" sensors are the other names of PIR sensors.

The output of the PIR motion sensor is connected to GPIO pin 23 of the Raspberry Pi. Whenever motion is detected, an image of the items in the fridge is taken and sent to the processor through the socket connection.

YOLO algorithms in a type of convolution neural network that is able to detect the various objects in a captured image by just analyzing the image once [17]. That is why it is called YOLO and its architecture is shown in Figure 11.3. The algorithm is capable of detecting a large number of items in the same image. It detects objects by providing bounding boxes for each item. It uses regression to detect the objects. The algorithm first predicts

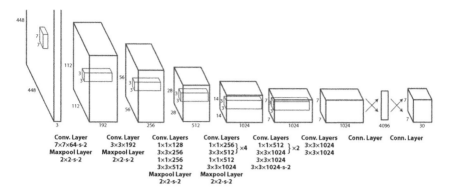

Figure 11.3 YOLO architecture.

where the object is inside the image and draws bounding boxes around it. Then, it predicts the class values of the objects inside each bounding box. There are a total of 24 convolutional layers that help in extracting the features of the image. There are two more dense layers that predict the class of the object. A neural network framework called DarkNet is used to implement the YOLO model.

11.3.3   Quality Detection

MQ-3 sensors are suitable for detecting alcohol, hexane, benzene, CH_4, LPG, and CO. This sensor has high sensitivity to alcohol and has high resistance to disturbance of gasoline, smoke, and vapor. This sensor offers an analog resistive output based on alcohol concentration. When the alcohol gas exists, the sensor's conductivity becomes higher along with the gas concentration increasing. The gas sensor connected to the NodeMCU detects the presence of any rotten gas and updates the status of the air inside the fridge to the database.

11.3.4   Android Application

The Android app is specifically developed to display what items are present in the refrigerator. The app also allows the user to set up a threshold for each of the products. The application is connected to the firebase database to receive the updated stock of contents in the refrigerator. There are four tabs: Grocery, Bottles, Quality, and Thresholds. The Grocery tab shows the items available in the fridge at that moment. It has to be updated concurrently with the database. The Bottles tab shows the quantity of liquid in the

apple:6
banana:4
bottle:4
capsicum:1
carrot:1
egg:1
juice:3
lemon:1
milk:2
orange:4
papaya:1
pineapple:2
tomato:1
watermelon:1

Gas Detected:NO
Humidity:74
Temperature:33

Figure 11.4 Pages in the Android app.

bottle and whether they are empty, full, or half full. The Quality tab shows the details of the temperature, humidity, and presence of any rotten gases inside the fridge (Figure 11.4).

11.4   Results and Discussion

The system consists of two microcontrollers, namely, Raspberry Pi and NodeMCU. It also has various sensors like the PIR sensor, pi camera, MQ3 sensor (gas sensor), and ultrasonic sensor. The object detection module consists of the PIR sensor and Pi camera connected to the Raspberry Pi microcontroller. Whenever a person opens the fridge, the PIR sensor detects motion and triggers the Pi camera to take an image of the contents of the refrigerator. The quality and quantity measuring module consists of the gas sensor and the ultrasonic sensor connected to the NodeMCU. All these are connected to the processor, in this case a computer. The experimental setup of the proposed system is shown in Figure 11.5.

The dataset used to train the YOLO algorithm to detect images was downloaded from Kaggle. It consists of some basic items in a refrigerator used in our daily lifestyle (Figure 11.6). The efficiency of the object detection system can be improved by using a larger dataset for training.

Figure 11.7 is an image of four capsicums. Figure 11.7a is the result got after training the YOLO model using 100 training images. From the

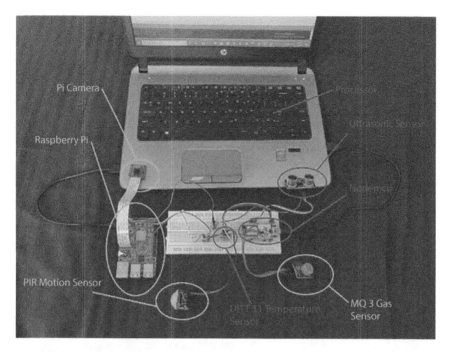

Figure 11.5 Experimental setup of the proposed system.

image, we see that along with the four capsicums, it has also given a few other extra detections, and also the detection of the fruits is not fully accurate. It shows some capsicums to be labeled as apples. Figures 11.7b and c show the same image but tested on a model trained by using 200 images and 500 images. They have now detected all the four capsicums and have not detected any other fruit or vegetable. So, the accuracy of the proposed system can be increased by including a larger dataset for training. I have trained my model to detect 14 types of items in the refrigerator: apples, oranges, capsicum, banana, juice box, cake, tomatoes, carrots, grapes, potatoes, chili, lemon, egg, and pineapple.

Figure 11.8 is an image of the inside of a refrigerator. Figure 11.8a is the result got after training the YOLO model using 100 training images. From the image, we see that the model has not detected most of the apples and capsicums. It has also wrongly classified capsicum as an orange. Figure 11.8b shows the same image but tested on a model trained by using 200 images. It has now detected all but one apple. It has detected only one capsicum and has done two misclassifications. Figure 11.8c shows the same image but tested on a model trained by using 500 images. It has detected all fruits except an orange. There are also no misclassifications.

(a)

(b)

Figure 11.6 (a) Annotating images in VoTT (b) Annotating images in VoTT.

Figure 11.7 Object detection using YOLO model trained with 100 (a) vs. 200 (b) vs. 500 (c) images.

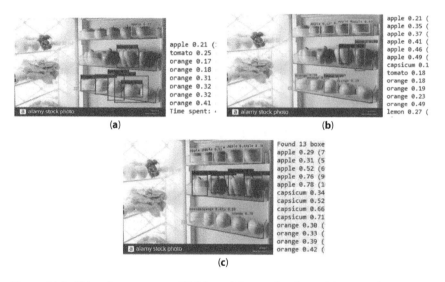

Figure 11.8 Object detection using YOLO model trained with 100 (a) vs. 200 (b) vs. 500 (c) images.

Table 11.3 shows the analysis of training the model. The model currently has an accuracy of about 95%. Ten random images were selected and were fed to the model trained using 100, 200, and 500 images. There were 40 items in all 10 images included. The accuracy was calculated using the following equation:

$$Accuracy = \frac{Number\ of\ Items\ detected\ correctly}{40} * 100$$

Table 11.3 Analysis of the model (10 testing images - 40 items).

No. of images used for training	Correct detection	Incorrect detection or not detected	Accuracy
100	28	20	70%
200	35	10	87.5%
500	38	5	95%

Figure 11.9 shows the graph of the number of epochs vs. the loss after each epoch. The model was trained for 80 epochs.

Figure 11.10 shows the output of the quality and liquid quantity measuring modules. The first image is for an empty bottle (21 cm in length). The second image is for the same bottle but half full of water (10 cm). Thus, the ultrasonic sensor can be used to determine the approximate amount of liquid in the bottle.

Epoch vs Value Loss

colour
— red

Figure 11.9 Graph of epoch vs. loss during training.

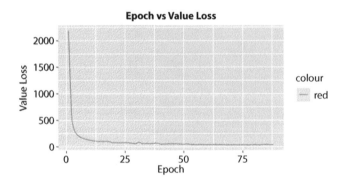

```
Current humidity = 73%  temperature = 33 C     Current humidity = 74%  temperature = 33 C
Centimeter : 21                                Centimeter : 9
1024                                           1024
Current humidity = 73%  temperature = 33 C     Current humidity = 73%  temperature = 33 C
Centimeter : 21                                Centimeter : 10
1024                                           1024
Current humidity = 73%  temperature = 33 C     Current humidity = 73%  temperature = 33 C
Centimeter : 21                                Centimeter : 10
1024                                           1024
                                               Current humidity = 73%  temperature = 33 C
                                               Centimeter : 11
                                               1024
```

Figure 11.10 Output from NodeMCU in serial monitor.

11.5 Conclusion

A smart refrigerator module that can help the user to know items present in the refrigerator without being at home has been developed. This intelligence alerts them to buy any missing items on the way home. The smart module has many advantages. The user does not have to go home, open the fridge, see what items are missing, and then go out to buy the things needed. The need for extra travel is avoided. It saves fuel and time. The product quality monitoring module can detect gases from rotten fruits. One important feature is that the user knows the presence of rotten fruits or vegetables in the refrigerator.

Further training can be done to make the system more accurate—more methods for recognizing spoiled food like image recognition can be introduced. The way of measuring liquid quantities using the ultrasonic sensor is also not very accurate. Measurements can be made better by using other methods like using load cells to calculate the weight of the bottles. To make it autonomous, this system can be connected to an e-commerce website so it can order items that are about to get over.

References

1. Mezgec, S. and Seljak, B.K., NutriNet: A Deep Learning Food and Drink Image Recognition System for Dietary Assessment. *Nutrients, 9*, 7, 657, 2017.
2. Zhang, J., Shao, K., Luo, X., Small sample image recognition using improved Convolutional Neural Network. *J. Vis. Commun. Image Represent.*, 55, 640–647, 2018.
3. Radovic, M., Adarkwa, O., Wang, Q., Object Recognition in Aerial Images Using Convolutional Neural Networks. *J. Imaging, 3*, 2, 21, 2017.
4. Zeng, G., Fruit and vegetables classification system using image saliency and convolutional neural network. *2017 IEEE 3rd Information Technology and Mechatronics Engineering Conference (ITOEC)*, 2017.
5. Gao, H., Zhu, F., Cai, J., A Review of Non-destructive Detection for Fruit Quality. *Computer and Computing Technologies in Agriculture III IFIP Advances in Information and Communication Technology*, pp. 133–140, 2010.
6. Muralidaran, S., Patil, S., Poddar, A., *Refrigerator Food Contamination Detection using Electronic Nose*, n.d. https://courses.engr.illinois.edu/ece445/getfile.asp?id=12210
7. Jayasankar, K., Karthika, B., Jeyashree, T., Deepalakshmi, R., Karthika, G., Fruit Freshness Detection Using Raspberry PI. *Int. J. Innov. Res. Appl. Sci. Eng., 1*, 10, 202, 2018.

8. Varun, K.S., Kumar, K.A., Chowdary, V.R., Raju, C.S.K., Water Level Management Using Ultrasonic Sensor(Automation). *Int. J. Comput. Sci. Eng.*, 6, 6, 799–804, 2018.

9. Sunmonu, R., Aduramo, S., Abdulai, O., Agboola, E., Development of An Ultrasonic Sensor Based Water Level Indicator With Pump Switching Technique. *J. Electr. Eng.*, 3, 5, 2018.

10. Kaner, A. and Rane, M., Automatic Water Level Indicator & Controller (To control water level of overhead tank). *Int. J. Adv. Res. Electr. Commun. Eng. (IJARECE)*, 6, 11, 1287–1290, 2017.

11. Vargas, E., Ceres, R., Marti´n, J., Caldero´n, L., Ultrasonic sensor for liquid-level inspection in bottles. *Sens. Actuators A: Phys.*, 61, 1–3, 256–259, 1997.

12. S., M.K., Nasikkar, B.S., Kulkarni, D.V., Kakuste, G.K., Smart Refrigerator Using Internet of Things (IoT). *Int. J. Adv. Res., Ideas Innovations Technol.*, 3, 1, 842–846, n.d.

13. Ringe, A., Dalavi, M., Kabugade, S., P, M.P., IoT Based Smart Refrigerator Using Raspberry PI. *Int. J. Res. Anal. Rev. (IJRAR)*, 6, 2, 605–619, 2019.

14. Wu, H. and Chuang, Y., Low-Cost Smart Refrigerator. *2017 IEEE International Conference on Edge Computing (EDGE)*, pp. 228–231, 2017.

15. Desai, S., Understanding IoT Management for Smart Refrigerator. *Presented at the National Conference on ICT & IoT*, 2016.

16. Miniaoui, S., Atalla, S., Hashim, K.F.B., Introducing Innovative Item Management Process Towards Providing Smart Fridges. *2019 2nd International Conference on Communication Engineering and Technology (ICCET)*, 2019.

17. Muehlemann, A., *How to train your own YOLOv3 detector from scratch*, 2019, November 18. https://blog.insightdatascience.com/how-to-train-your-own-yolov3-detector-from-scratch-224d10e55de2

12

Effective Methodologies in Pharmacovigilance for Identifying Adverse Drug Reactions Using IoT

Latha Parthiban[1]*, Maithili Devi Reddy[2] and A. Kumaravel[3]

[1]*Bharath Institute of Higher Education and Research, Tamilnadu, India*
[2]*Department of Computer Science and Engineering, Bharath Institute of Higher Education and Research, Tamilnadu, India*
[3]*School of Computing, Bharath Institute of Higher Education and Research, Tamilnadu, India*

Abstract

Nowadays, every recommended drug has some side effects based on the health of the patient. This negative impact leads to Adverse Drug Event (ADE) and the time of ADE association to the specified drug is called as **Adverse Drug Reaction** (ADR). With each and every day, more and more devices are getting connected to internet and IoT is becoming an evolving area. Since ADR results in fatality of humans, the primary analysis of any disease is a most significant process. As a result, the protection of a novel drug has been determined from its entire manufacturing. Unexpectedly, the potential of analyzing a drug's toxins has been restricted by several medicinal tools. At the time of modeling any kind of drug, it has been sampled on animals in order to test the function of drug applied, but the capability of inferring ADRs is minimized by the impotence of animal sampling which has to be completely understandable for human impacts. While a drug provides primary toxicity investigation, it is applied for testing on humans at the time of increased population. In this work, a novel neural predictive classifier for improving the prediction rate of ADR is proposed.

Keywords: ADR, IoT, Pharmacovigilance, feature selection, data mining, neural predictive classifier

---

Corresponding author: lathaparthiban@yahoo.com

R. Anandan, Suseendran Gopalakrishnan, Souvik Pal and Noor Zaman (eds.) The Industrial Internet of Things (IIoT): Intelligent Analytics for Predictive Maintenance, (301–320) © 2022 Scrivener Publishing LLC

12.1   Introduction

Generally, data is assumed to be the major source for several trading process and commercial applications. By identifying the information about medicinal fields is an optimal process from where data mining (DM) task has been considered as more crucial operation. Some of the database refers a collection of data that is correlated with certain structure as well as requirements. The process of developing different data is named as "Data Base Management System" (DBMS). Here, a new computation of Knowledge Discovery is applied for the complete database. DM can be determined by obtaining hidden data which is represented by massive number of data repositories. Knowledge Discovery in Databases (KDD) that is said to be non-trivial operation to find effective, novel, probably suitable, as well as readable patterns of data. According to the above definition, different types of data like numerical value, alphabets are determined by applying this method. The association among all data provides information and it is altered into knowledge about historical facts and future plans. In addition, there are some other parameters such as data pre-processing, selection, cleaning, and visualizing which are considered to be portions engaged in KDD operation.

Here, DM is connected with the study of database, Machine Learning (ML) and visualization. It is used to discover efficient remedy for many types of ailments and focus in exploring the required information from numerous set of data. DM is the crucial part of KDD which is applicable to derive the significant patterns from data that can be perceived in a simple manner and to orient the data. It is a model applied to find huge amount of data and to offer adaptable data. Also, KDD process involves in forming new information. Data warehouse is considered to be the major source to obtain data and pre-processing is an essential procedure to analyze various types of dataset. The final stage of KDD is to verify the pattern that has been generated with the help of DM methods which appears in huge database. Hence, the predefined data is composed with set of patterns that describe about features of data, patterns that are presented consecutively, and object that has been identified inside the clusters present in database which is described in Figure 12.1.

12.2   Literature Review

DM is used to find essential association, patterns, and movements between massive data that has been recorded in repositories, by using the pattern

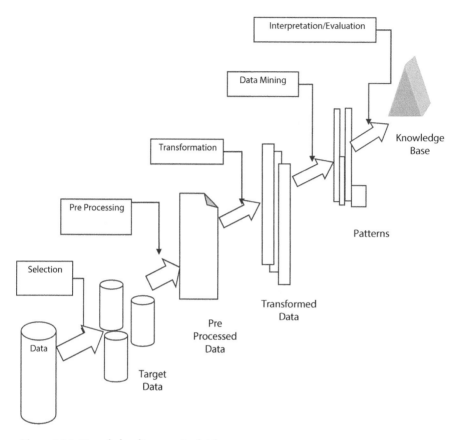

Figure 12.1 Knowledge discovery in databases.

recognition techniques as well as statistical models. The above method is assumed to be an evolving portion of scientific development, in educational sector and firms. Mining is one of the promising issues in clinical field. Medicinal DM deals with maximum capability to identify the hidden patterns from medical application.

DM is a logical task used to search maximum number of applicable data. By using the DM method, huge amount of information is capable of transforming essential as well as required data. Also, DM is more suitable for physicians to develop and improvise the disease prediction in a rapid manner, thus risk in detecting the ailments are minimized. Diverse models are assessable for every domain. DM is one of the mandatory factors in medical application which offers automatic prediction data that is obtained from huge dataset. In [1], the authors developed new ML technique that incorporates simulated annealing (SA) and support vector machine (SVM).

In [2], the authors discussed many feature selection algorithms. They also proposed a variant of the approach seeing the significance of each feature and verified the presentation of the proposed methods by experiments with various real-world datasets. Their feature collection methods based on the biologically inspired algorithms produced better presentation than other methods in terms of the classification accuracy and the feature significance. In particular, the modified method considering feature meaning demonstrated even more enhanced performance.

In [3], it was concluded that real-life data groups are often spread with noise. In [4], the authors presented supervised learning classification techniques. The results show that SVM with Data Gain and Wrapper method has the best results as related to others who tested. In [5], the authors presented medical diagnostic system. In [6–10], the authors discuss the ML algorithms using evolutionary computing for classification. In [11–14], the authors describe the various classification approaches for Pharmacovigilance. In [15], security requirement for medical diagnostic system was discussed.

12.3   Data Mining Tasks

The main objective of computer invention is to give assistance for humans by implementing difficult and prolonged task in an automated manner. The major advantage in discovering computer is that massive amount of digital information has been saved in the storage space provided by machines. Such data volumes could be applied to learn the facts, behaviors, and default aspects as well as to make decisions according to the human requirements. Several models are proposed for suggesting machines to read information. Specifically, ML is one of the scientific domains which have been treated as implementation of frameworks, rules, and techniques which may be obtained from data. These models are capable of constructing a detective method according to input data that is applied in decision making process. In recent times, DM is referred to be the region of computer science from where ML models are applied to identify the past unreliable features from numerous dataset. In addition, DM is used in examining the datasets which helps in discovering provocative, and essential patterns, and tendency. The DM process is comprised with models at interchanging AI, ML, statistics, arithmetic, database systems, and so on. The main objective of DM process is to obtain data from a dataset as well as to convert in a readable format that can be applied for future application. It is assumed to be the intermediary procedure of KDD process which concentrates in

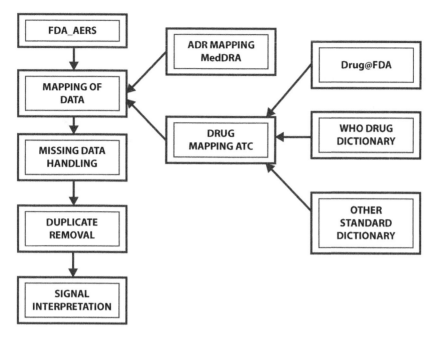

Figure 12.2 Data mining in Pharmacovigilance.

finding more reliable patterns and techniques that helps in predicting the data type. Also, few steps in KDD are data preparation, data selection, data cleaning, combination of essential data, and interpreting results obtained from mining process. Diverse DM techniques are developed as well as executed in various research fields like statistics, ML, mathematics, AI, and pattern recognition that applies particular models. There are commonly used DM processes, which are explained in the upcoming sections. Data mining procedure in Pharmacovigilance is shown in Figure 12.2.

12.3.1   Classification

The key objective of this model is to categorize a dataset into more than one predetermined classes. It can be achieved by implementing the mapping which is derived from a vector of values toward a classified parameter. From this classification, the membership of a data instance can be detected for provided predetermined classes. For example, collection of outlet can save customer information into three classes, namely, maximum spending, moderate spending, as well as minimum spending users. The classifying operation is applied for several other domains like economic sectors, bioinformatics, classification of document, multimedia, textual computation, social networks, and so on.

12.3.2   Regression

This method is considered as forecasting model which connect the dataset to quantitative features as well as computes the variable measure. Regression has various applications like using the likelihood where a patient acquires illness on the basis of analysis report and detection of spontaneous team according to the technical information of existing matches. It is generally applied in financial, ecological studies, market tendency, meteorology, as well as epidemiology.

12.3.3   Clustering

The DM operation is applied to find a group of clusters to define the data. Mostly, clustering techniques have been applied in the absence of class which has to be forecasted in an available input data and classified into set of identical instances. There are few applications of clustering which is applicable to find the similar subsets of customers present in database of business groups of objects including the same attributes. It is utilized for several applications like gene computing, intrusion of network, clinical imaging, analyzing the violation, and text mining. In contrary, the classification has predefined classes that should be obtained from data, and seeking for cluster which depends upon the measures of homogeneous data with no help of clients.

12.3.4   Summarization

It is one among the DM process which offers an accurate definition of subset of data. The summarization models are often applied to unstructured data such as classifying text and combine the document by distributing identical behavior. It also uses several tedious functions that have summary criteria as well as identifying the functional associations among variables. Hence, it is mostly employed in the communicative analysis of data and automated production of reports.

12.3.5   Dependency Modeling

It is employed for identifying the methods which explains the important base among variables. This method mainly concentrates in finding the dependencies of each data values. The dependency models can be divided into two phases. Initially, structural level of a method that is based on local variables, whereas quantitative level denotes the efficiency of dependency in a numeric scale. These modeling techniques are applied in retailing, commercial purpose, process management, software designing, and assembly line optimizing process.

12.3.6   Association Rule Discovery

This technique aims in finding the set of items that has been collected from records of a database as well as the correlation between this information is more useful to obtain maximum association which satisfy particular thresholds. It is mainly employed to discover robust patterns from huge datasets under the application of diverse values. Various domains apply this model to understand the intersection massive dataset. At this point, the association rule is named as market basket analysis. Also, there is alternate mandatory application from where the association discovery has been employed such that accessing web page, interacting network application, credit card facilities, medical analysis, bioinformatics, and so on.

12.3.7   Outlier Detection

Here, the outlier is said to be an observation which is more inconsistent by deviating from alternate items of dataset from where it has been originated. Even though the outlier is assumed to be fault or error, it carries more essential data. These models are presented for various domains like environmental analysis, credit card malfunctioning, medicinal trials, network intrusion detection, system process investigation, as well as alternate data analyzing issues.

12.3.8   Prediction

This operation seeks for association among temporary series of actions. The data instances looks like sequences of actions, from where all functions are composed with time of event. There is major problem in detecting the event sequences which is to discover the sequential segments, and set of events that happens frequently. For instance, identifying that a predefined event $E1$ happens, within a time interval t, also event $E2$ with maximum probability p. Instances of applications to apply for all alarm detection used in telecommunications, web log designing, client action series, error detection while developing plants, and environmental conditions.

12.4   Feature Selection Techniques in Data Mining

Feature selection is an important procedure in DM using different techniques as given below.

12.4.1   GAs for Feature Selection

In [4], the authors presented a integrative co-evolutionary technique for FS-based GA including three populations, where it mainly aims on FS process and on instance selection, as well as to concentrate on FS and instance selection. Here, the introduced model reports the FS and instance selection in a unique performance that minimizes the processing duration. These types of models undergo further investigations for the provided datasets with thousands of features that contributes unwanted features and noisy data. In addition, they established massive populations dependent GA for the purpose of FS technique, which is comprised with two adjacent populations distributed for interchanging data to improvise the searching potential. Here, local search has been computed on optimal individual for all population that tends to enhance the computation. This presented technique undergo testing with diverse filter as well as wrapper values, that showcased a powerful FS process, also sampled using datasets along with more number of features.

The authors in [5] projected a model to report the FS-based issue by using GAs for feature clustering, and GA has been applied to make optimized cluster middle values in clustering model which is essential to cluster the features as diverse clusters. Features present in every cluster undergoes ranking on the basis of distance measures to the intermediate cluster. The FS process could be attained by selecting top most features as a representative from every cluster. The deployed model shows an effective datasets including more amounts of features. They established a GA-relied FS technique by considering the domain knowledge about economical distress forecasting so that features are divided as various groups as well as GA have been employed for feature subsets that contains best candidate features from every cluster. The above process might consist of identical issue with respect to avoid feature communications. Subsequently, GA is applied in two-stage method, which uses a filter value for ranking the features and selects a first ranked feature which is then employed for GA based FS.

Bio-encoding method in GA which comprises of every chromosome along with pair of strings is applies in [6]. The primary string is a binary-encoded, which denotes the FS process while secondary string is encoded in the form of real-numbers by implying the feature weight. By integrating with Adaboost learning technique, the bio-encoding approach reaches a best performance when compared with conventional binary encoding. A novel representation, which includes FS as well as parameter optimization of assertive classifying method like SVM, was used by the authors. The length is defined as total count of features as well as parameters. They designed a three-level representation in GA and Multilayer Perceptron (MLP) which is useful in FS operation that signifies the election of features, also pruning of neurons, and the structure of MLP. The above mentioned instances recommend that combination of FS as well as optimizing the classification technique is very efficient to enhance the classifying operation as data and classification models has to be optimized.

12.4.2   GP for Feature Selection

Several works have been applied genetic programming (GP) for identifying optimized feature subset and concurrently equipped in the form of classifier. In this, a wrapper FS method which depends upon the multi-tree GP that selects optimal feature subset at the same time as well as a trained classification under the application of chosen features was modeled. Additionally, two novel crossover processes are established to improve the GP performance in selecting features. According to the two crossover operations developed in [7], it deployed an alternate crossover tool that operates in random selection of sub-tree from the primary parent and to search for effective location from alternate parent. It displayed a successful capability of GP to perform as simultaneous FS and in training a classifier. It has the same work that applies GAs in concurrent FS and to produce optimized classification process; however, it has the major variations of GP that applied for searching process to select features and in the form of classifier for classification technique (embedded FS) as GA is employed only for exploring purpose.

The authors also presented a mutual data metric technique for ranking single features as well as to eliminate the vulnerable unwanted features in a primary stage, where GP have been used for selecting a subset of residual features. In order to acquire various merits of diverse values, various filter values has been employed in ranking features and group of features have been selected on the basis of individual metric. By concatenating the above features, it might be applied as input for GP to improve the FS operation. Unfortunately, there is a potential shortcoming is that to eliminate the essential features with no consideration of communication with alternate features. In [7], the authors developed alternate type of single feature ranging technology, that consist of frequency embedded feature which has a unique score and ranked accordingly. Consequently, FS has been accomplished by applying most top ranged features which is induced for classification. It is the path of estimating the unique features to consider the adjacent ones that is capable of removing the shortcoming of individuals to rank features, respectively.

A GP relied multi-objective filter FS model has been presented here for binary classification issues. In contrast, many of the filter approaches can estimate the relation of individual feature of class labels, and the presented technique is capable of finding the correlation among hidden association from feature subset as well as the target classes, also to attain effective classification process. GP consists of minimum number of process in selecting features for multi-objective condition. It is more attractive to examine the upcoming process as GP shows a potential reporting of FS as well as multi-objective issues.

12.4.3   PSO for Feature Selection

Here, continuous PSO as well as binary PSO have been applied for filter and wrapper techniques with unique objective and multi-objective FS. The presentation of every particle within PSO has been applied in selecting features which is a typical operation where the dimension is same as total count of features present in the dataset. A bit-string could be a binary value where binary PSO in continuous PSO. While applying the binary representation, "1" refers the FS, whereas "0" symbolizes no selection. In case of employing the continuous representation, a threshold θ can be applied to compute the selection of specified feature, which has the value greater than θ, and then, adjacent features are selected. Else non-selected features are available. In [8], the authors presented the application of PSO and statistical clustering that helps to cluster the identical features into similar cluster for FS that has novel representation to combine the statistical feature clustering data at the time searching operation is carried out in PSO. The novel representation reveals that the features derived from similar cluster that has been organized together as well as individual feature have been chosen from all clusters. The projected technique shows the potential of minimizing the count of features. The technique was enhanced by enabling the selection process for many features from the identical cluster which helps to improvise the classifying operation.

By acquiring the knowledge from neighbors' experience, by interacting under the application of gbest, as well as by learning from every individual's self-experience by pbest are assumed to be the main suggestions of PSO. In [8], the authors deployed a gbest resetting model by adding zero features to suggest the swarm for searching tiny feature subsets. They assumed the count of features while upgrading pbest as well as gbest at the time of exploring PSO, that tends to decrease the amount of features than the conventional update of pbest and gbest techniques with no alleviation in classifying operation. All estimation present in local search has been improved by measuring the fitness relied on features which is often modified from required to non-required and vice versa. Therefore, the presented model again reduces the feature count and enhances the classifying performance than existing models as well as a reputed PSO. Any PSO with more number of swarms helps to share the experience which can be used in FS operation but tends in greater computation expense.

12.4.4   ACO for Feature Selection

In previous models, ACO as well as SVM have been employed for wrapper FS that is useful in face recognition, which consist of actual features that are obtained by applying the strategy of PCA from the images which is present in pre-processing phase. In [8], the authors projected the application of restricted pheromone measures in ACO that is applied for FS process as well as the deployed technique has been upgraded with pheromone trails of edges by linking diverse features of best-so-far solution. The final outcome displayed that the newly deployed technique attains good performance when compared with SA, a GA, and TS dependent models with respect to classification process and amount of features. Techniques applied in [8] use a ACO to select features concurrently as well as to parameter optimization of SVM, that consist of weighting model used in computing the probability of ant choosing specific feature. They also integrated ACO with DE for FS, and DE has been applied in searching the optimized feature subset on the basis of solutions derived by ACO. A classical FS technique has been presented for ACO, so that ACO starts with minimal number of core features. In [9], the authors referred an applicable ACO model including two colonies for FS task, where the initial feature allocated the feature value which is more essential and secondary colony is useful to choose unique features. They related the process of ACO along with GA-relied FS model that initiates ensemble classification. Hence, the simulation outcome depicts that ACO performs better in case of single classifiers are tiny at the time of GA performing optimal process while having maximum values.

Several ACO-based wrapper techniques are applied as fitness evaluation criteria and the fitness of ants have been measured with the help of entire classification process, as the operation of single features consider the further enhancing operation. Also, the fitness functions have been added for classifying process as well as count of features. Then, by expanding the process on individual objective ACO as well as a fuzzy classification that is applied for FS process, they deployed a multi-objective wrapper technique where the ACO focuses in reducing classification error as well as count of features. In [9], the authors introduced a novel multi-objective ACO which can be applied for filter FS operation that obtains elitism principle to improve the converging process that applied non-dominated solutions to include pheromone which results in reinforcing the exploitation, as well as to be used in a crowding relational operator to balance the diversity of solutions. The derived final outcome shows a better performance when compared with individual objective methodologies, since it is more attractive to analyze the application of multi-objective ACO in FS process.

12.5   Classification With Neural Predictive Classifier

The Semi-Convergent Matrix is constructed in SCM-NPC technique for discovering similarity information based on cloud user request on cloud big data with higher search accuracy. The SCM-NPC method employs Semi-Convergent Matrix techniques in parallel which maximize the flow of computation at the time of data extraction. Let us consider that there are numerous CN_{ij} Cloud nodes dispersed in Cloud platform. The cloud nodes which contain the similar user requested data in Cloud platform are arranged in Semi-Convergent Matrix to improve the rate of computation during data extraction. Therefore, Semi-Convergent Matrix structure M is represented as follows:

$$M = \begin{pmatrix} CN_{11} & CN_{12}... & CN_{1n} \\ CN_{21} & CN_{22}... & CN_{2n} \\ CN_{n1} & CN_{n2}... & CN_{nn} \end{pmatrix} \tag{12.1}$$

From Equation (12.1), CN_{ij} indicates the cloud nodes that consisting of resemblance user requested data. In Semi-Convergent Matrix, cloud nodes are arranged in row and column respectively. With the ever increasing size in big data, the issues that limit the applications are time complexity and space complexity. The Semi-Convergent Matrix in SCM-NPC technique significantly reduces the time complexity and space complexity through building the matrix with cloud nodes that includes similarity

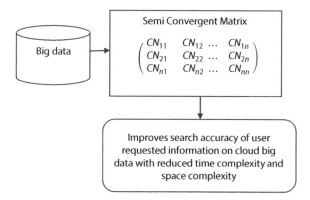

Figure 12.3 Semi-Convergent Matrix construction for improving search accuracy.

user requested data. The matrix M is a Semi-Convergent Matrix if the limit stratifies following conditions:

$$\lim_{k \to \infty} M^k \qquad (12.2)$$

The following diagram shows the Semi-Convergent Matrix construction process in SCM-NPC technique.

As shown in Figure 12.3, SCM-NPC technique efficiently identifies similarity information of cloud user requested data by creating the Semi-Convergent Matrix. This, in turn, helps for SCM-NPC technique to improve search accuracy on big data with minimum time complexity and space complexity.

12.5.1 Neural Predictive Classifier

The neural predictive classifier exploits the human neuron on a system. Billions of neurons are interconnected in human brain for conveying the information's with other layer using electric and chemical signals. A multi-layer network called neural predictive classifier which is made up of input layer neurons, hidden neuron, and output neurons.

Back propagation neural network is a supervised learning that is used to classify the medical data conditions on big data. The main aim of using neural predictive classifier is to reduce error rate during the classification. Back propagation is performed with the aid of three different layers. The construction of the neural network for classification of medical data on big data is shown in Figure 12.4.

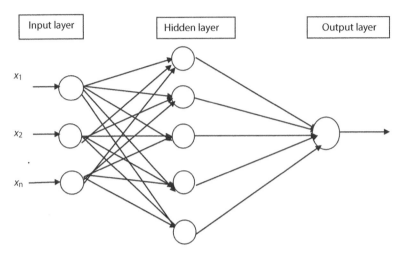

Figure 12.4 Structure of neural predictive classifier for classification.

Figure 12.5 demonstrates the processing diagram of activation function. The hidden layer is a processed layer that includes two functions, i.e., sum function and activation function. The activation function utilized sigmoid function since it unites nearly linear performance, curved behavior and nearly constant behaviors based on the input value. A sigmoid function is a statistical function that contains an "S" shaped curve as a sigmoid curve. A sigmoid function lies within the finite ranges at negative infinity and positive infinity, while the output can only be a number between −1 and 1. The sigmoid function is mathematically formulated as follows:

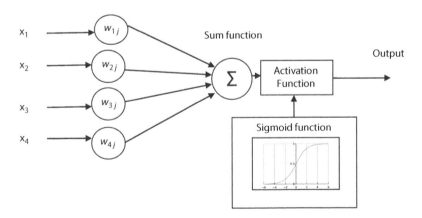

Figure 12.5 Processing diagram of activation function for classification.

$$\sigma(x) = \frac{1}{1 + e^{-x}} \tag{12.3}$$

From Equation (12.3), sigmoid function σ (x) is formulated. In hidden layer, product of the input similarity data from the input layer with the weight between input layer and hidden layer is summed with the aid of SUM function. The SUM is set of the output nodes from hidden layer which multiplied with the weights consigned to the each input value to get a single number and process through sigmoid function (activation function). Subsequently, a new weight among the hidden layer and the output layer transmitted from hidden layer output to the output layer. The output layer is the processing unit that contains summation function and activation function. In output layer, the multiplication of the activated output of hidden layer and the synaptic weight among the hidden layer and output layer is summed up with the support summation function. Then, it is transmitted to the activation function for choosing final output using threshold value of the activation function.

The resultant output of neural network is compared with the target for computing the error rate which is expressed as follows:

$$Error\ Rate\ (ER) = Desired\ output\ value\ (D_R) - \\ Actual\ output\ value(O_v) \tag{12.4}$$

The measured error value then passed backward to the input from the output by means of updating the synaptic weight. This process is repeatedly performed until the error is reduced during the classification of climate data on cloud big data. Thus, the learning rate and momentum rate are initiated for gradient fall to discover the weight that lessens the error. The error rate between the output layer and hidden layer are determined by using following mathematical formula:

$$ER = D_o - A_v$$
$$\delta = ER\ A_v\ (1 - A_v) \tag{12.5}$$

$$\delta = (D_o - A_v)\ A_v\ (1 - A_v) \tag{12.6}$$

From Equations (12.5) and (12.6), error rate is determined and then compared with target value, whereas D_o is represents desired output neuron value and A_v signifies the activation value using sigmoid function. Here, A_v $(1 - Av)$ indicates the derivative of the sigmoid function in hidden layer. Therefore, the synaptic weight is computed is represented as follows:

$$\Delta SW_{y,z} = \eta \, \delta \, X \qquad (12.7)$$

From Equation (12.7), $\Delta SWt_{y,z}$ demotes the updated synaptic weight between the output layer and the hidden layer, whereas η represents the learning factor that characterizes the relative variations in synaptic weights and input (X). As a result, the updated synaptic weight is described as the error multiplied with the input. Thus, the new weight is characterized as follows:

$$SW_{y,z} = SW_{y,z} + \Delta SW_{y,z} \qquad (12.8)$$

The above waiting function is utilized for computing the weight value. Hence, the new weight is formulated by using the following:

$$W_{new} = SW_{y,z} + \eta \, \delta \, X \qquad (12.9)$$

From Equation (12.9), the new weight is formulated depends on original weight is assigned with updated synaptic weight. Therefore, the SCM-NPC technique used neural predictive classifier to improve the classification accuracy of climate data on big data. The number of neurons (i.e., attributes) in the hidden layer is to find out the optimal number of neurons which supports to provide the better classification of climate data on cloud big data. There are two functions exploited in the hidden neurons, i.e., summation of the synaptic weight and the activation function. The activation function utilized in neural predictive classifier as sigmoid transfer function to handle complex problems during the classification of climate data on cloud big data. At last, the output layer generates the target output value for predicting climate data information on cloud big data.

The algorithmic process of neural predictive classifier for classification of medical data on cloud big data is shown in the following.

Algorithm 12.1 Neural predictive classifier.

// Neural Predictive Classifier Algorithm
Input: Similarity data obtained from Semi-Convergent Matrix
Output: Improves classification accuracy
Step 1: Begin
Step 2: Initialize the neural network with random weights
Step 3: For each similarity data, do
Step 4:   calculate the required activation rate output
Step 5:   compute the error rate using (12.4)
Step 6:   **For** each weight
Step 8:   Update the synaptic weight using (12.7) between the hidden and output layer
Step 9:   **End** for
Step 10: while (stop condition is met)
Step 11: if the activation output value is −1 then
Step 12:   Adverse Drug Reaction
Step 13: else
Step 14:   No Adverse Drug reaction
Step 15: end if
Step 16: end for
Step 17:End

As shown in Algorithm 12.1, at first, the neural network is created with random weights. For similarity data obtained from Semi-Convergent Matrix, the error rate is determined for updating the new weight in back propagation of classifier in order to get the activation output. The output of the activation is concluded, and the climate data is present in cloud big data. In SCM-NPC technique, the sigmoid function is used as an activation function. This produces the required output. If the activation produces the output as −1, then the data is classified as the Adverse Drug Reaction (ADR). Otherwise, the data is no ADR. The neural predictive classifier algorithm classifies the climate data from cloud big data through the activation function which resulting in improved classification accuracy.

12.5.2   MapReduce Function on Neural Class

The SCM-NPC technique employs MapReduce function on neural class to perform prediction analytics of ADR. The MapReduce function in

SCM-NPC technique process huge volumes of data in a parallel fashion. The SCM-NPC technique employs map-reduce function on neural class to perform predictive analytics of ADC as in Figure 12.6. In map reduce function, the input is taken by map task and revamps the content into Key-Value pair where the key has class, attributes, and value acquired from neural class which mathematically represented as follows:

$$Map(Y) \rightarrow (Key, Value) \tag{12.10}$$

$$(Key) \rightarrow (Class, Attributes) \tag{12.11}$$

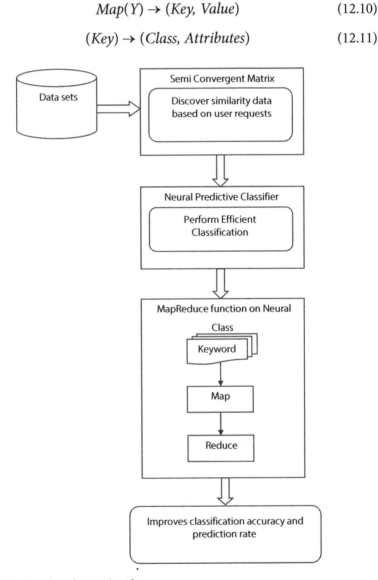

Figure 12.6 Neural predictive classifier.

12.6   Conclusions

In this paper, different computational techniques for feature selection in literature for pharmacovigilance is reviewed and discussed. Also various DM tasks for effective Pharmacovigilance are presented. The classification method proposed can find the presence of ADR and the proposed algorithm provides less computation time when compared to up-to-date works. With all medical devices slowly getting connected to internet, it has become more easy to get patient details and update ADRs.

References

1. Parthiban, L. and Subramanian, R., Intelligent heart disease prediction system using CANFIS and genetic algorithm. *Int. J. Biol., Biomed. Med. Sci.*, 3, 3, 157–160 2008.
2. Xue, B., Zhang, M., Browne, W.N., Particle swarm optimisation for feature selection in classification: Novel initialisation and updating mechanisms. *Appl. Soft Comput.*, 18, 261–276, 2014.
3. Venkatesan, A.S. and Parthiban, L., A novel nature inspired fuzzy tsallis entropy segmentation of magnetic resonance images. *Neuroquantology*, 12, 2, 221–229, 2014.
4. George, G., and Parthiban, L., Multi objective fractional cuckoo search for data clustering and its application to medical field. *J. Med. Imaging Health Inform.*, 5, 3, 423–434, 2015.
5. Nikfarjam, A., Sarker, A., O'Connor, K., Ginn, R., Gonzalez, G., Pharmacovigilance from social media: Mining adverse drug reaction mentions using sequence labeling with word embedding cluster features. *J. Am. Med. Inform. Assoc.*, 22, 3, 671–681, 2015.
6. Venkatesan, A. and Parthiban, L., Medical Image Segmentation With Fuzzy C-Means and Kernelized Fuzzy C-Means Hybridized on PSO and QPSO. *Int. Arab J. Inf. Technol. (IAJIT)*, 14, 1, 53–59, 2017.
7. Deborah, J.J. and Parthiban, L., Performance Evaluation of classification algorithms on Lymph disease prediction. *2018 International Conference on Smart Systems and Inventive Technology*.
8. George, G. and Parthiban, L., Multi objective hybridized firefly algorithm with group search optimization for data clustering. *2015 IEEE International Conference on Research in Computational Intelligence*.
9. Vaithinathan, K. and Parthiban, L., A novel texture extraction technique with T1 weighted MRI for the classification of Alzheimer's disease. *J. Neurosci. Methods*, 318, 84–99, 2019.

10. Latchoumi, T.P. and Parthiban, L., Abnormality detection using weighed particle swarm optimization and smooth support vector machine. *Biomed. Res.*, 28, 11, 4749–4751, 2017.

11. Thomas, S.C., Parthiban, L., Sriramakrishnan, G.V., Investigation of drug induced adverse effects and Disproportionality Analysis of Acetaminophen and Ibuprofen. *Int. J. Pure Appl. Math.*, 118, 7, 667–674, 2018.

12. Sriramakrishnan, G.V., Parthiban, L., Sankar, K., Thomas, S.C., Identifying the Safety Profile of Amiodarone and Dronedarone using Openvigil 2. *Int. J. Pure Appl. Math.*, 118, 18, 2779–2784, 2018.

13. Sankar, K. and Parthiban, L., Effective ways of finding Adverse Drug Reactions in Pharmacovigilance. *Int. J. Recent Technol. Eng. (IJRTE)*, 8, 2S4, 284–287, July 2019.

14. Balakrishnan, T.S. and Parthiban, L., Effective Pharmacovigilance using Natural Language Processing and Neural Network. *Int. J. Pure Appl. Math.*, 119, 15, 1825–1831, 2018.

15. Al Alkeem, E., Shehada, D., Yeun, C.Y., Zemerly, M.J., Hu, J., New secure healthcare system using cloud of things. *Clust. Comput.*, 20, 2211–2229, 1–19, 2017.

13

Impact of COVID-19 on IIoT

K. Priyadarsini[1]*, S. Karthik[2], K. Malathi[1] and M.V.V Rama Rao[3]

[1]Department of CSE, Vels Institute of Science, Technology and Advanced Studies, Chennai, India
[2]Department of ECE, Faculty of Engineering and Technology, Vadapalani Campus, SRMIST, Vadapalani, Chennai, India
[3]Department of CSE, Shri Vishnu Engineering College for Women, Andhra Pradesh, India

Abstract

Industrial Internet of Things (IIoT) technology has unprecedented potential to streamline processes and cut costs. From automation to data-driven insights, IIoT can augment existing assets and maximize workforce efficiency. However, challenges persist in the widespread implementation of IIoT. This book chapter aims to introduce the impact of COVID-19 on IIoT especially in industrial manufacturing, challenges, etc.

Keywords: IoT, IIoT, COVID, Coronavirus

13.1 Introduction

13.1.1 The Use of IoT During COVID-19

Internet of Things (IoT) is the method of linking intelligent (i.e., internet-connected) devices to the internet and rendering them unobtrusive. On the floor, IoT is a general-purpose computing network where several different types of computers interact with each other and exchange data via a universal programming language.

---

*Corresponding author: priyadarsini.se@velsuniv.ac.in

R. Anandan, Suseendran Gopalakrishnan, Souvik Pal and Noor Zaman (eds.) The Industrial Internet of Things (IIoT): Intelligent Analytics for Predictive Maintenance, (321–348) © 2022 Scrivener Publishing LLC

The information is gathered and then exchanged with other devices to improve user satisfaction. Here, we explore how IoT has had on everyone's daily lives, the advantages of IoT [1–7], and how it works inside the IoT network.

IoT has been part of our daily routine. Generally, this is being used for five different purposes: consumer, commercial, industrial, military, and infrastructure ("Internet of Things").

13.1.2   Consumer IoT

This type of IoT benefits the user by making their lives easier. These equipment, lights, and aids to communication can be found in homes, and Breville and BrewBrewGenie have invented automated espresso and coffee-making apps that allow you to prepare the brew while you are away from the kitchen. With these new tools, you do not have to brew your own coffee.

13.1.3   Commercial IoT

Traditionally, company applications are found in the transportation and healthcare sectors. For example, the health industry makes use of smart pacemakers and patients' vehicle transport vehicles to track the cardiovascular system, and the same IoT devices are used in industry (across all modes of transport). Patients using pacemakers that are embedded will be able to safely transmit data from home by way of the IoT will be able to consult with their doctors whenever they want.

13.1.4   Industrial Internet of Things (IIoT)

New technology, such as automated control systems, agriculture, and the use of big data in the industrial sector, are used to boost industry norms. Tracking the amount of moisture in the soil has decreased water use by 30%.

13.1.5   Infrastructure IoT

The battle robots use these systems to establish human-consumable surveillance. Efforts have been made to insert protocol chips into soldiers so that they can gain access to military bases, establishing a secure system with IoT devices.

13.1.6 Role of IoT in COVID-19 Response

IoT during CVID has helped in getting a better handle on infected patients through intertwined and linked systems. Now that the disease has been identified, the industry has naturally opted to maintain the flow of information to contain it.

13.1.7 Telehealth Consultations

It could be theorised that Coron doctors introduced video consultation to avoid the spread of Coron disease if there were no longer any physical meetings to be held. There is no question that advanced methods of health-care delivery allow us to keep patients at home for long periods of time, especially those with viral infections, where they can more effectively deal with their illnesses instead of being in the hospital for days. Since the E-coli outbreak, they have been able to see patients up to 620 a day, every day.

13.1.8 Digital Diagnostics

The number of IoT implementations uses diagnostics as a back-up. The Kinsetic is the only thermometer capable of mapping where outbreaks of the virus occur in the United States. Stripped-down thermometers may be useful data sharing tools for health professionals and governments to help protect populations from heat-related illness.

13.1.9 Remote Monitoring

Remotely embedded devices designed to track elderly patients who are at higher risk of dying of the Coronavirus have been able to discover innovative to exceed their budget; the first quarter revenue projection of $65 million has been invested in remote monitoring.

13.1.10 Robot Assistance

The rise of the IoT would facilitate the use of IoT robots. Robots will help decontaminate the machines, freeing up health-care workers' time for quality work. UVD robotics has begun producing patient care robots and hospital cleaning and theatre sanitization IoT machines. Although the COVID-19 has had taken to keeping their health care facilities spic and span, China has also kept up their caring practises.

On the whole, the spread of the pandemic has acted as a motivator for the adoption of IoTs in healthcare. Growing senior citizens, IoT has the ability to track and assist in day-to-day activities. Let us take the example of a Fitbit, which is also capable of measuring the consumer's calorie intake, determining the number of steps, blood pressure, and maintaining appointment reminders, for example. Many with heart disease or diabetes will benefit from these wireless devices, too.

COVID is notorious for production difficulties dating back to the spring of 2019, when the need for toilet paper and hand sanitizer were as acute as they are today.

Before they are able to administer shots, there are questions about whether the industrial supply chain can provide dry ice-filled pharmaceutical vials, cold storage space, and a long list of related products in a timely manner that is efficient enough.

Many of these issues can be minimised with sensors and actuators in addition to data analytics to track vaccine production.

Jared Weiner of VDC Research stated in an interview with FierceElectronics the difficulty of coping with people and producing the same with automation.

According to a May survey of more than 250 engineers and operators, 85% reported having had experienced supply chain disruption due to COVID-19, while 67% reported having reduced their output for their organization. Industries ranging from automobiles to building and heavy machinery, to consumer electronics were covered.

Consequently, 40% of the companies decreased the number of their on-site staff, but the others introduced new hardware and software to allow remote workers to function more effectively. In a variety of cases, IIoT increases quality, according to Weiner.

Weiner commented that some companies started to produce services such as pivoting during March and April of this year, when many distilleries began to make the switch to hand sanitizer.

Therefore, he said, "The ability to pivot on information technology is highly dependent on having been operationalized."

So, a company can quickly build a digital version of a real-world operation and continue with testing and improvements without rolling out the original. Managers like Siemens said companies could build digital counterparts to physical products by using their products like MindSphere.

The consequence of COVID CO's actions is that financial and organizational efficiency have become a much higher priority for businesses.

IIoT adoption continues to accelerate, with 35% reporting that their company has already started an IIoT program, with 27% of them saying that it is a large-project underway.

In the case of a pandemic, a company could introduce better production automation, instead of mandating that a plant maintenance worker use diagnostics on site. With COVID-19, there is a near-term urgency to keep staff from the site, but it also a much-longer long-term imperative to keep the operation streamlined.

Newby (USA investment firm) puts his tongue firmly in his cheek and says, "Today, tomorrow, and who knows about the rest of the week?" Actuators collect data; sensors turn the data through analysis, so manufacturers profit most from sensors and actuators. If you have sensors that generate loads of data, but do not analyze it effectively, then you have already squandered all your resources and investments.

The absolute need of AI, machine learning, machine learning, and advanced analytics and analytics is on the forefront. On the other hand, Covid has quite a significant effect, and the ability to help mitigate it. Data analysis and observations begin everything.

But while the overall IIoT movement is increasing, recent industry insights warrant a re-assessment. Manufacturers of smart sensors and other semic components for the auto industry began to return to an operational state in the second quarter, resulting in 3Q being good for the semiconductor market. By the end of 2020, however, Omdia forecasts automobile sales to be in the double digits.

Meanwhile, medical device manufacturers are expected to see increases in revenue, while other sectors will see mixed results, according to the Omdia analyst Kevin Anderson. In times of market volatility, investment appears to remain away from capital projects.

Not a positive news for the semiconductor industry: According to Infon Technologies, the automotive sector performed better than anticipated since the beginning of the summer. On the other side, the firm added, "machines in factories remain in the red"

Omia CEO Paul Pickering, however, said the industrial semiconductor sector does move slowly relative to the automotive and wireless sectors, and is highly diverse.

Pickering added, "Industrial semic providers have started to see a steady increase in demand for business during the first half of the year."

"On the other hand, IIoT in the industrial sector is lagging behind." An optimistic view of Covid is not supposed to have much of an impact over a short period of time.

According to Pickering, the pandemic has produced various outcomes for different industries: pharmaceuticals and medical, for example, have seen more growth. But adoption of factory 4.0 implemented networks will be hindered by the new 5G standards for industry, he mentioned. Measurement and test device growth will be lessened or delayed.

West talking about decades here, not years. "Covid can be a double-edged sword for IIT," concluded Alex West. But since plants have shut down, there has been the potential to repurpose and update old machinery.

West added, "Covid will contribute to IIoT adoption in the short term, but could turn out to be a net drain."

Industry 4.0 utilizes wireless automation to enhance performance. But in a world of increased cybersecurity risk, are the challenges of IIoT worth adopting this technology.

Industry 4.0, the revolution of industrial processes through smart technology, is all about wireless automation to enhance performance. But in a world of increased cybersecurity risk.

13.2 The Benefits of Industrial IoT

First off, it is useful to explain just what IIoT [8] is and how it can revitalize modern operations. IIoT is the application of connected smart devices to

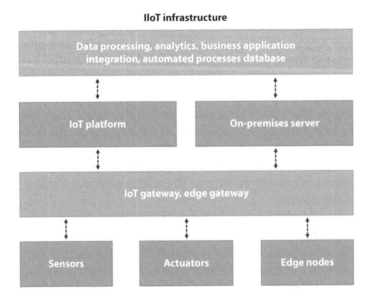

Figure 13.1 IIoT infrastructure.

monitor, automate, and predict all kinds of industrial processes and outcomes. Figure 13.1 shows basic IIoT infrastructure. These technologies offer everything from enhanced worker protections through factory floor monitoring systems to the predictive maintenance possibilities currently revolutionizing the fleet management industry.

Widespread implementation of such systems changes the ways manufacturers, supply chains, and warehouse managers function more effectively. With IIoT, data-driven insights power greater results. For many businesses, this can mean:

- Greater energy efficiency
- Reduced costs
- Better quality products
- Improved decision-making potential
- Less equipment downtime

In short, the automation and data-gathering capabilities of IIoT devices make for a more efficient workplace. As less energy is used, product efficiency is enhanced, and metrics are assessed, industrial businesses have the potential to streamline practices like never before. Since every downtime incident causes an average loss of $17,000, the application of IIoT in predictive maintenance alone can mean substantial saving.

These benefits of IIoT are the reason widespread adoption of this technology is so desirable. As of now, many companies across industries are already using it to great effect.

13.2.1   How IIoT is Being Used

The innovative potential of IIoT is virtually limitless. However, there are three primary categories in which this technology is applied within industries to promising results. These categories are remote monitoring, predictive maintenance, and automation.

Here are examples of IIoT shown in Figure 3.2 uses in each of these three categories to give you a better idea of what properly implemented smart devices can achieve.

13.2.2   Remote Monitoring

Radar-level sensors provide local displays so that operators can easily manage levels through a singular dashboard. These systems make for easy measuring points on moving and rotating machinery, so operators are constantly fed real-time data regarding the equipment's functionality.

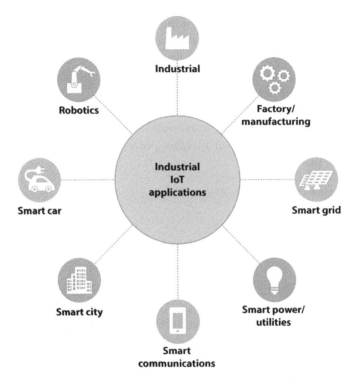

Figure 3.2 Applications of IIoT.

This, in turn, gives insights into overall equipment life-cycles and repair needs, allowing for predictive maintenance.

13.2.3   Predictive Maintenance

In the power industry, drones [30] with equipment monitors and sensors are being used to monitor powerline networks and evaluate risks. These drones can anticipate scenarios such as estimating when a tree is likely to fall on a line, resulting in costly maintenance and repair. That way, companies will be informed before the damage is done. In this fashion, predictive maintenance enables cost-effective repairs and intervention before the damage is even done.

One vital use of automation via IIoT is smart irrigation in industrial farming. Water is a precious resource, but farmers typically have to keep a consistent watering schedule to ensure proper plant care. Smart irrigation systems, however, are automating this process while conserving water. The IIoT device reads moisture levels in the soil and reports to the sprinkler system when water is needed. This way, water, money, and time are all saved.

These three categories of IIoT implementation give industries unprecedented precision and efficiency with the right application. Unfortunately, however, businesses must first overcome the challenges.

13.3   The Challenges of Wide-Spread IIoT Implementation

Only now are many realizing some of the broader challenges of managing an industrial IoT network complete with a repertoire of useful devices. Like with any networked device, IIoT components are open to cybersecurity risks. Meanwhile, the application of these devices to fill their potential requires pre-planning and assessment.

When implementing your IIoT system, consider these common challenges to wide-spread IoT success:

- Failure to align KPIs with clear business objectives
- Improper organizational alignment
- Lack of IoT experience
- IoT security threats

The dangers of not taking these challenges seriously can have more than just monetary risks. An autonomous machine can compromise employee safety like a vehicle that has been hacked or infected with malware. Overcoming many of these challenges requires running a cybersecurity risk assessment at consistent intervals during the IIoT device's lifecycle and training staff around the proper implementation.

Final Thoughts

IIoT can have powerful performance benefits for any industry. However, integrating such devices properly requires effective employee instruction and coordination. As part of the future of all industrial workplaces, IIoT sensors and autonomous machines can bring businesses valuable insights but overcoming common challenges like cybersecurity threats will take some time.

Thinking about 2021 is a welcome relief after a difficult year for many people, and a lot of us expect things to get better in the months ahead. That includes the manufacturing sector, which had to contend with supply chain issues, shutdowns, outbreaks, and demand-side challenges and is now looking at ways to work safer and more efficiently in the new year.

In 2021, we will see factories, food-service operators, and transportation companies get more out of the sensor networks and remote wireless monitoring capabilities they quickly adopted this year—and we will see more companies in these industries add remote sensor systems to stay competitive. But the biggest IIoT-related gains in 2021 may not be the ones that typically make tech news headlines.

13.3.1   Health and Safety Monitoring Will Accelerate Automation and Remote Monitoring

Safety for factory workers has been paramount this year, and that will continue through 2021. Many manufacturers have risen to the challenge of operating with social distancing and safety precautions in place to protect their people, and remote sensors and cameras have been important components in making factories safer. Others will need to do the same in 2021 to reduce the risk of outbreaks and shutdowns.

For example, combining camera coverage with door and activity sensors can allow plant security teams to make sure that workers are following safe traffic patterns through the building during shift changes. These sensors can also alert managers if there is unexpected activity in areas that are off-limits due to disinfection requirements or restricted to key personnel.

The pandemic has accelerated the trend toward automation and remote monitoring in other ways, too. As more facilities adopt these tools to protect their workforce and remain competitive, they are seeing how easy it is to add sensor capabilities and collect data that they can use to automate and monitor repetitive tasks [1]. This is another way to protect worker health while leveraging efficiency gains. For example, if you can automate and remotely monitor a repetitive task that you used to have five people doing in the same room, those people are now free to work on higher value tasks, presumably at a safe distance. We expect this trend to continue through 2021 and beyond.

13.3.2   Integrating Sensor and Camera Data Improves Safety and Efficiency

Another trend we expect to accelerate [10, 11] is pairing multiple types of sensors in the same location, aka sensor fusion. Sensor fusion can overcome one of the biggest challenges of relying on data from one type of device: Whether it is a video camera, a wireless motion sensor, or a remote temperature sensor, each device provides one kind of data with little or no other context.

For example, a video feed that shows an employee leaving a walk-in cooler door open cannot also show whether the temperature inside the cooler then rose to an unsafe level. If the cooler had a networked temperature sensor installed, then a manager could review the temperature while the door was left open to see if food safety had been compromised. If the sensor had a threshold set, then it could even notify the manager immediately if the temperature went out of safe range—and the video would show the manager why it happened.

Integrating sensor and camera data can show us more than the camera can see on its own, and as remote monitoring of workplaces continues to matter for safety, this type of integration is becoming more valuable to manufacturers, foodservice companies, and other employers.

Besides alerting managers to potential safety risks, combined sensor data can also help companies work more efficiently. For example, an air conditioner thermostat in a workspace that is set to turn on at 68° can stay off if nearby movement activity sensors indicate there is no one in the room. In a time of economic uncertainty, integrated sensor data can deliver efficiency gains and cost savings to help companies stay viable.

13.3.3 IIoT-Supported Safety for Customers Reduces Liability for Businesses

IIoT sensor networks [12–15] can also improve customer safety and compliance for businesses like restaurants, transportation companies, pharmacies, and clinics that need to store or move products at carefully maintained temperatures.

For example, remote temperature sensors that are capable of monitoring very low temperatures can help preserve the efficacy of temperature-sensitive health care products like vaccines, allergy shot serums, and biological treatments for diseases. Standard wireless temperature sensors can reduce the risk of foodborne illness for restaurant and food manufacturer customers. Mobile sensor networks installed in refrigerated trucks can help ensure that food and medications arrive in usable condition.

Preventing harm to customers and patients is a matter of ethics and trust, of course. It can also be a matter of financial survival, especially for businesses that are already dealing with economic uncertainty. A 2018 study in Public Health Reports found that the cost of a foodborne illness outbreak can be as high as $2.6 million—far more than the cost of the technology that could prevent the problem. For these reasons, we expect to see more businesses adopt low-cost sensor systems in 2021 to protect their customers and their revenue.

13.3.4   Predictive Maintenance Will Deliver for Organizations That Do the Work

Predictive maintenance has been a major topic in the IIoT world and in manufacturing for a few years now. This strategy relies on vibration sensor data, artificial intelligence (AI) and machine learning to analyze how a piece of equipment is operating, when it is likely to start operating outside of its ideal range, and when it will need maintenance for optimal functioning overits life span.

Organizations that do predictive maintenance right typically see a reduction in maintenance costs because they are only servicing equipment when it needs it, instead of on a calendar or hour-based schedule [2]. They also experience less unplanned downtime.

However, a remote sensor network alone is not enough to create an effective predictive maintenance program. PdM relies on machine learning and AI that have to be taught what to look for, and that requires human expertise. A June McKinsey report on IIoT also notes that a robust IT system and scalable IIoT capabilities are also required to build an effective PdM program.

In the year ahead, the manufacturers who get the most value from their PdM programs will be the ones who make a full commitment to getting the IT and machine-learning training right.

13.3.5   Building on the Lessons of 2020

As tempting as it may be to close the [16–20] books on 2020 and leave them closed, this year has offered a lot of lessons in the value of adopting new technology fast, pivoting to meet new demands, and coping with challenges to the standard ways of working. Companies that keep those lessons in mind, and maximize the value of their technology investments, will be ready to handle whatever 2021 brings.

13.4   Effects of COVID-19 on Industrial Manufacturing

In the immediate term, we are all involved in efficient and cost-effective supply chains, but long-lasting as well end-to-to-end value digitalization enables low-to-cost, flexibility, and scalability for supply chains. Finally, the use of data and AI-powered analytics would be an important success factor. When businesses engage in this revolution, they can gain better knowledge and increase the value they capture. While the more established businesses have started to feel the weight of time pressure to respond, CO19 has raised the stakes and required a swift response.

You can see the COVID-19 disease's impact in every industry, particularly in manufacturing. Supply chain delays, cargo concerns, and personnel difficulties have been cited as the biggest risks to the projects. In view of the current events, the focus in the manufacturing sector has changed from streamlining supply chain efficiencies to making IT and the core functions of the business interact seamlessly to remain current. The imagination and foresight to help predict and solve potential problems are important.

13.4.1 New Challenges for Industrial Manufacturing

The findings of COVID have broad-ranging consequences for the supply chain. Some of the problems that small businesses face in the industry include difficulties in sourcing of raw materials, increased demand, and insufficient delivery capability from suppliers. Abandoned and delayed deliveries take-offs result in a delivery delays that are on the order of 4 to 6 weeks.

Manufacturers report that maintaining workforce continuity is another staffing problem caused by the COVID-19 pandemic. Problems the company management has faced over the years include laws from the government, such as social distancing requirements [21–23], such as occurred at Amazon, and examples of this include sickouts from the target employees and labor conflicts.

To a large extent, these design obstacles undoubtedly diminish the efficiency of downstream customers, thus reducing downstream manufacturers' profitability. This is generating more problems that must be faced by manufacturers with creative approaches

13.4.2 Smarter Manufacturing for Actionable Insights

Because of the latest research on COVID-19, we are beginning to see industrial manufacturing adoptions of new technologies at a faster rate. Technology and connected devices are providing an increased demand for data analytics and insights. But broadly [24–27] speaking, the rate of digitization and implementation is only increasing, while the introduction of the latest Industry 4.0 definition is swift to the point of being a cliché.

We are increasingly expecting manufacturers to use technology that is more intelligent, like autonomous equipment and sensors, including forklifts or robotic cleaners, to become an important resource. The methods enable useful insights, leading to better decision-making for those who use the devices.

Proactive and preventive IoT-enabled technologies such as location data and critical asset tracking can assist manufacturers in maintaining their supply chains and helping them to anticipate risk [3]. Recently implemented IoT solutions provide real-time notifications that enable manufacturers to spot delayed, damaged, or missing inventory.

Companies in the industrial IoT are becoming more integrated with technologies such as eSIM, which allows for remote connection with self-to-service and over-air profiling without human interference. eSIM makes their linked goods easier to manage by offering a single interface. In addition, this drives improved resiliency over the lifecycle for design, manufacturing, and servicing of goods.

13.4.3   A Promising Future for IIoT Adoption

At this period of stress for industrial manufacturing, companies, which take advantage of technology and connectivity, will flourish and be able to withstand the storm. Such a catastrophe as the global COVID pandemic causes corporations to undergo. It is possible that combining modern and innovative technology with creative problem solving would speed the introduction of the implementation of industrial IoT, but it will also make it essential for manufacturers to remain profitable during disruptions and ensure continued competitiveness in a time of crisis.

The industries that are financially dependent (e.g., travel and fashion) will be more affected in the short term to the long term, while industries that rely on disposable income (such as utilities and medical services) will be more prominent in the medium term.

Other variations can be explained by the following market drivers:

- Owing to the prevalence of fragile global supply chains, companies will continue to increase their investment in industrial software.
- We will lead to increased investment in proven applications with short-term profit opportunities.
- Fewer resources are allocated to hard-to-sell or less profitable endeavors.
- There is no one solution that will work for all industries, especially for industries with a history of budgetary constraints and debt, but the negative impact of financial and social issues on all industries cannot be ignored.
- Reinforced proximity and security interventions in the time of a crisis.
- Faced with market change, enterprises are migrating to cloud-based applications that use the cloud as a catalyst.

13.5   Winners and Losers—The Impact on IoT/ Connected Applications and Digital Transformation due to COVID-19 Impact

Cambuys assessment [28] of the IIoT says the growth has been very strong in the past, and that CO19 is only short-term. Figure 13.3 highlights the continued development in all markets during the pandemic, followed by growth again in 2023. Figure 13.4 shows examples of "winners" in industrial IoT solutions.

Business areas benefit or damage because of the multiple market factors influencing the applications. This is very advantageous because it helps us to classify "winners and losers".

Creative and clever uses of predictive maintenance, for example, have already started to generate business value, while others are still underfunded.

When it comes [29] to implementing solutions to companies, there are two elements that need to be altered: company processes and application technologies and the network of providers. This matrix demonstrates the most promise in regards to technological capability and business effect. These times call for bold new approaches, imaginative ideas. The ecosystem comprising the top-consultants, systems integrators, and low-based

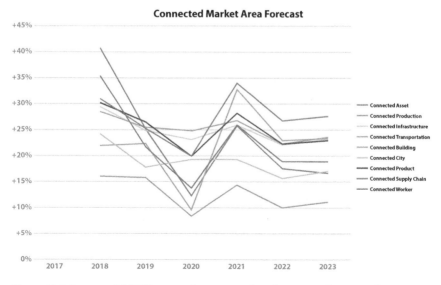

Figure 13.3 Impact of COVID-19 on the connected applications software market.

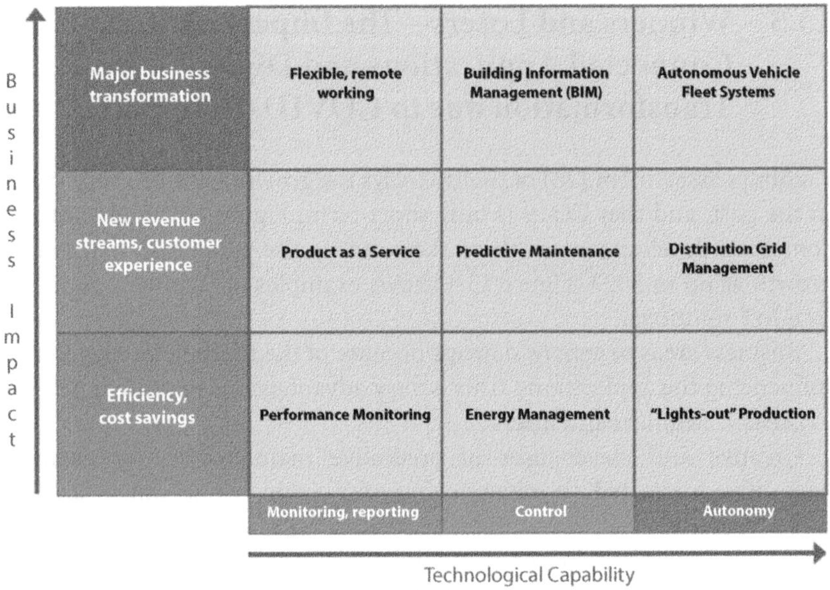

Business Impact	Monitoring, reporting	Control	Autonomy
Major business transformation	Flexible, remote working	Building Information Management (BIM)	Autonomous Vehicle Fleet Systems
New revenue streams, customer experience	Product as a Service	Predictive Maintenance	Distribution Grid Management
Efficiency, cost savings	Performance Monitoring	Energy Management	"Lights-out" Production

Technological Capability

Figure 13.4 Examples of "winners" in industrial IoT solutions.

software and technology providers -is needed to produce innovative solution providers.

According to Camb, most digital transformation initiatives will succeed because the number of organizations trying to exploit the versatility of working arrangements and location through digitalization will increase. Visionary businesses will view demand shock as an opportunity to put their money into digital technologies that can change how buildings and cars are designed and produced. Even though some transformations, in industries badly hit by the demand shock and cash-flow issues will go bankrupt, on the other hand, there will be others that do better.

Many companies will attempt to profit by marketing their goods as services, or using predictive maintenance or lights-out manufacturing, instead of profit and loss accounting. The kind of projects to which the organization is likely to devote time and money include extensive offshore oil and gas exploration—because of the price, as well as other complex and cutting-edge transportation technology such as self-driving shuttle taxis.

Mom-and-Pop companies which forecast a decline to result in a rise in business will probably ignore it, if it does not coincide with an opportunity, will miss out when the cycle goes up again. There is a good chance that the pandemic could spur greater digital transformation, but the evidence is not there yet [4].

For any digital transformation, a connected application like PLM (product lifecycle management), CAx (cloud), and BIM (modeling of building information) should be part of the solution. Computer-aided engineering (or CAE) allows production facilities to be continuously reconfigured according to operational laws. Sensor-enabled systems collect real-world data and merge it with the digital model.

When the COVID-19 pandemic affects connected applications, there will be big winners and losers; these, however, will only be temporary.

Very granular models display the sector, nation, and class effect. It also shows the effect at different levels, large levels, which helps to determine who the winners and losers are. This is still expected to remain a lucrative market, with still-to-be-be-determined estimated numbers. Owing to the complexities of the ecosystem, service providers would need to change their approach to stay ahead of the competition.

13.6   The Impact of COVID-19 on IoT Applications

The Figure 13.5 shows the impact of COVID-19 on IoT. Increased transparency, lower costs, and increased process automation for enterprise IoT deployments explain why some business-to-class applications [29] are now in high demand. The experiences that consumers get by using consumer IoT devices would be very different.

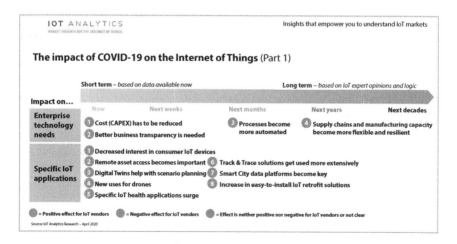

Figure 13.5 Impact of COVID-19 on IoT.

13.6.1 Decreased Interest in Consumer IoT Devices

Despite the fact that consumers spend a lot of time at home, it does not appear that they purchase IoT devices on a broad scale.

Big user IoT app downloads can serve as a good measure of sales volume. These apps (among their numbers of downloads) have fallen dramatically (for example, from the 233rd place in the US in 2 months ago, they are now at the 351st place). Figures 13.6 and 13.7 shows the download rank of the app "Philips Hue" on Android in the category "Lifestyle" in the USA and Usage of Librestram's Onsight and usage of Librestram's Onsight respectively. Figure 13.8 shows the download Rank of the app "Kinsa Health".

13.6.2 Remote Asset Access Becomes Important

One of the main reasons [29] why web conferencing tools like Zoom are booming is that they help you communicate to people around the country and around the world regardless of your location. Similarly, remote access tools are getting popular because they enable people to control their machines and their properties from any distance. One good thing about smart devices is that they allow people to talk to, conduct virtual

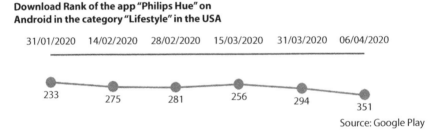

Figure 13.6 Download rank.

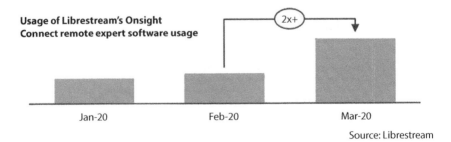

Figure 13.7 Usage of Librestram's Onsight.

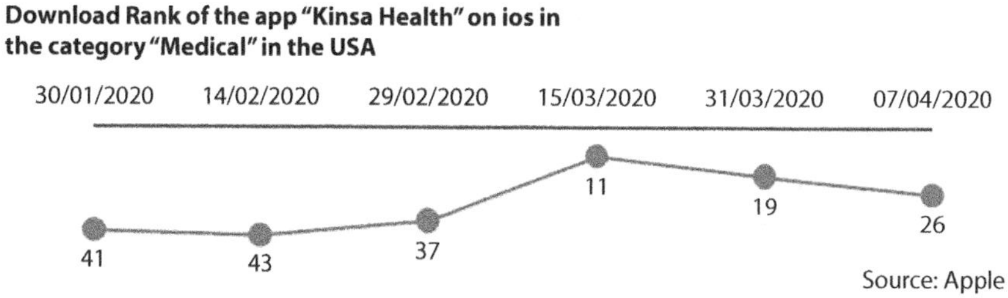

**Download Rank of the app "Kinsa Health" on ios in
the category "Medical" in the USA**

| 30/01/2020 | 14/02/2020 | 29/02/2020 | 15/03/2020 | 31/03/2020 | 07/04/2020 |

11

19

26

41

43

37

Source: Apple

Figure 13.8 Download Rank of the app "Kinsa Health".

inspections, and provide remote diagnosis, all at the same time. The number of remote device users in the field of computing has skyrocketed.

There is a trend of many new businesses setting up ProSoft Connect Remote Access to use their PLCs remotely, according to Keith Blod, a business director with Prosoft Technology.

13.6.3   Digital Twins Help With Scenario Planning

Currently, manufacturing, shipping and delivery delays, as well as demand variation under COVID-19 are affecting many businesses. In response, digital twins offer an end-to-end digital representation of the supply chain, allowing consumers to explore complex supply strategies, assess risks, and evaluate trade-offs to speed up or automate choices.

Llamasoft, for example, a US-based software supply chain analytics firm, integrates digital twins with information science, modeling and engineering fragile supply chain and developing resilient long-term risk management strategies.

13.6.4   New Uses for Drones

Drones [29] have been of help during the crisis.

- As far as parenthood is concerned, the sky is the limit. For instance, Zhao Liang Zhao, the Co-the Xinch County Chief Operations Officer, noted that their delivery system has helped hospitals do more than 300 flights with CO19 during the last month.
- Having a system in place is critical to ensuring that Surveillance and Monitoring goes on uninterrupted (used in many countries to monitor public spaces).
- Broadcasting ideas and letting people know.
- In addition, on January 30, XAG turned two of its agricultural robots and drones into disinfectant sprayers.

13.6.5   Specific IoT Health Applications Surge

Healthcare is obviously at the centre of the COVID-19 pandemic.

13.6.6   Track and Trace Solutions Get Used More Extensively

Today, real-time supply chain visibility is invaluable in order to business because of the current supply and demand trends.

This was reported by David Hewson, a manager of the Vesseltracking global network, who told us that "A great deal of our customers are telling us they find tracking highly advantageous". "Communities have experienced substantial delays because of local locking, so partners are turning to Vessel Tracker to verify whether or not a vessel has arrived."

IoT providers use their data to update the public on what is happening in their IoT networks.

- For instance, updates on the global cruises ship and freight operation recently published on Vesseltracker.com (in English).
- TER Geotab periodically updates the business operation of road transportation in North America.

13.6.7   Smart City Data Platforms Become Key

Although retrofitted solutions are simple to incorporate, the use of the IoT does not yield all of the same benefits.

The Bosch smart meter retrofit will enable utilities to continue reading meters that they have been reading for decades, without much effort on their part. To illustrate the sense of this term, we have chosen to use a Bosch business model which uses a micro generation from business premises as one example [5].

We are seeing a rise in demand for our IoT Meter Upgrade product during this period of trouble. The client gets a miniature gadget with a socket built into it, which they put on their meter. Finally, the data gets sent to the company in a safe fashion via Bosch IoT, and then, the customer does not have to dispatch anyone to read on-site meters.

He sees the same pattern, according to Graham Imman, VP of marketing for MachineMetrics: More and more of our original equipment manufacturers are sending cellular gateways to assist with remote computer diagnostics and servicing.

13.7   The Impact of COVID-19 on Technology in General

Before we look at the technology effect of COVID-19 on IoT, we will examine first how COVID-19 generally impacts technology. Figure 13.9 shows impact of COVID-19 on technology.

13.7.1   Ongoing Projects Are Paused

There is a common [29] consensus that technology budget cutbacks because many programs are cancelled or slowed down at the moment. A recent study by ETR has shown a 4% decrease in budgets.

Two exceptions to projects are not paused:

1. Significant policy measures
2. Technology ventures specifically aligned with COVID-19 Project (see next aspect)

13.7.2   Some Enterprise Technologies Take Off

There is a notable ramp-up in technologies such as follows:

1. Work-from-home infrastructure (e.g., laptops, screens, and connectivity)
2. Collaboration tools (e.g., video conferencing, team chat, and project planning)
3. Virtualization infrastructure (e.g., remote desktops)

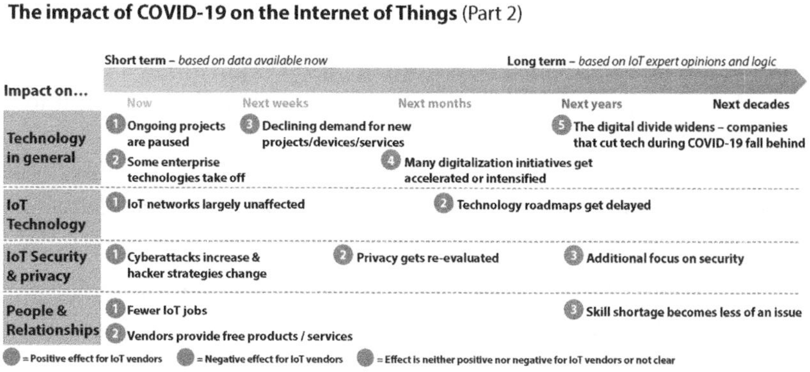

The impact of COVID-19 on the Internet of Things (Part 2)

Figure 13.9 Impact of COVID-19 on technology.

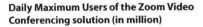

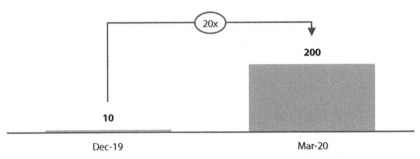

Source: https://blog.zoom.us/wordpress/2020/04/01/a-message-to-our-users/

Figure 13.10 Zoom usage analysis.

4. VPN networking
5. Mobile devices
6. Security
7. Desktop support

13.7.3   Declining Demand for New Projects/Devices/Services

On account of businesses becoming more vigilant about the potential procurement of new services, new ventures and the use of IoT, the sales pipelines for companies all over the world are depleting.

In the last 2 to 3 years, IoT analytics spoke with several experts on this subject: "A manager of a new company for venture capital consulting projects at an online marketplace announced in April". "We've seen a 50% decline in new projects."

In the last quarter of 2016, the head of business growth at a cellular IoT network provider remarked, "It's been a crazy year, and we expect it to get even better."

Our traffic has been decreased by 20%, resulting in fewer sales. "Currently, I anticipate March will produce 13% less sales than January."

13.7.4   Many Digitalization Initiatives Get Accelerated or Intensified

This seems to be a short-term problem that is associated with a drop in demand for digital technology and solutions. While there may be a medium-to-long-term effect, it is expected that COVID-19 will be positive in the long term [6]. Figure 13.10 shows zoom usage analysis.

It proved to have a tremendous impact on businesses and companies around the world, both in an immediate and lasting way. In order to leverage modern technology, all the employees (executives included) are expected to implement and discover the advantages of it (and challenges).

That is not to say that pandemics would not happen, but to say that businesses may want to develop additional means of dealing with future outbreaks. Additional money will be invested on the development of digital infrastructure is a guarantee.

The director of business solutions at an industrial communications company we spoke to in April of 20, 2020 supported this concept

More and more people are looking to use our remote asset-centric solutions. Customers and prospects suggest we are the first step in their digital strategy.

13.7.5 The Digital Divide Widens

COVID-19 could lead to a digital breakdown in the long run.

During the current crisis, IoT analytics experienced two intense reactions from various firms. The whole digital team was one of the first cost reduction initiatives taken by an organization that was consulted. Another corporation is cutting expenses elsewhere and ensuring the continuation of its digital projects.

COVID-19 may prove to be a crucial event which further broaden the digital divide between digital and priority initiatives. Many who have just taken digital initiatives along with them but have not taken them too seriously now have to go back, while others will pull ahead and will find new digital business models to lead them in their industries over the next few years.

13.8 The Impact of COVID-19 on Specific IoT Technologies

13.8.1 IoT Networks Largely Unaffected

That said, the IoT does not have the same data throughput as people are staying in their homes and using their teleconferencing devices.

The rate of IoT [27–30] use and the day before the crisis has not changed. In the short term, these improvements would have no effect on the network's bottom line, but in the long term, the organization claims, they could have a significant impact.

A cellular IoT network provider told us in the second quarter of March 2020 that "For us, the use has yet to begin because most of the applications on the network are currently in use. We do not expect any issues with attached to our network (and this ensures that data will be sent frequently) (yet) [9]. The only improvement we can certainly foresee is that telematics has many implementations, which has an effect of course."

They have the same opinion about Teppo Hemia, the CEO: they all think he is a complete ass.

More and more IoT devices are in service thanks to low-cost distributed local optimization is very happy to see. It is a company thing we really do not have to worry about; we are done with our ventures, so there is not much to be concerned about. Nonetheless, I am confident about the expected earnings during Q2 and Q3, as it is difficult for field workers to fly to different locations and set up new networks now.

13.8.2   Technology Roadmaps Get Delayed

Many new technologies and standards rest on an exchange of ideas with an influential group of experts and a decision by committee. COVID works against these experts, causing a delay in emerging technology adoption.

On March 23, 3GPP publicly announced that 5G will be delayed for an additional 3 months due to CO19, and consequently, its corresponding 17 release date would be delayed as well [12]. This release is very much needed for the Industrial IoT as it enhances network response time-to-to-live and distance-sensitive communication and improves network reliability (TSN).

The programs of other organizations (e.g., the Institute of Electrical and Electronics Engineers) are believed to face the same problem and to be further delayed.

13.9   Coronavirus With IoT, Can Coronavirus Be Restrained?

Global health officials are reporting an increase in the number of cases of Coronavirus infections, which have put Coronavirus on the International Emergency List of the World Health Organization (WHO). According to reports, the Indian Ministry of Health and Family Welfare has also become aware of the coronavirus and is providing daily updates to contain it.

The ministry of Health and Welfare has set out a simple campaign target to ensure people who come in touch with someone from Wuhan should be home quarantined for at least 14 days [13].

Since Coronavirus 741 was conducted, 738 of the total 741 studies have come out negative, and only 3 have proved positive. While the finishing touches are being applied, you have 342 items in operation. According to the Ministry, there are 5,123 individuals who have been put under constant watch at home arrest One can only wonder if things like the IoT, AI, and big data can bring an end to this while every step is taken to prevent its spread, Dilip Sarangan, Director of the Digital Practice, believes that health issues like Coronavirus can have the capacity to foment public hysteria and lead to millions of deaths.

13.10   The Potential of IoT in Coronavirus Like Disease Control

The IoT, which consists of interconnected networks, data analytics, and AI will allow us to cut the spread of infectious diseases, according to Dilip Sarangan's blog, and because China, which is the home of the IoT adoption, implementing this kind of technology should not be much of a problem [11].

In Sarangan's view, global organizations like corporations, towns, cities, and states should work together to put in place a huge network of sensors to detect Coronaviruses like this.

Once you have identified an infection, the only thing you can do is prevent it from spreading. Such a scheme is unlikely to be applied on a global scale, but China has the potential to enforce it locally. China has introduced several novel large-scale IoT initiatives (i.e., the installation of video surveillance) which no other countries have attempted. Would not a network of virus detectors be more practical? Connect that with existing surveillance cameras for facial recognition and you will have a system that will recognise, track, and watch people for coronavirus, suggests Dilip Sar.

"We can keep a log of every single person they have dealt with." While this can seem like a police state to many, using IoT and AI is the only rational approach to counteract the spread of highly infectious diseases in an ever-shrinking world, she contends.

13.11   Conclusion

Nowadays, IoT plays a key role in our daily routine applications as well as in industries. Due to COVID-19 pandemic, all the industries are going to be locked and some companies work from home. In these critical situations, IIoT plays a vital rule to keep our productivity as well before. In this paper, we discussed about the applications of IoT and impact of COVID-19 on some of the industries as detailed. The impacts of the COVID-19 pandemic will be serious, but short-term; the winners and losers will rely on market drivers.

Granular comparisons can be made between an industry, a country, and an application to name the winners and losers, since they are located in Cambashi and do this in different ways. According to this initiative, we expect the growth of this sector to be significant in the next step. Since the environment is so diverse, providers would need to consider their various growth opportunities in order to thrive. Physicians are now able to not only to keep track of their patients' health but also to control equipment, such as wheelchairs, for example, as well as the movement of the tanks with remote sensors IoT will keep track of the health equipment and check on the refrigerator levels, as well as monitor humidity and the overall machinery condition of the machinery. Healthcare IoT will continue to develop and evolve as diseases emerge in various parts of the world.

References

1. Aloi, A., Alonso, B., Benavente, J., Cordera, R., Echániz, E., González, F., Ladisa, C., Lezama-Romanelli, R., López-Parra, Á., Mazzei, V., Perrucci, L., Prieto-Quintana, D., Rodríguez, A., Sañudo, R., Effects of the COVID-19 Lockdown on Urban Mobility: Empirical Evidence from the City of Santander (Spain). *Sustainability*, 12, 9, 3870, 2020.
2. Ivanov, D., Predicting the impacts of epidemic outbreaks on global supply chains: A simulation-based analysis on the coronavirus outbreak (COVID-19/SARS-CoV-2) case. *Transport. Res. Part E: Log. Transport. Rev.*, 136, 101922, 2020.
3. Prather, K.A., Wang, C.C., Schooley, R.T., Reducing transmission of SARS-CoV-2. *Science*, 368, 6498, 1422–1424, 2020.
4. Arshad Ali, S., Baloch, M., Ahmed, N., Arshad Ali, A., Iqbal, A., The outbreak of Coronavirus Disease 2019 (COVID-19)—An emerging global health threat. *J. Infect. Public Health*, 13, 4, 644–646, 2020.
5. Pereira, R.M., Bertolini, D., Teixeira, L.O., Silla, C.N., Costa, Y.M.G., Covid-19 identi- fication in chest x-ray images on flat and hierarchical clas- sification scenarios. *Comput. Methods Programs Biomed.*, 194, 105532, 2020.

6. Cassaniti, I., Novazzi, F., Giardina, F., Salinaro, F., Michele, S., Perlini, S., Mojoli, R.B.F., Fausto, B., Performance of VivaDiag COVID-19 IgM/IgG Rapid Test is inadequate for diagnosis of COVID-19 in acute patients referring to emergency room department. *J. Med. Virol.*, 92, 1724–1727, 2020.

7. Charlton, C.L., Kanji, J.N., Johal, K., Bailey, A., Plitt, S.S., MacDonald, C., Kunst, A., Buss, E., Burnes, L.E., Fonseca, K., Berenger, B.M., Schnabl, K., Hu, J., Stokes, W., Zelyas, N., Tipples, G., Evaluation of six commercial mid-To high-volume antibody and six point-of-care lateral flow assays for detection of SARS-CoV-2 antibodies, *ASM J. J. Clin.* 59, 4, 2020.

8. Mayo Clinic Staff, *Coronavirus disease 2019 (COVID-19)—Symptoms and causes*, 2020, https://www.mayoclinic.org/diseases-conditions/coronavirus/symptoms-causes/syc-20479963 (accessed Apr. 14, 2020).

9. Johns Hopkins University, *COVID-19 Dashboard by the Center for Systems Science and Engineering (CSSE) at Johns Hopkins University (JHU).* https://systems.jhu.edu/research/public-health/ncov/

10. https://gisanddata.maps.arcgis.com/apps/opsdashboard/index.html#/bda7594740fd40299423467b48e9ecf6 (accessed Sep. 12, 2020).

11. World Health Organization, *Q&A on coronaviruses (COVID-19)*, 2020, https://www.who.int/emergencies/diseases/novel-coronavirus-2019/question-and-answers-hub/q-a-detail/q-a-coronaviruses (accessed Apr. 17, 2020).

12. U.S. Centers for Disease Control and Prevention (CDC), *How COVID-19 Spreads*, 2020, https://www.cdc.gov/coronavirus/2019-ncov/prevent-getting-sick/how-covid-spreads.html (accessed Apr. 03, 2020).

13. Xing, G., Lu, C., Pless, R., Huang, Q., On greedy geographic routing algorithms in sensing-covered networks, in: *Proceedings of the 5th ACM international symposium on Mobile ad hoc networking and computing - MobiHoc*, p. 31, 04, 2004.

14. Javaid, M., Haleem, A., Vaish, A., Vaishya, R., Iyengar, K.P., Robotics Applications in COVID-19: A Review. *J. Ind. Integr. Manag.*, 05, 04, 441–451, Dec. 2020.

15. Bahl, S., Singh, R.P., Javaid, M., Khan, I.H., Vaishya, R., Suman, R., Telemedicine Technologies for Confronting COVID-19 Pandemic: A Review. *J. Ind. Integr. Manag.*, 05, 04, 547–561, Dec. 2020.

16. Arora, R., Arora, P.K., Kumar, H., Pant, M., Additive Manufacturing Enabled Supply Chain in Combating COVID-19. *J. Ind. Integr. Manag.*, 05, 04, 495–505, Dec. 2020.

17. Javaid, M. and Haleem, A., Exploring Smart Material Applications for COVID-19 Pandemic Using 4D Printing Technology. *J. Ind. Integr. Manag.*, 05, 04, 481–494, Dec. 2020.

18. Haleem, A. and Javaid, M., Medical 4.0 and Its Role in Healthcare During COVID-19 Pandemic: A Review. *J. Ind. Integr. Manag.*, 05, 04, 531–545, Dec. 2020.

19. Ali, S. *et al.*, A Review of the Role of Smart Wireless Medical Sensor Network in COVID-19. *J. Ind. Integr. Manag.*, 05, 04, 413–425, Dec. 2020.

20. Singh, R.P., Javaid, M., Haleem, A., Vaishya, R., Bahl, S., Significance of Health Information Technology (HIT) in Context to COVID-19 Pandemic: Potential Roles and Challenges. *J. Ind. Integr. Manag.*, 05, 04, 427–440, Dec. 2020.

21. Sachs, J., Schmidt-Traub, G., Kroll, C., Lafortune, G., Fuller, G., Woelm, F., *The Sustainable Development Goals and COVID-19. The Sustainable Development Report 2020*, Cambridge University Press, Cambridge, 2020.

22. Sachs, J., Schmidt-Traub, G., Mazzucato, M., Messner, D., Nakicenovic, N., Rocjkstrom, J., Six Transformations to achieve the Sustainable Developnment Goals. *Nat. Sustainability*, 2, 9, 805–814, 2019.

23. Solberg, E., Akufo_Addo, N., *Why we cannot lose sight of the Sustainable Development Goals during coronavirus*, 2020, Available at:https://www.weforum.org/agenda/2020/04/coronavirus-pandemic-effect-sdg-un-progress/ (Accessed 29 June 2020).

24. American Academy of Pediatrics, *Children and COVID-19*, 2020, State level data report as of 6/11/20. https://services.aap.org/en/pages/2019-novel-coronavirus-covid-19- infections/children-and-covid-19-state-level-data-report.

25. Williams, S., Armitage, C.J., Tampe, T., Dienes, K., Public attitudes towards COVID-19 contact tracing apps: a UK-based focus group. *Health Expect.* 2021 Apr; 24(2): 377–385.

26. Wiertz, C., Banerjee, A., Acar, O.A., Ghosh, A., Predicted Adoption Rates of Contact Tracing App Configurations - Insights from a Choice-Based Conjoint Study with a Representative Sample of the UK population (April 28, 2020). Available at SSRN: https://ssrn.com/abstract=3589199 Accessed July 21, 2020.

27. Altmann, S., Milsom, L., Zillessen, H. *et al.*, *Support for app-based contact tracingof Covid-19: cross-country*, study.https://www.medrxiv.org/content/10.1101/2020.05.14.20102269v1.full.pdf; 2020, Accessed July 21, 2020.10.

28. Magro, G., COVID-19: Review on latest available drugs and therapies against SARS-CoV-2. Coagulation and inflammation cross-talking. *Virus Res.*, 286, 198070, 2020, https://doi.org/10.1016/j.virusres.2020.19807.

29. Lueth, K.L., https://iot-analytics.com/the-impact-of-covid-19-on-the-internet-of-things/

30. Ali, Z.H., Ali, H.A., Badawy, M.M., Intenet of Things (IoT): definitions, challenges and recent research directions. *Int. J. Comput. Appl.*, 128, 1, 37–47, 2015.

A Comprehensive Composite of Smart Ambulance Booking and Tracking Systems Using IoT for Digital Services

Sumanta Chatterjee*, Pabitra Kumar Bhunia, Poulami Mondal, Aishwarya Sadhu and Anusua Biswas

JIS College of Engineering, Kalyani/Nadia, India

Abstract

Technology is the primary force driving the lives of thousands on this planet. But being accustomed to the comforts of modernization, the curses are often being denied or ignored. The obsessed idea of being the superior race leads to a spike in the population curve which directly or indirectly threatens the comforts of the future era. The population density sheds a light on the threat to the ecological survival of mankind and further teases the phrase "survival of the fittest". Countries like India with more than 130 crore population are on the verge of exponential development obviously due to the huge availability of manpower and youth but the same population reasons the shortage of food, medical facility, and homes to lakhs of Indians. Further in the study, we focused works related to improving medical facilities (ambulance availability) in highly dense countries. Before the discussion regarding ambulance availabilities in medical infrastructure, shedding light on aspects like traffic congestion plays a vital role. In India, as per statistical data, a sharp rise of 4% in traffic had been noted and the curve is exponentially growing. Traffic congestion is becoming a major issue in India. Due to the increase in urban traffic congestion, the average time to reach hospitals is getting high. The ambulance is a transport vehicle that helps to connect patients with healthcare institutions like general hospitals or specialized hospitals. In India, traffic signals have a crucial role to play especially in metropolitan cities like Delhi, Mumbai, Bangalore, Chennai, and Kolkata. In emergency conditions, the time has a vital role to play. In any type of critical or emergency, medical condition ambulance

**Corresponding author*: sumanta.chatterjee@jiacollege.ac.in

R. Anandan, Suseendran Gopalakrishnan, Souvik Pal and Noor Zaman (eds.) The Industrial Internet of Things (IIoT): Intelligent Analytics for Predictive Maintenance, (349–368) © 2022 Scrivener Publishing LLC

is the first preference for the transport of the patient to the hospital or nursing home as well as for the first emergency medical services. In this book chapter, we propose an app-based real-time interface that will be made ambulance bookings easier in inimical situations and the definite algorithm will serve crowd management making ambulance ready to go for every patient. We are on a verge of digital evolution and smart ambulances require the hour and will prove an essential addition to the smart grid technology. Establishing secure servers and databases, our app will be enabled with data regarding ambulances and the following data will be served to the user in need using standard data transfer protocols HTTPS and to maintain live status TCP protocols using sockets will be integrated with our app. The app is also secured by standardized DES encryption ciphers and schemas, thus granting user data security. Databases associated with the app follows standard operation protocols and is primarily SQL based. This system can also be extended to the booking of all the High Priority Vehicle Booking through which the user can book by just one tap. Every data latency parameter is taken care of using high-end modules and efficient network algorithms hence, further enabling data flow from the patient's vitals to the hospital once the patient has been picked up by the ambulance. Due to the delay in ambulance service, many patients lose their life, and this has been increasing day by day. The main reason for traffic jams is the increased population which therefore leads to an increased number of vehicles. This affects the ambulance services. The ambulance also provides several emergency medical services to provide patient stability in his or her critical condition. Now, the design of an ambulance is mostly based on vans or pick-up trucks and sometimes also based on motorcycles, aircraft, cars, boats, buses, etc. In this era of digital revolution where traditional methods have lost their importance and are not efficient enough, our model is competent enough to serve the purpose effectively and can monitor the patients more efficiently than the age-old solutions already available. It works on real-time data provided by the users and thus will be a boon to the society. But being aware of the curses of the smart grid, tensions related to data security and the cyber secured network is always challenging and not being able to cope with such challenges will bring irreversible consequences. Although our proposed work defines security measures and is a definite boon still a further discussion over the threats is part of detailing in the further course of the book chapter.

Keywords: Smart ambulance, modernization, digital services, tracking system, IoT, infrastructure

14.1   Introduction

From ancient time, being medical services is the most important thing. Medical services are always the most demanding service all over the world. There are several types of equipment for health services. Among this equipment, ambulance is one of the most important medical service. Ambulance is used to transport patients. The word ambulance comes from the Latin word "ambulare". The meaning of this word is move out or to walk. In ancient times, carts were used as an ambulance to transfer patients. There are different types of ambulances according to their function like emergency ambulance which one is the mostly used most common type ambulance, patient transport ambulance that is generally used to transport patient from hospitals or nursing homes, ambulance bus that is a bus-type ambulance mainly used to transport more than one number of patients, charity ambulance that is a special type of ambulance arranged from any charity home for children or adults to take them on a trip from hospitals, and bariatric ambulance that is used to transport extremely fat people with proper equipment to maintain these patients and so on. Now, the design of an ambulance is mostly based on vans or pick-up-trucks and sometimes also based on motorcycles, aircrafts, cars, boats, buses, etc. Ambulance can be needed at any time anywhere. Mainly ambulance is used to transport patients in emergency cases. Patients who are in critical condition like stroke, heart attack, pregnancy, or any type of accident are mostly needed ambulance. Critical condition can come in any moment any time so ambulance is anytime anywhere the most needed and most unavoidable medical service. As ambulance is used in critical or emergency medical condition, so it contains light with flash and sirens to warn other vehicles in the road that there is an emergency condition so that the other vehicles can leave the path for the ambulance so that the ambulance can take the patient to hospital or nursing home without creating any late or any loss of patients' life. Sometimes, ambulance means a moving hospital because it serves the first treatment to the patient so the patients' condition can become stable for a short time before reaching hospital or nursing home. Inner place of an ambulance mainly has a place for a or more than one patient and some other places for some medical service provider like nurse who can give prior medical service to the patient in emergency or critical condition. Ambulance also provides several emergency medical services like first aid and oxygen cylinder facility to provide the patient stability in his or her critical condition. Beside this necessary medical equipment, ambulances also arrange some special equipment like two-way radio, mobile data terminal, tail lift, trauma lighting, CCTV, and data recorders. In any type of critical or emergency, medical condition ambulance is the first preference for transport of the patient to the hospital or nursing home as well as for the first emergency medical services. So, for this reason, sometimes, hospitals or nursing homes cannot provide ambulances for the patients in time, and this condition, some clubs or NGOs provide emergency ambulance services to the patients. Ambulance sometimes is also used for returning a patient from hospital or nursing home to home. But sometime, getting ambulance at time becomes so much tough like in the midnight if there is any emergency condition for patient, it sometimes difficult to get ambulance or if ambulance is got it cannot reach at time. So, it becomes so hard time of patient and his or her family to transfer patient to hospital or nursing home. So, in this flourishing era of technology where everything like daily necessities, grocery, clothes, and food, whatever we want is at the doorstep why medical services will be at backsteps. When peoples' every demand is fulfilled with one click on a mobile application, then also the most essential, i.e., medical service especially ambulance service, should be also be available through mobile application. Also, nowadays, IoT is the most popular technology to be applied for any technology-based smart device. Now, the question will grow everyone's mind is what is IoT and why it is so popular in the world of technology. IoT is the short form of Internet of Things (IoT) that means where we apply the idea of internet or something that is related to Internet. The IoT defines that how the "things" that are implanted with software, other technologies, and sensors are connected with other devices and exchange with other devices over the internet. Due to the interface of real-time investigation, various technologies and fixed systematical things have evolved in large numbers. To enable the traditional fields of machine learning and automation (including building and house automation), wireless sensor networks, control systems, and others contribution are included. In the shopper market, technology of IoT is mostly matches with the products containing the concept of the "smart home", that includes devices and appliances (like lighting fixtures, home security systems, thermostats and cameras, and other home appliances) that support more than one common ecosystem, and these devices are controlled by ecosystem, such as smartphones and smart speakers. In healthcare also, IoT technology is used. But there is also some danger in using the technology of IoT, especially in the fields of privacy and security. First IoT concept that is the network of smart devices was discovered in 1982 with a Coca-Cola vending machine with very first internet appliance. The application area of IoT can be differentiated mostly in four kinds like consumer, commercial or organizational, industrial, and infrastructure spaces. Most of the IoT applications are in consumer field like connected vehicles, home automation, wearable technology, connected health, and appliances with remote monitoring capabilities. In organizational applications, IoT is applied in medical and healthcare, transportation, and building and home automation. In industrial fields, IoT applications are in manufacturing, agriculture, and maritime. In infrastructure areas, it is in metropolitan scale deployments, energy managements, environmental monitoring, and living lab. Also, it is also applied in military fields and product digitization. So, we tried to develop a mobile application for fast ambulance service using IoT. This is an organizational application of IoT. Here in healthcare and medical fields, IoT is applied. Through this application, patients' family can get ambulance any time in there near about locality very soon and very easily. It will be a 24-hour service app where ambulance service will be active for any time. In this app, patient will be provided all types of facilities and there will be several options to be chosen like if patient needed oxygen facility or not, nurse facility or not, or if that will be a pregnancy case then some other special services will be provided. Beside ambulance facility, through this app, anyone can get facility of first aid, can get information about nearby pharmacy, hospitals, and blood banks, and also can get information about home health care, health insurance, etc. In this app, patients' family has to provide the current location of the patient and then by giving the nearby hospital name and also have to give the time that when the ambulance will be arriving and there will also be a drop down for special services like AC, oxygen, and nurse. Patient's family member can also contact with the ambulance driver or can see where the ambulance's location is. Also, in any emergency case there will be an emergency button or also there will be a transport and shifting button for any special type of transporting arrangements. So, in this way, all types of advantages will be provided through this app so that any patient's will not be fallen at danger. Our motto is to save each and everyone's life and fulfill all types of medical needs.

14.2   Literature Review

B. Janani Saradha *et al.* proposed a system of cloud networking which connect both ambulance and traffic controlling unit. RFID technology is used to achieve intelligent traffic signal control. The idea is to detect the ambulance near the signal, the ambulance is tracked by RFID reader which is attached with RFID tag and the data is send to the cloud. After sending the data through mobile app, the user receives the acknowledgment, then system changes to green signal automatically in the path of ambulance. This way, it provides undisturbed services to emergency vehicle [1].

Jay Lohokare *et al.* proposed an exclusive idea of handling live location of the emergency services. Using these locations, people who need emergency services can connect easily to the official centers. The main contribution of this paper is to provide a solution for the entire city where huge number of users will be using this system. For this application, the mandatory need according to the author is of Internet and GPS (Global Positioning System). This device can enable such a smart phone through which exact location can be sent to the server. This paper gives will help to handle huge number of users [2].

Omkar Udawant *et al.* proposed a smart ambulance system. The basic idea of this paper is to check that whether the range of the ambulance is within 100 m, then the color changes to green signal for some time. They use cloud and GPRS technology for tracking. Ambulance contains sensors like heart rate sensor, blood pressure, ECG to send data to hospital's database at the mean time. According to patient's condition, the treatment will be done by the hospital authorities. So, it saves time as well as patient's condition [3].

Homan Samani *et al.* have proposed an AED (Automated External Defibrillator) which is an ambulance robot termed as Ambubot. This Ambubot arrives and checks the pulse rate of the person who had a sudden cardiac attack and if it notices that the pulse rate is less, it suddenly gives permission to press a button which provides a shock to the cardiac captured person. So, the pulse rate improves and the person should be free from risk [4].

Arif Shalik has proposed GPS sensor which send data to the cloud, and from there, an alarm message will be received by whoever is brought into that vehicle. The flag will show the situation's condition and helps to locate the GPS area. The ambulance will use the GPS tracking system to get the location as fast as possible [5].

Venkatesh H *et al.* have proposed a system which makes use of embedded technology for Intelligent Traffic Control. In this system, the main aim is to control the traffic signal board to green whenever the ambulance is stuck in traffic and making the opposite traffic signal board to red signal. Using GPS and cloud, a request is send to traffic signal point to the user connecting to the cloud server by GSM technology. This proposed system does not have any other alternative method in case of technology failure such as embedded technology is mostly hardware based and failure in hardware would outcome into complete system failure. Secondly, the use of GSM technology is uncertain as network failure in GSM would mean that the request is not send to the traffic signal board on time and in such cases the proposed system will be of no use. Also, it does not specify the emergency and non-emergency situations [6].

Prashant Jadhav *et al.* have proposed work in makes use of Image Processing Technique. Over here, at first a film of lane is captured by a web camera which is placed in traffic lane that captures images of roads wherein we want to control the traffic. In order to have information about the traffic density these images are processed efficiently using the MATLAB software and then the controller sends the command to the traffic signal board to show particular time on the signal to manage traffic [7].

An advance warning system for ambulance passes for Indian scenarios was developed by Madhav Mishra *et al.* This research is basically based on the concept of IoT, along with other technologies. The architecture which is frequently used is server and client architecture. This is an android application using a client [8].

Buchenscheit, Andreas *et al.* have implemented an emergency vehicle warning system based on VANET. The system alerts the emergency vehicle that uses inter-vehicle communication and also surrounds roadside infrastructure like traffic lights. Through this system, other vehicles can be warned of an arriving emergency vehicle and also can receive detailed route information [9].

The Arduino-based RFID system that is used to change the traffic signal upon arrival at a traffic light junction was proposed by B. Janani Sharadha *et al.* The concept of this system is if an ambulance or any emergency vehicle stops at the signal, the installed RFID will control that emergency vehicle. The acknowledgement for the user through the mobile app where the particular signal is made Green for a particular duration and when ambulance passes by, it again gets back to its original sequence of signaling. If this system becomes automated, then it can fully track the route of the ambulance and can control the traffic signaling as per the ambulance route. Through this system the signaling process can be controlled and fully save the time for emergency services [10].

Toru Kobayashi *et al.* proposed a system of an IoT for ambulance to put a special application installed in a smartphone on a dashboard. The cloud side application also tried to control the position information of the ambulance distribution in consideration for the situation of other vehicles and the privacy of ambulance users. Functional effectiveness of this system was inspected by the proof experiment in the public road [11].

Mohamed N. Ashmawy *et al.* proposed the main target of the platform is to increase the likelihood of the patient's survival by having the ambulance arriving to the hospital as soon as possible while allowing the responsible doctor to monitor the patient's biomedical data. Hence, the doctor can provide the paramedics riding with the patient with helpful instructions or prepare the needed medical services to be received by the patient upon arrival. Furthermore, the platform applies machine learning techniques on the collected data to help the doctor identify possible medical threats. We adopt a layered approach in the design of the system. A prototype of the integrated system is implemented, and its performance is evaluated [12].

Puneet Kumar Aggarwal *et al.* proposed an autonomic computing allude as a self-managing feature that is autonomic nervous system, which manages the body. A system is autonomic if it can monitor changes by itself, analyze, plan actions according to it, and execute them automatically in order to become a reliable system. The present work focuses on a real-life case study of traffic light management system and plays an important role in our daily lives. In most places, "especially in developing countries", the traffic light system is time bounded, which sometimes does not allow an ambulance carrying a patient to pass through traffic light: red light. Hence, there should be a smart traffic light signal system which can overcome with such problems, allow the ambulance to pass through traffic signal whether it is red or green. This can be done using a wireless sensor network and voice recognition technology [13].

Tammishetty, Sneha *et al.* have proposed this method that allows the emergency vehicles like ambulances to get traffic signals controlled by the traffic area at the time of arrival so that the traffic can be regulated. This system is made of GSM, Arduino, and Android mobile system. In emergency cases, the user has to control the traffic signal by android app by travelling to ambulances [14].

The idea of traffic issues and providing the exact position of the train by using GPS was proposed by G. Hemanth Kumar *et al.* Through SMS, the communication will be made between train and the passenger. The second objective of this project is that it will provide an automatic spike control at a level crossing in place of the gates operated by the gatekeeper. It consists of two things. Firstly, it reduces time for which the gate is being kept closed. Secondly, for reduction of the traffic at the crossing, it also provides emergency path for ambulances [15].

14.3   Design of Smart Ambulance Booking System Through App

Nowadays, an ambulance has many facilities to comfort the patient but it is observed that ambulance online booking system is not yet launched. So, an effort has been taken to make easier service for the patient to book an ambulance in emergency purposes. Using mobile app, we are making an app for online booking system for ambulance. At first, the user has to register with their mobile number from where they have to put the pickup location and the exact destination of the patient. Now, while booking the ambulance enter card details for payment purpose and when the

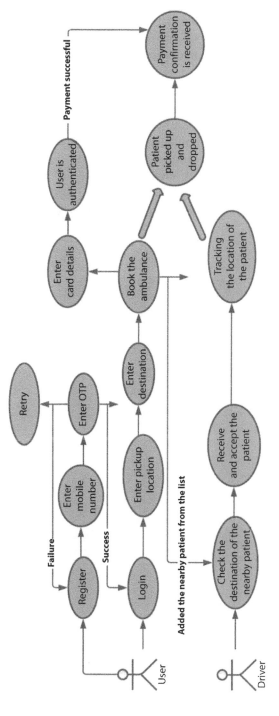

Figure 14.1 Use-case diagram.

ambulance is booked, the nearby driver checks the list of nearby patients and confirm the booking. After that, the driver tracks the location through Google map and picks up patients from the given location and dropped (Figure 14.1). Then, the payment process will be confirmed and the driver will receive the payment.

- Locate nearest ambulance.
- Get the assurance of your booking.
- Get ready for the ambulance to pick you up.
- Get the exact arrival time for ambulance.
- Choose your payment process carefully.
- Convenient to use ambulance booking app and find the nearby location of the ambulance for emergency booking.

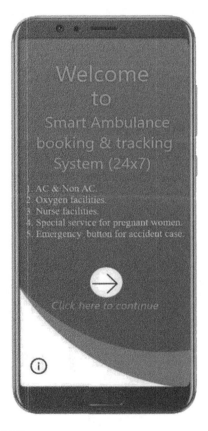

Figure 14.2 Welcome page.

14.4   Smart Ambulance Booking

Medical emergencies can happen anytime anywhere. Helping a patient in the transport system is a great work and should be handled under professional guidance. During emergency, the last thing you wish for is delay. This app will provide you with ambulance providers who are always on go with their vehicles. Our advanced algorithmic logic helps you to get the driver with the ambulance that matches your requirements in the shortest possible time. The idea of the introduction of an online ambulance service is to handle the critical situation in a far better and structured manner and assures the patients that the chances of life and death situations can be reduced the maximum. Just like you book cabs over a few taps on your smartphone, similarly, you can book an ambulance now in the same way.

Figure 14.3 Signup page.

14.4.1   Welcome Page

This is the welcome page of "Smart ambulance booking and tracking system". Here, we can find all the facilities provided by us. By clicking on the continue button, the app will be redirect to the next page (Figure 14.2).

14.4.2   Sign Up

Through this page, one can easily signup to this app by putting their basic details (e.g., name, email address, and choosing their password to access the service). For the instant and secure process, user can also sign up using their social media account (e.g., Email id, Google pulse, and Facebook). By clicking on the Sign-Up button, the user will be redirect to the next page (Figure 14.3).

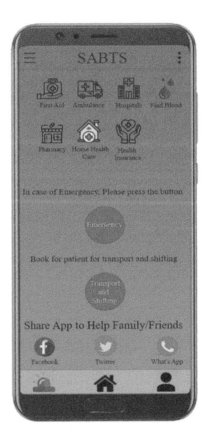

Figure 14.4 Home page.

14.4.3   Home Page

On this home page, user can find all the facilities provided by the app. They can choose any option as per their requirement (e.g., first aid service, ambulance service, nearby hospitals, blood bank, pharmacy, and health insurance). For any emergency cases (e.g., road accident), they can find the "Emergency" button to book the ambulance instantly. For shifting the patient to one hospital to another place user can choose the "Transport and shifting" button (Figure 14.4).

14.4.4   Ambulance Section

This is the main and vital part of the app where a user can book the ambulance by providing some basic details (e.g., pickup location, drop

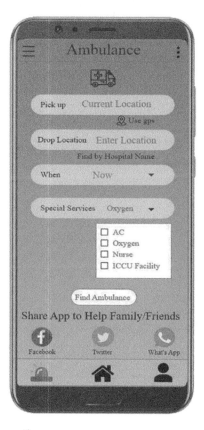

Figure 14.5 Ambulance section.

location, and time when the ambulance is required, if any special services are needed like Oxygen, Nurse, ICCU, AC they can choose). After filling-up all the required information the user can press the "Find Ambulance" button to redirect the next page where user can find the nearby ambulance (Figure 14.5).

14.4.5   Ambulance Selection Page

Here, user can get their nearby ambulance services from where user can select any option as per their choice to successfully book the ambulance (Figure 14.6).

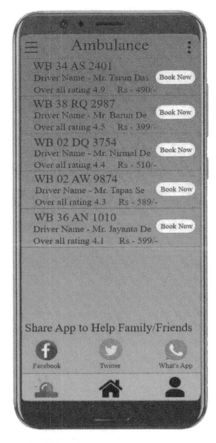

Figure 14.6 Ambulance selection page.

Figure 14.7 Confirmation of booking.

14.4.6 Confirmation of Booking and Tracking

From here, user can view the booked ambulance as well as user also track the ambulance. User can choose any payment option from there (e.g., cash, card, net banking, wallet) (Figure 14.7).

14.5 Result and Discussion

- One-Touch Emergency Booking: Easily book emergency ambulance with a press of a button.
- Estimated Time to Arrival: Contact the ambulance driver via phone call to know his location.

- Easy to Use: Convenient to use and find an ambulance nearby your location for elective or emergency booking.
- Freedom of Choice: You can get to choose a free or paid ambulance available near you.
- Direct On-Call Communication: Engage effortlessly with ambulance drivers over the phone.
- Book Ambulance for Others: Be a good human being and help the patient who need emergency medical treatment (Figure 14.8).

Figure 14.8 Ambulance booking app.

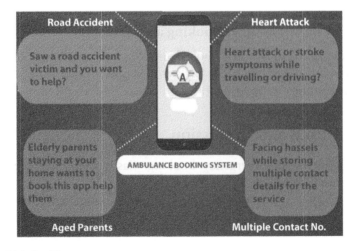

Figure 14.9 Booking system.

14.5.1 How It Works?

- Install the app on any Android phone or iPhone through Playstore.
- After opening the app, select Free or Paid Ambulance and choose from available options.
- You can enter the details of the location where the patient needs to be transported by simply entering the destination name or proper address.
- Get estimated arrival time for ambulance and their contact number (Figure 14.9).

14.6 Conclusion

The most important thing to remember is that ambulance is little different from cab booking. When you will book an ambulance, if you are booking it for emergency purpose, the app will immediately give the present location of the nearby ambulances so that you can get the ambulance as fast as possible.

The driver will immediately contact you to find out the nature of the emergency and know your exact location before the ambulance even arrives. At the same time, nearby hospitals will be informed about the emergency and will also offer some emergency advice on the spot, so that the patient's health do not get worse before the ambulance gets there.

That is utterly important, and the problems where were centralized in the existing systems became apparent to us first-hand in present scenario. A big cricket match was going on in the weekend held by a company, and a critical accident on the ground takes place to a player breaking his leg badly, with the bone coming out badly.

At that time, everyone was in a dilemma—whether you should move the victim to keep him still, how to call an ambulance, and what to do after the ambulance came. When an ambulance was finally tracked down, it was a very incomprehensible situation in getting it to reach the actual location.

We should have a prior knowledge of what kind of emergency the patient is having and complete few formalities before booking.

In the hospitals, having their own ambulances, the ambulances are provided by the government for emergency services. As the demand keeps on increasing, it became a big challenge. Now, the faster you respond, the faster is the chances of recovery.

14.7   Future Scope

Our existing model can efficiently arrange for an ambulance according to the demand of the situation. But in future, it can be extended to book all the High Priority Vehicle Booking through which the user can avail Fire Brigade service, Police service at the earliest, by just one tap and can track the HPVB (High Priority Vehicle Booking) using GPS on the device.

The mobile application can be formulated in such a way that, it could be made to monitor the vital body parameters of the patients and necessarily take due actions within the smart ambulance itself to reduce time wastage in treatment after reaching hospitals. Accordingly, all these steps if implemented successfully could bring a new shape to the existing Smart Ambulance System benefitting the entire society at large.

References

1. Udawant, O., Thombare, N., Chauhan, D., Hadke, A., Waghole, D., Smart ambulance system using IoT, in: *2017 International Conference on Big Data, IoT and Data Science (BID)*, Pune, India, 20-22 Dec. 2017, IEEE, 12 April 2018.
2. Saha, H.N., Raun, N.F., Saha, M., Monitoring Patient's Health with Smart Ambulance system using Internet of Things (IOTs). *8th Annual Industrial Automation and Electromechanical Engineering Conference (IEMECON)*, 2017.
3. Samani, H. and Zhu, R., Robotic Automatetd External Defibrillator Ambulance for Emergency Medical Service in Smart Cities. *IEEE Access*, 4, 268–283, 2016.
4. Shaik, A., Bowen, N., Bole, J., Kunzi, G., Bruce, D., Abdelgawad, A., Yelamarthi, K., Smart Car: An IoT Based Accident Detection System. *2018 IEEE Global Conference on Internet of Things (GCIoT)*, 2018.
5. Beri, G., Ganjare, P., Gate, A., Channawar, A., Gaikwad, V., Intelligent Ambulance with Traffic Control. *Int. Jour. Of Elect, Electron. Comp. Syst.*, 4, 43–46, Feb. 2016.
6. Karkar, A.G., Smart Ambulance System for Highlighting Emergency-Routes, in: *2019 Third World Conference on Smart Trends in Systems Security and Sustainablity (WorldS4)*, London, United Kingdom, United Kingdom, 30-31 July 2019, IEEE, 21 November 2019.
7. Kobayashi, T., Kimura, F., Arai, K., Smart Ambulance Approach Alarm System Using Smartphone, in: *2019 IEEE International Conference on Consumer Electronics (ICCE)*, Las Vegas, NV, USA, 11-13 Jan. 2019.

8. Karthikeyan, S., Srinivasan, S.R., Ali, J.S., Veeraraghavan, A.K., Smart Summoning Of Ambulance during a Vehicle Accident, Bangalore, India16-18 Aug. 2018, IEEE, 04 July 2019.

9. Joshi, Y., Gharate, P., Ahire, C., Alai, N., Sonavane, S., Smart parking management system using RFID and OCR, in: *2015 International Conference on Energy Systems and Applications*, Pune, India, 30 Oct.-1 Nov. 2015, IEEE, 04 July 2016.

10. El-Masri, S. and Saddik, B., Mobile Emergency System and Integration, in: *2011 IEEE 12th International Conference on Mobile Data Management*, Lulea, Sweden, 6-9 June 2011, IEEE, 03 November 2011.

11. Call ambulance smart elderly monitoring system with nearest ambulance detection using Android and Bluetooth, in: *2016 Second International Conference on Science Technology Engineering and Management (ICONSTEM)*, Chennai, India, 30-31 March 2016, IEEE, 08 September 2016.

12. Kumar, G.H. and Ramesh, G.P., Intelligent gateway for real time train tracking and railway crossing including emergency path using D2D communication, in: *2017 International Conference on Information Communication and Embedded Systems (ICICES)*, Chennai, India, 23-24 Feb. 2017, IEEE, 19 October 2017.

13. Karmokar, P., Bairagi, S., Mondal, A., Nur, F.N., Moon, N.N., Karim, A., Yeo, K.C., A Novel IoT based Accident Detection and Rescue System, in: *Third International Conference on Smart Systems and Inventive Technology (ICSSIT)*, Tirunelveli, India, India, 20-22 Aug. 2020, IEEE, 06 October 2020.

14. Alhomsi, Y., Alsalemi, A., Al Disi, M., Bensaali, F., Amira, A., Alinier, G., CouchDB Based Real-Time Wireless Communication System for Clinical Simulation. *2018 IEEE 20th International Conference on High Performance Computing and Communications; IEEE 16th International Conference on Smart City; IEEE 4th International Conference on Data Science and Systems (HPCC/SmartCity/DSS)*, Exeter, United Kingdom, pp. 1094–1098, 2018.

15. Kiss, G., Using Smartphones in Healthcare and to Save Lives. *2011 International Conference on Internet of Things and 4th International Conference on Cyber, Physical and Social Computing*, Dalian, China, pp. 614–619, 2011.

15

An Efficient Elderly Disease Prediction and Privacy Preservation Using Internet of Things

Resmi G. Nair* and N. Kumar

Department of Computer Science and Engineering, Vels Institute of Science, Technology & Advanced Studies (VISTAS), Pallavaram, Chennai, India

Abstract

IoT (Internet of Things) is the physical object network that connects many inbuilt devices to the Internet for data collection and exchange. The ability to link such systems to vast pools of data, such as the cloud, is an essential improvement. IoT is widely applicable in many aspects of our life by integrating integrated appliances and cloud servers. Embedding devices with a cloud server will give aged people a more versatile facility without going to hospitals with the ageing population. While the sensor-cloud paradigm has benefits, there are still many security challenges. Therefore, it is important to understand the architecture and integration of security problems such as authentication and data protection to protect elderly people's privacy. An intelligent and safe health control system is proposed in this article with an IoT sensor focused on cloud storage and encryption. Here, initially, using the IoT devices, a smart wearable device can be designed using ESP 32. Then, the obtained data can be normalized, and pointed features can be extracted by using the semantic component analysis method. Then, by implementing the iterative multistate uplift, ANN can classify and identify the diseased data precisely. Then, the data is stored on a cloud server or maintained and monitored. The PHR must be protected from the attack in the cloud. To comply with this privacy preservation system, techniques of cryptography are used. The polynomial HMAC encryption algorithm is initially used for the PHR service. The cloud server produces the key for authentication purposes as the data owner queries the file and checks it out with the user. The user will access the decrypted file when the key is given using

Corresponding author: reshmign@gmail.com

R. Anandan, Suseendran Gopalakrishnan, Souvik Pal and Noor Zaman (eds.) The Industrial Internet of Things (IIoT): Intelligent Analytics for Predictive Maintenance, (369–392) © 2022 Scrivener Publishing LLC

a polynomial HMAC algorithm. Then, the emergency message and the generated key can be sent to the patient and doctor for earlier treatment. Finally, the performance analysis is performed, and the proposed and the existing techniques are analyzed to demonstrate the scheme's efficiency. The proposed scheme achieves authentication and provides essential security requirements.

Keywords: IoT, sensor-cloud, cryptography, ESP 32, ANN, cloud server, HMAC encryption

15.1 Introduction

Over the last years, the Internet of Things (IoT), medical sensors, and Internet software have exponentially expanded to provide remote patient care. It is worth remembering that, every year, there are an increased number of elders with chronic illness. An ageing community refers to a demographic paradigm that meets or exceeds a certain percentage of the ageing population. According to the UN Norm, a city is regarded as a culture of the age, in which 10% of the population is individuals over 60 years of age and 7% of the population over 65. People aged 65 years are included under the new norm. From 12% to 22% between 2015 and 2050, the world population is expected to nearly double over 60. Ageing means low fertility, ageing, and social care scheme lagging behind. Meanwhile, elderly well-being has been a global concern illuminated. When more and more elders need long-term care, they choose independence and involve themselves to remain in their own homes as long as possible. They cannot be handled properly because of the scarcity of medical facilities. A central process in hospitals is the continuous surveillance of essential vital symptoms of patients. This is normally done today using a range of cable sensors connecting to patients and bedside monitors. The limit is for elderly people to be hooked to bedding devices. Consequently, it was practicable and necessary to identify medical conditions personally through a repository without hospitals. This situation opens up the modern body sensor networks with the growing availability of IoT and health sensors for personal use. This conditions new technologies which can play an important role in many applications, Wireless Sensor Network (WSN). The exponential Development of physiological sensors allowed a new generation of WSNs now being used for traffic monitoring, crops, utilities, and welfare. The body area network area is an interdisciplinary area that provides cost-effective and consistent health monitoring by medical information online in real-time. However, sensor networks have posed several challenges: mobility, scalability, and heterogeneous information services. The WSN cloud integration provides increased connectivity, endless resources, immense computing power, and customer reaction. The modern data infrastructure paradigm of cloud computing is offered to researchers. The provision (and inclusion within the current infrastructure) of computing services and storage resources and software is pay-per-use. Cloud storage has become much more versatile for personal use in order to offer more appropriate and convenient network services. Since the cloud is a wide range of resources, companies can select when, where, and how to use cloud storage. Cloud platforms are widely known as "software as a service" (SaaS), "platform as a service" (PaaS), and "infrastructure as a service" (IaaS). Various surveys have shown that the future trend is simply cloud-based services. The online programming applications, apps, and data are supported through a browser with cloud computing services. To ensure confidentiality and protection of user data, cloud services need to adhere to security and privacy policies.

Despite the consensus and certification of parties to browse patient records, due to theft, data transmission times, and long-lasting data retention issues, the public is also concerned about the electronic medical record systems. However, several systems are suggested that do not guarantee the anonymity and non-repudiation of a patient. This chapter suggests a smart and stable surveillance regime using cloud-based IoT sensors to safeguard elders' privacy. The biggest issue here is that the elderly increase daily and do not have to be linked to their beds with surveillance devices, leading to disadvantages and the waste of medical services. The elderly, on the other hand, are at great risk of acute pain or episodes like heart attacks. Without adequate medical aid, the consequences would be very severe. The EHR will provide our system with a diverse and appropriate medical service. The suggested system should focus on the advantages of cloud computing and the safety of information for elderly people because of the importance of the privacy of the elderly.

15.2   Literature Survey

Chavan Patil and Sonawane [1] proposed microcontroller (AAB) that is a passway for communication with different sensors, for example, the pulse sensor, ECG sensor, drip trace sensor (blood or saline), and sensors to track motion, which is the AVR-328 microcontroller (Arduino board). The microcontroller captures the sensor data and passes it into the network via Wi-Fi and thus tracks medical parameters in real-time. The physician will view the data at any time. The controller is also attached to a buzzer to alert the controller to sensor output variations. The Android-based application attached to the cloud service sends alerts to the doctor when the extremity is present. The doctor can then conveniently use NFC tags to quickly take provisional prescriptions without looking manually at patient records. With low power consumption, simple setup, high efficiency, and time-to-time response, this device are efficient. Sow *et al.* [18] proposed variations in data, including biodiversity and climate, that were used to predict the result of a particular disease in supervised learning. Bui and Zorzi [6] proposed applications for healthcare focused on an Internet-based solution to things. Islam *et al.* [9] proposed the IoT for health care. Birje *et al.* [5] proposed the IoT. Kumar [11] proposed the novel IoT Architecture and Healthcare System Design. Ženko *et al.* [22] proposed variability of pulse rate and detection of the quality of blood oxidation by the wearable mini-skill system. Shu *et al.* [17] proposed a heart rate tracking pressure sensor device with polymer-based pressure sensors and a post-processing interference circuit. An *et al.* [3] proposed a versatile, uncontrolled R.F. pulse detection sensor based on array resonators. Larson *et al.* [12] proposed a lung monitoring system that can be easily updated on any of the android devices. Milici *et al.* [14] proposed the air sensor based on a wearable modulated frequency selective surface. Baker *et al.* [4], on the web, proposed for smart healthcare things, barriers, and opportunities. Gubbi and Amrutur [8] proposed for low pulse oximetry adjustment pulse width monitoring and sampling. Von Rosenberg *et al.* [19] proposed smart helmet that can be activated by using the ECG and EEG multichannel. The proposed wearable can be very effective. Schäck *et al.* [16] proposed on the computer effective atrial fibrillation detection algorithm for photoplethysmography using smartphones. Yuce [21] proposed the implementation of wireless health services area networks. Lei Clifton [13] proposed mobile monitoring of patients by combining wearable and clinical observations. Parae *et al.* [15] proposed Smart Healthcare Monitoring System focused on the cloud. Wang *et al.* [20] proposed a hybrid mobile-cloud approach to smart, customized health care with ECG telemonitoring. Dunsmuir *et al.* [7] proposed the production of pre-eclampsia triage m-health applications.

15.3   Problem Statement

Owing to the diverse, healthy habitats, the well-being of elderly people in the digital world has been bad every day. They do not have the time to track their own condition. A person's relative state of well-being and disease reflects the nature of the biochemical or neurological disorder, signs, and physical disability. Health beliefs are individual assessments of the person's health status. A safe automated health management system is therefore essential to provide the individual with an appropriate human health rating and take the necessary measures to improve his or her health and to preserve his or her health data.

15.4 Proposed Methodology

The IoT in the area of health will attempt to initialize the accurate tracking of elderly health and will be able to provide people with wake-up information about their ailments at an acceptable time. In this chapter, we suggested a method in which patients have read the findings of a monitoring system of the body temperature, heart rate, body movements, blood pressure, etc. This is an automatically coded system in which elders can monitor the condition of the person without any further work on the health status tracking process. The extraction and classification of this information will then be performed. Confidential data can be saved in a cloud server, and a warning letter can be sent to the family doctor and patients, along with a clone key to access their confidential private health records, depending on the classified results. The proposed flow diagram will clearly show how the new monitoring system is developed. The data collection is performed using the sensor components of the IoT.

The schematic description of the proposed flow is shown in Figure 15.1. In this context, all IoT components will form a well-connected network, all connected with the health care system. Even the person may simply feed personal information to the computer to instantly connect the person to a hospital or healthcare unit.

15.4.1 Design a Smart Wearable Device

The device is implemented with hardware modules combined. During the implementation process, all hardware parts are assembled. In Figure 15.2, the circuit diagram of the device formed is shown. With physical pins, all sensors are connected to ESP32. The Wi-Fi module is built-in, so ESP32 is used as a computing unit. The Vcc and GND are attached to all sensors by the ESP32 Vcc and GND pin. The signal pin is wired to the D26 pin of the ESP32 in the case of the heartbeat sensor.

The LM35 data pin has a D35 microcontroller pin mapping (ESP32). This applies to a certain patient. The DHT11 database pin is connected to the D14 pin of ESP32 for room state tracking. DHT11 is only used for the calculation of room moisture. For testing poisonous gases in the room

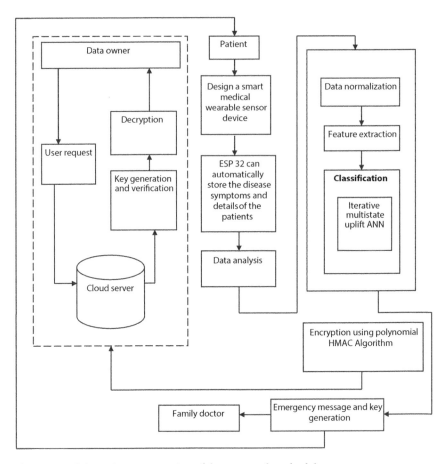

Figure 15.1 Schematic representation of the suggested methodology.

surroundings, the MQ-9 and MQ-135 optical outlet pins are attached to ESP32 D27 and D34, respectively. The data will then be reviewed after the collection of all health data from the elders and safely deposited on the server.

15.4.2 Normalization

The normalization of values calculated at a differing balance to a notionally common scale is often needed for the operation of data processing, often before the average. Certain normalization forms only require a rescaling method to retrieve the values correlated with certain other elements.

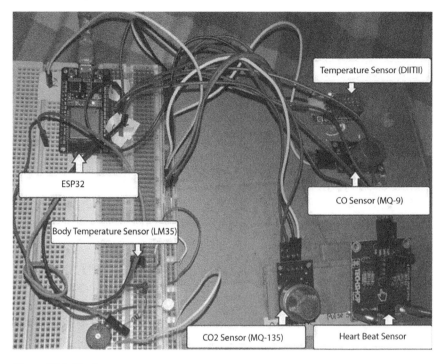

Figure 15.2 Hardware prototype.

We need to change the mistakes by making easy changes as we know data parameters. Following the adjustment of the errors, the health data values will usually not be spread randomly. The first step in the normalization process is to get the z-point. The Z-score will be represented in Equation (15.1):

$$Z = [(L-)/\sigma]$$ (15.1)

where μ is the mean of the health data and σ is the standard deviation of the health data.

$$Z = \frac{L - \overline{L}}{S}$$ (15.2)

where $\overline{L}$ is the mean of the sample and S is the standard deviation of the sample.

Then, the Hat matrix (H) can be calculated by using Equation (15.2):

$$H = L^*$$

$$(L^T L)^{-1L^T} \tag{15.3}$$

The variance for the Hat matrix is represented in Equation (15.4):

$$Var(\hat{\epsilon}_i) = \sigma^2 (1 - h_{ii}) \tag{15.4}$$

$$Var(\hat{\epsilon}_i) = \sigma^2 (1 - \frac{1}{n} - [(x_i - \overline{x}^2) / \Sigma_{j=1}^i (x_j - \overline{x}^2)]) \tag{15.5}$$

Then the residual can be calculated by using Equation (15.6)

$$t_i = \frac{\hat{\epsilon}_i}{\overline{\sigma}} \sqrt{1 - h_{ii}} \tag{15.6}$$

where $\overline{\sigma}$ is an estimate if the σ which is the mean values

$$o^k = (\sqrt{E(L - \mu)^\wedge K})^\wedge 2 \tag{15.7}$$

where L is a random variable and E is the expected value.

Use the mean μ particularly for the usually ordered distribution to standardize the distribution of the variable.

$$C_v = \frac{S}{\overline{L}} \tag{15.8}$$

where C_v is the coefficient of the variance.

In order to obtain all values from 0 to 1, the feature scale procedure should be performed. This approach is known as standardization based on continuity. The normalized equation will be in the form of L'

$$L' = \frac{(L - L_{min})}{(L_{max} - L_{min})} \tag{15.9}$$

Since standardizing the data in the data collection, the spectrum and data variability will then be equalized. The redundancy of data is mostly reduced or evenly removed. The normalized data could then be entered in the compilation steps as an input.

15.4.3 Feature Extraction

We can then delete the unwanted features by using the SCA process. This is a means of excluding second-degree mathematical dimensions. This approach was used in many applications. This is a mathematical activity that normally eliminates errors efficiently. The accuracy of the data can also be seen. It is important to distinguish the data during the study period. SCA defines the frequency of the effects in a given exact differential field. The details were challenged, and other information is pointed to as Ø route l and m adjacent. Generally, m only gets one benefit, and Ø is good in the way. The directional value then obtained will delete the data attributes. The method of removing functions is as follows:

$$K(1,m) = G(1,m,o,\emptyset) / \sum_{l=1}^{H} \sum_{m=1}^{H} G(\cdot 1,m,o,\emptyset) \qquad (15.10)$$

where G is the frequency vector, m, n, and o are that the frequencies of that particular constituent normally has the l and m values, k is the data characteristic (l,m), and l is variable, Ø is the uniform constant. The multiple attributes can be obtained using the SCA approach. You can also display the features with this method. This is one of the most popular methods of extraction. The maximum variance is seen when removing the axis from the results. This SCA measurement method evaluates whether or not data consistency is helpful. Certain correlation parameters use the criterion value dependent on the absolute and partial combining of goal and unnecessary results. SCA is mainly feedback to the evaluation of the features of controlled and unregulated classification applications. The whole procedure depends on the device's load, input changes, and IDS output. Using the removal process, the modified objects are produced during the selection phase. The unwanted details are separated. We would then point out any of the most significant characteristics below. The details are set as follows, duration and characteristics:

$$Information\ length = \frac{1}{l} - 1\sum_{l-1}^{l-1} a(r+1) - y_i(r) \qquad (15.11)$$

$$\text{Log entropy} = \Sigma_{i,j=0}^{M-1} F(i,j)[\frac{(i-\mu i)(j-\mu j)}{\sqrt{(\sigma i^2)}\sqrt{(\sigma j^2)}}] \qquad (15.12)$$

$$\text{Homogeneity} = \Sigma_{i,j=0}^{n-1} \frac{r(l,m)}{l} - (r+2) \qquad (15.13)$$

15.4.4   Classification

Back propagation absorbs results that include symptoms of the disease by matching the symptoms of the disease to the disease forecast using the known real goal value by the replicated processing. For the sake of estimation, the target value might be the known value. A weight set is modified for each data in order to reduce the average squared error between the network prediction and the real value. This modification is made from the output layer to the first hidden layer and the expression "backward". These revisions take the "reverse" direction. The steps concerned some of the parameters include inputs, outputs, and errors. The first step is to measure the value of the data set to reduce problems with the binary classification, where F(l) is a functional matrix that can be represented by Equation (15.14)

$$F(1) = W^t(l) + b \qquad (15.14)$$

where W is the classifier of the dual variables.

After that need to discuss the relationship among the data

$$F(l) = \Sigma_{a_{i>0}} a_i y_i K(l_i, X) + b \qquad (15.15)$$

The error can be the classification by using the below equation

$$\varphi(W) = -\emptyset(\|W\|)^2 \qquad (15.16)$$

Finally, a ranking is generated for the abnormality matching distance of database data

$$obj_{ED} = -20 * q(-2 * \sqrt{\Sigma V_v})/2 - \exp(\Sigma \cos(2\pi * V_v)/d_b) + 20\exp * ED \qquad (15.17)$$

where the E.D. signifies the Euclidean distance, q denotes the query data, and s is the signal score value.

$$\text{classify}(c) = ED_j^l \qquad (15.18)$$

The classification was concluded as

$$c_d = N(ED)_j^l - N(E_j^l D_j^l)^2 \qquad (15.19)$$

Algorithm 15.1 Interative Multistate Uplift ANN Algorithm

Input: details of symptoms of the disease
Output: Diagnosis of the disease

Initialize all weights and prejudice in the Network
while termination is not fulfilled X in D/ {
   // for the data proliferation is:
      for each input-layer in unit j { OJ = Ij;
   / / output of the input unit is the real input value of each unit secret or output-layer
input unit J {
   / / Compute the input net in unit j in relation to the previous input-layer;
For the output layer of each unit $\varphi(W) = -\varnothing(\| W \|)^2$
   // Calculate the errors of each unit j of the hidden layers from last up to first hidden layer –
      //Calculate an error of each unit j of the hidden layers,
         – Σk Errj Oj Oj Err wjkk 1(
         k of each network weight wi j.
// Calculate the error of the next layer /
c d=N direction(ED)
} }
End
End

15.4.5   Polynomial HMAC Algorithm

The proposed security framework ensures stable and effective data sharing in the cloud. For public-key encryption, the polynomial HMAC algorithm provides an alternative to the RSA. Many modern ABE strategies can handle private and public keys with only one authority. Device operators exchange data with actual users controlled by a different entity in some cases. In order to deal with this issue, many multi-authorities have been set up. The data holder includes ciphertext update access control structures and related status attributes. In the suggested scheme, a protection algorithm is used to weight cloud storage data. The 64-bit symmetrical polynomial HMAC algorithm has a variable-long address between 32 and 448 bit (14 bytes). The algorithm has been developed to correctly and continuously encrypt 64-bit plaintext in a 64-bit chip.

In choosing the operations of the algorithm, the table scan, node, addition, and bit by bit are used or to reduce the necessary 32-bit processor encryption and decryption time. The algorithm has been built purposefully, so that code functions remain simple, straightforward, and secure. Polynomial HMAC algorithm has a 16 round Feistel network for encryption and decoding, much like the DES (Data Encryption Standard). However, 32-bit knowledge on the left and right is changed for each round of polynomial HMAC algorithms relative to DES, changing only the proper 32-bit at the next round and eventually turning left. Included on the left before modification to the F function or 32-bit right for the next round, the Polynomial HMAC Algorithm was a bit exclusive 32-bit operation. Polynomial HMAC algorithm also consists of two proprietary trade and exchange operations after 16 checks. The method is based on the DES permutation shape.

In the proposed device configuration, the polynomial HMAC algorithm is given for the encryption, decryption, and generation of keys. The results are also authenticated via a code matching operation. Instead, the software generates user weight according to its capabilities. The polynomial HMAC algorithm is typically divided into two components, e.g., key extension and coding. In 16 rings, the data is encrypted. The main- and data-dependent displacement or substitution are often carried out at all times. In relation to 32 bits, this add-on (four indexed search tables). All of this is seen in the polynomial HMAC algorithm. The CA must have a user I.D. as a single user linked to the customer.

Nevertheless, the individual ciphers the features and sends them their signature to the authority. The legitimacy trait authenticates the user's personality. The hidden keys and weight will be set if the current person is the right one. CA and officials forward a hidden key to the network and issue the new recipient a secret key separately. With configuration and program algorithms from the central government and with public keys to the intruder, the challenger will be supplied with the correct keys. A single I.D. is logged in, and an asymmetrical dataset key is automatically selected before a data file is sent to the server. First, the device user downloads and uses a decryption algorithm to decode cloud storage. The method calculates these weights by value if the secret key given by the data owner has been accepted. The receiver will decode the weighted text data file.

Algorithm 15.2 Polynomial HMAC Algorithm

Launch (& ctx, key,); Polynomial HMAC Algorithm;
printf("Plaintext string is: percent s\n, "string of plaintext");
/ * Crypt plaintext of the response list * /
printf("Crypted string is:);
Though (len of plaintext)
Left response = Wrong request = UL;
Crack the message string of 64-bit (ok, 2 truly 32-bit); zero pad, if required
* / / *
For (len block = 0; len block > < 4;)
Left Message = Left Answer < minus 8;
Where (len plaintext)
+ * string++ plaintext; len — plaintext;
}
Left post + = 0;
}
(Strength block = 0; power of block < 4; strands of block + +)
message row = message row < 8; message row
When (len lens plaintext).
Right message + = * string++ plaintext;
complaints: complaints —; complaints;
}
Right to message + = 0 else;
}
/ * Encrypt and show reports * / *
Polynomial HMAC Algorithm encryption (& ctx, & wrong post, & correct post);
printf('%lx%lx,' left message, right message);
/ * Decryption performance update under * /
* ciphertext(left message)>24)(link message). * (link message).

(string++ = (uint8 t)(name > > 16);
* ciphertext string++(message left > > 8);
[122] Rd+= [108](1)capture back; back capture;
* string++= ciphertext (uint8 t)(communication > > 24);
(string++) (uint8 t)(droit>>16 message);
(uint 8 t)(message right > > 8)); * ciphertext string++

```
(uint8 t)message right; (1)message right;
+ = 8; ciphertext len
square("\n);
/ * Invert the cycle * / if decryption is required
}

square("\n);
return 0;
}
```

Finally, after the process of secret cryptography key can be generated. The secret key, along with a message, can send to the elders and the doctors. By using the secret key, the family doctors and the patient can access their personal health records safely and securely.

15.5   Result and Discussion

By comparing, it with the other current approaches, the efficiency of the proposed classification system was evaluated.

15.5.1   Accuracy

It shows the ordered errors, an indicator of the predisposition of arithmetic; the poor precision creates a difference between a result and the "real" value. This news is named ISO. This ensures that rare samples or data are checked using the same algorithm frequently and how accurate the data are collected from the device. Precise outcomes are the proportion of really positive and negative results in the overall data.

$$\text{Accuracy (A)} = (TP + TN)/(TP + TN + FP + FN) \quad (15.20)$$

15.5.2   Positive Predictive Value

Precision is a random error portrayal that reflects an algebraic variability metric

$$PPV = TP/(TP + FP) \quad (15.21)$$

15.5.3   Sensitivity

Also called sensitivity is the true optimistic rate, the reminder or identification in Any fields calculate the proportion of real positives found correctly.

$$\text{Sensitivity} = TP/ (TP+FN) \qquad (15.22)$$

15.5.4   Specificity

In addition, the specificity of the actual pessimistic rate tests the number of actual negatives defined correctly.

$$\text{Specificity}) = TP/(TP+FP) \qquad (15.23)$$

15.5.5   False Out

The false-positive rate of incorrect rate of incidence is measured as a combination of the number of incorrectly classified negative events and the overall number of negative events.

$$\text{False out} = FP/(FP + TN) \qquad (15.24)$$

15.5.6   False Discovery Rate

In zero hypothesis testing when making multiple comparisons, the false discovery rate (FDR) is a way to design a type-I error rate. FDR monitoring protocols are designed to control the anticipated percentage (no hypotheses rejected) of incorrect discoveries (incorrect rejections).

15.5.7   Miss Rate

The false-negative rate is the proportion of positive results produced by the test.

15.5.8   F-Score

F-score is the harmonic mean for consistency and recalls the average balance.

$$\text{F-Score} = 2 * \text{precision} * \text{recall}/ \text{precision} + \text{recall} \qquad (15.25)$$

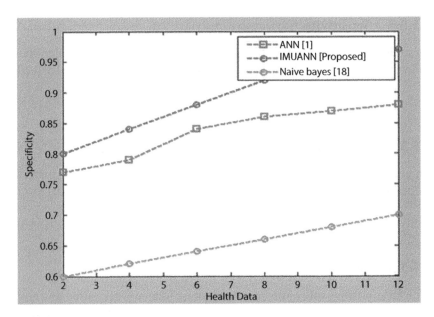

Figure 15.3 Health data vs. specificity.

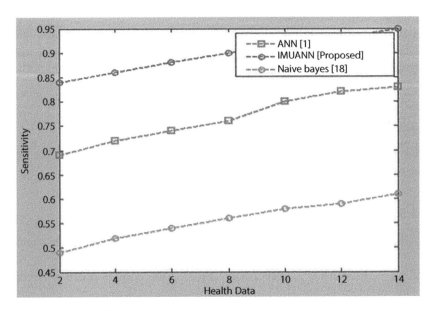

Figure 15.4 Health data vs. sensitivity.

The relation of precision for the suggested iterative multistate uplift ANN with other known approaches is seen in Figure 15.3. The suggested approach clearly achieves classification precision of 97% and forecasts the disorder with accuracy by its symptoms.

Figure 15.4 provides a contrast of sensitivity to other existing approaches for the suggested iterative multistate uplift ANN-raising classifier. The suggested approach clearly achieves a sensitivity for classification of 95% and predicts the disorder correctly from its symptoms.

In Figure 15.5, the proposed false out probability is estimated for other current approaches by iterative multistate uplifting ANN. It is clear that in comparison with the current scheme, the proposed approach achieves a false classification rate of less than 0.011%.

Figure 15.6 shows the positive predictive value with the other current approaches of the iterative multistate uplifting ANN. It is apparent that in contrast with the current procedure, the proposed approach produces a positive predictive value score of less than 0.16%.

Figure 15.7 represents the determination of the FDR of the proposed iterative multistate uplift ANN classifier with the other existing methods. It is clear that the proposed method achieves a FDR of less than 0.057% when compared to the existing system. It is very low.

Figure 15.8 represents the determination of the miss rate of the proposed iterative multistate uplift ANN classifier with the other existing methods.

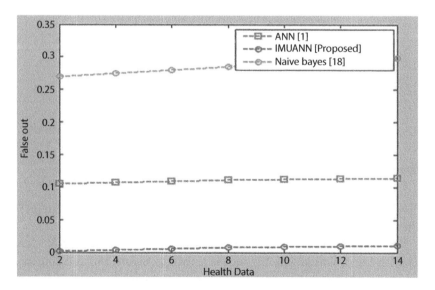

Figure 15.5 Health data vs. false out.

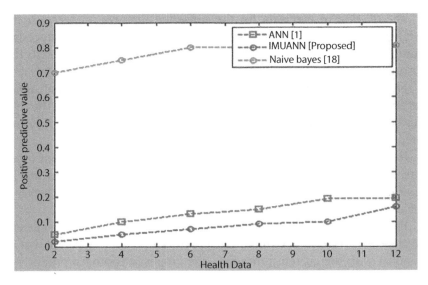

Figure 15.6 Health data vs. positive predictive value.

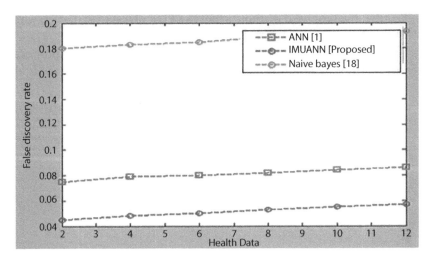

Figure 15.7 Health data vs. false discovery rate.

It is clear that the proposed method achieves a miss rate of less than 0.15% when compared to the existing system. It is very low.

The F-score for the suggested iterative multistate uplift ANN classifier with the other current methods is shown in Figure 15.9. Of course, as opposed to the current scheme, the proposed approach earns a 97% F-score.

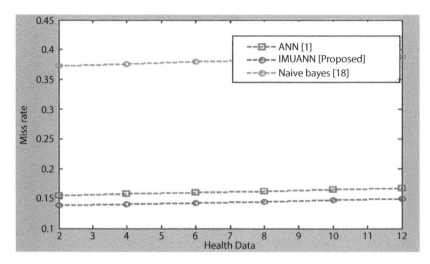

Figure 15.8 Health data vs. miss rate.

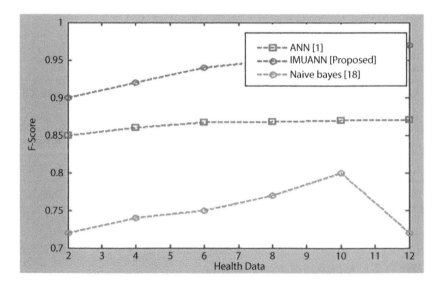

Figure 15.9 Health data vs. F-score.

The consistency of the proposed iterative multistate uplift ANN classifier with the other current methods is seen in Figure 5.10. It is obvious that, relative to the current scheme, the proposed approach achieved an F-score of 97%. The suggested method, therefore, yields successful results in comparison to all other established approaches. Therefore, the suggested

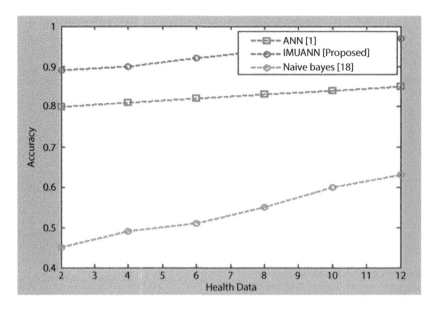

Figure 15.10 Health data vs. accuracy.

Table 15.1 Comparison of encryption time.

Algorithm	20 KB	50 KB	150 KB	300 KB
MDRSA [10]	0.051	0.078	0.093	0.25
DES [2]	0.038	0.042	0.08	0.129
AES [2]	0.027	0.037	0.06	0.076
Proposed	0.012	0.016	0.018	0.065

Table 15.2 Comparison of decryption time.

Algorithms	20 KB	50 KB	150 KB	300 KB
MDRSA [10]	0.035	0.05	0.085	0.1
DES [2]	0.005	0.012	0.036	0.076
AES [2]	0.011	0.017	0.028	0.048
Proposed	0.009	0.0092	0.013	0.02

solution provides efficient efficiency contrary to all other established approaches. The suggested cloud protection, polynomial HMAC efficiency metrics, is measured by its useful time in order to demonstrate the usefulness of the polynomial HMAC algorithm, as described in Tables 5.1 and 5.2. The suggested cloud security metrics were contrasted with the current security algorithm.

The re-encrypted ciphertext is decrypted by the medical professionals' private key. The period required to encrypt re-encrypted data over the

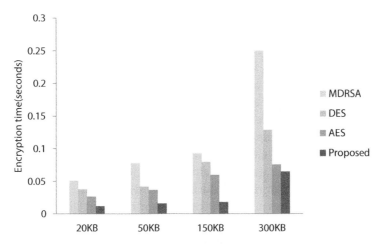

Figure 15.11 Time taken for encryption.

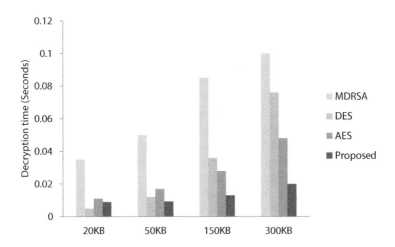

Figure 15.12 Time taken for decryption.

re-encrypted file size is described in Table 15.2. Figure 15.11 shows the time required for encryption simulation data.

In the encryption and decryption time between 20 and 300 KB, as seen in Figure 15.12, the polynomial HMAC algorithm is faster than AES, MDRSA, and DES. We checked and compared the four algorithms with different file sizes, which results in the encryption and decryption of small files faster than the other existing methodologies. The suggested speed approach is sharply increased on larger files. The results showed finally that the polynomial HMAC algorithm is more effective, quicker, and elegant.

15.6   Conclusion

In predicting the disease of wearable people, the new smart wearable device proposed would be very useful. Hence, the iterative multistate uplift ANN approach has been developed, which depicts diseases by studied their effects. The goal is to improve the user-friendly framework. Here, iterative multistate uplift ANN elevation is a new and efficient approach used to forecast diseases accurately. The aim of this new technology application is to alert patients beforehand during illnesses. Instead, the polynomial HMAC algorithm does not only provide a semi-trustful cloud service provider with data security and central authorities, but it also builds a lightweight key management system for large-scale applications. Overall, the proposed approach is superior to other current approaches.

References

1. Chavan Patil, A.B. and Prof. Sonawane, S. S., To Predict Heart Disease Risk and Medications Using Data Mining Techniques With an IoT Based Monitoring System For Post Operative Heart Disease Patients. *Sixth Post Graduate Conference for Computer Engineering (cPGCON 2017) Procedia International Journal on Emerging Trends in Technology (IJETT)*.
2. Al-gohany, N.A. and Almotairi, S., Comparative Study of Database Security In Cloud Computing Using AES and DES Encryption Algorithms. *J. Inf. Secur. Cybercrimes Res.*, 2, 1, 102–109, 2019.
3. An, Y.J., Kim, B.H., Yun, G.H., Kim, S.W., Hong, S.B., York, J.G., Flexible non-constrained R.F. wrist pulse detection sensor based on array resonators. *IEEE Trans. Biomed. Circuits Syst.*, 10, 2, 300–308, 2016, *Informatics*, 18, 3, 722–730, May.

4. Baker, S.B., Xiang, W., Atkinson, I., Internet of things for smart healthcare: technologies, challenges, and opportunities. *IEEE Access*, 5, 26521–26544, 2017.

5. Birje, M.N., Kumbi, A.A., Sutagundar, A.V., Internet of things: a survey of architecture, requirements, and applications. *Int. J. Hyperconnectivity Internet Things (IJHIoT)*, 1, 2, 45–71, 2017.

6. Bui, N. and Zorzi, M., Health care applications: a solution based on the Internet of things, in: *Proceedings of the 4th International Symposium on Applied Sciences in Bio-medical and Communication Technologies*, ACM, 2011.

7. Dunsmuir, D., Payne, B., Cloete, G., Petersen, C., Development of m-Health Applications for Pre-eclampsia Triage. *IEEE J. Biomed. Health Inf.*, P.P, 99, 2168–219, 2014. January.

8. Gubbi, S.V. and Amrutur, B., Adaptive pulse width control and sampling for low power pulse oximetry. *IEEE Trans. Biomed. Circuits Syst.*, 9, 2, 272–283, 2015.

9. Islam, S.M.R. *et al.*, The Internet of things for health care: a comprehensive survey. *IEEE Access*, 3, 678–708, 2015.

10. Kiran Kumar, Y. and Mahammad Shafi, R., An efficient and secure data storage in cloud computing using modified RSA public-key cryptosystem. *Int. J. Electrical & Comput. Eng.*, 10, 1, 2088–8708, 2020.

11. Kumar, N., IoT architecture and system design for healthcare systems, in: *2017 International Conference on Smart Technologies for Smart Nation (SmartTechCon)*, IEEE, pp. 1118–1123, 2017.

12. Larson, E.C., Goel, M., Redfield, M., Boriello, G., Rosenfeld, M., Patel, S.N., Tracking lung function on any phone, in: *Proceedings of the 3rd ACM Symposium on Computing for Development*, ACM, p. 29, 2013.

13. Clifton, L., Clifton, D.A., Pimentel, M.A.F., Watkinson, P.J., Tarassenko, L., Predictive Monitoring of Mobile Patients by Combining Clinical Observations with Data From Wearable Sensors. *IEEE J. Biomed. Health*, 2014.

14. Milici, S., Lorenzo, J., Lázaro, A., Villarino, R., Girbau, D., Wireless breathing sensor based on wearable modulated frequency selective surface. *IEEE Sens. J.*, 17, 5, 1285–1292, 2017.

15. Parade, K.A., Patil, N.C., Poojara, S.R., Kamble, T.S., Cloud-based Intelligent Healthcare Monitoring System, in: *In the proceedings of International Conference on Issues and Challenges in Intelligent Computing Techniques (ICICT)*, Ghaziabad, Indian, February 7-8, pp. 697–701, 2014.

16. Schäck, T., Harb, Y.S., Muma, M., Zoubir, A.M., A computationally efficient algorithm for photoplethysmography-based atrial fibrillation detection using smartphones. *39th Annual International Conference of the IEEE Engineering in Medicine and Biology Society (EMBC)*, 2017, pp. 104–108.

17. Shu, Y., Li, C., Wang, Z., Ma, W., Li, Y., Ren, T.L., A pressure sensing system for heart rate monitoring with polymer-based pressure sensors and an anti-interference post-processing circuit. *Sensors*, 15, 2, 3224–3235, 2015.

18. Sow, B., Mukhtar, H., Ahmad, H.F., Suguri, H., Assessing the relative importance of social determinants of health in malaria and anemia classification based on machine learning techniques. *Inf. Health Soc. Care*, 1–13, 2019.

19. Von Rosenberg, W., Chanwimalueang, T., Goverdovsky, V., Looney, D., Sharp, D., Mandic, D.P., Smart helmet: wearable multichannel ECG and EEG. *IEEE J. Transl. Eng. Health Med.*, 4, 4, 1–11 2016.

20. Wang, X., Gui, Q., Liu, B., Jin, Z. *et al.*, Enabling Smart Personalized Healthcare: A Hybrid Mobile-Cloud Approach for ECG Telemonitoring. *IEEE J. Biomed. Health Inf.*, 18, 3, 739–745, 2014, May.

21. Yuce, M.R., Implementation of wireless body area networks for healthcare systems. *Sensor Actuators A: Phys.*, 162, 1, 116–129, 2010, July.

22. Ženko, J., Kos, M., Kramberger, I., Pulse rate variability and blood oxidation content identification using miniature wearable wrist device, in: *2016 International Conference on Systems, Signals and Image Processing (IWSSIP)*, IEEE, 2016.

Index

Also of Interest

Check out these published and forthcoming titles in the "Advances in Learning Analytics for Intelligent Cloud-IoT Systems" series from Scrivener Publishing

Artificial Intelligence for Cyber Security
An IoT Perspective
Edited by Noor Zaman, Mamoona Humayun, Vasaki Ponnusamy and G. Suseendran
Forthcoming 2022. ISBN 978-1-119-76226-3

Industrial Internet of Things (IIoT)
Intelligent Analytics for Predictive Maintenance
Edited by R. Anandan, G. Suseendran, Souvik Pal and Noor Zaman
Published 2022. ISBN 978-1-119-76877-7

The Internet of Medical Things (IoMT)
Healthcare Transformation
Edited by R. J. Hemalatha, D. Akila, D. Balaganesh and Anand Paul
Published 2022. ISBN 978-1-119-76883-8

Integration of Cloud Computing with Internet of Things
Foundations, Analytics, and Applications
Edited by Monika Mangla, Suneeta Satpathy, Bhagirathi Nayak and Sachi Nandan Mohanty
Published 2021. ISBN 978-1-119-76887-6

Digital Cities Roadmap
IoT-Based Architecture and Sustainable Buildings
Edited by Arun Solanki, Adarsh Kumar and Anand Nayyar
Published 2021. ISBN 978-1-119-79159-1

Agricultural Informatics
Automation Using IoT and Machine Learning
Edited by Amitava Choudhury, Arindam Biswas, Manish Prateek and Amlan Chakraborty
Published 2021. ISBN 978-1-119-76884-5

Smart Healthcare System Design
Security and Privacy Aspects
Edited by SK Hafizul Islam and Debabrata Samanta
Published 2021. ISBN 978-1-119-79168-3

Machine Learning Techniques and Analytics for Cloud Security
Edited by Rajdeep Chakraborty, Anupam Ghosh and Jyotsna Kumar Mandal
Published 2021. ISBN 978-1-119-76225-6

www.scrivenerpublishing.com

Printed and bound by CPI Group (UK) Ltd, Croydon, CR0 4YY

27/10/2024

14580173-0004